IMAGINARY FUTURES

The designers were populists, you see; they were trying to give the public what it wanted. What the public wanted was the future.

WILLIAM GIBSON, *THE GERNSBACK CONTINUUM*

IMAGINARY FUTURES

From Thinking Machines to the Global Village

RICHARD BARBROOK

Pluto  Press

LONDON • ANN ARBOR, MI

First published 2007 by Pluto Press
345 Archway Road, London N6 5AA
and 839 Greene Street, Ann Arbor, MI 48106

www.plutobooks.com

Copyright © Richard Barbrook 2007
Artworks © Alex Veness 2007

The right of Richard Barbrook to be identified as the author of this work has been
asserted by him in accordance with the Copyright, Designs and Patents Act 1988.

British Library Cataloguing in Publication Data
A catalogue record for this book is available from the British Library

Hardback
ISBN-13   978 0 7453 2661 0
ISBN-10   0 7453 2661 7

Paperback
ISBN-13   978 0 7453 2660 3
ISBN-10   0 7453 2660 9

Library of Congress Cataloging in Publication Data applied for

10   9   8   7   6   5   4   3   2   1

Designed by Sacha Davison Lunt
Produced for Pluto Press by Chase Publishing Services Ltd, Sidmouth, EX10 9QG
Typeset from disk by Stanford DTP Services, Northampton
Printed and bound in the European Union by
Antony Rowe Ltd, Chippenham and Eastbourne, England

CONTENTS

ARTWORKS

ABOUT THE ARTIST

Alex Veness (born 1965) is an English artist based in London. He is a part-time Lecturer in Fine Art at the Winchester School of Art, University of Southampton.

www.alexveness.net

RESPECT DUE

The Cybersalon crew; CREAM/University of Westminster; Alex Veness; Alexandre Freire; Andy Cameron; Annette Hill; Armin Medosch; Ben Lunt; Boris Kagarlitsky; David Campany; Doug Rushkoff; Eva Pascoe; Gilberto Gil; Gilson Schwartz; Graham Barrett; Graham Seaman; Fred Vermorel; Helen Barbrook; Ilze Black; Joan Smith; John Barker; Jon Agar; Ken Wark; Kosta Papagiannopoulos; Lance Strate; Leonid Levkovich; Les Levidow; Lewis Sykes; Marcos Dantas; Mare Tralla; Maren Hartmann; Mark Osborn; Mark Stahlman; Martin Housden; Martin Thomas; Marty Lucas; Matt Miller; Murray Glickman; Pat McMath; Peter McLoughlin; Rasa Smite; Ricardo Ruiz; Rick Harrington; Rosie Thomas; Sacha Davison Lunt; Simon Schaffer; Sookie Choi; Sonya Williams; Sophia Drakopoulou; Tatiana Wells; Tom Campbell; Trebor Scholz; the UoW library staff; the UCU; *Mute*; nettime.org; *Melancholic Troglodytes*; thething.net; 16 Beaver; Mídia Tática Brasil; abebooks.co.uk; and the staff and students of the MA in Hypermedia Studies (1996–2005).

IMAGINARY FUTURES

www.imagineryfutures.net

THE
FUTURE
IS WHAT IT
USED TO
BE

01

It was Monday 25 April 2005 in New York and I was in search of
frozen time. From Manhattan, I had taken the 7 train eastwards out
to Flushing Meadows in Queens. Arriving at the station, I headed
straight towards the park. Almost immediately, I found what I was
looking for: relics of the 1964 New York World's Fair. At the
entrance of the park, I was welcomed by a series of mosaics in the
tarmac celebrating the organisers and themes of the exposition.
Along one of its paths, I spotted the 'The Rocket Thrower': a
statue of a mythological space traveller. Meeting a friendly Japanese
tourist, we had fun taking pictures of each other standing in front
of the 'Unisphere': the massive 45-metres-high metal globe which
dominates the park. I chatted with a 50-something couple from the
neighbourhood about their teenage visits to the World's Fair. The
cloudy skies of the morning had disappeared and Flushing Meadows
was now basking in the sunshine. Skateboarders performed tricks
under the Unisphere, families wandered along the paths and couples
relaxed on the grass.[1] The next day I would be taking the long
flight back home to London. But, in that afternoon at Flushing
Meadows, the tasks of tomorrow seemed far away. I had succeeded
in discovering frozen time. Everything else could wait while I
savoured the moment.

The photograph on the cover of this book provided the inspiration
for my trip to Flushing Meadows. Early on in my research into the
origins of the Net, I'd come across a fascinating reference to the
1964 New York World's Fair. I was sure that I'd been there as a
child. When I spoke to my mother that weekend on the phone, she
confirmed my suspicion. A few days later, looking through the photo
albums that I'd inherited from my father Alec, I couldn't believe
my luck when I found the picture he had taken in June 1964 of
the Barbrook family at the New York World's Fair. On the right
stands the 7-year-old Richard, wearing what I instantly recognised
as my favourite polo shirt. In the centre, my 30-year-old mother Pat
looks as glamorous as Jackie Kennedy in her sleeveless top, pencil
skirt and sling-backs.[2] Sitting in the pushchair, my 3-year-old sister
Helen is suffering from the 30°C heat. Carefully posed in front of the

---

[1] For more information about this park, see New York City Department of Parks and
Recreation, 'Flushing Meadows Corona Park Virtual Tour'.
[2] Jackie Kennedy was the photogenic wife of the 1961–63 US president, John Kennedy.

Unisphere, the Barbrook family is captured admiring the wonderful spectacle of the World's Fair.

When I think back to this visit, my only clear memory of the exposition is seeing the giant rockets in its Space Park. However, I'm not surprised that I can recall very little about our visit to the New York World's Fair. So many other exciting things happened to me during this formative period of my childhood. Between 1964 and 1965, I lived for a year in a foreign country with very different customs and beliefs from those back home. At my junior school, the class began the day by reciting a loyalty oath to the US flag instead of mumbling their way through a few prayers. During our history lessons on the 1776 American Revolution, this English boy was taught that England was the villain not the hero. While I was living in the USA, I also experienced the extremes of its continental climate and the pleasures of its popular culture. Best of all, I had my first crush, when I held hands with Donna in the school playground. Compared to these seminal events in my life, the details of our family visit to the New York World's Fair were easily forgotten. When I look at the cover of this book, I don't just see an image of my physical presence in a specific place at a particular time. What intrigues me is how this snapshot evokes what it felt like to be a small child living in a strange country. 'Family photographs are supposed to show not so much that we were once there, as how we once were ...'[3]

While writing this book, I realised that this happy period of my childhood in America had a more sinister side which – as a 7-year-old boy – I wasn't aware of at the time. When the Barbrook family went to the New York World's Fair in June 1964, my father was in transit to Boston to begin a twelve-month residency at the political science department of MIT on an exchange scheme funded by the US intelligence services.[4] As a student union official in the early 1950s, he'd been involved in a pro-American faction of the British Labour Party. By the mid 1960s, my father had become an academic specialising in the politics of his ideological homeland: the USA. While doing the research for this book, I recognised from my

3 Annette Kuhn, 'Remembrance', page 18.
4 The Massachusetts Institute of Technology (MIT) is based in Cambridge on the outskirts of Boston, Massachusetts. During his year there, my father carried out the research for his book on the electoral politics of the local state: Alec Barbrook, *God Save the Commonwealth*.

childhood some of the dubious characters – like Walt Rostow – and dodgy organisations – such as the Congress of Cultural Freedom – who play leading roles in the following chapters. My father knew them and he supported their cause. Finding a photograph of the Barbrook family at the New York World's Fair no longer seems like a fortunate coincidence. Given my father's geopolitical loyalties, it was almost inevitable.

When I took the decision to begin work on this book, the last thing on my mind was exploring my own childhood. On the contrary, my starting point was a theoretical conundrum: the uncritical advocacy of old visions of the future. Back in 1995, when we were writing 'The Californian Ideology', Andy Cameron and I had taken delight in pointing out that the dotcom boosters of *Wired* magazine were championing the early-1980s neo-liberal model of the Net.[5] A few years later, I'd made a similar connection in 'The Hi-Tech Gift Economy' between the dreams of the open source software movement in the late 1990s and those of the 1960s community media activists.[6] What fascinated me then as now was that both Right and Left were advocating futures of the Net from the past. For decades, the shape of things to come has remained the same. The hi-tech utopia is always just around the corner, but we never get there. As I began work on this book, I set myself the task of explaining one of the strangest phenomena of the early twenty-first century: the future is what it used to be.

When I found the photograph of the Barbrook family in front of the Unisphere, I knew that I had discovered the image which could provide a focus for my investigation. I decided that the starting point for this book would be exploring a strange paradox: the model of the future offered to me as an adult in late-2000s London is the same future promised to me as a child at the 1964 New York World's Fair. What is even weirder is that – according to the prophecies made more than four decades ago – I should already be living in this wonderful future. Within the developed world, this longevity has created familiarity with the predictions of the computer visionaries. From infancy, we have been told that these machines will one day be able to reason – and even feel emotions – just like humans. Some

---

[5] See Richard Barbrook and Andy Cameron, 'The Californian Ideology'.
[6] See Richard Barbrook, 'The Hi-Tech Gift Economy'.

of the most popular characters in science fiction stories are artificial intelligences. Audiences have grown up with images of loyal robot buddies like Data in *Star Trek TNG* and of pitiless mechanical monsters like the android in *The Terminator*.[7] These sci-fi fantasies are encouraged by confident predictions from prominent computer scientists. In 2006, Honda's website boasted that the current model of its Asimo robot was the precursor of sentient machines which will be able to perform complex tasks such as caring for the elderly or fighting fires.[8] Some computer scientists even believe that the invention of artificial intelligence is a spiritual quest. In California, Ray Kurzweil and Vernor Vinge have been patiently waiting since the 1980s for the Singularity: the Incarnation of the Robot Redeemer.[9] Whether inspired by money or mysticism, all these advocates of artificial intelligence share the conviction that they know the future of computing – and their task is to get there as fast as possible.

> Biological intelligence is fixed, because it is an old, mature paradigm, but the new paradigm of non-biological computation and intelligence is growing exponentially. The crossover will be in the 2020s and after that, at least from a hardware perspective, non-biological computation will dominate ...[10]

Like artificial intelligence, the concept of the information society is also an old acquaintance. For decades, politicians, pundits and experts have been telling the citizens of the developed world that the arrival of this digital utopia is imminent. These premonitions have been confirmed by media coverage of the increasing sophistication and rapid proliferation of iconic technologies: personal computers, satellite television, cable systems, mobile phones, games consoles and, above all, the Net. During the late-1990s dotcom boom, the Californian acolytes of the information society became intoxicated with millennial fervour. Kevin Kelly claimed that the Net had created a 'new paradigm' which had abolished the boom-and-bust economic cycle.[11] Manuel Castells published a multi-volume celebration of the

---

[7] See Startrek.com, 'Data'; and James Cameron, *The Terminator*.
[8] See Honda, 'Asimo'.
[9] See James Bell, 'Exploring the "Singularity"'; and Vernor Vinge, 'The Technological Singularity'.
[10] Ray Kurzweil, 'The Intelligent Universe', page 3.
[11] See Kevin Kelly, *New Rules for the New Economy*.

transition from the miseries of industrial nationalism to the marvels of post-industrial globalism.[12]

When the share bubble imploded in 2001, this tale of sunny optimism lost its core audience. Shattering the dreams of the Californian ideology, boom had been followed by bust. The business cycle still regulated the economy. With *jihadi* terrorism and imperial adventures dominating the headlines, new media seemed so last century. However, this fall from favour was only temporary. As more people went on-line and connection speeds increased, confidence slowly returned to the new-media sector. By the mid 2000s, dotcom shares were once again trading at premium prices on the stock exchange. As if the bubble had never burst, the United Nations hosted a conference on 16–18 November 2005 in Tunis promoting the hi-tech future: the World Summit on the Information Society.[13] The Net had regained its status as the epitome of modernity. As the European Commissioner for the Information Society and Media explained in the run-up to the conference:

> For many years, experts have been talking about digital convergence of communication networks, media content and devices. ... Today [1 June 2005], we see digital convergence actually happening. Voice over IP, Web TV, on-line music, movies on mobile telephones – all this is now reality.[14]

In the prophecies of artificial intelligence and the information society, ideology is used to warp time. The importance of a new technology lies not in what it can do in the here and now, but in what more advanced models might be able to do one day. The present is understood as the future in embryo – and the future illuminates the potential of the present. Every step forward in computing technology is further progress towards the final goal of artificial intelligence. The prophecy of the information society comes closer to fulfilment with the launch of each new piece of software and hardware. The present already contains the future and this future explains the present. What is now is what will be one

---

[12] See Manuel Castells, *The Rise of the Network Society; The Power of Identity; End of Millennium.*

[13] See World Summit on the Information Society, 'Second Phase, Tunis'.

[14] Viviane Reding, in Commission of the European Communities, 'Commission Launches Five-Year Strategy to Boost the Digital Economy', page 1.

day. Contemporary reality is the beta version of a science fiction dream: *the imaginary future*.

When I made my trip to Flushing Meadows, I was searching for evidence of 40-year-old visions of this computer utopia. The Unisphere, the Rocket Thrower and other survivors of the World's Fair aren't just historical curiosities. The frozen time of the 1960s past is almost indistinguishable from our imaginary futures in the 2000s. Thinking about what has happened over the last four decades, this proposition seems counter-intuitive. Between my two visits to Flushing Meadows, the international political and economic system has gone through a process of radical restructuring. The Cold War ended. The Russian empire collapsed. American hegemony has declined. Europe became a single trading zone. East Asia has rapidly industrialised. Electoral democracy became the dominant form of politics. Economic globalisation has imposed strict limits upon national autonomy. Some of the most pressing problems facing the world today weren't even heard of 40 years ago: climate change, the Aids epidemic, Islamist terrorism and debt relief for the impoverished South. Yet, throughout this period of turmoil and transformation, our conception of the computerised future is the one thing which has remained fixed. As in the mid 1960s, the invention of artificial intelligence and the advent of the information society are still only a couple of decades away. The present is continually changing, but the imaginary future is always the same.

Living in pre-modern societies, both Aristotle and Muhammad Ibn Khaldûn observed similar historical cycles. The slow pace of social evolution limited the impact of political upheavals. When the system changed, the present was forced to repeat the past.[15] According to the gurus of postmodernism, this phenomenon of circular time returned in the late twentieth century. Ever since the Enlightenment, the 'grand narrative' of history had imposed the logic of progress upon humanity.[16] But, now that the process of industrialisation had been completed, these philosophers believed that modernity had lost its driving force. Linear time had become obsolete. For the more pessimistic postmodernists, this rebirth of cyclical time proved that there could be no better future. Historical

---

[15] See Aristotle, *The Politics*, pages 101–234; and Muhammad Ibn Khaldûn, *The Mugaddimah*, pages 91–261.

[16] See Jean-François Lyotard, *The Post-Modern Condition*.

evolution had ended. Cultural innovation was impossible. Political progress had stopped. The future is nothing more than the 'eternal return' of the present.[17]

When the concept of postmodernism was first proposed in the mid 1970s, its founding fathers argued that the spread of information technologies was responsible for the emergence of this new social paradigm. Jean-François Lyotard claimed that the fusion of media, computing and telecommunications was sweeping away the ideological and economic structures of the industrial age.[18] Jean Baudrillard denounced the new form of domination imposed by the hypnotic power of audio-visual imagery over the public imagination.[19] Ironically, although both philosophers were critical of techno-optimism, their analysis required an uncritical belief in the hi-tech prophecies of the New York World's Fair. The 1960s future of modernism explained the 1970s present of postmodernism. Because they didn't question the validity of the previous decade's predictions, their revival of cyclical time was founded upon their certainty about the direction of linear progress. The perpetual present was justified by the immutable future.

Contrary to its self-image as the new theory of the information age, postmodernism was itself an ideological symptom of the hegemony of hi-tech prophecies. Most tellingly, its concept of cyclical time was derived from the continual repetition of the same model of the sci-fi utopia. In contrast, the premise of this book is asking *why* the imaginary futures of the past have survived into the present. Despite their cultural prominence, the semiotic ghosts of sentient machines and post-industrial economies are vulnerable to theoretical exorcism. Far from being free-floating signifiers, these predictions are deeply rooted in time and space. As this book will show, it is no accident that their intellectual origins can be traced back to Cold War America. By data-mining the history of these two imaginary futures, the social underpinning of these techno-ideologies can be revealed. Not surprisingly, contemporary boosters of artificial intelligence and the information society rarely acknowledge the

---

[17] See Gilles Deleuze, *Difference and Repetition.*
[18] See Lyotard, *Post-Modern Condition*, pages 3–4, 60–67.
[19] See Jean Baudrillard, *Simulations; The Ecstasy of Communication.*

antiquity of their predictions. They want to move forwards rather than look backwards. Time is fluid, never frozen.

In contrast, this book insists that the imaginary futures of artificial intelligence and the information society have a long history. It's over 40 years since the dreams of thinking machines and post-industrial cornucopia gripped the American public's imagination at the New York World's Fair. Examining these earlier attempts to propagate these prophecies is a requisite for understanding their contemporary iterations. Frozen time illuminates fluid time. Rather than being a diversion, looking backwards is the precondition for moving forwards. While researching this book, revisiting that June 1964 day as a child in Flushing Meadows was an essential step in constructing – as an adult – my analysis of the prophecies of the imaginary future. With this motivation in mind, let's go back to the second decade of the Cold War, when the most powerful and wealthiest nation on the planet put on a show in New York to celebrate the wonders of new technologies ...

THE AMERICAN CENTURY

02

On the 22 April 1964, the New York World's Fair was opened to the general public. During the next two years, this modern wonderland welcomed over 51 million visitors. Every section of the American elite was represented among the 140 pavilions of the World's Fair: the federal government, local state administrations, public bodies, large corporations, financial institutions, industry lobbies and religious groups. After over 20 years of uninterrupted economic expansion, there were plenty of organisations willing to spend serious money on exhibition space at the World's Fair. Here was a wonderful opportunity for combining self-promotion with patriotic duty. The New York World's Fair proved that the USA was the world leader in everything: consumer goods, democratic politics, show business, modernist architecture, fine art, religious tolerance, domestic living and, above all else, new technology. A 'millennium of progress' had culminated in the wonders of American civilisation.[1]

Not surprisingly, this fusion of hucksterism and patriotism was most pronounced among the corporate exhibitors at the World's Fair. Located at addresses like the Pool of Industry or the Avenue of Transportation, the pavilions of big business and its lobby groups loudly advertised the virtues of their sponsors. Every trick was used to attract the punters. Pepsi hired Disney to build a theme-park ride which featured singing and dancing models of children, animals and birds. The US Rubber Company managed to combine funfair entertainment with Pop Art aesthetics by constructing a big wheel in the shape of 'a giant whitewall tire'.[2] Although they were very popular, these exhibits never became the stars of the show. What really impressed the 7-year-old Richard and millions of other visitors were the awe-inspiring displays of new technologies. Writers and film-makers had long fantasised about travelling to other worlds. Now, in NASA's Space Park at the 1964 World's Fair, the public could admire the huge rockets which had taken the first Americans into earth orbit.[3] Before their own eyes, science fiction was transformed into science fact.

[1] 'A Millennium of Progress' was one of the three feel-good themes used to promote the World's Fair.

[2] See Editors of Time–Life Books, *Official Guide*, pages 94, 96, 212.

[3] See Editors of Time–Life Books, *Official Guide*, page 208; and William Laurence, *Science at the Fair*, pages 2–14. NASA was set up in 1958 as the US government's civilian space exploration agency.

Ever since the Russians launched the Sputnik satellite in 1957, the two superpowers had been locked in the 'space race': a competition to prove technological supremacy by carrying out spectacular feats outside the earth's atmosphere. By the time that the World's Fair opened, the US media was obsessed with every detail of this contest. The astronauts were idolised as all-American heroes who were taking on the Cold War enemy in the heavens.[4] Although the Russians had humiliated the USA again in 1961, when Yuri Gagarin became the first person to orbit the earth, their technical lead was slowly being eroded. In the same year as Gagarin's flight, US President John Kennedy felt confident enough to announce a new goal for his nation's space programme: landing an astronaut on the moon within ten years. When the crowds were looking at the giant rockets in the Space Park, this ambition was already well on the way to being realised.[5] Visitors to New York City's Hall of Science could wonder at a model of NASA space shuttles taking people and supplies to an orbiting laboratory. Inside the United States pavilion, they were shown a film depicting American astronauts making the first lunar landing.[6] Despite the early setbacks, Yankee ingenuity and inventiveness were winning out in the space race. America was still Number One.

As in the Space Park, the corporate pavilions also took pride in the USA's technological prowess. At the DuPont exhibition, the main attraction was the 'Wonderful World of Chemistry' musical which celebrated American scientists' contributions to the consumer society with songs like 'The Happy Plastic Family'.[7] In pavilion after pavilion, big business predicted that the achievements of the present would soon be surpassed by the triumphs of tomorrow. Visitors to General Motors' exhibit could take a theme-park ride to a future of elevated multi-lane motorways, giant skyscrapers, underwater settlements, desert cities and, as a grand finale, a holiday resort on the moon. At the nearby Ford pavilion, motor cars were praised as the prototypes of rocket ships. The corporation boasted that

4 See Tom Wolfe, The Right Stuff, pages 109–177, 212–351.
5 See John Kennedy, 'Special Message to Congress on Urgent Needs'; and James Schefter, The Race, pages 145–231.
6 See Editors of Time–Life Books, Official Guide, pages 180, 182, 206, 208, 212, 214; and Laurence, Science at the Fair, pages, 16–18.
7 See Editors of Time–Life Books, Official Guide, page 102; and Laurence, Science at the Fair, pages 54–56.

passengers on its space ride would go '... gliding on a superskyway over the City of Tomorrow with towering spires and the glittering glass of "bubble dome" buildings'.[8] Both General Motors and Ford shared the same vision: visiting other planets in the future would be as cheap and easy as travelling to other cities was in the present. Within a few decades, every American would be an astronaut.

When the World's Fair opened, General Electric created a media sensation by putting on '... the first demonstration of controlled thermonuclear fusion to be witnessed by a general audience'. In its Progressland pavilion, an intense burst of light and noise was created every six seconds by squeezing plasma with a giant magnet.[9] General Electric claimed that this awe-inspiring experiment was the first step towards developing a source of limitless supplies of free energy: nuclear fusion. During the previous decade, this builder of power plants had profited handsomely from the US government's enthusiasm for generating electricity from nuclear fission. In the Hall of Science, the state agency directing this project organised a children's exhibit which explained how the new form of energy was improving the lives of every American: 'Atomsville, USA'.[10] In its pavilion, General Electric predicted that the wonders of nuclear fusion would soon surpass even those of nuclear fission. This futuristic method of generating electricity promised to be so efficient that there would no longer be any point in metering its use by consumers. The era of free energy was imminent.

Whatever the technology, the message of these corporate exhibits was the same. Big business was building a brighter and better American future. Nowhere was this self-congratulatory attitude more in evidence than in the exhibits featuring the latest innovations in information technology. The corporate pavilions emphasised their sponsors' control over the rapid developments in media, telecommunications and computing. RCA participated in the World's Fair to celebrate the successful launch of colour television in the USA. At its exhibition, the public could tour the studios

[8] See Editors of Time–Life Books, *Official Guide*, pages 52–53, 220, 222, 204. Also see Sheldon Reaven, 'New Frontiers', pages 76–82.

[9] See Editors of Time–Life Books, *Official Guide*, pages 90, 92; and Laurence, *Science at the Fair*, pages 40–43.

[10] See Editors of Time–Life Books, *Official Guide*, pages 206, 208; Laurence, *Science at the Fair*, pages 19–20; and Reaven, 'New Frontiers', pages 90–93.

making the programmes that were broadcast live to 250 screens around the site. Inside the Bell pavilion, there were demonstrations of videophones, voice synthesisers, lasers, electronic games and other gadgets from its research laboratories.[11] For many corporations, the most effective method of proving their technological modernity was showcasing a computer. The Clairol pavilion contained a machine which could choose 'the most flattering hair shades' for female visitors. The Parker Pen exhibit featured a computer which matched American kids with 'pen pals' in foreign countries.[12] In each of these shows, the presence of a computer loudly proclaimed that US corporations were the makers of the future.

Ironically, although they played a prominent role in the media coverage of the World's Fair, almost all of these expensive mainframes were hi-tech gimmicks. It would be nearly two decades before the first personal computers appeared in the office and the home. It would take even longer before chips were incorporated into everyday consumer items. In contrast, IBM was able to dedicate its pavilion exclusively to the wonders of computing as a distinct technology. For over a decade, this corporation had been America's leading mainframe manufacturer. Back in the mid 1950s, it had developed the IBM 650, which became the best-selling computer of the decade.[13] When this model became obsolete, its replacement – the IBM 1401 – was even more successful. In 1961, this one single product accounted for a quarter of all the computers operating in the USA.[14] Despite their best efforts over the years, none of the corporation's rivals had ever seriously threatened its control over the industry. The vast resources of IBM ensured that any competitive advantage acquired by its competitors was only temporary. By the time that the 1964 World's Fair began, the corporation enjoyed a near monopoly over the mainframe and peripheral markets in both the USA and Western Europe.[15] In the minds of most visitors to the World's Fair, IBM *was* computing.

---

[11] See Editors of Time–Life Books, *Official Guide*, pages 82, 113–114; and Laurence, *Science at the Fair*, pages 43–54.

[12] See Editors of Time–Life Books, *Official Guide*, pages 86, 90.

[13] See Emerson Pugh, Lyle Johnson and John Palmer, *IBM's 360 and Early 370 Systems*, pages 17–19.

[14] See Emerson Pugh, *Building IBM*, pages 265–267.

[15] See Paul Ceruzzi, *A History of Modern Computing*, pages 110–112; and Richard Thomas DeLamarter, *Big Blue*, pages 47–49.

Just before the World's Fair opened to the public, the corporation launched a series of products which would further tighten its grip over the computer industry: the System/360.[16] Since the early 1950s, IBM had produced different mainframes and peripherals for each segment of the market. There were low-cost and high-cost machines. There were commercial, academic and military models. As well as increasing research and development costs, this business strategy meant that IBM's products often didn't work with each other. Even worse, customers complained that upgrading mainframes or adding peripherals could be a technical nightmare.[17] Fearful that this problem helped its competitors, IBM in the early 1960s invested heavily in developing the industry's first fully compatible range of computers. The monopolistic ambitions of the System/360 project were symbolised by the inspiration for its name: all the points of the compass. From IBM's new range of compatible products, customers would be able to 'pick 'n' mix' the combination of mainframes and peripherals which best suited their particular needs.[18] Over the next decade, the System/360 became the de facto standard for computing across the world and entrenched the corporation's hegemony over the industry for another 20 years.[19] However, in 1964, the success of this ambitious project was still in doubt. Having already 'bet the company' on developing the System/360, the bosses of IBM weren't going to waste the opportunity for self-promotion offered by the World's Fair. They decided to celebrate the computer colossus' technological and economic achievements by building a pavilion which would eclipse all others at the exposition.

Eero Saarinen – the renowned Finnish architect – created the stunning look of the IBM building: a white, corporate-logo-embossed, egg-shaped theatre held aloft by 45 rust-coloured metal trees. Underneath this striking feature, Charles and Ray Eames – the couple epitomising American modernist design – were commissioned to produce the exhibits celebrating the corporation's leading role within the computer industry. Inside the ground-floor

16 See IBM, 'System/360 Announcement'; and Pugh, Johnson and Palmer, *IBM's 360 and Early 370 Systems*, pages 165–169.
17 See Pugh, *Building IBM*, pages 113–114.
18 See Pugh, Johnson and Palmer, *IBM's 360 and Early 370 Systems*, pages 114–367; and Ceruzzi, *Modern Computing*, pages 144–158.
19 See DeLamarter, *Big Blue*, pages 54–146.

space, IBM mainframes demonstrated their ability to recognise human handwriting and to translate Russian into English. On stages surrounding the building, visitors could watch 'mechanical figures act out playlets ... about such topics as speed, computer logic and information handling systems'. For the theatre itself, Charles and Ray Eames directed the main attraction at the IBM pavilion: 'The Information Machine'. After taking their places in the 500-seat 'People Wall', visitors were elevated upwards into the egg-shaped structure. Once inside, a narrator introduced a 12-minute, 9-screen, 14-projector, slide and film performance with a stereophonic sound commentary provided in a choice of five languages. The theme of this 'mind-blowing' multimedia show was how computers solved problems in the same way as the human mind.[20] The audience learnt that the System/360 mainframes exhibited in the IBM pavilion were in the process of acquiring consciousness: *artificial intelligence.* 'Don't be surprised if your own mind stretches a bit, as you see how computers use your own everyday way of reasoning to solve some of the universe's most mystifying riddles.'[21] IBM's multimedia show communicated an important message to the American public. The corporation was much more than just a commercial operation. Selling computers to big government and big business was simply a way of providing money for achieving IBM's primary goal: the creation of artificial intelligence. For over a decade, Herbert Simon, Marvin Minsky and other prominent scientists in the USA had been arguing that improvements in hardware and software would sooner or later make machines indistinguishable from humans.[22] Once the technology was sophisticated enough, the emergence of thinking machines would be inevitable. In 1961, IBM had announced that its newly opened laboratories were going to prioritise the development of artificial intelligence.[23] As the System/360 mainframes were developed and improved, hardware would become powerful enough to construct the prototypes of thinking machines.

---

[20] See Charles and Ray Eames, *IBM at the Fair*; Editors of Time–Life Books, *Official Guide*, pages 70, 74, 129; and Robert Stern, Thomas Mellins and David Fishman, *New York 1960*, page 1046.

[21] Advert for the IBM pavilion in Editors of Time–Life Books, *Official Guide*, page 129.

[22] See Herbert Simon, *The Shape of Automation for Men and Management*; and Marvin Minsky, 'Steps Towards Artificial Intelligence'.

[23] See Pugh, *Building IBM*, pages 240–242.

Simon, Minsky and their fellow experts in artificial intelligence agreed that the appearance of the first fully conscious computers was imminent. For over two decades, the optimistic vision of sentient machines serving humanity had been ubiquitous within popular science fiction.[24] During the 1950s, human interaction with a friendly android had become a well-loved plot line within American mass culture. In the hit 1956 sci-fi film *Forbidden Planet*, the most popular – and memorable – character was a loyal and obedient sentient machine: Robby the Robot.[25] At the 1964 World's Fair, IBM proudly announced that this fantasy was about to be realised. The System/360 mainframe might be shaped like a box, but – if you looked hard enough – you could see that this computer was the prototype of a humanoid artificial intelligence. In the near future, American consumers would be able to buy their own Robby the Robot. 'Duplicating the problem-solving and information-handling capabilities of the [human] brain is not far off; it would be surprising if it were not accomplished within the next decade.'[26]

The IBM pavilion's impressive combination of avant-garde architecture and multimedia performance was a huge hit with both the press and the public. Many believed that the corporation had commissioned by far the best exhibit at the 1964 World's Fair. For once, product promotion had been successfully combined with 'an integrated architectural-design concept'.[27] What impressed visitors most of all was Charles and Ray Eames' audio-visual extravaganza about artificial intelligence. IBM had spent its money well. Alongside space rockets and nuclear reactors, the computer had confirmed its place in the public imagination as one of the three iconic technologies of modern America. IBM was the builder of electronic brains: the proof in the present of the marvels of the future.

In the early 1960s, this confusion between science fact and science fiction dominated the public's perception of technological innovation. Before they arrived at the New York World's Fair, most visitors already knew the moral of the show: the machines on display were prototypes of better things to come. NASA's spaceships would

[24] See Charles and Ray Eames, *A Computer Perspective*, pages 105, 147–149.
[25] See Fred Wilcox, *Forbidden Planet*.
[26] Simon, *Shape of Automation*, page 39. This firm prediction was made in 1960.
[27] Ada Louise Huxtable, in Stern, Mellins and Fishman, *New York 1960*, page 1046.

evolve into luxurious interplanetary passenger liners.[28] General Electric's fission reactors would become fusion plants providing almost limitless amounts of energy. Crucially, these fantasies of the future explained how new technologies would eventually benefit everyone. The promise of space travel for everyone justified spending enormous sums of money on sending a few astronauts into earth orbit. The prediction of electricity 'too cheap to meter' showed that the massive investments in nuclear power were worthwhile. The present was the harbinger of the future – and the future fulfilled the promise of the present.

Like space rockets and nuclear reactors, computers also existed in two time frames at once. On the one hand, the current models displayed at the IBM pavilion were prototypes of the sentient machines of the future. Visitors could see a computer which was already capable of translating Russian into English. On the other hand, the dream of artificial intelligence showed the true potential of the mainframes exhibited in the IBM pavilion. The audience of Charles and Ray Eames' multimedia performance learnt how machines were in the process of becoming as smart as humans. The System/360 mainframe was Version 1.0 of Robby the Robot. Artificial intelligence was both imminent and inherent within the new technology of computing. At the New York World's Fair, the exhibitors' enthusiasm for merging science fiction with science fact reflected their optimistic vision of contemporary America. In both the Space Park and the corporate pavilions, big government and big business identified the present with the future to emphasise the technological supremacy of their homeland. Scientific advances were making sci-fi dreams come true and – simultaneously – these predictions were inspiring the invention of amazing new machines. What was happening and what would happen were indistinguishable from each other. In the IBM pavilion, the new technology of computing was displayed as the fulfilment of science fiction fantasy: *the imaginary future of artificial intelligence.*

When the New York World's Fair opened, Americans had good reasons for feeling optimistic. The holding of the exposition coincided with a very special historical moment: the peak of US

---

28 A few years later, this fantasy was portrayed on film in the famous scenes of a space flight between the earth and the moon in Stanley Kubrick's *2001*.

hegemony over the planet. During the previous 50 years, the American elite had outfought, outproduced and outsmarted all of its imperial rivals. By 1964, the USA had become an economic and military superpower without comparison.[29] More than anything else, American pre-eminence was demonstrated by its technological superiority. It was not surprising that the most popular exhibits at the New York World's Fair were the latest triumphs of US science: space rockets, colour television sets, videophones, nuclear reactors and, above all, mainframe computers. This identification of new technologies with the imaginary future had been a leitmotif of international expositions for over a century. In 1851, flush with the wealth and power which flowed from owning the 'workshop of the world', the British elite had organised the inaugural celebration of the wonders of economic progress: the Great Exhibition of the Works of Industry of All Nations. The Crystal Palace – a futuristic iron and glass building – was erected in a central London park. Inside, visitors were treated to a dazzling display of new products from the factories and exotic imports from the colonies. For the first time, the icons of industrial modernity were the main attractions at a large international festival.

Ironically, in their original proposal, its organisers had identified the primary purpose of the Great Exhibition as the promotion of faux-medieval design. When the Crystal Palace was laid out, the best location in the middle of the main hall was allocated to the Gothic Revival exhibit.[30] By seeing so many examples of this elevating design at the Great Exhibition, consumers would become more discerning in their purchases and businesses would be inspired to create better products. When they were given a retro-makeover, factory goods became socially acceptable. The new was only beautiful when imitating the old.[31] In Victorian England, the Gothic Revival was much more than just an art movement. The British elite took delight in disguising their hi-tech commercial republic as a romantic medieval monarchy. In the most modern nation in the world, the latest industrial innovation masqueraded as an archaic feudal custom:

[29] See Stephen Ambrose, *The Rise to Globalism*, pages 102–296.
[30] See Jeffrey Auerbach, *The Great Exhibition of 1851*, pages 113–118. Auguste Pugin – the organiser of the Gothic Revival exhibit – had recently designed the mock-Tudor interior of the new Parliament buildings in London.
[31] See Auerbach, *Great Exhibition*, pages 91–98.

the invented tradition.[32] '[England's] essence is strong with the strength of modern simplicity; its exterior is august with the Gothic grandeur of a more imposing age.'[33]

Despite the best efforts of the organisers, their admiration for faux-medieval design wasn't shared by most of the people who flocked to the Great Exhibition. Instead, it was the Machinery Hall which became the most popular section of the Crystal Palace. For working-class visitors in particular, highly decorated Gothic Revival furniture and reliquaries were never going to have the emotional impact of the new technologies which had turned Britain into an economic and military superpower: cotton looms, telegraphy, harvesters, rotary printing presses and, best of all, steam engines.[34] In Victorian England, these machines were potent symbols of modernity. Industrial capitalism had surpassed the achievements of all previous civilisations. For the first time in human history, people could travel, on a railway train, faster than a horse and communicate across vast distances with telegraphy. Above all, their everyday lives had been reshaped by the new products of the factory system.[35] For millennia, the aristocratic elite had kept the peoples of Europe in poverty and ignorance. The 1851 Great Exhibition was the public celebration of England's leading role in destroying this oppressive social order. In the two centuries following the 1642 Revolution, free trade had swept away the feudal economy in this part of Europe. By privatising land ownership and mechanising handicraft production, the English pioneered a new – and more advanced – economic system: liberal capitalism. Entrepreneurs proved that deregulated markets could coordinate human labour indirectly, much more efficiently than by the direct methods of feudalism. Adventurers discovered that selling commodities in the world market was much more profitable than rack-renting peasants in one locality.[36]

[32] See Eric Hobsbawm, 'The Invention of Tradition'.
[33] Walter Bagehot, *The English Constitution*, page 65.
[34] See Robert Brain, *Going to the Fair*, pages 97–103; and Auerbach, *Great Exhibition*, pages 104–108.
[35] See J.M. Golby and A.W. Purdue, *The Civilisation of the Crowd*; and Eric Hobsbawm, *Industry and Empire*; pages 1–173.
[36] See Adam Smith, *The Wealth of Nations*, Volume 1, pages 1–287, 401–445; Karl Marx, *Capital*, Volume 1, pages 762–940; and Ellen Meiksins Wood, *The Pristine Culture of Capitalism*, pages 95–116.

As competition intensified, English capitalists had initiated the reorganisation of the manufacturing process itself. Investing in machinery increased the productivity of their employees. Developing new products led to more consumers for their firms.[37] Inside the Crystal Palace, the fruits of this new economic system were placed on display. Free trade had created the conditions for the manufacture of its wonderful exhibits. Industrialisation had provided the advanced technologies to build a global empire. Yet, at the same time, these exhibits inside the Crystal Palace systematically ignored the labour of the people who had produced them. The silk dresses betrayed no traces of the horrors of the sweatshops where they were made. The glassware from Ireland contained no reminders of the made-in-Britain famine which had recently decimated the peasantry of the country.[38] As in the marketplace, the marvels of the product were more important than the conditions of the producers at the Great Exhibition. Public display was – paradoxically – the most effective method of social concealment.[39]

The modernity of the English was demonstrated by the Great Exhibition's emphasis on products rather than producers. In the first industrial nation, material goods were no longer just symbols of social status. People were now required to interact with each other through things: commodities, money and capital. The distribution and division of labour across the economy was regulated by the prices and wages set by market competition. However, the demise of the aristocracy hadn't ended class rule in England. When labour was bought and sold in the capitalist economy, equality within the marketplace resulted in inequality inside the workplace.[40] Because commodities were exchanged with others of equivalent value, this new form of class rule was very different from its predecessor. Indirect exploitation had replaced direct domination. Under liberal capitalism, the impersonal movements of the markets now determined the destiny of individuals. When the economy was

[37] See Smith, *Wealth of Nations, Volume 1*, pages 7–25, 72–160, 401–445; David Ricardo, *The Principles of Political Economy*, pages 263–271; and Marx, *Capital, Volume 1*, pages 429–639, 943–1084.

[38] See Auerbach, *Great Exhibition*, pages 100–104, 132–134.

[39] See Walter Benjamin, *The Arcades Project*, pages 17–18.

[40] See Marx, *Capital, Volume 1*, pages 270–280; and Isaac Rubin, *Essays on Marx's Theory of Value*, pages 77–253.

expanding, workers' living standards rose as competition among employers for their labour intensified. But, when the business cycle turned, the situation was reversed. Rising unemployment impoverished those who lost their jobs and weakened the bargaining position of those who remained in work. For the proletarians of Victorian England, the market was – at one and the same time – the provider of plenty and the creator of misery. When trading goods and services directed the distribution and division of labour within the economy, fetishised commodities determined the destiny of their human creators.[41]

In the mid nineteenth century, both bourgeois liberals and working-class socialists could find confirmation of their political beliefs in the steam engines of the Great Exhibition. Since the moment of production had disappeared from view, the specific doctrine materialised in these machines was open to interpretation. Despite their deep differences about the politics of industrialisation, both Right and Left agreed upon one thing: new technology represented the future. The rapid transformation of society by the combined efforts of scientific researchers and factory labourers had taken a fetishised form. Instead of rival political projects to improve the lives of human beings, the next stage of modernity was increasingly symbolised by predictions of fantastic new machines. In turn, as technology influenced politics, class struggles over economic power were expressed through ideological disputes over the social meaning of technological innovation. With human creativity hidden behind the commodity, the process of modernity had acquired a highly visible object as its subject: the '... *automatic system of machinery* ... a moving power that moves itself'.[42]

The triumph of the 1851 Great Exhibition was the beginning of the global exposition movement. Within two years, New York had held its first World's Fair and, a couple of years later, Paris also hosted its inaugural show. The trend had been established. Organising an exposition became one of the best ways of proving the modernity of a nation. Like the Great Exhibition, these subsequent events were much more than just trade fairs. The 1893 Chicago Columbian Exposition had more than 21 million visitors and the 1900 Paris

---

41 See Marx, *Capital, Volume 1*, pages 163–177; and Rubin, *Essays*, pages 5–60.
42 Karl Marx, *Grundrisse*, page 692. Also see Marx, *Capital, Volume 1*, pages 501–506.

Universal Exposition attracted nearly 48 million spectators.[43] These unprecedented movements of people demonstrated the important social role of these events. Before the advent of cheap air travel, going to an exposition was one of the few chances to experience the cultures of other nations. World expositions appeared to be prefiguring world peace.

Although their locations and historical circumstances were different, each of these events followed the template laid down by the 1851 Great Exhibition: the public celebration of economic progress. Above all, in exposition after exposition, the stars of the show were the cutting-edge technologies of the time. The 1889 Paris Universal Exposition was immortalised by the superb engineering achievement of the Eiffel Tower.[44] However, by the time that this exhibition opened, the European powers were beginning to fall behind the rapid pace of innovation taking place across the Atlantic. Only a few years after the Eiffel Tower was built, the Palace of Electricity – the most popular exhibit at the 1893 Chicago World's Exposition – provided spectacular proof of the technological superiority of US industry over its European rivals.[45] During the first half of the twentieth century, the disparity between the two continents became ever more obvious. While the European powers destroyed each other in disastrous wars, the USA took the path to global dominance. In the late 1930s, these diverging fortunes were dramatically demonstrated by the expositions held in Paris and New York. Visitors to the 1937 Paris International Exhibition were confronted with a sombre image of the world. Directly opposite to each other in the middle of the main boulevard, Nazi Germany and Stalinist Russia had erected massive buildings to champion their rival visions of the totalitarian future. The political and ideological divisions which were driving Europe towards catastrophe were starkly symbolised in brick and concrete.[46]

In complete contrast, visitors to the 1939 New York World's Fair were greeted by a feast of optimistic symbolism. At the centre of the exposition stood New York State's stunning contributions to

[43] See Brain, *Going to the Fair*, page 10.
[44] See Urso Chappell, *Expomuseum*.
[45] See Julie Rose, 'Reactions to the Fair'.
[46] See Xavier Ryckelynck, 'L'Expo de 1937'.

the show: the Trylon – an Art Deco obelisk – and the Perisphere – a shimmering white globe. Inside the latter was the hugely popular Democracity exhibition which promoted a utopian vision of suburban living and motorised transport for all.[47] This imaginary future also inspired the most successful corporate pavilion at the 1939 World's Fair: General Motors' Futurama. Visitors flocked to admire its diorama showing what the USA would look like in 20 years time. As in the Democracity model, this exhibit also predicted that most people would be living in suburbs and commuting to work in motor cars.[48] Both big government and big business were convinced that – within a couple of decades – America would be a consumer society.[49]

> 'Democracity' [is] a perfectly integrated, futuristic metropolis pulsing with life and rhythm and music. ... Here is a city of a million people with a working population of 250,000, whose homes are located beyond the city-proper, in five satellite towns. Like great arteries, broad highways traverse expansive areas of vivid green countryside, connecting outlying industrial towns with the city's heart.[50]

Facing such strong competition for the attention of visitors, other corporations showcased machines which up to then had only been found in sci-fi stories. The star exhibit of the Westinghouse pavilion was Electro: 'an 8-foot metal man that talks, sees, smells, sings, and counts with his fingers'.[51] Although it was only a gimmick, this machine was one of the earliest iterations of the imaginary future of artificial intelligence. Until the 1939 World's Fair, almost every sci-fi story about synthetic beings had imitated the plot of Mary Shelley's *Frankenstein*. Sooner or later, the fabricated creature turned into a psychotic monster which tried to kill its human creator. Only a year after the exposition closed, Isaac Asimov – a New York sci-fi author – set out to change this negative image. Reversing the

---

[47] See New York World's Fair 1939, *Official Guide Book*, pages 42–45; and Jeffrey Hart, 'Yesterday's America of Tomorrow'.

[48] See New York World's Fair 1939, *Official Guide Book*, pages 207–209; and David Gelernter, *1939*, pages 25, 34–35.

[49] Visitors to the Futurama exhibit were given a badge with the slogan 'I have seen the future'. See Gelernter, *1939*, page 154.

[50] New York World's Fair 1939, *Official Guide Book*, page 44.

[51] New York World's Fair 1939, *Official Guide Book*, page 195. Also see Charles and Ray Eames, *A Computer Perspective*, page 105.

popular stereotype, his tales described robots with loyalty to their human masters hard-wired into their 'positronic brains'.[52] Like Electro in the Westinghouse pavilion, Asimov's artificial beings were safe and friendly products of a large corporation. This new approach proved to be a hit with the American public. Reflecting this change of image, the US media became fascinated by the scientists who were working hard to turn Asimov's fantasy of friendly robots into really existing thinking machines. In both science fiction and science fact, artificial intelligence had become the promise of better times to come.

In their exhibits for the 1939 World's Fair, big government and big business had proved that the USA was already implementing the theme of the exposition: 'Building a World of Tomorrow'.[53] The managerial present was building the imaginary future. While the dominant imagery of the 1937 Paris International Exhibition represented the unchecked violence of the totalitarian state, the enduring icons of the 1939 New York World's Fair expressed the productive potential of American industry. The technology of militarism was pitted against the technology of consumerism. For this competition of ideological symbolisms between the two international expositions, the USA had provided by far the most attractive – and utopian – vision of the imaginary future. In 1941, as the nations of Europe tore themselves apart in another disastrous war, Henry Luce – publishing magnate and intimate of the US president – proclaimed the manifesto of the rising superpower across the Atlantic:

> [The] ... promise of adequate production for all mankind, the 'more abundant life' – be it noted that this is characteristically an American promise. It is a promise easily made by demagogues and proponents of all manner of sick schemes and 'planned economies.' What we must insist on is that the abundant life is predicated on Freedom – on the Freedom which has created its possibility – on a vision of Freedom under the Law. Without Freedom, there will be no abundant life. With Freedom, there can be.[54]

---

[52] See Isaac Asimov, *I, Robot; The Rest of the Robots*.
[53] See *New York World's Fair 1939, Official Guide Book*.
[54] Henry Luce, *The American Century*, pages 14–15.

COLD WAR
COMPUTING

03

For most visitors to the 1939 New York World's Fair, its imaginary future of consumer prosperity must have seemed like a utopian dream. The American economy was still recovering from the worst recession in the nation's history. Europe was on the brink of another devastating civil war and East Asia was already engulfed by murderous conflicts. Yet, by the time that the 1964 World's Fair opened, the most famous prediction of the 1939 exposition appeared to have been realised. The Democracity and Futurama dioramas had portrayed a future where most workers would live in family houses in the suburbs and commute into work in their own motor cars. However sceptical visitors might have been back in 1939, this prophecy seemed remarkably accurate 25 years later. Most tellingly, like other American cities, New York itself had been rebuilt around a vast network of multi-lane motorways. Just as Democracity and Futurama had foreseen in 1939, large numbers of the city's workers were car-owning commuters who lived in the suburbs. The imaginary future had become everyday reality.[1]

Since the most famous prophecy of the 1939 exposition had largely come true, visitors to the 1964 New York World's Fair might have been forgiven for thinking that *its* three main imaginary futures would also be realised during the next 25 years. Considering what had already been accomplished, its hi-tech predictions didn't look like wild fantasies. Over the previous two and a half decades, big government and big business had repeatedly proved their ability to turn sci-fi dreams into ubiquitous commodities. Who could doubt that – by 1990 at the latest – the majority of Americans would be enjoying the delights of space tourism and unmetered electricity? Best of all, they would be living in a world where sentient machines were their devoted servants. The Robot Age was only a generation away.

The American public's confidence in these imaginary futures was founded upon a mistaken sense of continuity. Despite being held on the same site and having many of the same exhibitors, the 1964 World's Fair had a very different technological iconography from its 1939 antecedent. Two and a half decades earlier, the centrepiece of

[1] Robert Moses – the chief organiser of both the 1939 and 1964 World's Fairs – had led the redevelopment of New York into the world's first city dominated by roads designed for commuter traffic. See Marshall Berman, *All That Is Solid Melts into Air*, pages 287–312; and Ric Burns and James Sanders with Lisa Ades, *New York*, pages 404–413, 456–465, 494–510, 518–519.

the exposition had been the motor car: a mass-produced consumer product. In contrast, the stars of the show at the 1964 World's Fair were space rockets, atomic reactors and high-speed mainframes: state-funded technologies for fighting the Cold War. When combined together into computer-guided nuclear missiles, these technologies became horrific weapons which could destroy entire Russian cities and their unfortunate inhabitants. While its 1939 predecessor had showcased motorised transportation for the masses, the icons of the 1964 World's Fair were the machines of atomic Armageddon. In earlier expositions, the public display of new products had intensified the effects of commodity fetishism. By adding another degree of separation between creation and consumption, these events concentrated the public's attention on the symbolic role of new technologies. Inside the 1939 Futurama pavilion, the stands showing off General Motors' brand-new automobiles played a supporting role to the huge diorama which portrayed the corporation's ambition to turn the majority of the US population into suburban-dwelling, car-owning consumers. This showcasing of awe-inspiring machines and innovative products was designed to win converts for the ruling elite's hierarchical concept of society. Since there were so many wonderful things in the present, the managerial system had proved its ability to build the imaginary future. But, despite the prioritising of their symbolic role, this exposition couldn't totally ignore the use values of new technologies. Almost everyone at the 1939 World's Fair had at some point travelled in a motor car. Imaginary futures expressed the potential of a really existing present.

The 1964 New York World's Fair needed a much higher level of fetishisation. For the first time, iconography had to deny the principal use value of new technologies. Whatever their drawbacks, motor cars provided many benefits for the general public. In contrast, space rockets, nuclear reactors and mainframe computers had been invented for a diabolic purpose: murdering millions of people. Although imperial hegemony depended upon nuclear weapons, this threat of mutual annihilation made their possession increasingly problematic. The ruling elites of the USA and Russia had difficulties in admitting to themselves – let alone to their citizens – the deep irrationality of the new form of military competition. The Cold War never became a hot war between the two superpowers because both sides could threaten each other with nuclear weapons. Neither nation would have 'won' if most of their citizens were dead and all of their major cities had been turned into radioactive rubble. In the bizarre logic of the Cold War, the prevention of an all-out military confrontation between the two superpowers depended upon the continual growth in the number of nuclear weapons held by both sides. Deterrence meant escalation. Perpetual peace was permanent war. In a rare moment of lucidity, American analysts invented an ironic acronym for this high-risk strategy of 'mutually assured destruction': MAD.[2]

Not surprisingly, the propagandists of both sides justified the enormous waste of resources on the arms race by promoting the peaceful applications of the leading Cold War technologies. By the time that the 1964 New York World's Fair opened, the weaponry of genocide had been successfully repackaged into people-friendly products. Nuclear reactors were generators of cheap electricity, not atomic bomb factories. Rockets were built to take heroic astronauts into space, not to drop nuclear warheads on Russian cities. When placed on public show, almost all traces of the military origins of these technologies had disappeared. Like nuclear reactors and space rockets, the mainframe computers at the 1964 New York World's Fair were also progeny of the Cold War. During the previous two decades, the US military had dominated each stage in the development of this new technology. ENIAC – the first media icon of the computer age in America – was a machine for calculating tables to improve the accuracy of artillery guns and determining the explosive power of nuclear bombs.[3] When IBM started making mainframes in the late 1940s, its corporate strategy was focused on winning military orders. Expensive research had to be subsidised by participating in the Cold War arms race. In 1952, the dependence of IBM upon the US military was symbolised by the patriotic name given to its new 701 computer: the Defense Calculator. This moniker was accurate. The US military and its armaments manufacturers were the only purchasers of this mainframe.[4]

[2] See Jeremy Isaacs and Taylor Dowling, *Cold War*, pages 230–243; and Herman Kahn, *On Thermonuclear War*, pages 119–189.
[3] See Paul Ceruzzi, *A History of Modern Computing*, page 15; and Mike Hally, *Electronic Brains*, pages 2–27.
[4] See Ceruzzi, *Modern Computing*, pages 34–36; and Emerson Pugh, *Building IBM*, pages 167–172.

In 1953, IBM secured the contract to build the computers for the Air Defense Command: the control centre for fighting a nuclear war with Russia. Over the next five years, the corporation constructed the SAGE system, which could track Russian aircraft and order US bombers to destroy the enemy's cities. Flush with government money, IBM had the resources to pioneer the control of computers by graphic user interfaces and networked terminals.[5] When the survival of the nation was at stake, technological excellence wasn't constrained by financial limitations. By the time that the 1964 World's Fair opened, IBM's products were playing a central role in the confrontation between the two superpowers. By simulating an all-out nuclear war, using computer games, American strategists had devised the chilling strategy of mutually assured destruction.[6] With IBM mainframes, the US military could plan the destruction of Russian cities, organise the invasion of 'unfriendly' countries, direct the bombing of enemy targets, pay the wages of its troops and manage its supply chain.[7] Best of all, the generals were always eager to buy the latest version of the corporation's machines to gain the edge over their Russian opponents. Thanks to the generosity of the American taxpayers, IBM had become the technological leader of the global computer industry.

This dependency upon state funding had an excellent pedigree. In the early nineteenth century, the English government had subsidised Charles Babbage's pioneering research into mechanical calculation. Providing the best equipment for the Royal Navy was the price of maintaining British hegemony over the international trading system.[8] When Babbage's project ended in failure, other inventors of calculating engines soon emerged to take his place. As well as improving its military capabilities, the modern state also needed mathematical machinery to administer the increasingly complex industrial economy. In the late nineteenth century, Herman Hollerith founded the precursor of IBM to sell tabulators for processing the findings of national censuses. As the US government had discovered in the early 1890s, adopting this new technology was the only way to deliver the results of this survey on time.[9] Having succeeded in

---

5 See Pugh, *Building IBM*, pages 199–219.

6 See Andrew Wilson, *The Bomb and the Computer*, pages 91–117.

7 See Edmund Berkeley, *The Computer Revolution*, pages 56–7, 59–60, 137–145.

8 See Philip Morrison and Emily Morrison, 'Introduction', pages xiii-xvi.

9 See Robert Sobel, *IBM*, pages 3–22.

overcoming this problem, Hollerith's calculating machines rapidly became an essential tool of public administration across the developed world. As the state was forced to take more and more responsibility for policing the population, regulating the economy and providing welfare, its bureaucracy had to collect and collate increasing amounts of data. The dispassionate rationality of the 'government machine' was symbolised by the smooth working of the machinery of government: card indexes, filing systems, typewriters, telephones and, as a premonition of things to come, Hollerith tabulators.[10]

During the first half of the twentieth century, the mobilisation of resources for industrialised warfare consolidated the state's ascendancy over the market. Back in the Victorian era, liberal orthodoxy had emphasised that individual initiative was the only efficient method of organising the economy. This dogma was quickly abandoned when winning the battle for production became the prerequisite of military victory. In the epoch of mechanised warfare, the nation which equipped its armed forces with the greatest numbers of the most advanced weaponry would eventually prevail.[11] With so much at stake, political leadership was needed to impose the priorities of the battlefield upon private enterprise. As the conflict dragged on, state intervention was steadily extended beyond the day-to-day direction of the economy. Having usurped the managerial functions of the capitalist class, the government bureaucracy also began to take over its entrepreneurial role. State planners were given the responsibility for conceiving and implementing a long-term growth strategy for the national economy. Their task was to maximise output by organising the optimum allocation of skilled labour and scarce resources.[12] As was dramatically proved between 1914 and 1918, the state's ability to organise production had become the foundation of geopolitical supremacy.

When the war between the European powers recommenced in 1939, the combatants were well aware that military strength depended upon industrial prowess. As one of their primary goals, the planners had to prioritise the development of new technologies.

---

[10] See Jon Agar, *The Government Machine*, pages 121–199.
[11] See Paul Kennedy, *The Rise and Fall of Great Powers*, pages 330–354.
[12] See Eric Hobsbawm, *Age of Extremes*, pages 21–53; and Keith Middlemas, *Politics in Industrial Society*, pages 68–151.

Scientists on the home front invented the weapons which secured victory for soldiers on the battlefield. In the opening rounds of the Second World War, the German military demonstrated its mastery of the new tactics of mechanised warfare by routing the armies of Poland and France. However, when its air force tried to seize control of the skies over southern England, its pilots soon discovered that their opponents now had the technological edge. During the 1930s, as well as developing the best fighter planes, British scientists had also invented radar detection systems. In this vital air battle, superiority in the collection, analysis and dissemination of information gave victory to the numerically inferior side. The mastery of technology had halted the fascist advance in Europe.[13]

After the German invasion of Britain was abandoned, encryption became the main front in the information war. Radio broadcasting provided the communications infrastructure for the command and control of military forces operating over huge distances. But, because the enemy could intercept these messages, security had to be protected by transmitting information in unbreakable codes. At the outbreak of the war, the German high command was convinced that its Enigma machine provided the technological solution to this problem. Determined to prove them wrong, the British government created an organisation dedicated to breaking this new form of encryption: Bletchley Park. Faced with the problem of analysing vast amounts of scrambled information, multi-disciplinary teams of academics and engineers were mobilised to develop machines which could decipher codes generated by machines.[14]

Alan Turing was the intellectual guru of this technological project. In 1936, this Cambridge mathematician had published an article describing the abstract model for a programmable computer: the 'universal machine'.[15] At Bletchley Park, Turing was given the opportunity to turn theory into reality. By developing sophisticated mechanical calculators to process their decrypting formulas, his colleagues were able not only to break the unbreakable Enigma code, but also, just as importantly, to decode large quantities of enemy

[13] See Agar, *Government Machine*, pages 209–217.
[14] See Agar, *Government Machine*, pages 203–206; and Jack Copeland, 'Enigma'.
[15] See Alan Turing, 'On Computable Numbers'; and Jon Agar, *Turing and the Universal Machine*, pages 85–100.

signals.[16] Frustrated by the limitations of analogue tabulators, Turing persuaded his bosses to fund research into electronic calculation. Led by Tommy Flowers, a group of telephone engineers took responsibility for completing this vital project. By the end of 1943, this team had successfully built their prototype of the electronic computer: Colossus.[17] Britain had retained its technological lead in the information war.

For Turing, the invention of Colossus proved that his theoretical speculations could be turned into practical applications. Every improvement in tabulator technology was another step towards the creation of the universal machine.[18] When the war was over, Turing devoted himself to realising his dream. Thanks to their experiences at Bletchley Park, British scientists were now at the forefront of the new technology of computing. Moving to Manchester, Turing joined a team of researchers who were building a programmable machine. As proposed in his 1936 article, software would be used to enable the hardware to perform a variety of different tasks. On 21 June 1948, before he'd even taken up his new post, Turing's colleagues switched on the world's first electronic stored-program computer: Baby. The theoretical concept described in an academic journal had taken material form as an enormous metal box filled with valves, switches, wires and dials.[19]

Turing was convinced that the Baby computer was much more than just an improved version of the Hollerith tabulator. In a series of seminal articles, he argued that this mathematical machine was the precursor of an entirely new life form: the mechanical mathematician. When software could control hardware, counting became consciousness. Back in Victorian England, Charles Babbage had promoted an early version of this vision of artificial intelligence. When his Difference and Analytical engines carried out calculations, they were 'thinking' like humans.[20] Inspired by Babbage's insight,

[16] See Andrew Hodges, *Alan Turing*, pages 160–241; and Michael Smith, *Station X*, pages 52–53, 67–68, 110.

[17] See Hodges, *Turing*, pages 263–268, 277–278; Agar, *Government Machine*, pages 208–209; and Smith, *Station X*, pages 147–151, 170.

[18] See Hodges, *Turing*, pages 289–305.

[19] See Alan Turing, 'Lecture on the Automatic Computing Engine'; Agar, *Turing*, pages 3–5, 113–124; and Hodges, *Turing*, pages 314–402.

[20] See Simon Schaffer, 'Babbage's Dancer'.

Turing defined human intelligence as what computers could do. Since calculating was a sophisticated type of thinking, calculating machines must be able to think. If children acquired knowledge through education, educational software would create knowledgeable computers. Because the human brain worked like a machine, it was obvious that a machine could behave like an electronic brain.[21]

According to Turing, computers would soon even acquire the essence of human subjectivity: 'free will'. By using a random-choice generator, mainframes were also able to make arbitrary decisions.[22] Everything human was replicable by machines. But, as Turing emphasised, it would take at least five decades before the goal of artificial intelligence was reached. In the early 1950s, computers weren't yet powerful enough to fulfil their true potential. Fortunately, continual improvements in hardware and software would – sooner or later – overcome these limitations. In the second half of the twentieth century, computing technology was rapidly evolving towards its preordained destiny: artificial intelligence.

> The memory capacity of the human brain is probably of the order of ten thousand million binary digits. But most of this is probably used in remembering visual impressions, and other comparatively wasteful ways. One might reasonably hope to be able to make some real progress [towards artificial intelligence] with a few million digits [of computer memory].[23]

In his most famous article, Turing described a test for identifying the winner of this race to the future. At Bletchley Park, he had become fascinated by the possibility of programming a computer to play chess. Because intellectuals enjoyed this game, he became convinced that machines which could play chess must be intelligent.[24] Mesmerised by technological fetishism, Turing claimed that the labour of the programmers disappeared when the computer was running the programs which they had written. Extrapolating upon this assertion, this academic devised his own idiosyncratic test of machine intelligence: the 'imitation game'. Once an observer

---

[21] See Alan Turing, 'Automatic Computing Engine'; 'Intelligent Machinery'; 'Intelligent Machinery, a Heretical Theory'; 'Can Digital Computers Think?'.

[22] See Turing, 'Can Digital Computers Think?', pages 484–485.

[23] Turing, 'Automatic Computing Engine', page 393.

[24] See Alan Turing, 'Chess'; and Hodges, Turing, pages 210–217.

couldn't tell whether they were talking with a human or a computer in an on-line conversation, then there was no longer any substantial difference between the two types of consciousness. If the imitation was indistinguishable from the original, the machine must be thinking. The computer had passed the test.[25]

In the late 1940s and early 1950s, Alan Turing became the first prophet of the imaginary future of artificial intelligence. The musings of Babbage and the fantasies of Asimov had been turned into a scientific research project. From this point onwards, computers existed in two time zones at once. In the present, these machines were practical tools and tradable commodities. Yet, as Turing's articles proved, computers were also endowed with immense symbolic value. The imaginary future of artificial intelligence revealed the transformative potential of this new technology. Despite their shortcomings, the current models of computers were forerunners of the sentient machines to come. The passing of the Turing test was always imminent. Inside the fetishised economy, machines were becoming indistinguishable from human beings.

By the late 1940s, the catechism of artificial intelligence had been defined. Within computing, what was and what will be were one and the same thing. Despite this achievement, Turing was a prophet whose influence was waning within his own country. The computer might have been invented in Britain, but its indebted government lacked the resources to dominate the development of this technology.[26] Across the Atlantic, the situation was very different. During the Second World War, the US government had created its own multi-disciplinary research teams to develop advanced weaponry. By pouring money into the Manhattan Project, its military scientists were able to build the first nuclear bomb. As an important part of the war effort, the American government had also provided generous funding for research into electronic calculation. Crucially, when the victory over fascism was won, scientists working on these projects didn't have to worry about losing their grants. Once the Cold War got underway, American politicians

---

25 See Alan Turing, 'Computing Machinery and Intelligence', pages 441–448; and Agar, *Turing*, pages 122–126.

26 See Hodges, *Turing*, pages 456–527; and Agar, *Government Machine*, pages 266–278.

had no problem in justifying these subsidies to their constituents.[27] Since the late 1930s, scientists in the leading industrial nations had been working in parallel towards the realisation of Turing's goal of building a universal machine. At different moments, the British, Germans and Russians had been at the forefront of this collective project. By the early 1950s, the USA's academic and corporate research teams had seized the leadership of computing from their rivals. Above all, American companies like IBM had also learnt how to turn this cutting-edge science into reliable products for military and corporate customers. In the mid 1960s, there was no doubt that the most advanced machines were made-in-the-USA.[28]

---

[27] See Stuart Leslie, *The Cold War and American Science*, pages 1–13; and R.C. Lewontin, 'The Cold War and the Transformation of the Academy'.
[28] See Ceruzzi, *Modern Computing*, pages 13–46.

THE HUMAN
MACHINE

04

In 1946, a group of prominent American intellectuals held the first of a series of meetings dedicated to breaking down the barriers between the various academic disciplines: the Macy conferences.[1] Inspired by their wartime experiences of collaborative research, they were looking for a meta-theory which could be applied within both the natural sciences and the social sciences. If everyone shared a common language, academics with different areas of expertise would be able to work together.[2] After the first few meetings, Norbert Wiener emerged as the theoretical guru of the Macy conferences.[3] During the Second World War, this MIT mathematician had worked on a project to improve the accuracy of anti-aircraft guns. When firing at a moving plane, the operator had to anticipate the future positions of the target. Because of the speed of hi-tech warfare, the most effective method of achieving this goal was developing technology which automatically corrected the gunner's aim. When acting in symbiosis, the soldier and the weapon could outwit their enemy.[4]

From this research for the US military, Wiener developed a theoretical framework for analysing the behaviour of both humans and machines. Soldiers aimed their anti-aircraft guns by guessing the flight path of the enemy. Whether carried out by a human or a machine, the input of information about the surrounding environment led to the output of actions designed to transform this environment. Dubbed 'feedback', these cycles of stimulus and response weren't restricted to the battlefield. According to Wiener, this concept applied to any action which reversed the spread of entropy within the universe. The second law of thermodynamics was only determinant in the last instance. Thanks to feedback, order could be created out of chaos.[5] Wiener argued that this master theory described all forms of purposeful behaviour. Whether in humans or

---

[1] This series of conferences was named after their sponsoring organisation, the Josiah Macy Jr. Foundation. As well as giving away the oil fortune of its eponymous benefactor to good causes, this charity also subsidised academic research projects with clandestine funding from the US intelligence services. See Steve Heims, *The Cybernetics Group*, pages 14–18, 164–169.

[2] See Heims, *Cybernetics Group*, pages 14–30. Also see American Society for Cybernetics, 'Summary: The Macy Conferences'.

[3] See Flo Conway and Jim Siegelman, *Dark Hero of the Information Age*, pages 154–170.

[4] See Norbert Wiener, *Cybernetics*, pages 9–13, 133–134.

[5] See Wiener, *Cybernetics*, pages 74–136; and Arturo Rosenblueth, Norbert Wiener and Julian Bigelow, 'Behaviour, Purpose and Teleology'.

machines, there was continual feedback between information and action. The same mathematical equations could be used to analyse the impact on the world of both living organisms and technological systems.[6] Echoing Turing, this approach implied that it was difficult to tell the difference between humans and their machines.[7] In 1948, Wiener outlined his new master theory in a book filled with pages of mathematical proofs: *Cybernetics – or command and control in the animal and the machine.*

Much to his surprise, this academic had written a best-seller. For the first time, a common set of abstract concepts covered both the natural sciences and the social sciences. Above all, Wiener's text provided potent metaphors for describing the new hi-tech world of Cold War America. Even if they didn't understand his mathematical equations, readers could easily recognise cybernetic systems within the social institutions and communication networks which dominated their everyday lives. Across the American sphere of influence, the media promoted this meta-theory as the epitome of computerised modernity. The metaphors of feedback, information and cybernetic systems soon became part of everyday speech.[8] Despite this public acclamation, Wiener remained an outsider within the US intelligentsia. The high priest of the Macy conferences was also a heretic who spoke out against the Cold War arms race.

Back in the early 1940s, Wiener – like almost every American scientist – had believed that developing weapons to defeat Nazi Germany benefited humanity. When the Cold War started, military-funded researchers claimed that their work was also contributing to the struggle against an aggressive totalitarian enemy.[9] Challenging this patriotic consensus, Wiener argued that American scientists should adopt a very different stance in the confrontation with Russia. He warned that the nuclear arms race could lead to the destruction of humanity. Faced with this dangerous new situation, responsible scientists should refuse to carry out military research.[10]

[6] See Rosenblueth, Wiener and Bigelow, 'Behaviour, Purpose and Teleology'; and Wiener, *Cybernetics*, pages 168–191.

[7] For Turing's influence on Wiener, see Wiener, *Cybernetics*, pages 21, 32–33.

[8] See Conway and Siegelman, *Dark Hero*, pages 171–194; and Heims, *Cybernetics Group*, pages 271–272.

[9] See R.C. Lewontin, 'The Cold War and the Transformation of the Academy'.

[10] See Norbert Wiener, *The Human Use of Human Beings*, page 174; and Conway and Siegelman, *Dark Hero*, pages 237–243, 255–271.

During the 1950s and early 1960s, Wiener's political dissidence inspired his advocacy of a socialist interpretation of cybernetics. In the epoch of corporate monopolies and atomic weaponry, the theory that explained the behaviour of both humans and machines must be used to place humans in control of their machines. Abandoning his earlier enthusiasm for Turing's prophecy of artificial intelligence, Wiener now emphasised the dangers posed by sentient computers.[11] Like the protagonists of the *Thousand and One Nights*, humans might find themselves unable to control their new hi-tech jinnees.[12] Above all, this attempt to build artificial intelligences was a diversion from the urgent task of creating social justice and global peace. 'The world of the future will be an ever more demanding struggle against the limitations of our own intelligence, not a comfortable hammock in which we can lie down to be waited upon by our robot slaves.'[13]

For the sponsors of the Macy conferences, Wiener's cybernetics had provided a master theory for Cold War America. But, by opposing the militarisation of scientific research, this sage had embarrassed his sponsors among the US elite. Even worse, his left-wing version of cybernetics had transformed this celebration of multi-disciplinary collaboration into a critique of the intellectual establishment. Fortunately for its US military sponsors, there was another brilliant mathematician at the Macy conferences who was also a fanatical Cold War warrior: John von Neumann. Traumatised by the nationalisation of his family's bank during the 1919 Hungarian Revolution, this anti-socialist ideologue had written the founding text of games theory which – among other things – set out to prove that there was no economic alternative to liberal capitalism. In a tautological argument, the utility-maximising egoists of neo-classical economics were equated with the rational individuals who played to win against their opponents.[14] At the outbreak of the Cold War, von Neumann's political position was so extreme that he'd advocated the USA's launching of a pre-emptive strike against Russia to stop

---

[11] See Wiener, *Human Beings*, pages 239–254.

[12] See Norbert Wiener, *God & Golem, Inc.*, pages 52–60.

[13] Wiener, *God and Golem, Inc.*, page 69.

[14] See John von Neumann and Oskar Morgenstern, *Theory of Games and Economic Behaviour*; and Steve Heims, *John von Neumann and Norbert Wiener*, pages 43–46, 79–95, 193–194, 292–293.

its leaders from acquiring nuclear weapons.[15] Not surprisingly, this hawk was deeply involved in military-funded research. While playing a leading role in developing the atomic bomb, von Neumann had also applied his mathematical and organisational talents to the new field of computing. When the first Macy conference was held in 1946, his team of researchers was already working on building a prototype mainframe for the US Navy.[16] In von Neumann, the American empire had found a guru without any trace of heresy.

At the early Macy conferences, the political differences among its attendees weren't apparent. United by the anti-fascist struggle, Wiener and von Neumann were not only intellectual collaborators, but also close friends. Both Left and Right could champion the same meta-theory of cybernetics. But, within a few years, these two stars of the Macy conferences were divided by their incompatible positions on the Cold War. As their politics diverged, Wiener and von Neumann began advocating rival interpretations of cybernetics. In its left-wing version, artificial intelligence was denounced as the apotheosis of technological domination. When he formulated his right-wing remix, von Neumann took cybernetics in exactly the opposite direction. Tellingly, his interpretation emphasised that this master theory had been inspired by the prophecy of thinking machines. By taking this approach, Wiener's critique of the corruption of science by the Cold War was countered by undermining his status as the guru of computerised modernity. By promoting Turing's concept of artificial intelligence, von Neumann had elevated himself into the position of the founding father of cybernetics.[17] Ironically, the English scientist who had inspired the builders of the first computer had been relegated to being a forerunner of the pre-eminent prophet of the American scientists who claimed that they'd built the first computer.

Back in the mid 1930s, von Neumann had briefly worked with Turing at Princeton University. A decade before his involvement

[15] See Heims, *Von Neumann and Wiener*, pages 235–236, 244–251. If this horrifying plan had been carried out, the resulting nuclear war would have wiped out most of the inhabitants of his Hungarian homeland who were living on the frontline in Europe.

[16] See Paul Ceruzzi, *Modern Computing*, pages 21–24; and Heims, *Von Neumann and Wiener*, pages 238–239.

[17] See John von Neumann, 'The General and Logical Theory of Automata', pages 313–315; *Theory of Self-Reproducing Automata*, pages 49–51.

in computing, this Hungarian scientist already knew about the concept of the universal machine.[18] When, in the early 1940s, Warren McCulloch and Walter Pitts applied Turing's theory to explaining the process of thinking, von Neumann was fascinated by the implications of their speculations. Since the mechanical calculator was modelled on the human brain, these two Chicago psychologists decided that consciousness must be synonymous with calculation. Like the electrical contacts of an IBM tabulator, neurons were switches which transmitted information in binary form.[19] Entranced by this inversion of Turing's line of argument, von Neumann became convinced that it was theoretically possible to build a thinking machine. If neurons acted as switches within the human brain, then valves could be used to create an electronic brain.[20] Moving into computer research, he was given large sums of money by the US military to realise his dream. Just like Turing, this prophet believed that continual improvements in hardware must eventually culminate in the emergence of artificial intelligence. As the number of valves in a computer approached that of the neurons in the brain, the machine would begin to think.[21] Within a decade, von Neuman and his colleagues would be equipping the US military with cybernetic soldiers capable of fighting and winning a nuclear war.

> Dr McCulloch: How about designing computing machines so that if they were damaged in air raids ... they could replace parts ... and continue to work?
> Dr von Neumann: These are really quantitative rather than qualitative questions.[22]

By the early 1950s, von Neumann had successfully created cybernetics without Wiener. The metaphor of feedback now proved that computers operated like humans. Like the rational players in his

---

[18] See B. Jack Copeland, 'Computable Numbers: a guide', pages 21–22.

[19] See Warren McCulloch and Walter Pitts, 'A Logical Calculus of the Ideas Immanent in Nervous Activity'.

[20] See von Neumann, 'General and Logical Theory of Automata', pages 308–311; Theory of Self-Reproducing Automata, pages 43–46.

[21] See von Neumann, 'General and Logical Theory of Automata', pages 296–300; Theory of Self-Reproducing Automata, pages 36–41; The Computer and the Brain, pages 39–52.

[22] Von Neumann, 'General and Logical Theory of Automata', page 324.

book on games theory, both living and mechanical beings responded to stimuli from their surrounding environment. Inputs of information led to outputs of action. Since the behaviour of both humans and machines could be described mathematically, calculation became the leitmotif of consciousness. Through this line of argument, von Neumann was able to define the research mission of the new computer science departments being set up in American universities: building artificial intelligence. Language was a set of rules which could be codified as software. Learning from new experiences could be programmed into computers.[23] As they began to evolve like living organisms, machines were becoming 'self-reproducing automata'.[24] In this right-wing version, the theory of cybernetics had been redefined as the study of artificial intelligence. Led by McCulloch, von Neumann's admirers at the Macy conferences pioneered the application of this new orthodoxy within other academic disciplines. If human brains were calculating machines, social institutions should be studied as cybernetic systems. Just like computers, individuals were information processors who responded to orders given by their programmers.[25] For over a century, commodity fetishism had inspired the fetishisation of technology. Now, in von Neumann's remix of cybernetics, technological fetishism explained a society founded upon the fetishisation of commodities. Instead of the computer successfully imitating a human, this new Turing test was passed when humans were indistinguishable from computers.

This conservative version of cybernetics provided philosophical reassurance for the moral dilemmas faced by academic researchers in American universities. From the early 1950s onwards, the US military enthusiastically funded the development of computer games simulating an atomic war between the superpowers. By running these programs, its experts formulated the paradoxical concept of mutually assured destruction. According to the cruel logic of game theory, the benefits of treachery outweighed those of mutual trust: 'the prisoner's dilemma'. Based on this premise, the computer

23 See Marvin Minsky, 'Matter, Mind and Models'; 'Steps Towards Artificial Intelligence'.
24 See von Neumann, 'General and Logical Theory of Automata', pages 315–318; Theory of Self-Reproducing Automata, pages 74–87.
25 See Talcott Parsons and Edward Shils, Toward a General Theory of Action; and B.F. Skinner, Science and Human Behaviour. Also see Heims, Cybernetics Group, pages 52–247; and Christopher Rand, Cambridge U.S.A., pages 129–158.

simulations proved that the preservation of peace between America and Russia required a continual escalation of the nuclear arms race. Embodying Turing and von Neumann's concept of artificial intelligence, game-playing IBM mainframes had scientifically produced the most intelligent military strategy for fighting the Cold War. The irrational had become rational.[26] For military-funded researchers in American universities, von Neumann's interpretation of cybernetics provided a self-congratulatory cover story for their dubious activities. Programming computers to guide missiles, control bombers, direct armies and play war games was no longer helping to plan the nuclear holocaust. On the contrary, as Turing and von Neumann had proved, these military applications were an essential step towards the final goal of artificial intelligence. Technological fetishism had absolved computer scientists of any responsibility for the consequences of their own actions.

At the 1964 New York World's Fair, IBM copied this strategy when designing its exhibit. Like university computer science departments, the corporation needed von Neumann's cybernetic remix to distract attention away from its deep involvement in questionable military projects. IBM had recently sold a 704 mainframe to the US Air Force for guiding nuclear missiles that were designed to massacre the civilian population of Russia and its dependencies. The first order for a System/360 computer had come from a manufacturer of fighter planes whose products would soon be raining death and destruction upon the villages of Vietnam.[27] However, just like the displays of fission reactors and space rockets, the IBM pavilion carefully avoided showing the military applications of its computers. The only hint of the corporation's massive involvement in fighting the Cold War was the presence of the computer which could translate Russian into English.

As with the predictions of unmetered energy and space tourism, the imaginary future of artificial intelligence disguised the original motivation for developing IBM's mainframes: killing large numbers of people. During the Cold War, smart advertising had to hide

[26] See Anatol Rapoport, *Fights, Games and Debates*, pages 107–179; and Andrew Wilson, *The Bomb and the Computer*, pages 140–153.
[27] See Edmund Berkeley, *The Computer Revolution*, pages 142–3; and Emerson Pugh, Lyle Johnson and John Palmer, *IBM's 360 and Early 370 Systems*, page 171.

horrific use values. The American elite certainly didn't want tourists on a fun day out at the New York World's Fair to leave terrified by displays about the ever-present danger of a nuclear holocaust. The machines of death were therefore repackaged as prototypes of science fiction technologies. In symbiosis, the different imaginary futures also gave credibility to each other. The promise of interplanetary tourism had transformed the main function of computerised rocket guidance systems from destroying Russian cities with nuclear bombs into taking intrepid astronauts into outer space. The horrors of the Cold War present had been successfully hidden by the marvels of the imaginary futures.

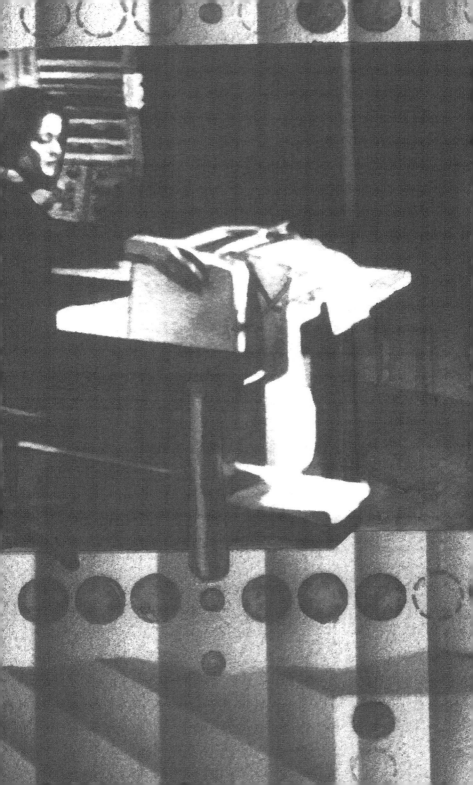

CYBERNETIC SUPREMACY

05

Although it was very popular at the time, the hyper-reality of the 1964 World's Fair didn't age well. During the subsequent 25 years, none of the predictions made at the exposition about the key Cold War technologies were realised. Energy remained metered, tourists didn't visit the moon and computers never became intelligent. At the 1964 World's Fair, imaginary futures had succeeded in concealing the primary purpose of the three main Cold War technologies from the American public. Instruments of genocide were successfully disguised as benefactors of humanity. However, this subterfuge could only be temporary. Sooner or later, even the finest-crafted advertising was no longer able to hide dodgy use values. When the 1990s eventually arrived, producing significant amounts of power from nuclear fusion was still impractical. By then, it also had become obvious that fission reactors were an economic and environmental disaster. The explosion in 1986 at the Chernobyl plant in Ukraine had dramatically demonstrated the inherent dangers of this exotic method of generating electricity.[1] By the early 1990s, most people had also realised that manned space flight would long remain an expensive luxury. It had been two decades since NASA's astronauts had last landed on the moon and there were no plans to restart the programme.[2] When the Cold War eventually ended in 1991, even most of the military applications of nuclear power and space travel appeared largely redundant. Unlike the prescient vision of motoring for the masses at the 1939 World's Fair, the prophecies about these two star technologies of the 1964 exposition seemed almost absurd a quarter of a century later. The epoch of unmetered electricity and holidays on the moon was indefinitely postponed. Hyper-reality had collided with reality − and lost.

Just like the displays of nuclear reactors and space rockets, the computer exhibits at the 1964 World's Fair also totally misread the direction of technological progress. Led by IBM, American corporations had foreseen the triumph of artificial intelligence. But, as more and more people used computers over the next 25 years, the myth of thinking machines lost most of its credibility. Like almost free energy for nuclear power and moon tourism for space travel, the iconography of artificial intelligence could only temporarily

---

[1] See Arjun Makhijani and Scott Saleska, 'The Nuclear Power Deception'.
[2] The final US Apollo moon mission took place in December 1972.

obscure the underlying use value of computing. However, there was one crucial difference between the collapse of the first two prophecies and that of the last one. What eventually discredited the predictions of unmetered electricity and holidays on the moon was their failure to appear over time. In contrast, scepticism about the imaginary future of artificial intelligence was encouraged by exactly the opposite phenomenon: the increased likelihood of people having personal experience of computers. After using these imperfect tools for manipulating information, it was much more difficult for them to believe that calculating machines could evolve into sentient super-beings. Artificial intelligence had been exposed as a contradiction in terms.[3]

Despite the increasing scepticism about its favourite prophecy, IBM suffered no damage. In stark contrast with nuclear power and space travel, computing was the Cold War technology which successfully escaped from the Cold War. Right from the beginning, machines made for the US military were also sold to commercial clients. In the late 1940s, IBM had developed its CPC computer for a defence contractor to calculate missile trajectories. Yet, within a few years, this machine had become the corporation's best-selling product in the business market.[4] More than anything else, the 'spin-off' of computing into the civilian sector was encouraged by the increasing bureaucratisation of both the military and the economy.[5] What had originated as a Cold War weapon quickly evolved into a technology with multiple commercial applications. In 1962, one of the pioneering analysts of the social impact of computing explained that:

> The growth of a great civilisation which is complex engineering-wise and technologically on the one hand, and complex business–wise and industrially on the other, has produced an enormous growth in the information to be handled and operated with. This provides the push, the energy, the urgency behind the great development of

[3] Ted Nelson pointed out that: '... "artificial intelligence" is an ever-receding frontier: as techniques become well-worked out and understood, their *appearance* of intelligence, to the sophisticated, continually recedes.' Ted Nelson, *Computer Lib*, 'Dream Machines' section, page 120.

[4] See Emerson Pugh, *Building IBM*, pages 153–155.

[5] The first commercial application of computing in the USA was running the payroll of General Electric. See Paul Ceruzzi, *Modern Computing*, pages 33–34.

the automatic handling of information, expressed in computers and data-processing systems, the Computer Revolution.[6]

When IBM built its pavilion for the 1964 World's Fair, the imaginary future of electronic brains had to hide more than the unsavoury military applications of computing. This fetishised ideology also performed its classic function of concealing the role of human labour within production. Computers were described as 'thinking', so the hard work involved in designing, building, programming and operating them could be discounted. This process of technological fetishisation didn't just shape social attitudes towards those who worked for the corporation itself. Above all, the imaginary future of artificial intelligence diverted attention away from the hard economics driving the computerisation of the workplace in 1950s and early-1960s America. Back in the late nineteenth century, IBM's forerunner had started out as a producer of tabulators, typewriters and other types of office equipment. Even without the encouragement of US military contracts, the corporation would eventually have had to move into computing to protect itself against technological obsolescence. By the mid 1950s, what had once been calculated by hordes of tabulator operators could now be done much more quickly and cheaply by a few engineers with a mainframe.

The introduction of computers into the workplace came at an opportune moment. During the first half of the twentieth century, large corporations had become the dominant institutions of the American economy. More than anything else, this unprecedented centralisation of capital was driven by the need to increase the productivity of labour. When market competition was replaced by managerial authority, the costs of organising large numbers of workers could be substantially reduced.[7] When many different individuals invested in the same company, the expenses of technological innovation were more easily met.[8] Since family firms lacked these advantages, capital and labour became increasingly concentrated under the control of large corporations. Indirect association was replaced by direct supervision. As the twentieth

---

[6] Edmund Berkeley, *The Computer Revolution*, page 41.
[7] See R.H. Coase, 'The Nature of the Firm'.
[8] See Karl Marx, *Capital, Volume 3*, pages 566–573.

century progressed, the corporate restructuring of the economy was widely imitated within politics, the arts and everyday life. Henry Ford's giant car factory became the eponymous symbol of the new social paradigm: *Fordism*.[9]

Large corporations depended upon a specialist caste of bureaucrats to run their organisations. They ran the managerial 'Panopticon' which ensured that employees obeyed the orders imposed from above.[10] They supervised the financing, manufacture, marketing and distribution of the corporation's products. Above all, they were responsible for improving working methods and introducing new technologies. As Frederick Winslow Taylor's manuals pointed out, 'scientific management' could compel people to toil harder.[11] As Henry Ford's assembly lines demonstrated, machinery could determine the pace of work.[12] This pressure to separate conception from execution encouraged the collection of more and more information. Corporate bureaucrats wanted to know what was happening within the workplace and the marketplace. They had to manage invoices, payrolls, supplies and stocktaking. They needed to organise consumer surveys, product development, market research, political lobbying and advertising campaigns. As the demand for information kept on growing, corporations recruited ever larger numbers of clerical workers.[13] As the wage bill for white-collar employees steadily rose, managers purchased increasing amounts of equipment to raise productivity within the office. Long before the invention of the computer, the bureaucracies of Fordist corporations were running an information economy with tabulators, typewriters and other types of office equipment.[14]

At the beginning of the 1950s, the mechanisation of clerical labour had stalled. Increases in productivity in the office were lagging

[9] See Michel Aglietta, A Theory of Capitalist Regulation, pages 215–272; and Alain Lipietz, Mirages and Miracles, pages 29–46.

[10] According to Michel Foucault, the Panopticon – a late-eighteenth-century prison designed to keep its inmates under constant surveillance – pioneered the disciplinary model which was later used to control the workers of the factories and offices of Fordism. See Michel Foucault, Discipline and Punish.

[11] See Frederick Winslow Taylor, The Principles of Scientific Management.

[12] See Henry Ford, My Life and Work, pages 77–90.

[13] See Fritz Machlup, The Production and Distribution of Knowledge in the United States, pages 381–400.

[14] See James Beniger, The Control Revolution, pages 291–425.

well behind those in the factory. When the first computers appeared on the market, corporate managers quickly realised that the new technology offered a solution to this pressing problem. Buying a mainframe could increase their company's profits.[15] Just like new machines in the factory, computers were – first and foremost – purchased to replace skilled labour within the office. Even better, the new technology of computing enabled capitalists to deepen their control over their organisations. Like big government, big business was delighted that much more information about a wider variety of topics could now be collected and processed in increasingly complex ways. Managers were masters of all that they surveyed.

Almost from its first appearance in the workplace, the mainframe was caricatured – with good reason – as the mechanical perfection of bureaucratic tyranny: the 'information Panopticon'.[16] For the first time since the early 1940s, Asimov's optimistic vision of artificial intelligence was widely questioned. In his sci-fi stories, thinking machines were consumer goods just like motor cars. Mr and Mrs Average were the owners of robot servants. But, when the first computers arrived in America's factories and offices, economic reality contradicted Asimov's imaginary future. The new technology was the servant of the bosses, not of the workers. In 1952, Kurt Vonnegut published a sci-fi novel which satirised the authoritarian ambitions of the information Panopticon. In his dystopian future, the ruling elite had outsourced the management of society to an omniscient artificial intelligence.

> EPICAC XIV ... decided how many [of] everything America and her customers could have and how much they would cost. And it ... would decide how many engineers and managers and research men and civil servants, and of what skills, would be needed to deliver the goods; and what I.Q. and aptitude levels would separate the useful men from the useless ones, and how many ... [women and] men [on public works schemes] and how many soldiers could be supported at what pay level ...[17]

For big business even more than for big government, Vonnegut's nightmare was their computer daydream. At the 1964 World's Fair,

15 See Robert Sobel, *IBM*, pages 95–184.
16 See Shoshana Zuboff, *In the Age of the Smart Machine*, pages 315–361.
17 Kurt Vonnegut, *Player Piano*, page 106.

the IBM pavilion promised that thinking machines would be the servants of all of humanity. Yet, at the same time, its sales personnel were telling the bosses of large corporations that computers were hard-wiring bureaucratic authority into modern society. Herbert Simon – a former colleague of von Neumann – believed that the increasing power of mainframes would enable companies to automate more and more clerical tasks.[18] For its new System/360 machines, IBM had constructed the world's most advanced computer-controlled assembly line to increase the productivity of its high-skill, high-wage employees.[19] When artificial intelligence arrived, mainframes would almost completely replace bureaucratic and technical labour within manufacturing. The ultimate goal was the creation of the fully automated economy. Companies would then no longer need either blue-collar or white-collar workers to make products or provide services. Even most managers would become surplus to requirements.[20] Instead, thinking machines would be running the factories and offices of America. In the imaginary future of artificial intelligence, the corporation and the computer would be one and the same thing. Capitalist firms would have become self-reproducing automata.

This prophecy was founded upon the conservative appropriation of cybernetics. During the 1950s, Simon had pursued a twin-track career. On the one hand, he worked on research projects into artificial intelligence for the US Air Force. On the other hand, he pioneered the application of systems theory within business studies.[21] By the beginning of the 1960s, Simon had combined his two areas of expertise into one. Since both were cybernetic systems, the fusion of the computer and the corporation was inevitable. By making this prediction, Simon had updated Turing's original goals for artificial intelligence. Back in the late 1940s, this Cambridge mathematician had argued that his universal machine would eventually replace most routine forms of mental labour.[22] In Turing's original version, the

[18] See Herbert Simon, *The Shape of Automation for Men and Management*.

[19] See Emerson Pugh, Lyle Johnson and John Palmer, *IBM's 360 and Early 370 Systems*, pages 87–105, 204–210.

[20] See Simon, *Shape of Automation*, page 47.

[21] See Herbert Simon, *Administrative Behaviour*; and Paul Edwards, *The Closed World*, pages 250–256.

[22] See Alan Turing, 'Lecture on the Automatic Computing Engine', pages 391–394; 'Intelligent Machinery, a Heretical Theory', pages 474–475.

bureaucratic hierarchy of the British state provided the model for the ordered structure of the intelligent computer. The government machine was evolving into a physical machine. Political fetishism had inspired technological fetishism.

In his managerial theory, Simon substituted the American corporation for the British civil service. The operations of a computer now resembled the workings of a firm. Both were cybernetic systems which processed information. As in McCulloch and Pitts' psychology, this identification was made in two directions. Managing workers was equated with programming a computer. Writing software was like drawing up a business plan. Both employees and machinery were controlled by orders issued from above. Ironically, the credibility of Simon's managerial ideology depended upon his readers forgetting the fierce criticisms of corporate computing made by the founding father of cybernetics. Echoing Marx, Wiener had warned that the role of new technology under capitalism was to intensify the exploitation of the workers. Instead of creating more leisure time and improving living standards, the computerisation of the economy under Fordism would increase unemployment and cut wages.[23] If Vonnegut's dystopia was to be avoided, American trade unionists and political activists must mobilise against the corporate Golem.[24] According to Wiener, cybernetics proved that artificial intelligence threatened the freedoms of humanity. 'Let us remember that the automatic machine ... is the precise equivalent of slave labour. Any labour which competes with slave labour must accept the economic conditions of slave labour.'[25]

Like the US military, the academic boosters of the American corporations also needed a new guru. As von Neumann had shown, smart intellectuals knew how to create cybernetics without Wiener. The key move was rewriting the historical origins of this meta-theory. If someone else had helped to invent cybernetics, Wiener's subversive opinions could be safely downplayed. By appropriating Turing's concept of artificial intelligence, von Neumann had taken over the role of the first prophet. Within managerial theory,

[23] See Norbert Wiener, *Cybernetics*, pages 36–39; *The Human Use of Human Beings*, pages 206–221.
[24] See Norbert Wiener, *God & Golem, Inc.*, pages 54–55.
[25] Wiener, *Human Beings*, page 220.

the Hungarian hero was given an American sidekick: Claude Shannon. In the early 1940s, this Bell engineer had used Wiener's cybernetic metaphors to improve the transmission of messages across telephone networks. For countering the deterioration of signals over long distances, feedback showed how to create error-correcting mechanisms. When quantifying the traffic on a telephone network, information provided an exact unit of measurement.[26] As well as helping to solve Bell's technical problems, Shannon's analysis also provided a business-friendly interpretation of cybernetics. Learning from how engineers controlled the telephone network, employers could apply the abstract concepts of feedback and information to improving the management of their employees. In both cases, they were optimising the efficient use of scarce resources. Within the fetishised economy of capitalism, information about labour was indistinguishable from the labour embodied in information.

By the late 1950s, the process of airbrushing Wiener out of the history of cybernetics had been completed. Von Neumann and Shannon were now the founding fathers of this master theory. By minimising Wiener's importance, his socialist interpretation of cybernetics had been marginalised. Taking its place, conservative remixes now defined the academic orthodoxy. In Simon's managerial theory, von Neumann and Shannon's versions were fused into a hagiography of cybernetic Fordism. Just like computers, corporations were prototypes of artificial intelligence. As in the telephone networks, management hierarchies were feedback systems of information inputs and action outputs. In this late-1950s update of the Turing test, the most rational form of human behaviour was doing what computers did.

The corporate vision of cybernetic Fordism meant forgetting the history of Fordism itself. This economic and social paradigm had been founded upon the successful coordination of mass production with mass consumption. Henry Ford's famous factory symbolised this imperative to transform expensive luxuries for the few into cheap commodities for the many. At the 1939 World's Fair, the dioramas of a car-owning consumer society in the Democracity and Futurama pavilions portrayed an imaginary future extrapolated

[26] See Claude Shannon and Warren Weaver, *The Mathematical Theory of Communication*, pages 31–125.

from an optimistic interpretation of contemporary America. But, by the time that the 1964 exposition opened, the IBM pavilion was promoting the sci-fi fantasy of thinking machines. The imaginary future was now disconnected from contemporary America. Ironically, since their advertising message was more closely connected to social reality, Democracity and Futurama in 1939 provided a much more accurate prediction of the development path of computing than the IBM pavilion did in 1964. Just like motor cars 25 years earlier, this new technology was also slowly being transformed from a rare, hand-made artefact into a ubiquitous, factory-produced commodity. IBM's own System/360 series was at the cutting edge of this process. For the rest of US industry, the corporation was the pioneer of computer-controlled automated production. IBM mainframes were being used to make IBM mainframes. These opening moves towards the mass production of computers anticipated what would be the most important advance in this sector 25 years later: the mass consumption of computers. In its formal design, the 1964 System/360 mainframe was a bulky and expensive prototype of the much smaller and cheaper IBM PCs of the 1980s.

The imaginary future of artificial intelligence was a way of avoiding thinking about the likely social consequences of the mass ownership of computers. In the early 1960s, Big Brother mainframe was the technological materialisation of the hierarchical structures of big government and big business. Feedback was knowledge of the ruled, monopolised by the rulers. However, as Wiener himself had pointed out, Fordist production would inevitably transform expensive mainframes into ever cheaper commodities.[27] In turn, increasing ownership of computers was likely to disrupt the existing social order. For the feedback of information within human institutions was limited when decision making was concentrated into the hands of a few top managers. Instead, the most effective method of operating was the uninhibited two-way flow of communications and creativity across the whole organisation. By reconnecting conception and execution, cybernetic Fordism threatened the social hierarchies which underpinned Fordism itself.

> [T]he simple coexistence of two items of information is of relatively small value, unless these two items can be effectively combined in

27 See Wiener, *Human Beings*, pages 210–211.

some mind ... which is able to fertilise one by means of the other. This is the very opposite of the organisation in which every member travels a pre-assigned path ...[28]

At the 1964 World's Fair, this possibility was definitely not part of IBM's imaginary future. Rather than aiming to produce ever greater numbers of more efficient machines at cheaper prices, the corporation was focused on steadily increasing the capabilities of its computers to preserve its near monopoly over the military and corporate mainframe market. Instead of room-sized machines shrinking down into desktops, laptops and, eventually, mobile phones, IBM was convinced that computers would always be large and bulky mainframes.[29] If this path of technological progress was extrapolated, artificial intelligence must surely result. After over two decades of improvements, the number of switches in the machine was on the verge of surpassing the number of neurons in the brain. Just as Turing and von Neumann had predicted, computers would soon become powerful enough to replicate all the functions of consciousness. In a fetishised economy, this vision of self-directing computers took its inspiration from social reality. Since commodities already determined the destiny of their creators, the inanimate must be capable of superseding the living. The Fordist separation between conception and execution was about to achieve its technological apotheosis. It was this prophecy of sentient super-beings replacing humanity which was the existential flaw at the core of the imaginary future of artificial intelligence. Under cybernetic Fordism, people would be lesser life forms than machines. Ironically, the optimistic fantasy of 1960s computer gurus confirmed the pessimistic nightmare of 1930s sci-fi writers: artificial intelligence was the enemy of humanity.

Not surprisingly, IBM was determined to counter this unsettling interpretation of its own futurist propaganda. At the 1964 World's Fair, the corporation's pavilion emphasised the utopian possibilities of computing. Yet, despite its best efforts, IBM couldn't entirely avoid the ambiguity inherent within the imaginary future of artificial

[28] Wiener, *Human Beings*, page 172.
[29] In Stanley Kubrick's *2001*, the astronaut hero floats inside the huge memory banks of the HAL 9000: a sentient machine. By a remarkable coincidence, 'HAL' is 'IBM' transposed down one letter.

intelligence. This fetishised ideology could only appeal to all sections of American society if computers fulfilled the deepest desires of both sides within the workplace. Therefore, in the exhibits at its pavilion, IBM promoted a single vision of the imaginary future, which combined two incompatible interpretations of artificial intelligence. On the one hand, workers were told that all their needs would be satisfied by sentient robots: servants who never tired, complained or questioned orders. On the other hand, capitalists were promised that their factories and offices would be run by thinking machines: producers who never slacked off, expressed opinions or went on strike. Robby the Robot had become indistinguishable from EPICAC XIV. If only at the level of ideology, IBM had reconciled the class divisions of 1960s America. In the imaginary future, workers would no longer need to work and employers would no longer need employees. Just like the Gothic invented traditions of Victorian England, the computerised imaginary future of Cold War America acted as an ideological defence against the social disruption unleashed by perpetual modernisation. After visiting IBM's pavilion at the 1964 World's Fair, it was all too easy to believe that everyone would win when the machines acquired consciousness.

THE GLOBAL VILLAGE

06

At the centre of the 1964 New York World's Fair stood the icon of the exhibition: the Unisphere. Built by US Steel, this edifice was a triumph of American engineering. Never before had anyone been able to create a representation of the earth on this scale. Just like the Eiffel Tower at the 1889 Paris Exposition, the Unisphere became the instantly recognisable symbol of the World's Fair. Its image adorned magazine front covers, newspaper reports, posters and souvenirs. The meaning of this planetary logo was obvious: the New York World's Fair was a gathering of the whole of humanity. During the two years of the exposition, the Unisphere was the focal point of the entire earth.[1] In its international edition, *Life* magazine promoted the opening of the New York World's Fair as the ideal moment for foreigners to visit America. A global exhibition deserved a global audience.[2] By the early 1960s, the long and arduous journey by sea to the USA had been replaced by a quick and uneventful plane flight. But, despite this technological leap forward, moving between continents was still expensive. In contrast, the iconography of the Unisphere anticipated the democratisation of international mobility. As larger and more efficient machines were introduced into service, aeroplanes were in the process of becoming a means of mass transportation. Even better, as the NASA, General Motors and Ford exhibits at the 1964 World's Fair promised, space travel would soon be available to all. Within 25 years at most, ordinary people would be taking their holidays on the moon. Reflecting this optimism, the Unisphere was surrounded by three rings which celebrated famous space flights: Yuri Gagarin – the first person to orbit the earth; John Glenn – the first American to repeat this feat; and Telstar – the first satellite to transmit television signals from the USA to Europe.[3] When holiday makers in the 1990s looked back at the earth from their lunar resorts, it would be obvious to them that all of humanity shared a common home.

The rings surrounding the Unisphere didn't just encourage fantasies about space travel. Alongside models of Gagarin's and Glenn's capsules, a miniature version of Telstar was also depicted

---

[1] See Editors of Time–Life Books, *Official Guide*, page 180.
[2] On 23 March 1964, *Life* magazine published a special 'Vacationland USA' double issue to coincide with the opening of the World's Fair.
[3] See Neil deGrasse Tyson, 'Unisphere'.

circling US Steel's giant globe. On 10 July 1962, audiences in America and Europe had watched in amazement as the first live television broadcast was made across the Atlantic using this communications satellite. Back in the 1930s, the formation of radio networks had enabled people living in different parts of the USA to listen simultaneously to the same programmes transmitted from studios in New York.[4] With the launch of Telstar, the same process was beginning to happen on a global scale. Viewers in different countries were now able to see the same images on their screens. By 1964, live feeds were already an essential ingredient of television news coverage. The model of Telstar circling the Unisphere promised much more. When large numbers of communications satellites were in operation, people across the world would be watching the same channels at the same time. Television was uniting humanity.

At the same time as the first visitors to the 1964 World's Fair were admiring the Unisphere, Marshall McLuhan – a Canadian professor – published a book which provided the theoretical explanation of this dream of audio-visual harmony: *Understanding Media*. The symbolism of the Telstar satellite had been given written form. As soon as it appeared, *Understanding Media* became a publishing sensation. Unlike most academics, McLuhan wrote for a non-specialist audience. He rejected the stylistic conventions of his profession: dense prose, detailed investigation and careful referencing. Instead, McLuhan's analysis utilised 'thought probes': a dazzling combination of snappy headlines, sweeping generalisations and unsupported assertions. Although this approach outraged his university colleagues, his populist style appealed to the large numbers of educated readers outside the academy. Difficult concepts were turned into wacky catchphrases. Human history was explained through paradoxical exaggerations. In contrast with run-of-the-mill academic texts, *Understanding Media* made social theory fun to read.

McLuhan's book hit the zeitgeist of the mid 1960s. After perusing *Understanding Media*, any intelligent person was able to talk about how television, satellites, computers and other new technologies were radically transforming American society. Best of all, they

---

[4] See Daniel Glover, 'Telstar'; and Erik Barnouw, *A Tower In Babel*, pages 235–285.

could impress people by dropping its evocative thought probes into newspaper articles, public lectures and dinner-party conversations. The popularity of *Understanding Media* quickly turned McLuhan into an A-list celebrity. Within a couple of years of its publication, this once obscure Canadian professor had become one of the most famous people in the world.[5] His books were international best-sellers. His musings appeared in leading newspapers. He starred in his own television shows. He was a consultant for major corporations. Across the world, McLuhan was hailed as a heroic genius: 'the oracle of the modern times'.[6]

The massive success of *Understanding Media* was the culmination of a long intellectual journey. When the book was published, McLuhan was a professor of English literature at Toronto University. He had been educated to appreciate the traditional forms of cultural expression: novels, poems and plays. Devoted to the artistic legacy of the past, English professors were expected to be contemptuous of modern media: films, radio and television. Confounding this stereotype, McLuhan had long been fascinated by the vibrancy of popular culture. While teaching in the mid-West of the USA in the late 1930s, he had applied the techniques of literary criticism to the analysis of advertising and comics. Initially, he had believed that exposing the limitations of popular culture would prove the superiority of high culture.[7] During the 1950s, McLuhan slowly abandoned this conventional wisdom and started to discover his own voice. Suspicion of popular culture turned into celebration of new technologies. Nostalgia for the past became hope for the future.

McLuhan's intellectual transformation was aided by the gift of a book: Wiener's *Cybernetics*. For the first time, he realised that the computer wasn't just a digital calculator, but also a communications device. Above all, like many of his peers, McLuhan became convinced that this new technology had created a new theoretical paradigm. Following the Macy conference example, he set up his own multi-disciplinary research project at Toronto University. During the 1950s, McLuhan and his colleagues dedicated themselves to the task

[5] See Warren Hinckle, 'Marshall McLuhan'.
[6] Tom Wolfe, 'What If He Is Right?', page 110. Also see Philip Marchand, *Marshall McLuhan*, pages 136–211.
[7] See Marshall McLuhan, *The Mechanical Bride*; and Marchand, *McLuhan*, pages 42–110.

of developing a cybernetic analysis of the mass media and popular culture. Adopting Shannon's interpretation of this meta-theory, they decided to focus their research upon the role of information within society.[8] Like many of their American peers, McLuhan's team believed that they were now working at the cutting edge of social theory: cybernetics without Wiener. Their enthusiasm for Shannon's approach was inspired by their deep and long-held fascination with the writings of Harold Innis. In the late 1940s and early 1950s, this Canadian thinker had developed a theory which also proposed that the 'movement of information' played the primary role in shaping human societies. From this premise, Innis explained the process of historical evolution. The invention of a new form of media had always led to the emergence of a new civilisation.[9]

Making his final break with cultural snobbery, McLuhan became the 'greatest disciple' of Innis' idiosyncratic form of technological determinism.[10] Despite being a professor of English literature, he argued that the ideological meaning of cultural products was irrelevant. Instead, it was the media technologies used to create these products that took precedence. McLuhan believed that Innis had discovered how human behaviour was shaped by the psychological impact of the media. Like Pavlov's dogs, people were much more responsive to the stimulation of their senses than of their imaginations. According to McLuhan, every technology was an 'extension of man' which shaped human perception of the surrounding environment. When a new form of media was introduced, this sensory relationship was always reconfigured. Because this cybernetic process changed people's behaviour, a new social system would inevitably be created. Technological innovation was the driving force of history. The fetishism of machinery had explained the evolution of humanity. 'The effects of [media] technology do not occur at the level of opinions or concepts, but alter sense ratios or patterns of perception steadily and without resistance.'[11]

---

[8] See Donald Theall, *The Virtual Marshall McLuhan*, page 7; and Flo Conway and Jim Siegelman, *Dark Hero of the Information Age*, page 277.

[9] See Harold Innis, *Empire and Communications*, pages 166–167; and William Kuhns, *The Post-Industrial Prophets*, pages 139–168.

[10] Kuhns, *Post-Industrial Prophets*, page 169. Also see McLuhan's 'Foreword' in Innis, *Empire and Communications*, pages v–xii.

[11] Marshall McLuhan, *Understanding Media*, page 18.

McLuhan summarised his theoretical position in a famous slogan: 'The medium is the message'.[12] It was not what was said which was important, but with what machinery it was said. This insight meant that the history of humanity was understood as a series of 'break boundaries' between different media technologies.[13] Crucially, McLuhan rejected all political, economic and cultural explanations for the advent of modernity. Instead, the introduction of printing was solely responsible for this profound social transformation. Supplanting the traditional oral culture, this new technology had stimulated human senses in completely new ways. In response to this altered media environment, people were forced to adopt the psychological attitudes of modernity: individuality, rationality and self-discipline. Just as the uniqueness of each illuminated letter had been replaced by standard pieces of type, the diversity of medieval communities had been supplanted by the homogeneity of industrial societies. Everyone was now the same: equal citizens of the nation state; anonymous employees of large corporations; and identical consumers in the marketplace.[14] The whole of society had been reconstructed in the image of the new media technology. Johann Gutenberg's print shop had led inexorably to Henry Ford's factory.

Since printing had created modern society, McLuhan was convinced that the advent of the electronic media marked the next break boundary in human history. Beginning with telegraphy and radio in the Victorian era, this new technological paradigm had slowly but surely undermined the hegemony of the written word. During the 1950s, the spread of television had led to the electronic media finally supplanting printing as the dominant extension of man. Although important, this historical moment wasn't the end of the process of social transformation. Inspired by Wiener's and Shannon's cybernetic theories, McLuhan believed that the electronic media was already evolving beyond television. In the near future, broadcasting would fuse with computing and telecommunications into one demiurgic technology.[15] What radio and television had

---

[12] See McLuhan, *Understanding Media*, pages 7–21.
[13] See McLuhan, *Understanding Media*, page 39.
[14] See Marshall McLuhan, *Gutenberg Galaxy*, pages 155–279; *Understanding Media*, pages 7–32, 170–178.
[15] See McLuhan, *Understanding Media*, page 354–359; and Eric Norden, 'The Playboy Interview: Marshall McLuhan', pages 20–21.

begun, the 'electric global network' was going to complete.[16] By the time that convergence was fully realised, this new media technology would have created a new – and better – social order. Five years before its first nodes were connected together, McLuhan had already identified the hi-tech saviour of humanity: *the Net*.[17]

> Playboy: Isn't this prediction of an electronically induced world consciousness more mystical than technological?
> McLuhan: Yes ... Mysticism is just tomorrow's science dreamed today.[18]

Like its predecessor, this new information technology imposed its own specific psychological outlook upon humanity by stimulating the senses in new ways. Instead of dividing society into isolated individuals as printing had done, the electronic media encouraged communal feelings between people.[19] This radical shift in mental attitudes was hastened by the transformation of the workplace. In the same way as the printing press had replaced the farm with the factory, the computer provided the prototype for the new methods of fully automated production. With the spread of radio and television, the manufacture of physical goods was already beginning to lose its predominant role within the economy to the creation of information. This meant that the narrowly focused experts of the industrial age would soon become redundant. In their place, the new economy required a new type of worker: multitasking generalists.[20] According to McLuhan, the social consequences of these changes within the workplace were obvious. In a very short time, print consciousness – the indifference of rationalism – would be superseded by electronic media consciousness – the empathy of intuition.

Marshall McLuhan was convinced that the emergence of a new economy would be accompanied by a radical transformation of the political system. The printing press had not only created the factory, but also the nation state. If the Net was going to abolish the former, it would also get rid of the latter. In *Understanding Media*, McLuhan

[16] See McLuhan, *Understanding Media*, page 351.
[17] See McLuhan, *Understanding Media*, page 346–359; and Norden, 'Marshall McLuhan', pages 8–9, 18–19.
[18] Norden, 'Marshall McLuhan', page 19.
[19] See McLuhan, *Understanding Media*, pages 50–51.
[20] See McLuhan, *Understanding Media*, pages 138, 207, 354.

explained that the combination of the printing press and the wheel had enabled political leaders to extend their control beyond the limits of the tribal community: the 'explosion of the social'. As these technologies spread across the world, humanity had been divided into the rival nation states of the 'Gutenberg galaxy'. Internally, the political institutions of modernity had imposed cultural and linguistic homogeneity. Externally, these nation states had emphasised their cultural and linguistic specificity.[21] McLuhan believed that – after centuries of dominance – this political system was now in crisis. When printing had dominated society, people had accepted the limitations of representative democracy. But, with the advent of the electronic media, they now wanted more direct participation in political decision making. Sooner or later, choosing between candidates in infrequent elections would be replaced by on-line voting in daily referendums. The new information technologies were beginning to impose a new paradigm: the 'implosion of the social'.[22]

No one could stop this process. Television was replacing printing and '... Telstar [was] threatening the wheel'.[23] When everyone across the world was watching the same programmes, national hatreds and cultural differences would inevitably disappear. The computer was already deepening the social impact of television and satellites. As shown by the Russian–English translation machine on display in the IBM pavilion at the 1964 World's Fair, artificial intelligences would soon be able to remove the linguistic barriers between people.[24] The printing press and the wheel had imprisoned individuals inside nation states. Televisions, telephones and computers were now linking the peoples of the world together. The electric global network would create a global political system. The Net was about to unite a divided humanity into one.

> After three thousand years of specialist explosion and of increasing specialism and alienation in the technological extensions of our bodies, our world has become compressional by dramatic reversal. As electricity contracted, the globe is no more than a village. Electric

21 See McLuhan, *Understanding Media*, pages 170–178.
22 See McLuhan, *Understanding Media*, pages 204, 308–337; and Norden, 'Marshall McLuhan', pages 18–19.
23 McLuhan, *Understanding Media*, page 256.
24 See McLuhan, *Understanding Media*, page 80.

speed in bringing all social and political functions together in a sudden implosion has heightened human awareness and responsibility to an intense degree.[25]

This utopian vision of world unity inspired McLuhan's most famous catchphrase: the 'global village'.[26] The technological convergence of television, satellites and computers into the Net would – at one and the same time – create a single social system for the whole of humanity and restore the intimacy of living in a tribal community. The best of the new would be combined with the best of the old. This feel-good prophecy contributed greatly to the huge popularity of *Understanding Media*. Readers were delighted to be told that the rapid pace of technological innovation would lead to peace and prosperity for all. Ironically, in private, McLuhan was much more pessimistic about the prospects for humanity than he admitted in his writings. As a devout Catholic, he believed that there were no technological fixes for the problems of this world.[27] However, in *Understanding Media*, these caveats were so well hidden that most of McLuhan's readers missed them entirely. Instead they saw what they wanted to see. Led by Tom Wolfe, admirers of *Understanding Media* took the most optimistic interpretation of its analysis and turned it into a distinctive ideological position: *McLuhanism*.[28]

According to this new orthodoxy, human history was a succession of cybernetic systems created by feedback from different types of media. The modern phenomenon of commodity fetishism had been transformed into the universal principle of technological fetishism. Every leap in social evolution was identified with the advent of a new type of media. By ending the dominance of the spoken word, the invention of the printing press had led to the rise of nationalism, individualism and industrial capitalism. After four centuries of modernity, the convergence of television, telecommunications and computing was once again transforming the media environment.

[25] McLuhan, *Understanding Media*, page 5.
[26] See McLuhan, *Understanding Media*, 92–93.
[27] McLuhan even suggested that the Net might be the work of the Devil: 'Electric information environments ... [are] now a reasonable facsimile of the mystical body, a blatant manifestation of the Anti-Christ. After all, the Prince of this World [Satan] is a very great electric engineer.' Marshall McLuhan, 'Letter to Jacques Maritain', page 370.
[28] For the founding text of McLuhanism, see Tom Wolfe, 'What If He Is Right?'.

More than anything else, McLuhanism was identified with this prediction that the Net was going to create the new – and much better – social system of the global village. Under its new sensory dispensation, the downsides of the Gutenberg galaxy – war, egoism and exploitation – which had afflicted humanity for generations would disappear. The imminent arrival of the Net meant that people would soon be living, thinking and working in a peaceful, equalitarian and participatory civilisation.

For the McLuhanists, this vision of the future explained what was happening in the here-and-now. Five years before it was invented, portents of the Net could already be seen in the present. At the 1964 New York World's Fair, RCA's colour television sets, Telstar communications satellites and IBM's mainframe computers were all harbingers of the marvellous hi-tech society to come. In turn, the full potential of these machines could only be comprehended by envisioning humanity living in a world where the liberating process of their convergence into the Net had been completed. While the prophets of artificial intelligence looked forward to the emergence of the synthetic individual, the McLuhanists believed that computerisation would remake the whole of humanity. Living in a fetishised economy, they were convinced technology was the demiurge of a new stage in social evolution. The meaning of the present was revealed in the anticipation of this path of progress. Just like IBM's obsession with artificial intelligence, the advocates of McLuhanism were dedicated to the promotion of their own imaginary future: *the information society*.

THE
COLD WAR
LEFT

07

Understanding Media was a publishing sensation built upon a paradox. A professor of English literature had written a book which had become a best-seller because it told its readers that they should be watching television instead of reading books. Ironically, McLuhan needed the printed word to become the prophet of the imminent demise of print culture. Writing an important book was still the prerequisite for becoming a prominent intellectual. The worth of the thinker was measured by the quality of the text. During the twentieth century, the iconic role of the book within intellectual life had been reinforced by the growth of the mass media. McLuhan's own career demonstrated how newspapers, magazines, radio stations and television channels were eager to disseminate new ideas coming out of the universities among the general public and – as in his case – to transform some academics into celebrities. Contrary to the assumptions of McLuhanism, the famous book remained the signifier of the influential intellectual in the age of the electronic media.

In the early 1960s, McLuhan achieved a degree of public recognition beyond that of almost any other academic within the American sphere of influence. *Understanding Media* was one of the rare books which crossed over from the specialist university market into the best-seller lists. Crucially, its worldwide popularity wasn't the result of a short-lived fad. As Tom Wolfe had quickly realised, McLuhan's writings provided the theoretical source material for the construction of the new ideology of McLuhanism. By removing the ambiguities and qualifications from *Understanding Media*, its analysis could be reinterpreted as an enthusiastic celebration of the imaginary future of the information society. Best of all, this prophecy identified America as the prototype of the emerging global village. In the mid 1960s, McLuhanism was the latest model of the new-style ideologies specially developed for the Cold War struggle. Because the two superpowers had no desire to destroy each other with nuclear weapons, the military confrontation between them on the European continent was largely symbolic. Despite being sold as the struggle against an external enemy, the Cold War was – first and foremost – aimed at internal opponents. Both sides needed the threat of attack by its rival as the justification for imposing discipline not only at home, but also within their spheres of influence.

At the outbreak of the Cold War in 1948, the leader of the Republican opposition in the legislature had urged US President

Harry Truman to 'scare the hell out of the American people', with lurid fantasies about ruthless Russian totalitarians plotting to take over the world.[1] Admiration for the Red Army's victory over Nazi Germany had to be quickly replaced with fear of the 'Red Menace' overwhelming Western civilisation. During the 1950s, show trials of Russian spies, public humiliations of left-wing dissidents, political purges of state institutions, civil defence drills and loyalty oaths were all used to terrify the US population into the new ideological orthodoxy.[2] From sci-fi films about alien invasions to TV shows with secret agents as heroes, American popular culture became dominated by the imagery of Cold War mythology.[3] In an electoral democracy like the United States, the inculcation of paranoia and patriotism was the most effective method for winning the consent of the many to the hegemony of the few. More than four centuries earlier, in the disguise of a courtier's advice to 'the Prince' who wished to rule over Renaissance Italy, Niccolò Machiavelli had exposed the cynical reasoning behind this manipulative form of politics:

> Everyone realises how praiseworthy it is for a prince to ... be straightforward rather than crafty in his dealings; nonetheless contemporary experience shows that princes who achieved great things have been those who have ... known how to trick men [and women] with their cunning and who, in the end, have overcome those abiding by honest principles.[4]

During the economic crisis of the 1930s, an upsurge of radical trade union and political struggles had challenged the social order in the USA. But, in contrast with their European comrades, American working-class militants had never been able to establish their own independent mass political party.[5] This failure to escape from the sectarian ghetto had disastrous consequences in the 1950s. Once the Cold War was under way, it became increasingly difficult to advocate any form of socialism in America. Already marginalised,

---

[1] Arthur Vandenberg in Stephen Ambrose, *Rise to Globalism*, page 151.
[2] See Frank Donner, *The Un-Americans*; and Joel Kovel, *Red Hunting in the Promised Land*, pages 87–136.
[3] See Todd Gitlin, 'Television's Screens'; and Tom Engelhardt, 'Ambush at Kamikaze Pass'.
[4] Niccolò Machiavelli, *The Prince*, page 99.
[5] See Mike Davis, *Prisoners of the American Dream*, pages 3–7, 55–69; and Seymour Martin Lipset and Gary Marks, *It Didn't Happen Here*, pages 203–235.

the US Left was now tainted by its ideological affinities with the nation's foreign enemy. Back in the 1920s and 1930s, American radicals – like their European and Asian comrades – had argued passionately over the political implications of the 1917 Russian Revolution and the theoretical maxims of its charismatic leader, Vladimir Lenin. Holding to the orthodox position, Social Democrats believed that the new regime had betrayed its Marxist principles by abolishing parliamentary democracy and banning independent trade unions.[6] In contrast, embracing the new line from Moscow, Leninists claimed that the revolutionary dictatorship was modernising a backward country in the interests of the masses. Crucially, they were also convinced that this Russian model of political activism had universal significance. While the Social Democrats aimed to create a mass membership organisation for fighting elections, the Leninists saw their primary task as building a small and disciplined group of professional revolutionaries: *the vanguard party.*[7]

Contesting the orthodox interpretation of Marxism, this revolutionary elite proclaimed itself as the harbinger of the post-capitalist future. By becoming Communists with a capital C, the vanguard party staked its claim to monopolise the leadership of the workers' struggles for communism with a small c. In 1924, the death of Lenin quickly led to bitter divisions between his followers. Like the Fordist factory, the Communist Party needed an autocratic managing director to decide who did what. During the late 1920s, the struggle between Joseph Stalin and Leon Trotsky to succeed Lenin as the absolute ruler of Russia was expressed through a theoretical dispute between competing definitions of the Leninist version of Marxism. Forced to take sides in this quarrel, the members of the American Communist Party – like their counterparts in Europe and Asia – soon split into rival factions of Stalinists and Trotskyists. While both sides identified themselves with the 1917 Revolution, they loudly disagreed over whether Stalin's regime or the exiled Trotsky was the legitimate heir of Lenin's revolutionary legacy. At the outbreak of the Second World War, the US Left was bitterly

---

[6] In 1918, the chief theoretician of German Social Democracy had defined this critique of Lenin's authoritarian politics: Karl Kautsky, *The Dictatorship of the Proletariat.*

[7] For the founding 1902 manifesto of this political institution, see V.I. Lenin, *What Is to Be Done?* Also see Marcel Liebman, *Leninism under Lenin,* pages 25–83.

divided over the meaning of socialism. Differences between Social Democrats, Stalinists and Trotskyists had become symbolised by incompatible interpretations of the same political ideal.[8]

In Western Europe, these ideological disputes took place within large and powerful labour movements. No one group could monopolise the theoretical analysis of the Left. Socialism didn't always mean Stalinism and some Communists were fervent anti-Stalinists. In contrast, the American Left was far too weak to protect its own ideological integrity.[9] Because Social Democrats and Trotskyists had little political influence in America, the US elite had no problems in adopting the terminology of its Cold War enemy. Socialism was synonymous with Stalinism and all Communists were Stalinists. At the beginning of the 1950s, the American Left found itself ideologically dispossessed. If Russian totalitarianism was the only form of socialism, it was almost impossible to advocate any radical alternative to capitalism in the USA. Even worse, the political language of the Left had become tainted by the rhetoric of Stalinist propaganda. Criticising capitalism literally sounded unpatriotic. All forms of socialism were inherently un-American. For conservatives, the Red Menace provided the long-awaited opportunity for clamping down on trade union and political activism.[10] Initially, their opponents were thrown into confusion. While some prioritised defending civil liberties at home, most of them were convinced that the first priority of the American Left was to prove its anti-Stalinist credentials in the Cold War confrontation. Since socialism – in all its interpretations – was a dangerous foreign concept, a more patriotic form of radical politics had to be developed. During the long period of conservative rule of the 1950s, this aspiration became the rallying call for a new movement of progressive intellectuals: *the Cold War Left.*

> ... one cannot pretend to be neutral or indifferent in regard to the world struggle. ... Between the West and 'ourselves' there is, not a full identity of interest, but a sharing of certain limited goals, the

---

[8] See James Cannon, *The History of American Trotskyism*, pages 100–101; and Vivian Gornick, *The Romance of American Communism*, pages 27–106.

[9] In 1946, the Socialist Workers Party – the leading Trotskyist group in the USA – had only 1,470 members out of the 145 million inhabitants of America. See Alan Wald, *The New York Intellectuals*, page 300.

[10] See Davis, *American Dream*, pages 82–101.

realisation of which requires us to depend upon Western power and also to put forward a variety of radical proposals.[11]

For over a decade, the thinkers of the Cold War Left dedicated themselves to developing a distinctively American form of progressive politics. Throughout the 1950s, they lamented that the right-wing Republican administration epitomised many of the worst aspects of their nation's culture: philistinism, parochialism and bigotry.[12] As well as exacerbating social problems at home, these attitudes damaged the US position abroad. Because of the nuclear stalemate in Europe, the most important front in the Cold War was the propaganda battle. Each side dedicated massive resources to the task of convincing people across the world of the righteousness of its cause: 'psychological operations'.[13] The long-term security of America's sphere of influence now required more than the 'hard power' of military and economic pre-eminence. The US elite also had to achieve supremacy in the 'soft power' of ideological and cultural hegemony.[14] In this vital struggle, the symbol of the racist and narrow-minded American was a propaganda disaster.[15] What was needed instead was the creation of a more positive and attractive image for the USA. Since conservatives were incapable of fulfilling this task, left-wing intellectuals seized the opportunity to invent new ideologies for the American empire. By taking this key role in the Cold War, they could demonstrate that the Republican Party was no longer the most effective opponent of Stalinism. Above all, by becoming the public face of America overseas, these intellectuals had proved that a left-of-centre Democrat – as US president – would be able to defend the nation's interests within the global arena. Progressive policies were not only morally preferable, but also politically rewarding.

In the ideological struggle against the Russian enemy, the most important achievement of the Cold War Left was reconciling the irreconcilable: the liberal ideals of the 1776 American Revolution

[11] Irving Howe, *Steady Work*, page 238. Howe was a former Trotskyist turned guru of the Democratic Party.
[12] See Richard Hofstadter, *Anti-Intellectualism in American Life*, pages 1–23.
[13] See Christopher Simpson, *Science of Coercion*.
[14] See Joseph Nye, *Soft Power*.
[15] See Benjamin Mays, 'Race in America'; and Frances Stonor Saunders, *Who Paid the Piper?* pages 190–198.

with the imperial ambitions of the 1950s American ruling class. Back in the late eighteenth century, the founders of the USA had believed that the primary purpose of constitutional government was to provide a legal framework for the spontaneous activities of property-owning individuals.[16] According to John Locke and his admirers, this form of social organisation promised a degree of freedom unprecedented in human history.[17] When the American revolutionaries finally won their nation's independence, the principles of liberalism were enshrined in the constitution of the new republic: minimal government, the rule of law and laissez-faire economics. Thomas Jefferson – the drafter of the American Declaration of Independence and third US president – took pride that the United States was a nation where: '... a wise and frugal government, which shall restrain people from injuring one another, shall leave them otherwise free to regulate their own pursuits of industry and improvement ...'.[18]

Compared to the absolute monarchies of Europe and Asia, the USA was the homeland of personal liberty. Yet, at the same time, freedom remained circumscribed. Women were second-class citizens. Some individuals were the property of other individuals. The indigenous population of America was subjected to a ruthless campaign of extermination. Liberalism meant freedom for some of the people not for all of the people.[19] Despite its many faults, this creed served the Americans well as their republic grew from a narrow strip of settlements on the east coast of the continent to the dominant power within its hemisphere. But, by the middle of the twentieth century, circumstances had dramatically changed. However pliable liberalism was as an ideology, its believers were now faced by the intractable problem that two of its central principles – minimal government and laissez-faire economics – had become impossible to put into practice.

When the Royal Navy had dominated the world's oceans, the United States had been protected from external aggression. But, as

[16] See Alexander Hamilton, James Madison and John Jay, *The Federalist*, pages 13–83.

[17] See John Locke, *Two Treatises of Government*, pages 374–427. John Locke was the chief theorist of the 1688 English Revolution.

[18] Thomas Jefferson, 'First Inaugural Address', pages 2–3.

[19] See Alexis de Tocqueville, *Democracy in America, Volume 1*, pages 343–432; *Democracy in America, Volume 2*, pages 222–225.

the British empire disintegrated, America's isolation came to an end. For the first time, the nation needed a large military establishment to protect its interests. By the end of the Second World War, the USA possessed the most powerful army, navy and air force on the planet. Any hope of military demobilisation after the victory over Germany and Japan disappeared when Russia quickly moved from being an ally into an enemy. In the age of nuclear weapons, the possession of large and expensive armed forces was incompatible with minimal government. The Cold War mobilisation of American military power had forced the abandonment of one of the fundamental principles of liberalism.

The expansion of the US state was also encouraged by the spread of Fordism. By the 1950s, big business had become dependent upon big government to oversee and direct the national economy. In the early nineteenth century, it had been possible for a small caste of politicians, entrepreneurs and financiers to run the country in an intimate and informal manner. But, now that America was the world's leading economy, unregulated markets and unashamed corruption looked like relics from another age. In their place, both capitalist corporations and the US state were using rational and efficient managerial bureaucracies to administer their affairs. Market competition had been supplemented with top-down planning. Like minimal government, laissez-faire economics was an anachronism in Cold War America. Fordism had replaced liberalism.

The bureaucratisation of both business and politics transformed the make-up of the American ruling class. Although political office and inherited wealth still guaranteed membership, new routes into the US elite had opened up. The managers of the huge corporate and state bureaucracies were now among the most important decision makers in the nation. Generals, admirals and spy chiefs exercised immense power both at home and abroad.[20] For the first time, significant numbers of academics also found themselves admitted into the inner circles of the American elite. During the Second World War, scientists had been mobilised to develop new military technologies. With the invention of the atom bomb, these intellectuals had emphatically demonstrated their vital importance to the modern state. While earlier generations of scientists had been

[20] See C. Wright Mills, *The Power Elite*.

haphazardly absorbed into the ruling class, the US government now began systematically recruiting their successors into leadership positions. Thanks to his leading role in the development of the atomic bomb, von Neumann became a prominent member of the political and military leadership of America. Where he led, others soon followed. As well as working on advanced weaponry and teaching their students, these favoured academics also managed large organisations, contributed to military planning, participated in fact-finding committees and created Cold War propaganda. The intellectual in the ivory tower had morphed into the scientist–warrior–bureaucrat.[21] '... [T]hey are ... leaders of a new type ... academic entrepreneurs, who know how to raise money, and put an organisation together and get results in the outside world.'[22]

In the opening phases of the Cold War, military spending was concentrated on the development of hi-tech armaments. As the superpower confrontation became institutionalised, increasing amounts of money were also committed to research into the social sciences. Locked into a propaganda struggle with the Russians, the US government recruited intellectuals to boost its psychological operations across the world. Above all, America urgently needed a credible replacement for laissez-faire liberalism. In the same way that natural scientists were employed to invent new weaponry, social scientists now received large grants from military sponsors to develop new ideologies.[23] Even when the Republicans were in power in the 1950s, the US government accepted that the success of this mission depended upon the participation of left-wing intellectuals. Although they were critics of conservatism at home, radicals possessed the knowledge needed to convince sceptical foreigners that the American empire represented progress and modernity. Hard power needed to be backed up with soft power.

Back in the 1930s, radical intellectuals in the United States had lived an impoverished existence on the margins of society. Despite these hardships, the American Left had fostered a cultural renaissance which inspired some of the most innovative theorists, writers and

[21] See Stuart Leslie, The Cold War and American Science; and André Schiffrin, The Cold War and the University.
[22] Christopher Rand, Cambridge U.S.A. page 4.
[23] By 1952, the Department of Defense was providing 96 per cent of government funding for social science research. See Christopher Simpson, Science of Coercion, page 52.

artists of the decade.[24] This brief moment of creativity was cut short
by the outbreak of another world war. Fearful of a Nazi victory,
most of the American Left rallied to the anti-fascist cause. Those
who had once been excluded now became an integral part of the
military effort. After Germany was defeated, this reconciliation
with mainstream society was consolidated by the Cold War.
Heavily influenced by Trotsky's critique of totalitarianism, many
of the leading intellectuals of the American Left had long been
anti-Stalinist. When the Cold War began, this hostility towards
Russian imperialism convinced many of them that radicals had to
continue supporting American imperialism. No longer content with
criticising impotently from the sidelines, these thinkers believed that
they should shape US policy at home and abroad in a progressive
direction. The Trotskyist Left had grown up and become the Cold
War Left.[25]

> [The] ... men of power ... need a way of perceiving the consequences
> of what they do if the actions are not to be brutal, stupid, bureaucratic
> but rather intelligent and humane. The only hope for humane
> government is through the extensive use of social sciences by
> government.[26]

For the US elite, these radical intellectuals possessed an invaluable
asset: an intimate knowledge of Marxism. Because laissez-faire
liberalism was an anachronism in the epoch of Fordism, the
Americans unexpectedly found themselves at a disadvantage in the
propaganda war with the Russians. Despite its economic inferiority,
political authoritarianism and military weakness, their Stalinist enemy
enjoyed superiority on the all-important ideological battlefield. This
moment of crisis for the American empire created an opportunity
for disillusioned Social Democrats and repentant Leninists to enter
into the inner sanctum of the US elite. Just like nuclear physicists
during the war against Germany and Japan, they were the only
people with the esoteric knowledge which could ensure victory for

[24] See Daniel Bell, *Sociological Journeys*, pages 119–137; and Wald, *New York
Intellectuals*, pages 27–192.
[25] See Wald, *New York Intellectuals*, pages 193–225, 267–310; Bell, *Sociological
Journeys*, pages 119–137; and Saunders, *Who Paid the Piper?* pages 7–56.
[26] Ithiel de Sola Pool, 'The Necessity for Social Scientists Doing Research for
Governments', page 111.

the United States in this geopolitical contest. Soft power was now as important as hard power. Once military money began to pour into social-science research, these intellectuals quickly emerged as the gurus of the multi-disciplinary teams developing the ideological weapons for psychological operations against the Russian enemy. The US state had discovered that the most effective way of creating attractive alternatives to Marxism was to employ former Marxists to do the job. 'The final struggle [for global hegemony] ... will be between the Communists and the ex-Communists.'[27]

---

27 Ignazio Silone, 'The Initiates', page 118.

THE
CHOSEN FEW

08

James Burnham was the pioneer of the move by left-wing intellectuals from the margins into the mainstream of US society. During the 1930s, along with James Cannon, Max Schachtman, and C.L.R. James, he had been one of the paramount leaders of the American Trotskyist movement. But, by the end of the 1930s, he had become increasingly sceptical about revolutionary politics. After a bitter theoretical quarrel with Trotsky, he suddenly announced that he was quitting the movement and that 'I [can] no longer regard myself ... as a Marxist.'[1] Soon afterwards, Burnham published a book which proposed a new theory of social evolution: *The Managerial Revolution*. In this best-seller, he argued that Marx's prediction that laissez-faire capitalism would be replaced by a classless communist society had been disproved by recent history. Although market competition was rapidly disappearing, the workers who formed the majority of the population were no nearer to becoming the masters of society. On the contrary, as could be seen not only in Stalinist Russia and Nazi Germany, but also in Fordist America, the bureaucrats who directed the giant state and corporate institutions were becoming the new ruling class. The Leninist vanguard had morphed into the 'managerial elite'.[2] Using ideas taken from some of the most advanced Marxist theorists of the time, Burnham had challenged the theoretical credibility of Marxism itself.[3]

> The Russian Revolution was not a socialist revolution – which, from all the evidence, cannot take place in our time – but a managerial revolution. ... [Marxism-]Leninism ... is not a scientific hypothesis but a great social ideology rationalising the social interests of the new rulers and making them acceptable to the minds of the masses ... the task of the ideology is to give fitting expression to the [Russian managerial] regime of ... purges, tyrannies, privileges and aggressions.[4]

[1] James Burnham, 'Letter of Resignation of James Burnham from the Workers' Party', page 257.

[2] See James Burnham, *The Managerial Revolution*, pages 20–87, 188–245.

[3] In particular, Burnham's hypothesis drew upon – and generalised to cover all industrial societies – the work of Marxists who argued that the Stalinist bureaucracy had become the new ruling elite in post-revolutionary Russia. See Karl Kautsky, *The Dictatorship of the Proletariat*; Rudolf Hilferding, 'State Capitalism or Totalitarian State Economy?'; Leon Trotsky, *The Class Nature of the Soviet Union*; and C.L.R. James, 'The USSR is a Fascist State Capitalism'.

[4] Burnham, *Managerial Revolution*, pages 200–201.

This intellectual achievement was Burnham's entrance ticket into the top echelons of the US elite. During the Second World War, he began a long career as a consultant and propagandist for the American intelligence services.[5] One of Burnham's most urgent tasks was finding a theoretical underpinning for his managerial analysis which couldn't be traced back to Marxism. Because laissez-faire liberalism was also unusable, he turned to a group of political thinkers whose ideas were popular in Fascist Italy: Gaetano Mosca, Robert Michels and Vilfredo Pareto.[6] In the work of these theorists, Burnham found a hard-headed approach which explained why the domination of one class over another was inevitable within human societies. The rise of the managerial elite in the twentieth century could now be interpreted as the modern manifestation of an eternal sociological imperative. Best of all, this analysis explained that – far from leading the workers towards the classless utopia – the Leninist vanguard party was nothing more than the Russian variant of the new bureaucratic form of class rule which was sweeping the industrialised world.[7] However, because Michels and Pareto had supported Italian Fascism, Burnham had to adapt their ideas for an American audience. Emphasising their concept of the 'circulation of elites', he argued that class domination was – paradoxically – the precondition of electoral democracy. The masses might not be able to rule themselves, but they could choose which minority was going to rule over them.[8] According to Burnham's reinterpretation, elite theorists were no longer apologists for America's totalitarian enemy in Italy. Instead, as the subtitle of his aptly named 1943 book *The Machiavellians* proclaimed, they had become the 'defenders of freedom'.

As soon as Germany and Japan were defeated, Burnham launched himself into a campaign to warn his fellow citizens about the dangers of Russian totalitarianism. Educated in the Trotskyist movement, he had no illusions about the imperialist ambitions of America's erstwhile ally. In *The Struggle for the World* and *The Coming Defeat*

[5] See Daniel Kelly, *James Burnham and the Struggle for the World*, page 121, 149–150.
[6] See Gaetano Mosca, *The Ruling Elite*; Robert Michels, *Political Parties*; and Vilfredo Pareto, *Sociological Writings*.
[7] See James Burnham, *The Machiavellians*, pages 160–175.
[8] See Burnham, *Machiavellians*, pages 115–118, 175–189; and Pareto, *Sociological Writings*, pages 111–114, 275–278.

of Communism, Burnham advocated an all-out effort by the United States to liberate the peoples of Europe and Asia from Stalinist tyranny.[9] Being a lapsed Leninist, he was well aware that the credibility of this democratic crusade was threatened by Lenin's celebrated dissection of global power politics in *Imperialism: the highest stage of capitalism*. To meet this challenge, Burnham turned to a theoretical celebration of the civilising mission of world empires: Arnold Toynbee's *A Study of History*. Living through the collapse of British imperial power, this English Classics professor had sought to explain his country's dramatic reversal of fortune by making comparisons between his own times and those of the ancient world. According to Toynbee, the history of humanity comprised a recurrent succession of predetermined cycles: a 'Universal State' was founded; stability led to stagnation; the old order collapsed into a 'Time of Troubles'; and, completing the process, a new 'Universal State' took over.[10] Far from being something extraordinary, the ebbing of British hegemony in the early twentieth century could now be understood as the latest iteration of this transcendent temporal rhythm. The collapse of one global empire would be inevitably followed by the rise of a new – and more advanced – Universal State.[11]

For Burnham, this sweeping theory of human history provided a flattering explanation of the USA's recently acquired mastery over the world system. In the same way that Rome had replaced Greece after a long period of instability, the American empire was the new Universal State emerging victorious from the Time of Troubles unleashed by the fall of the British empire.[12] Out of Toynbee's writings, Burnham developed a compelling theory of geopolitics for the US elite's ideological struggle in the Cold War. Like Marx's anticipation of the classless society, Lenin's call for the abolition of imperialism was dismissed as a utopian fantasy. Instead, in the same way that voters had to decide between competing political elites in elections, the peoples of the world were forced to choose which

---

[9] See James Burnham, *The Struggle for the World*, pages 181–199, 242–246; *The Coming Defeat of Communism*, pages 135–148, 272–278.

[10] See Arnold Toynbee, *A Study of History*, pages 12–34, 187–208, 555–558.

[11] See Toynbee, *Study of History*, pages 318–319.

[12] See Burnham, *Struggle*, pages 40–55, 134–135, 187–199; *Defeat of Communism*, pages 44–59.

Universal State was going to rule over them: democratic America or totalitarian Russia.[13] In the epoch of the Cold War, there was no other option. 'The reality is that the only alternative to the Communist World Empire is an American Empire which will be, if not literally worldwide in formal boundaries, capable of exercising decisive world control.'[14]

Where Burnham led, large sections of the American Left followed. Just like him, many others also found that anti-Stalinism – the politics of their revolutionary youth – was now driving them towards a rapprochement with the US elite. As Burnham had discovered, this apostasy had its material rewards. The US military and the CIA – the new intelligence agency set up to fight the Cold War – were providing academic jobs and research money for repentant socialists. Publishing anti-Marxist books could bring fame and fortune to disenchanted revolutionaries. Like Burnham, they might even get the chance to become influential members of the US elite. Crucially, many of them believed that helping themselves could be combined with helping others. As the Machiavellian advisers to the 'Modern Prince', progressive intellectuals would be able to improve the lives of ordinary people, both at home and abroad.[15] Ironically, despite being the founder of this new and increasingly influential Cold War Left, Burnham soon became disillusioned with his own creation. By the mid 1950s, he had abandoned any pretence of radicalism and moved to the extreme right of American conservatism.[16] With Burnham having discredited himself among progressives, other thinkers had to take over the role of building upon the ideas with which he had launched the Cold War Left in the early 1940s.

The primary task of these American intellectuals was to continue the theoretical demolition of Marxism. Like Burnham, they faced the conundrum that the materialist conception of history was first proposed by two of the greatest liberal philosophers: Adam Smith

[13] See Burnham, *Struggle*, pages 53–55, 140–143, 221; *Defeat of Communism*, pages 18–19.

[14] Burnham, *Struggle*, page 182.

[15] According to Antonio Gramsci, these experts were the contemporary equivalents of the courtiers who counselled the princes of Renaissance Italy. See Antonio Gramsci, *Selections from the Prison Notebooks*, pages 5–14, 147–158.

[16] See Kelly, *Burnham*, pages 183–237.

and Adam Ferguson. Back in the late eighteenth century, these Scottish thinkers had realised that human societies were constantly evolving. Living on the borderline between the tribal Highlands and proto-industrial England, the contrast between tradition and modernity had been stark.[17] Rejecting the prevailing belief in the immutability of human nature, these two philosophers argued that changes in the methods of creating wealth inevitably led to a transformation of the whole social structure. In a flash of brilliance, Adam Smith summarised the process of history as the movement through four successive stages of economic development: hunting, herding, agriculture and commerce.[18]

In the early nineteenth century, this analysis became one of the principle theoretical inspirations of the emerging labour movements. While Adam Smith had ended his investigations with the advent of commerce, the European Left began to argue that human evolution would continue towards a further stage: socialism.[19] In their 1848 pamphlet *The Communist Manifesto*, Karl Marx and Friedrich Engels popularised this new interpretation of the materialist conception of history. Like Adam Smith and Adam Ferguson, they also welcomed the destruction of feudalism by capitalism. Yet, at the same time, they were keenly aware of the suffering and exploitation caused by this new economic system. In a masterpiece of prophecy, they looked forward to a time when the majority of the population would use the productive powers of modern technology to create a truly democratic and equalitarian society.

> The advance of industry, whose involuntary promoter is the bourgeoisie, replaces the isolation of the labourers, due to competition, by their revolutionary combination, due to association. The development of modern industry, therefore, cuts from under its feet the very foundation on which the bourgeoisie produces and appropriates products. What the bourgeoisie, therefore, produces, above all, is its own gravediggers. Its fall and the victory of the proletariat are equally inevitable.[20]

[17] See Christopher Berry, *Social Theory of the Scottish Enlightenment*, pages 1–19, 74–90.
[18] See Adam Smith, *Wealth of Nations*, Volume 1, pages 401–445; Volume 2, pages 213–253. Also see Adam Ferguson, *An Essay on the History of Civil Society*, pages 74–146.
[19] See Robert Owen, *A New View of Society*; and Henri Saint-Simon, *Selected Writings on Science, Industry and Social Organisation*.
[20] Karl Marx and Friedrich Engels, *The Communist Manifesto*, page 35.

During the late nineteenth and early twentieth centuries, Marxism provided a distinctive ideological identity for the increasingly powerful parliamentary socialist parties and industrial trade unions in Europe. Their day-to-day struggles for reforms within capitalism were inevitably leading to the revolutionary moment of socialist emancipation.[21] However, like laissez-faire liberalism, the credibility of this optimistic prophecy was fatally weakened by the outbreak of the First World War: the Time of Troubles precipitated by the waning of the British empire. Political and economic turmoil rapidly led to theoretical confusion. During the 1920s and 1930s, bitter divisions inside the European labour movements were expressed through incompatible interpretations of Marxism. Although Social Democrats and Communists quoted the same authors and the same texts, the two sides drew completely different conclusions from them. As Europe headed towards another catastrophic war, Marxism was – at one and the same time – the theory of parliamentary reformism and that of revolutionary dictatorship.

Lacking mass working-class parties, these ideological disputes in the USA had taken place outside of mainstream politics. Yet, it was the relative safety offered by this life on the margins which encouraged the theoretical creativity of the American Left. Unencumbered by rigid party discipline, Trotskyist intellectuals were free to experiment with the most avant-garde versions of historical materialism. When they abandoned their belief in revolutionary politics, this innovatory spirit soon became focused on finding alternatives to Marxism in all of its many varieties. In *The Managerial Revolution* and *The Machiavellians*, Burnham had begun the task of constructing a specifically American version of the materialist conception of history. Once the Cold War had started, the geopolitical importance of these books became clear. Both superpowers were in agreement on the terminology of their ideological confrontation: Marxism meant Stalinism and all Communists were Stalinists. Instead of arguing over the correct interpretation of socialism, as the European Left had done in the 1920s and 1930s, these imperial rivals wanted to champion their own distinctive versions of historical materialism. For Russian propagandists, the problem was how to impose a rigid orthodoxy upon Marx's subversive analysis of human social

---

[21] See Karl Kautsky, *The Class Struggle*, pages 199–202.

evolution. In contrast, for their American rivals, the challenge was
how to create a credible version of the materialist conception of
history without admitting any debt to their Russian opponent's
favourite theorist.

Just like producing cybernetics without Wiener, inventing
Marxism without Marx had now become an ideological priority.
For the members of the Cold War Left charged with this vital task,
Burnham had shown the way forward. Any theory from any social
theorist – including those who were Marxists – could be adapted
for the task as long as the final product wasn't explicitly Marxist in
inspiration. While Russian intellectuals were forced to work within
the confines of the one true faith of Stalinism, American academics
were able to explore a multiplicity of different approaches. With
nothing theoretically in common except their rejection of Marxism
as the ideology of Communism with a capital C, the thinkers of the
Cold War Left became the gurus of a new philosophical position:
Anti-Communism.

> My generation was raised [in the 1930s] in the conviction that the
> basic motive power in political behaviour is the economic interest
> of groups ... However much importance we continue to attach to
> economic interests ... we are still confronted from time to time with
> a wide range of behaviour for which the economic interpretation of
> politics seems to be inadequate or misleading or altogether irrelevant.
> It is to account for this range of behaviour that we need a different
> conceptual framework ...[22]

For the successors of Burnham, their ideological mission was aided
by the increasing availability of military funding and technological
tools. By the early 1950s, as in the natural sciences, multi-disciplinary
teams had become the cutting edge of intellectual research within
the social sciences in American universities. As well as weakening
traditional academic rivalries, this form of collaborative working
was also designed to encourage a common methodology across
disciplines. Just like physicists or chemists, sociologists would also
discover the truth by measuring, surveying and quantifying. Above
all, they too would use the new technology of computing to make

---

[22] Richard Hofstadter, 'Status Politics', page 191. 'The economic interpretation of politics'
is a euphemism for Marxism.

sense of their findings.[23] By adopting this up-to-date methodology, American social scientists claimed that their research had become as 'value free' as that of natural scientists. Yet, at the same time, these academics were also promoting their work as a vital part of the Cold War struggle for soft-power supremacy. Expensive computers and large numbers of data-collectors were needed to verify the different Anti-Communist theories which proved the USA's superiority over its Russian opponent. In the social science departments of 1950s America, there was nothing more qualitatively ideological than quantitative value-free research carried out on computers.

The disingenuous nature of US academics' hi-tech impartiality was revealed by their continued devotion to the cult of the famous book. As had happened for centuries, leading intellectuals were still expected to provide the theoretical framework for other less influential academics to draw conclusions from their empirical research. Although these gurus had to back up their arguments with references from quantitative studies, their books and articles only became essential reading if they were identified with a specific qualitative judgement about human societies. In Cold War America, the ultimate goal of any ambitious social scientist was writing a canonical text of Anti-Communism. As Burnham had shown, discrediting the ideological authority of the Russian enemy wasn't only a patriotic duty, but also an excellent career move. Among all the difficulties facing Anti-Communist academics in the 1950s, the most intractable problem was devising a credible theory for the analysis of economic history. Although quantitative surveys and empirical studies could challenge minor details in Marx's writings, American social science lacked a replacement for his grand narrative explaining the rise of capitalism. Surprisingly, their colleagues in the economics departments were completely incapable of solving this problem. From the late nineteenth century onwards, liberal theorists had concentrated on celebrating the mathematical perfection of the immutable laws of market competition. Because they believed that private enterprise reflected the eternal verities of human nature,

---

[23] See Lance Davis, J.R.T. Hughes and Stanley Reiter, 'Econometrics'; Christopher Rand, *Cambridge U.S.A.*, pages 129–158; and Steve Heims, *Cybernetics Group*, pages 1–13, 164–179, 248–272.

anything unfamiliar about life in pre-capitalist societies was dismissed as nothing more than a nascent form of capitalism.[24]

In 1950s America, this ahistorical interpretation of liberalism remained the credo of academic economics. Yet, when this theory was applied to other social sciences, its spatial and temporal limitations were quickly revealed. In the mid twentieth century, the majority of the world's population were still living in pre-capitalist societies. Within the most advanced economies, laissez-faire liberalism was no longer the dominant paradigm. For American academics wanting to analyse contemporary social reality, the invention of a patriotic version of historical materialism was a top priority. In *The Managerial Revolution*, Burnham had begun the task of constructing an Anti-Communist account of the development of capitalism. But, because this book was focused on the transition from liberalism to Fordism, his managerial analysis didn't provide a grand narrative which explained the emergence and evolution of market economies. Since an all-encompassing approach couldn't be found in Burnham's writings, the completion of this theoretical assignment was left to other thinkers of the Cold War Left.

In 1960, Walt Rostow – a prominent academic from the CIA-funded CENIS research centre at MIT – published the book which finally provided the American empire with its own distinctive grand narrative of modernity: *The Stages of Economic Growth*.[25] Just like Burnham, this intellectual had also used his Marxist past as an entry into the US elite. As the child of Russian–Jewish émigrés, he had been brought up within a socialist milieu.[26] While studying at Yale in the late 1930s, he had 'argued the virtues of communism' to his classmates.[27] Like many other American leftists, it was the Second World War that transformed this outsider into an insider. After working with the US intelligence services in the anti-fascist struggle, Rostow went on to a successful career as an academic analyst

---

[24] See Eugen Böhm-Bawerk, *Karl Marx and the Close of his System*; and Rudolf Hilferding, 'Böhm-Bawerk's Criticism of Marx'.

[25] The Centre for International Studies (CENIS) was set up in 1950. See Victor Marchetti and John Marks, *The CIA and the Cult of Intelligence*, page 181, 224–225; Christopher Simpson, *Science of Coercion*, pages 81–84; and Rand, *Cambridge U.S.A.*, pages 95–105.

[26] See W.W. Rostow, *Concept and Controversy*, pages 2–7. Rostow's parents named him after Walt Whitman – the radical American poet.

[27] Michael Carson, 'David Dellinger'.

and propagandist for the CIA.[28] Even though he'd broken with Marxism and was funded from dodgy sources, Rostow still identified himself as a leftist. Unlike Burnham, who was advocating a return to laissez-faire liberalism by the late 1950s, Rostow's research into economic history was inspired by a progressive vision of America as an advanced welfare democracy. He was convinced that the Cold War Left would not only prevail in the struggle against Russian totalitarianism overseas, but would also succeed in constructing a fairer and more humane society at home.

> [T]he agenda of American domestic life for ... [the 1960s] consists in large part of issues where the problem is ... for the community to act ... as a collectivity on an expanded range of common interests. This is the case with the problem of inflation; with school buildings and teachers' salaries; with enlarged road building programmes; with the rebuilding of old cities, including the clearance of slums; with public health; with care of the aged.[29]

In *The Stages of Economic Growth*, Rostow proposed his own replacement for Adam Smith's and Karl Marx's abstract schemas of social development. As in *The Wealth of Nations* and *The Communist Manifesto*, human history was explained as the movement from one economic paradigm to another. First and foremost, this approach allowed Rostow to theorise the existence of traditional societies that had existed before capitalism. Unlike his academic colleagues in the economics departments, he understood that market competition was a historical creation rather than an immutable law of nature. According to Rostow, this insight explained why the opening phase of the transition from a traditional society to capitalism was a complex and lengthy process. But, once certain socio-psychological preconditions for modernisation were met, then a country would experience the rapid 'take-off' of economic growth. Within a relatively short period, the nation would reach the stage of industrial maturity, with factory production, the rule of law, free markets and constitutional government. Inspired by Burnham, Rostow emphasised that this liberal phase of capitalism wasn't the culmination of the process of modernisation. In the next stage of

[28] See Rostow, *Concept and Controversy*, pages 28–58.
[29] W.W. Rostow, 'The National Style', page 131.

growth, a nation evolved into a mass-consumption society where the benefits of industrialisation were extended to the majority of the population. Under Fordism, workers became car-owning, suburban-dwelling, TV-watching inhabitants of a democratic and pluralist welfare state.[30] At the end of the grand narrative of human history, the social programme of the Cold War Left would be realised across the entire world.

As soon it appeared, *The Stages of Economic Growth* became one of the canonical texts of the new American credo. In the subtitle to his book, Rostow proudly announced that he had written the 'non-communist manifesto'. For the first time, an American social scientist from the Cold War Left had created a plausible version of the materialist conception of history. Best of all, Rostow had directly challenged Marx on his own intellectual territory. In *Capital*, the economic modernisation of England had provided the empirical evidence for Marx's theoretical analysis of the rise of capitalism and, in turn, its eventual replacement by socialism. In his book, Rostow had examined the same history to draw entirely different conclusions. Both theorists were in agreement that England had pioneered the model of modernity which the rest of world had to follow.[31] But, while Marx had emphasised class conflicts as the driving force of capitalist development, Rostow concluded that social consensus was the best way to encourage rapid economic growth.[32] Above all, instead of the grand narrative culminating in socialism, he argued that the process of modernity led to welfare Fordism. In the ideological battle of the Cold War, America now possessed an attractive alternative to the Stalinist interpretation of Marxism. After a long wait, its propagandists finally had the theoretical proof that the USA was the hope of humanity.

> American domestic political skills and social habits are accommodated to achieving order and direction from situations of diffused power, where regional, class, cultural and economic interests clash and intertwine in complex patterns. If the [US] nation can evoke and sustain the best in its own interests and experience, it ought to do

[30] See W.W. Rostow, *The Stages of Economic Growth*, pages 17–92.
[31] See Karl Marx, *Capital, Volume 1*, page 90; and Rostow, *Stages of Economic Growth*, pages 33–35.
[32] See W.W. Rostow, *Essays on a Half-Century*, pages 65–78.

reasonably well in a world where history is likely to impose a larger version of [American] continental politics as the working basis for international life.[33]

For Rostow, this analysis of the economic history proved that – as they adopted the US model of capitalism – the whole of humanity would soon be enjoying the benefits of the mass-consumption society. Like social consensus at home, international cooperation was rewarded by faster economic growth.[34] In contrast, Stalinism was denounced as the pathology of modernisation. By fermenting nationalist revolts in developing countries, its proponents sabotaged the take-off of their economies. By promoting class conflicts within industrialising nations, they delayed the advent of the mass-consumption society. By initiating the Cold War, the Russian patrons of this aberrant ideology had forced the nations of the American-led 'Free World' to divert scarce resources from welfare into warfare.[35] Marxism wasn't simply an obsolete version of the materialist conception of history. Worst of all, this dangerous theory encouraged irrational and violent opposition to modernisation across the globe. In the penultimate subheading of his celebrated book, Rostow summarised his position in one line: 'Communism: a disease of the transition'.[36]

Although Stalinism was in ascendancy in some parts of the world, this was seen as only a temporary phenomenon. Rostow was convinced that – in the long run – the inherent logic of modernity would prevail. Every nation had a different history and a different culture, but, sooner or later, all of them would have to follow the same path of progress pioneered first by England and then by the United States. The stages of growth were a universal model applicable to the whole of humanity. This meant that Stalinism was a historical dead end. In the grand narrative of progress, all countries were heading towards convergence with the American model of modernity. It was inevitable that – at some point in the

---

33 W.W. Rostow, *The United States in the World Arena*, page 442.

34 See Rostow, *Stages of Economic Growth*, pages 87–88; *United States*, pages 214–217.

35 See Rostow, *United States*, pages 141–3, 515–518; *Essays*, pages 100–101.

36 Rostow, *Stages of Economic Growth*, page 162. Whether consciously or not, Rostow was echoing Lenin's assertion that the European socialists who criticised the repressive policies of his regime were suffering from 'an infantile disorder'. See V.I. Lenin, *'Left Wing' Communism*.

future – even Russia and China would evolve into US-style mass-consumption societies.[37] However, Rostow had difficulties in providing an explanation of why all the nations of the world were progressing through the stages of growth to the promised land of welfare Fordism. In both liberalism and Marxism, human subjectivity – in the form of either self-interest or class conflict – was celebrated as the driving force of modernity. In contrast, Rostow described this history as a process without a subject. People might create the conditions for the take-off of industrialisation but, from then on, capitalism developed through the stages of growth according to its own internal rationale.[38] As suggested by his aeroplane metaphor, Rostow believed that the economy operated like an autonomous machine. Computer modelling at CENIS had provided scientific proof that strictly observing the rules of the capitalist game was the precondition of progress through the stages of growth.[39] Unlike Marx, Rostow ruled out the possibility that underdeveloped countries of the South might be able to learn from the mistakes of the North and industrialise in a more enlightened manner.[40] The calculations of the CENIS mainframes had proved that all nations had to follow the same predetermined route to modernity. For Rostow, the hubris of Stalinism was daring to tamper with this transcendent cybernetic mechanism. Freedom and prosperity could only be achieved by humanity submitting itself to the impersonal priorities of capitalist modernisation. In Rostow's canonical text, commodity fetishism had become the driving force of social evolution.

As well as promoting America as the prototype of the Fordist future of the rest of the world, *The Stages of Economic Growth* also provided the grand narrative which justified the Cold War Left's rewriting of the history of the United States itself. During the first half of the twentieth century, most intellectuals had understood that the gargantuan bureaucracy of the modern American state had little

[37] See Rostow, *Stages of Economic Growth*, pages 133–137; and *United States*, pages 423–430.
[38] See Rostow, *Stages of Economic Growth*, pages 36–58; *The Process of Economic Growth*, pages 274–306.
[39] See Rand, *Cambridge U.S.A.*, page 100.
[40] In 1861, Marx had reassured a Russian advocate of agrarian socialism that her country wasn't necessarily condemned to follow the English path of economic development. See Karl Marx, 'Letter to Vera Ivanovna Zasulich'; and Theodor Shanin, *Late Marx and the Russian Road*, pages 3–93.

in common with the minimal government of the early years of the republic. In contrast, in the Cold War Left's new interpretation of the nation's history, the evolution of the USA had been a linear and uninterrupted process, from the War of Independence to global dominance. Although political, social and economic conditions had changed out of all recognition, the liberal principles of the 1776 Revolution still defined modern America.[41] For the Cold War Left, the primary purpose of this historical analysis wasn't to provide a more accurate interpretation of the facts of their nation's history. Far more important was the ideological role of this invented tradition. By denying that there had been a radical break in recent American history, the Cold War Left was able to argue that there was no incompatibility between liberalism and Fordism. Even if minimal government and laissez-faire economics had disappeared, the ideological foundations of the USA remained unchanged. Like Humpty Dumpty in *Through the Looking Glass*, the leaders of the Cold War Left insisted that liberalism meant what they wanted it to mean.[42]

For the promoters of Anti-Communism, this redefinition was essential. Because Stalinist totalitarianism claimed to be socialist, the Cold War Left didn't want to be identified as socialists. Needing an alternative, they instead described themselves as liberals. By the end of the 1950s, the Cold War Left had succeeded in capturing this political term. Since the eighteenth century, liberalism had meant advocating minimal government and laissez-faire economics. Now, in mid-twentieth-century America, this word defined supporters of the militarised state and welfare Fordism. For the Cold War Left, adopting the moniker of liberalism also symbolised their search for an Anti-Communist ideology of progressive politics to replace working-class forms of socialism. Looking across the Atlantic, many of them believed that they'd found the answer in a faction of the British Labour Party: the Fabians. Set up in the late nineteenth century, this group of intellectuals had always rejected revolutionary politics in favour of cautious reforms. Just like the Cold War Left, they too had simultaneously supported social improvements at home

---

[41] See W.W. Rostow, 'The National Style'; and Richard Hofstadter, *The American Political Tradition*, pages 315–352.
[42] See Lewis Carroll, *Through the Looking Glass*, page 223.

and imperial expansion overseas. Above all, the Fabians provided a model of how progressive intellectuals could influence events by the 'permeation' of the institutions of the establishment. As civil servants, politicians, academics, artists and journalists, their members had formed an enlightened managerial elite overseeing the building of the British welfare state.[43] In their non-Marxist version of socialism, Fabians were better at organising the lives of workers than the workers were themselves.

> If ... we lose the delusive comfort of belief in that magic giant, the Proletariat, who will dictate, arrange, restore and create, ... we clear the way for the recognition of an elite of intelligent ... people ... and for a study of the method of making this creative element effective in human affairs against the massive oppressiveness of selfishness and unimaginative self-protective conservatism.[44]

During the 1950s, the Cold War Left adapted the Fabians' bureaucratic ideology to create its own distinctively American version of progressive politics. Pragmatic thinkers would provide guidance on how to introduce reforms at home and to protect the nation's interests abroad. However, unlike the Fabians, the Cold War Left never organised themselves into a formal political faction. Since many of them were former Trotskyists, these intellectuals had acquired a distrust of group discipline. Instead, they created a diffuse elite linked together by academic institutions, government departments, specialist journals, art galleries, corporate foundations, military projects, political patrons and personal ties. The Cold War Left was a vanguard which didn't need to organise itself as a party. What distinguished them from their fellow Americans wasn't formal membership of a faction, but a shared ideology and a common culture.[45] At the beginning of the twentieth century, many intellectuals of the US elite had held insular and conservative attitudes. Fifty years later, the thinkers of the Cold War Left took

---

[43] See Sidney Webb, 'Introduction to the 1920 Reprint'; and Henry Pelling, Origins of the Labour Party.
[44] H.G. Wells, The Open Conspiracy, page 56.
[45] The group identity of the Cold War Left was reinforced by the leading role in the movement of a group of intellectuals who had grown up together in New York's Jewish community. See Daniel Bell, Sociological Journeys, pages 118–137; and Irving Howe, Steady Work, pages 349–364.

pride in their cosmopolitan and modern outlook. There was no need for a conspiratorial organisation when cultural sophistication was as efficient as any party card in marking out the members of their movement.

This group cohesion amplified their influence within the US managerial elite. Although each pursued their own individual careers, these intellectuals were united by a common goal: advocating progressive policies for the American empire. By writing canonical texts of Anti-Communism, they demonstrated that the adoption of the Cold War Left's social and foreign policies was inevitable. By processing their findings through the latest computers, they proved that their political programme was backed up by impartial research. As Rostow had shown, both their conservative opponents at home and their totalitarian enemies abroad were vainly resisting the onward rush of the grand narrative of human history. Above all, although it might seem that laissez-faire liberalism and Stalinist Marxism had nothing in common, these obsolete ideologies produced the same results when put into practice: social instability and global confrontation. If the American empire wanted to avoid these dangers, the US government would have to implement the progressive policies of the Cold War Left. Under its guidance, the modernisation of the political and economic system would create the conditions for peace and prosperity within the global village.

09

FREE WORKERS IN THE AFFLUENT SOCIETY

In 1949, Arthur Schlesinger, Jr., produced the political manifesto of the new American pragmatism: *The Vital Center*. Rejecting the two obsolete ideological extremes of tooth-and-claw capitalism and messianic totalitarianism, this prophet of the Cold War Left claimed to have discovered a new third way to modernity. Instead of being polarised into rival camps, political parties were increasingly learning to work with each other. Toleration of different viewpoints had created a bipartisan consensus over most major issues. Not surprisingly, Schlesinger argued that America provided the best model for this pluralist political system. The imposition of outdated laissez-faire and Marxist dogmas was impossible under the US constitution. However much Republicans and Democrats might disagree, the two parties had to collaborate when power was divided between the executive and the legislature. In the USA, political decisions were arrived at through informed debate and impartial investigation.[1] Now that modern techniques of consensus management were available, the ideologies of class confrontation were no longer relevant. Schlesinger was convinced that this pragmatic dispensation was the modern iteration of the principles of the 1776 Revolution. Even though minimal government and laissez-faire economics had been discarded, modern America was still the global champion of liberalism.

> The spirit of the centre ... [is] the spirit of human decency against the extremes of tyranny. ... The new radicalism, drawing strength from a realistic conception of ... [humanity], dedicates itself to problems as they come, attacking them in terms which ... best secure the freedom and fulfilment of the individual.[2]

During the 1950s, the Cold War Left transformed the pragmatic politics of *The Vital Center* into an all-embracing philosophy. Capturing the zeitgeist, Daniel Bell announced in *The End of Ideology* that the increasing irrelevance of laissez-faire liberalism and totalitarian Communism marked the imminent disappearance of all forms of political partisanship.[3] Like Burnham and Rostow, this guru had also been a fervent socialist in the 1930s and had acquired a detailed knowledge of Marxist theory in the process. When he

---

[1] See Arthur Schlesinger, Jr., *The Vital Center*, pages 11–34, 51–91, 131–218.

[2] Schlesinger, *Vital Center*, page 256.

[3] See Daniel Bell, *The End of Ideology*, pages 39–45, 75–94, 275–314, 393–407.

lost his faith in the workers' revolution, Bell redirected his learning into the advocacy of class compromise as the only credible form of politics in the modern world. Echoing Schlesinger, he argued that social consensus had removed any need for revolutionary intransigence. If the class war was over, then class parties were also obsolete.[4] Now that progressive politics were focused on making pragmatic improvements in public administration, no intelligent person could believe in a redemptive ideology like socialism. Modern left-wing intellectuals should be proud of their scepticism about all belief systems.[5] However, as in other examples of value-free social science, this Anti-Communist celebration of consensual politics and administrative efficiency disguised a deep commitment to the self-interested policies of the American empire. A lack of convictions meant unquestioning loyalty to one side in the superpower confrontation. The Cold War Left had invented a political creed which denied its own existence: the 'ideology of the end of ideology'.[6]

In his analysis, Bell appropriated the populist Marxist argument that economics played the determining role in social evolution to explain the triumph of political consensus. Like Burnham and Rostow, he'd also learnt from his socialist teachers that the increasing concentration of ownership was an integral part of the capitalist system. The economy of small businesses had already evolved into one dominated by large corporations. But, as Bell emphasised, this disappearance of laissez-faire liberalism hadn't led to the socialist revolution. Back in the 1930s, Stalinist state planning may have seemed like an attractive option when the only alternative was mass unemployment and widespread poverty under free-market capitalism. Fortunately, in the 1950s, ordinary people were no longer required to give up their personal freedom in return for economic security. As in politics, America had discovered a third way between the two obsolete ideologies of laissez-faire liberalism and Stalinist Marxism. On the one hand, the US state regulated markets to prevent another slump and provided welfare for the

---

[4] Bell argued that the struggle between capital and labour had been replaced in the USA by the competition between 'new prosperity-created "status groups" ... for recognition and respectability'. Daniel Bell, *The Radical Right*, page 39.

[5] See Daniel Bell and Henry David Aiken, 'Ideology – a Debate', pages 261–262.

[6] See C. Wright Mills, 'Letter to the New Left'.

poor. On the other hand, the American economy was dominated by private businesses and powered by entrepreneurial innovation. In the USA, capitalists and workers might have their quarrels, but they also collaborated to ensure that everyone got richer.[7] Bell argued that the political consensus was founded upon this economic compromise. Instead of bitterly fighting each other for control over the means of production, the two sides had a mutual interest in improving efficiency and raising output. Partisan ideologies were disappearing because class enemies had become economic partners.

> Few serious minds believe any longer that one can ... through 'social engineering' bring about a new utopia of social harmony. ... Few 'classic' liberals insist that the State should play no role in the economy ... In the Western world, therefore, there is today a rough consensus among intellectuals on political issues: the acceptance of a Welfare State; the desirability of decentralised power; a system of mixed economy and of political pluralism.[8]

Although reconciled with capitalism, the Cold War Left contemptuously dismissed the theoretical presuppositions of liberal economics as anachronistic. During the 1930s, the old dogma of self-correcting markets had been discredited by the worst slump in American history. This economic disaster had driven the founders of the movement to embrace revolutionary socialism in their youth. When they finally realised that this Russian-inspired panacea threatened the life and liberty of every citizen, these intellectuals were left without an economic model. Looking again at the New Deal policies of US President Franklin Roosevelt during the 1930s, they discovered that state intervention could be used to manage the business cycle and improve workers' living standards without any requirement for mass nationalisations. From its earliest days, the Cold War Left championed this pragmatic solution as the third way beyond market instability and planned tyranny. During the 1950s, their programme of class compromise was vindicated by the rapid growth of the US economy. Prosperity had become a permanent feature of American life.[9]

---

[7] See Bell, *End of Ideology*, pages 75–94, 211–226.

[8] Bell, *End of Ideology*, pages 402–403.

[9] See W.W. Rostow, *The Stages of Economic Growth*, pages 75–81, 154–155; *The United States in the World Arena*, pages 8–12, 515–529.

What the Cold War Left found difficult to explain was how the economics of welfare Fordism operated. Crucially, as the high priests of Anti-Communism, they weren't allowed to find the replacement for the pieties of laissez-faire liberalism in the most obvious place: Karl Marx's *Capital*. In his masterpiece, the pre-eminent theorist of the socialist movement had provided two key insights into the evolutionary path of industrial capitalism. Firstly, building on the work of the French Physiocrats, Marx in *Capital, Volume 2* developed an abstract model of the national economy as a dynamic feedback system. The continuous cycle of production and consumption not only connected its different sectors together, but also compelled them to expand in parallel.[10] Secondly, in the other two volumes, Marx analysed the institutional changes within capitalism which were facilitating the rapid growth of the late-nineteenth-century English economy. Under pressure from the trade unions, the state had been forced to regulate the working conditions of the factory proletariat. When this political intervention into the economy was combined with market competition, family firms were compelled to evolve into capitalist corporations.[11] From his studies of Victorian England, Marx was able to equip the labour movement with a remarkably accurate prognosis of what would become the defining features of Fordism: big government and big business. Ironically, by constructing a cybernetic model of capitalism, this socialist critic had also inadvertently revealed to the emerging managerial elite how they could control the national economy in their own interests.

Not surprisingly, Marx's *Capital* initially had little overt influence outside intellectual circles of the radical Left. Yet, at the same time, the hardening of liberal dogma within academic economics in the closing decades of the nineteenth century demonstrated the political threat to the established order posed by his subversive interpretation of Adam Smith's *The Wealth of Nations*. Similarly, on the respectable Left, the Fabians felt that it was essential to found their hierarchical version of socialism upon a rejection of Marx's price theory.[12] In 1910, Rudolf Hilferding – an Austrian Social Democrat – published

---

[10] See Karl Marx, *Capital, Volume 2*, pages 427–599.
[11] See Karl Marx, *Capital, Volume 1*, pages 340–416; *Capital, Volume 3*, pages 505–514, 566–573.
[12] See George Bernard Shaw, 'Sixty Years of Fabianism', page 313.

a book which challenged this complacent attitude: *Finance Capital*. As its title suggested, his text took Marx's masterpiece as its starting point. Hilferding explained that – during the three decades separating the two works – the evolution of capitalism beyond laissez-faire liberalism had continued unabated. Aided by the state, a cartel of industrial corporations and financial institutions was now directing the economy.[13] Although it was still subject to the fluctuations of the business cycle, this organised form of capitalism was a premonition of the socialist emancipation to come. If politicians, industrialists and bankers were already successfully regulating market competition, then the labour movement must be on the brink of being able to take over running the economy. The spontaneous coordination of individual initiatives was giving way to the conscious planning of collective labour.

> Capital now appears as a unitary power which exercises sovereign sway over the life process of society: a power which arises directly from ownership of the means of production, of natural resources, and of the whole accumulated labour of the past, and from command of living labour as a direct consequence of property relations. ... The problem of property thus attains its clearest, most unequivocal and sharpest expression at the same time as the development of finance capital itself is successfully resolving the problem of the organisation of the social economy.[14]

For decades after its publication, Hilferding's *Finance Capital* represented the cutting edge of Marxist theory for not only his Social Democratic comrades, but also their Communist opponents. Responding to the outbreak of the First World War, Lenin – aided by Nikolai Bukharin – had used his analysis of cartelised capitalism to provide a historical materialist explanation for the imperialist rivalries which had unleashed this disastrous Time of Troubles.[15] When their party seized power in the 1917 Revolution, the new government's economic policy also took its inspiration from an idiosyncratic reading of Hilferding's book. Lenin and Bukharin were convinced that – under the firm leadership of the Communist vanguard – peasant Russia was leaping forward into the most

[13] See Rudolf Hilferding, *Finance Capital*, pages 107–235.
[14] Hilferding, *Finance Capital*, page 235.
[15] See V.I. Lenin, *Imperialism*; and Nikolai Bukharin, *Imperialism and World Economy*.

advanced form of organised industrial modernity: 'state capitalism'.[16] Forced requisitions, hyperinflation and payments in kind were premonitions of conscious planning. One-party rule and one-man management were precursors of proletarian democracy. The militarised economy of the First World War had become the Marxist imaginary future realised in the present: 'War Communism'.[17] In response, their left-wing critics denounced the hypocrisy of a regime which claimed to be fighting for proletarian freedom while ruling as a bureaucratic despotism. By the time that the Communists had won the civil war with the monarchists in 1921, Lenin and Bukharin had also become disillusioned with their own tyrannical version of state capitalism. Faced with rebellion among its own supporters, the revolutionary dictatorship needed a new economic strategy. Chastened by their recent experiences, Lenin and Bukharin adopted a more sober interpretation of Hildferding's analysis. As an underdeveloped country, Russia couldn't leap into hi-tech socialism in one bound. Instead, state-owned industrial enterprises would act as the modernising vanguard of an economy which consisted overwhelmingly of small businesses, artisan workshops and, above all, peasant farms. The future of Leninist Russia was American Fordism.[18]

Tellingly, the Communist regime hired Social Democrat economists to implement its new policies. As recommended in *Capital, Volume 2*, they saw the Russian economy as a feedback system which linked the different sectors of production. With an intelligent combination of taxes, regulations and investments, the state would be able to plan the symbiotic growth of industrial and agricultural output. Over a long period of transition, Russia would slowly evolve into a modern urban economy. Having studied Marx and Hilferding, the Social Democrats knew that this self-styled Communist country was many decades away from even arriving

---

[16] See V.I. Lenin, *State and Revolution*, pages 35, 39–40, 75; *The Threatening Catastrophe*, pages 11–16

[17] See Nikolai Bukharin and Eugeni Preobrazhensky, *The ABC of Communism*. Also see E.H. Carr, *The Bolshevik Revolution, Volume 2*, pages 151–268.

[18] Reflecting the new party line of the mid 1920s, Stalin defined Communism as a combination of 'Russian revolutionary sweep' with 'American efficiency'. See Joseph Stalin, 'Foundations of Leninism', page 109. Also see Moshe Lewin, *Political Undercurrents in Soviet Economic Debates*, pages 84–96.

at the Fordist stage of capitalism.[19] Following the death of Lenin in 1924, a fierce succession struggle quickly broke out within the ruling party. As well as dividing over foreign policy, the different factions also argued passionately over the pace of industrialisation in Russia. While Bukharin and his allies held to Lenin's cautious approach, Trotsky's group championed a more vigorous strategy. If the Communist vanguard didn't change course, the socialist plan was in danger of being overwhelmed by the capitalist market. Applying the analysis in *Capital, Volume 1* of the English path of modernisation to Russia, Eugeni Preobrazhensky – the leading Trotskyist economist – advocated the systematic exploitation of the peasantry to pay for a faster tempo of industrialisation: 'primitive socialist accumulation'.[20]

By the late 1920s, the Leninist dictatorship's relationship with the countryside had reached a crisis point. With the nationalised industries unable to supply the goods required to purchase sufficient food supplies from the peasantry for the urban population, the economy stood on the verge of a catastrophic collapse.[21] Playing on the fear of social unrest among the regime's supporters, Stalin – the chief of the party bureaucracy – seized this opportunity to become the undisputed master of Russia. Having already excluded Trotsky's faction from political power, he now turned on Bukharin and his supporters. Private businesses and family farms were blamed for destabilising the entire economy. The survival of the Communist Party required a dramatic about-turn in policy: the revival of War Communism. Stalin no longer had any need for Social Democrat planners. State terror and mass mobilisation were more effective – and faster – methods of organising the take-off of the Russian economy than financial methods like prices, profits, wages, taxes and subsidies.[22]

In Stalin's Five Year Plan, the totalitarian state decided the production targets which maximised industrial growth. Wielding

[19] See Naum Jasny, *Soviet Economists of the Twenties*, pages 16–36, 89–157; and Meghnad Desai, *Marx's Revenge*, 69–74.

[20] See Eugeni Preobrazhensky, *The New Economics*, pages 77–146. For the inspiration of this concept of primitive accumulation, see Marx, *Capital, Volume 1*, pages 873–904.

[21] See Alec Nove, *An Economic History of the USSR*, pages 136–159.

[22] See Joseph Stalin, 'The Right Deviation in the CPSU (B)'; and Lewin, *Political Undercurrents*, pages 97–124.

absolute power, it could direct millions of people and vast resources into building tractor factories, steel mills, dams, electricity generators, canals and railway lines. As a result, measuring outputs increasingly replaced monetary accounting as the primary regulator of the economy. Following Preobrazhensky's advice, Stalin ruthlessly exploited the Russian peasantry to pay for his modernisation drive. Along with food and taxes, the rural population also supplied the new labour force needed for the rapidly expanding industrial sector. Aided by this influx, the Stalinist dictatorship was able to drive down the wages and conditions of Russian workers. With the production targets prioritising heavy industry, the provision of consumer goods inevitably suffered. In the workers' state, the workers had no say in the management of their own workplaces. Feedback between the different sectors of the economy had been replaced by Taylorist discipline imposed from above.[23] Having imposed his will on the peasantry and the proletariat, Stalin launched a brutal purge of the ruling party itself. Like his erstwhile opponent Bukharin, Preobrazhensky was one of the many Communists who fell victim to the tyrant's wrath.[24] When he had championed the policy of primitive accumulation in the mid 1920s, this thinker had somehow overlooked Marx's exposition of the crucial role played by 'conquest, enslavement, robbery, [and] murder' during this stage of growth.[25] As Preobrazhensky learnt to his cost, Stalin had no compunctions about imitating – and surpassing – the most unpleasant features of the English path to modernity. The libertarian promise of proletarian communism had morphed into the grim reality of totalitarian Communism.

Outside Russia, the human costs of the Stalinist system were all too often overlooked in the rush to admire its economic achievements. In the early 1930s, Communism was the future that worked. Following the 1929 Wall Street Crash, the global economy went into free fall. The sudden disappearance of cheap credit had precipitated the worst recession in human history. Trapped by the

---

[23] See Joseph Stalin, 'New Conditions – New Tasks of Socialist Construction'; and Jasny, *Soviet Economists of the Twenties*, pages 37–55. For a description of an iconic Stalinist industrial project, see Stephen Kotkin, *Magnetic Mountain*.

[24] Preobrazhensky was executed in 1937. For Stalin's destruction of his former comrades, see Isaac Deutscher and David King, *The Great Purges*.

[25] Marx, *Capital*, Volume 1, page 874.

shibboleths of liberalism, the rulers of America and Europe in the early 1930s seemed to have no remedies for shrinking markets and mass unemployment. In stark contrast, Russia was the one country which had successfully escaped from the economic crisis sweeping the world. As Stalin boasted, Communism had delivered the goods: more steel, more tractors, more coal and more wheat. What the Russians had successfully pioneered, the rest of the world should imitate.[26] For Social Democrats, Stalin's industrialisation drive presented a political conundrum. On the one hand, Hilferding's prognosis that capitalism was entering into the Fordist stage of growth had been vindicated. However, on the other hand, the cruelty and conformity of Stalinism horrified the Social Democrats. Looking at what happened in Russia, Hilferding warned that the nationalisation of industry and agriculture might also lead to the imposition of a new totalitarian form of class rule. Instead of market competition being superseded by democratic planning, the will of the tyrant and his coterie had become the driving force of the economy.[27] Fortunately, in Hilferding's native country of Austria, the Social Democrats had broken with liberal economics in a more enlightened manner. Their interventionist policies were designed not only to increase production within the industrial sector, but also to provide housing, hospitals, schools and cultural facilities for their working-class supporters. With incremental reforms, the Left was building the welfare state which would lift the masses out of poverty, ignorance and disease.[28]

For Social Democrats, the Russian experience had proved that it was impossible to leap over capitalism into socialism. Contrary to the hopes of 1917, there was no such thing as 'the revolution against *Capital*'.[29] Drawing on Hilferding's analysis, Social Democrats now envisioned a long transition period between the capitalist present and the socialist future. Léon Blum – the leader of the French Socialist Party during the 1920s and 1930s – argued that this reformist strategy also involved entering into national government. Faced with the rise

[26] See Joseph Stalin, 'Report to the Seventeenth Congress of the CPSU (B)'.

[27] See Rudolf Hilferding, 'State Capitalism or Totalitarian State Economy?'

[28] See Helmut Gruber, *Red Vienna*.

[29] This phrase was the title of a famous article welcoming the 1917 Russian Revolution written by Antonio Gramsci – a founding father of the Italian Communist Party. See James Joll, *Gramsci*, pages 34–5.

of fascism across Europe, the Marxist Left had to combine with all other progressive forces to protect the republican liberties which were the precondition for working-class activism. With the proletariat's 'conquest of power' postponed to the succeeding generations, Social Democrats were going to have to take responsibility for managing the capitalist system in the here and now: the 'exercise of power'.[30] As Marxists, their reforming administrations were committed to an interventionist economic strategy: nationalising key industries; long-term planning; welfare provision and employment protection. But, unlike their Communist rivals, the Social Democrats placed limits on their ambitions. Given the historical conjuncture, the Left would have to learn to coexist with the private sector.

Since the late nineteenth century, John Hobson – an English socialist – had been anticipating this progressive alternative to liberal economics. As long as the working class remained impoverished, businesses had to focus on selling their goods in foreign marketplaces – and politicians would continue starting imperialist wars to make sure that their nation's capitalists had privileged access to them. Having studied *Capital*, Hobson realised that – even for its winners – this global economic struggle was leading to disaster. As mechanisation gathered pace, the supply of goods and services was increasing exponentially. Sooner or later, the capitalist system would face its nemesis: the crisis of overproduction.[31] By the 1920s, Hobson was convinced that the Left had discovered the solution to this economic impasse. Through a combination of cheap credit, public works and welfare spending, a radical government could create jobs, increase wages and eliminate poverty. Hobson argued that these policies benefited both sides of the class divide. With higher living standards, workers would become consumers of the goods and services which the capitalists couldn't sell to foreign customers. The cure for overproduction in the global market was ending underconsumption in the home market. Like Hilferding, Hobson was convinced that this reformist economic strategy had revolutionary implications. The measures required to end the slump were also important steps forward in the transition to socialism.

[30] See Léon Blum, 'Exercise et Conquête du Pouvoir'.
[31] See J.A. Hobson, *The Evolution of Modern Capitalism*. Also see J.A. Hobson, *Imperialism*, pages 71–93.

> An equitable distribution of the product, evoking full productivity through the best technique and the utmost economy of labour, and providing for all the labour 'saved' in standardised mass production by a higher standard of consumption ... would require a cooperation of all the economic factors, including the consumer, in the regulation of industry.[32]

During the 1920s and 1930s, Social Democrats developed a distinctive strategy for the transition from capitalism to socialism. As in Stalin's Russia, the state would also take the leading role in the economy. The plan had priority over the market. But, in contrast with the Communists, the Social Democrats didn't favour the immediate nationalisation of the entire economy. Instead, the state would implement expansionary policies to maximise the balanced growth of both the public and private sectors. By the mid 1930s, with liberalism in disgrace, right-wing governments had also started to appreciate the advantages of the mixed economy. In Britain, the Conservatives adopted an interventionist programme which included devaluing the currency, running public deficits, nationalising key industries, regulating trade and negotiating with the trade unions.[33] The predictions of Hilferding and Hobson appeared to have been confirmed. Even capitalists were now helping to build the economic institutions of socialism.

Taking a more sceptical position, Michal Kalecki – a Polish Marxist – argued that the Left and the Right could adopt the same statist strategy for countering recessions while still continuing to fight for very different social objectives. Both sides of the class divide had embraced the new economics in response to the arrival of Fordism. As capitalism had expanded and concentrated, rising production hadn't been matched by increasing consumption. Since market competition was incapable of regulating this process, the state was forced to provide the 'effective demand' whose absence had precipitated the catastrophic crisis of the 1930s. In this new Fordist dispensation, the political struggle was now centred on which class gained the most from this reflationary programme. Learning from the experience of the First World War, the Right preferred military spending as the primary method of stimulating the economy because its greatest

32 J.A. Hobson, *Rationalisation and Unemployment*, pages 104–105.
33 See Keith Middlemas, *Politics in Industrial Society*, pages 214–265.

beneficiaries were the most conservative elements in society. In contrast, the Left prioritised welfare measures which strengthened the position of their working-class voters.[34] For Marxists, these short-term reforms served a long-term goal. By freeing itself from unemployment, ignorance and poverty, the proletariat was preparing to become the master of society. Although they passionately disagreed about strategy and tactics, Social Democrats and Communists both shared the same revolutionary ambition: the abolition of capitalism and its replacement with socialism.

For Burnham, Bell and Rostow, this quarrel over the correct interpretation of Marxism had provided their political training ground. In 1930s America, as elsewhere, Communists and Social Democrats had argued passionately about the lessons of the Russian Revolution and the possibility of an electoral road to socialism. From their involvement in this radical milieu, these gurus of the Cold War Left acquired the theoretical knowledge which would turn them into leading members of the US establishment. In the struggle for soft-power primacy with Stalinist Russia, the American empire needed former Marxists to invent Marxism without Marx. During the 1940s and 1950s, these master thinkers set to work on this vital task. Burnham replaced the proletariat with the managerial class as the principle beneficiary of the new post-liberal society. Bell transformed revolutionary ideology into the end of ideology when defining the political credo of organised industrialism. Rostow turned the next stage of growth from socialism into consumerism in his grand narrative of modernity. For the Cold War Left, this creation of Marxism without Marx wasn't only a refutation of the Stalinist and Trotskyist versions of Marxism. Just as importantly, in their American remix, historical materialism was also Marxism without Hilferding, Hobson and Kalecki. Back in the 1920s and 1930s, Social Democracy had been the original third way between totalitarianism and liberalism. In order to appropriate this concept for themselves, the champions of the Vital Centre required an economic analysis which justified the short-term reformist programme of orthodox Marxism without endorsing its long-term revolutionary aspirations. The third way went through New York, not Vienna, Paris, London or Warsaw.

[34] See Michal Kalecki, *The Last Phase in the Transformation of Capitalism*, pages 65–97.

By emphasising the trailblazing role of the New Deal in the rise of Fordism, the Cold War Left identified America as the vanguard of human civilisation. According to Rostow's calculations of the difference in living standards, the USA was 30 to 40 years ahead of its Russian rival in economic development.[35] Where this nation led, the rest of the world would have to follow. From this insight, it followed that – in the epoch of Fordism – the cutting edge of historical materialist theory was explaining the American path to modernity. For this task, the Cold War Left looked to the canonical texts which reflected the intellectual attitudes of the architects of the New Deal. When Roosevelt became US president in 1933, his interventionist programme had drawn upon a long tradition of state activism dating back to the 1776 Revolution. Like their Populist predecessors, the Democrats were convinced that the elected representatives of the people should legislate, finance and implement the measures needed to correct the deficiencies of liberal economics.[36] For the rest of the decade, the conflict over recalibrating the relationship between the plan and the market had dominated American politics. At the 1939 New York World's Fair, big government and big business celebrated the victory of the New Deal modernists over their traditionalist opponents. The utopian potential of the new Fordist paradigm was there for all to see in the Democracity and Futurama dioramas of the futurist city. Although the Marxist Left remained marginalised in America, its post-liberal economic policies had become the leitmotif of progressive politics.

In 1930, a few years before Roosevelt was elected president, Adolf Berle and Gardiner Means – two intellectuals associated with the Democratic Party – published a detailed analysis of the new institutional structure of American Fordism: *The Modern Corporation and Private Property*. Like Marx and Hilferding, they described how an economy of small businesses and family farms had evolved into one of giant corporations and large banks. Under the law, the shareholders were still the owners of big business. However, in practice, real control had passed into the hands of the managers

35 See Rostow, *Stages of Economic Growth*, pages 93–105; *The Process of Economic Growth*, pages 317–325.
36 For the historical background to the New Deal, see Donald McCoy, *Coming of Age*, pages 193–334.

who had day-to-day responsibility for running the factories and offices of the Fordist economy. Individual entrepreneurship had been replaced with bureaucratic hierarchy.[37] Crucially, as Burnham later emphasised, the political conclusions of their account of the rise of the corporations were very different from those of the Marxists. In contrast with Hilferding, Berle and Means didn't locate Fordism as a transient stage in the transition from liberalism to socialism. Looking at the data, they had concluded that the corporation was building the emerging collectivist society in its own image. Instead of preparing the way for proletarian democracy, the demise of liberalism was creating a new and powerful ruling class: the managerial elite. With market competition curtailed, the planners now dominated the American economy.

> The communist thinks of the community in terms of a state; the corporation director thinks of it in terms of an enterprise; and though this difference between the two might lead to a radical divergence in results, it still remains true that the corporation director who would subordinate the interests of the individual stockholder to those of the group more nearly resembles the communist in thought than he does the protagonist of private property.[38]

Anticipating the New Deal, Berle and Means in the conclusion of their book argued that the democratic potential of Fordism could only be fulfilled through enlightened leadership.[39] The few had to ensure that the many also participated in the new prosperity. In the early 1930s, Berle put this theory into practice as a prominent member of Roosevelt's group of intellectual advisers, the 'Brains Trust'. During the New Deal, he played an active role in reforming the regulatory structure of the American economy, especially within the financial sector.[40] By the 1950s, Berle had become one of the intellectual godfathers of the Cold War Left. His career path was a role model for its members: a combination of groundbreaking academic research and distinguished public service. Above all, two decades after its publication, his New Deal analysis of the rise of

---

[37] See Adolf Berle and Gardiner Means, *The Modern Corporation and Private Property*, pages 3–140.
[38] Berle and Means, *Modern Corporation*, page 245.
[39] See Berle and Means, *Modern Corporation*, pages 309–313.
[40] See McCoy, *Coming of Age*, pages 200–218.

Fordism was one of the founding texts of the American version of historical materialism. Along with Means, Berle had created the core concepts for the Cold War Left's Anti-Communist theory of organised capitalism.

In their search for replacements for *Capital*, the master thinkers of the Vital Centre also needed a cybernetic theory of the national economy. Luckily for them, John Maynard Keynes – an English mandarin – had already produced an impeccably respectable explanation of the emerging Fordist paradigm: *The General Theory of Employment, Interest and Money*. By the time of its publication in 1936, the innovative ideas in the second volume of Marx's *Capital* could no longer be ignored by the academic mainstream. From Russia to America, governments were intervening within the economy in ways which flouted all of the laissez-faire shibboleths. Whether consciously or not, their policies treated the national economy as a feedback system. In the *General Theory*, Keynes provided a non-Marxist explanation of this new paradigm. Above all, in an impressive piece of scholasticism, his book managed to preserve the appearance of orthodoxy while abandoning the substance of liberal economics. According to Keynes, the old precepts of competitive individualism now only applied at the micro-level. In the mid twentieth century, the liberal rules of the game were obsolete at the macro-level. As the catastrophic slump following the 1929 Wall Street Crash had proved, the private sector was incapable of generating sufficient effective demand on its own. Under Fordism, the state must take responsibility for managing the marketplace.[41]

Like the Social Democrats, Keynes understood that welfare reforms were not only morally desirable, but also economically essential. Inspired by Hobson, he argued that the most effective method of dealing with the crisis of overproduction was ending the underconsumption of the working class. Echoing Kalecki, Keynes explained that the big rise in public spending needed to achieve this ambitious goal would pay for itself by stimulating economic recovery: the 'multiplier effect'. Like the Russian Social Democratic planners, he produced a feedback model of the national economy which showed how public spending could be used to synchronise

[41] See John Maynard Keynes, *The General Theory of Employment, Interest and Money*, pages 3–34, 245–254, 372–384.

mass production with mass consumption.[42] However, in contrast with his Marxist contemporaries, Keynes was convinced that this cybernetic system could be controlled without any dramatic redistribution of wealth and power. By 'pump-priming' with cheap credit, more welfare spending and bigger budget deficits, a left-of-centre government was able to prevent the economy falling into a recession. By 'fine-tuning' its policies in response to the business cycle, the state could maximise the growth rate in the interests of both capital and labour.[43] During the 1930s, Keynes' analysis won admirers across the political spectrum in Britain. In particular, the Fabians believed that his consensual form of economic interventionism offered a third way between deflationary liberalism and full-blown socialism. Although theoretically inconsistent, Keynesianism was ideologically comforting for the various English opponents of Marxism. Social Democratic reforms were no longer the building blocks of proletarian communism. On the contrary, as Keynes kept emphasising, state supervision of the nation's economy was the saviour of bourgeois civilisation.[44] The ending of unemployment and poverty would create the conditions for class compromise and social stability. Keynes, not Marx, was the prophet of Fordism.

Taking their cue from the Fabians, the Cold War Left also became adepts of the multiplier, pump-priming and fine-tuning. By quoting Keynes, they could analyse the national economies of Fordism without any danger of contamination by not only Marx, but also Hilferding, Hobson and Kalecki. During the 1950s, this British Fabian ideology became orthodoxy within the more progressive American universities. In the same way that the public and private sectors cooperated within the mixed economy, Keynesian academics taught that Fordist macroeconomics and liberal microeconomics were symbiotic theories. The state and the market each knew their place in the outside world as in the textbook.[45] In 1958, John Kenneth Galbraith – a Canadian economist at Harvard University

---

[42] See Keynes, *General Theory*, pages 3–34, 313–332, 372–384. Also see Toni Negri, 'Keynes and the Capitalist Theory of the State'.

[43] For the implications of Keynes' book for political policy-makers, see Michael Stewart, *Keynes and After*, pages 78–181.

[44] See John Maynard Keynes, *The Economic Consequences of the Peace*; and Negri, 'Keynes and the Capitalist Theory of the State'.

[45] This doublethink was exemplified by the most popular undergraduate textbook of the period: Paul Samuelson, *Economics*.

who had worked for the Roosevelt administration – published the key text of Cold War Left Keynesianism, *The Affluent Society*. Backing up Rostow and Bell's findings, he argued that the United States had combined the best elements of both market competition and state intervention into a new system: 'planned capitalism'. Under government supervision, a virtuous circle had been created between rising production and increasing consumption. With more money to spend, workers were buying more goods and services. With profits rising, capitalists were paying higher dividends, increasing wages and creating employment. As a result, ordinary Americans were experiencing an unprecedented rise in their standard of living. For the first time, the majority of the population who produced the nation's wealth was also consuming it.[46]

Like Rostow, Galbraith was convinced that 1950s America was the economic model for the rest of world. In the same way as the English had launched the process of industrialisation in the late eighteenth century, the United States was now building the first consumer society in human history. Despite the opposition of laissez-faire ideologues, the federal government was also steadily improving the scope and extent of its welfare services.[47] According to Galbraith, this social transformation had been made possible by the increasing cooperation of big government and big business. Thanks to Keynesian demand management, the 'technostructure' of state and corporate bureaucracies was now able to plan for a continual expansion in output without – as had happened in the past – being destabilised by the cycle of boom and bust.[48] During the 1950s, the US government had turned to Galbraith's academic colleagues to develop the knowledge needed for fine-tuning the Fordist system. Just like the Russian planners three decades earlier, American researchers also constructed a cybernetic model of the dynamic interaction between production and consumption: 'input–output economics'. Appropriating the liberals' mathematical theory of price formation, these Keynesians explained how the state could direct this feedback mechanism by manipulating its financial flows.[49]

[46] See John Kenneth Galbraith, *The Affluent Society*, pages 91–164.
[47] See Galbraith, *Affluent Society*, pages 221–257.
[48] See John Kenneth Galbraith, *The New Industrial State*, pages 117–134.
[49] See Wassily Leontieff, *The Structure of the American Economy*; and Desai, *Marx's Revenge*, pages 220–230.

By collecting data, studying the business cycle and running computer simulations, the US government was able to determine the correct combination of credit expansion, public spending and tax rates for minimising the fluctuations of the business cycle and optimising the growth rate. Just like an IBM mainframe, the technostructure of the American economy was a programmable machine. The Cold War Left had upgraded the Keynesian theory of Fordism for the computer age.

Applied to 1920s Russia, Preobrazhensky's concept of primitive socialist accumulation described a national economy where the public sector grew at the expense of the private sector. Three decades later, Galbraith was convinced that American Fordism had overcome this evolutionary barrier. Under Keynesian management, the state and the corporations were collaborators, not competitors. In a positive feedback loop, the public and private sectors helped each other to grow faster. By simultaneously tackling overproduction and underconsumption, state spending now benefited both capital and labour: advanced Fordist accumulation. In American Cold War propaganda, the lesson of Keynesian economics was clear. Stalinism had promised to build a socialist paradise, but the Russian people remained impoverished as their leaders concentrated resources on heavy industry and the arms race. In contrast, planned capitalism in 1950s America delivered the goods. Keynesian interventionism had created unprecedented prosperity not just for employers, but also, more importantly, for workers as well. According to Galbraith, Rostow and their Cold War Left colleagues, the new prosperity of America would inevitably spread beyond its shores. Even Russia would eventually have to abandon totalitarianism so it could evolve into a US-style consumer society. Sooner or later, every country in the world would imitate the American system of planned capitalism, which ensured that ordinary people not only owned family homes, motor cars and television sets, but also were provided with universal education, high-quality health care and generous pensions. Welfare Fordism meant the good life for everyone: the affluent society.

Within the global village, the implications of Keynesianism were unambiguous. Instead of being duped by backward Marxist ideology, the nations of the world should copy the up-to-date American model of political consensus, ideological moderation and economic compromise. The third way was the only path to hi-tech modernity. In constructing their materialist conception of history, the Cold War Left had carefully covered up their intellectual debts to Marx, Hilferding, Hobson and Kalecki. By the end of the 1950s, they had successfully incorporated the key insights of *Capital* into their economic analysis in more politically acceptable disguises. Organised capitalism had been renamed planned capitalism. State intervention was no longer the proletarian regulation of private enterprise. The model of the cybernetic national economy in *Capital, Volume 2* had been transformed into a computer simulation of the feedback between outputs and inputs. By crediting others for the theoretical achievements of Marx and his admirers, the Cold War Left could dismiss Marxism itself as a Stalinist relic. Far from pioneering the theorisation of Fordism, *Capital* was an irrelevance now that the managerial elite knew how to apply the multiplier effect to the economy, pump-prime the growth rate and fine-tune the business cycle.

> The [Marxist] revolution was to be catalysed by the capitalist crisis – the apocalyptic depression which would bring the already attenuated structure down in ruins. But the industrial system has, as an integral requirement, an arrangement for regulating aggregate demand which, while permitting it to plan, gives promise of preventing or mitigating depression. ... Everything on which the revolution seemed to depend, and even the revolution itself, has disintegrated.[50]

Being apostles of the third way, the sages of the Cold War Left were determined to prove that Marxism wasn't the only steam-age ideology which had been rendered obsolete by Keynesianism. Back in the 1930s, many American employers had bitterly opposed the New Deal's reflationary programme of public works schemes, banking controls, trade union recognition and agricultural subsidies. Drawing the same conclusions as Marx, Hilferding and Hobson for opposite reasons, the Right had convinced itself that the social reforms of the New Deal were the beginnings of the socialist revolution. Roosevelt's rapid expansion of the public sector was denounced as the imminent end of private property, individual freedom and moral order. There was no stage of capitalism beyond liberalism.[51]

---

50 Galbraith, *New Industrial State*, page 294.
51 See Walter Lippmann, *The Good Society*.

Two decades later, the Right's attitudes towards state regulation of the economy had completely changed. As Kalecki had pointed out, fighting wars was good for business. In contrast with welfare measures, this military form of Keynesianism created effective demand without weakening the power of capital over labour at the point of production. When orders were slack, buying more weapons and increasing the size of the armed forces was the business-friendly method of managing the economic cycle. Back in the early 1940s, the waging of total war against Germany and Japan had ended the slump which had plagued America for over a decade. By the time that the USA emerged victorious from this struggle, the business community had learned to love military Keynesianism. After a brief scare when peace threatened a return to recession, the outbreak of the Cold War ensured that this form of fiscal stimulation became a permanent feature of the US economy. For companies like IBM, the advantages of the superpower confrontation were obvious. In Cold War USA, the 'permanent arms economy' delivered the rapid growth which provided both large profits for capital and high wages for labour.[52]

Back in the mid 1930s, the Nazi leadership had warned the German population that the rearmament of the country demanded sacrifices in their living standards: 'guns *or* butter'.[53] Two decades later, the US government didn't have to confront its citizens with this choice. Under Fordism, military spending now acted as a Keynesian multiplier which benefited all sectors of the economy. In Cold War America, warfare was welfare. As part of the struggle against the Red Menace, conservatives had finally accepted that the US state should build motorways, finance education, provide health care and subsidise academic research. In this post-liberal stage of growth, the divisions over economic policy which had polarised the Right and the Left in the 1930s were disappearing. Under Keynesian demand management, American industry was so productive that the military and social requirements of the nation could be met at the same time: guns *and* butter. With the correct mix of regulatory and financial stimuli, the US government was now able to programme

---

[52] See Kalecki, *The Last Phase*, pages 65–97; and Michael Kidron, *Western Capitalism since the War*, pages 48–64.
[53] See Richard Evans, *The Third Reich in Power*, pages 322–411.

the feedback system of the economic machine in the interests of both capital and labour. As its critics pointed out, it was mainly thanks to this military-funded class compromise that America had become the home of political quiescence.[54] Not surprisingly, the Cold War Left downplayed this barbaric precondition for the ascendancy of advanced Fordist accumulation. For them, the arms race was an unfortunate by-product of the struggle against Communist aggression. Of much more importance was the democratic potential of US-style planned capitalism. In contrast with their Marxist rivals, American progressives possessed the up-to-date economic theory which – when properly put into practice – could provide jobs, welfare and prosperity for everyone. The third way was the fast lane to modernity.

When Kennedy became US president in 1961, the long march of the Cold War Left through the institutions was finally over. Emerging from obscure Trotskyist sects in the early 1940s, this movement had spent two decades reaching the pinnacles of power. Former revolutionary socialists like Rostow and Bell were now the confidants of the rulers of the world's dominant empire. More than anything else, the Cold War Left had been responsible for defining the ideological style of this new Democratic administration. During the long period of conservative hegemony, its thinkers had devoted themselves to developing a patriotic and pragmatic form of progressive politics. Rejecting both laissez-faire liberalism and totalitarian Stalinism, they had discovered the third way to modernity: political consensus, economic compromise and efficient administration. Above all, this vanguard of Vital Centre intellectuals had demonstrated their abilities and energy by taking charge of the propaganda struggle against the Russian enemy. They were the only people who were capable of inventing the Anti-Communist grand narrative of history which proved that the American present was the rest of the world's future. In 1961, after a long apprenticeship, the Cold War Left was ready to take office. Under its tutelage, America would become a truly modern and progressive empire.

> We who now bear a measure of responsibility in ... [the Democratic administration] are building on all those who have gone before. ... We are the trustees of the principles of national independence

54 See C. Wright Mills, *The Power Elite*, pages 198–224, 325–361.

and human freedom all over the globe, and ... this is a proud and natural responsibility.[55]

At the head of the new administration was the charismatic figure of John F. Kennedy. This skilful politician personified many of the virtues prized by the Cold War Left: youthful energy, cultural sophistication and social tolerance. While his Republican predecessor had been formal and traditional, the new president cultivated his image as an open-minded man of the modern world.[56] Best of all, Kennedy was a master of the new technology of television. Many pundits at the time believed that he had won the presidential election because of his superb performance during the televised debates with his opponent. With a beautiful wife and cute children, Kennedy epitomised the political leader as media celebrity.[57] Under the American constitutional system, a change of regime required the appointment of party loyalists to direct the state bureaucracy. Not surprisingly, when the new Democratic government was formed, the authors of the canonical texts of Anti-Communism were rewarded with important jobs. Rostow became a presidential adviser. Schlesinger was an intimate of the Kennedy family. Berle was given the responsibility for developing the administration's Latin American policy. Galbraith was appointed US ambassador to India.[58] As recommended by the Cold War Left, the Kennedy administration fostered political consensus by also giving top posts to people who weren't card-carrying Democrats. The prize recruit of the new government was Robert McNamara, the managing director of the Ford motor company. Run by the man dubbed by the media as 'an IBM machine on legs', managerial efficiency rather than ideological fervour would determine the priorities of the US military.[59]

The resilience of the new Democratic administration was demonstrated when Kennedy was assassinated in 1963. Apart from a few minor changes, Lyndon Johnson – his successor as US

---

[55] W.W. Rostow, *View from the Seventh Floor*, page 53.

[56] See Arthur Schlesinger, Jr., *A Thousand Days*, pages 113–117, 725–729, 739–749; and Robert Dallek, *John F. Kennedy*, pages 274–275.

[57] See Erik Barnouw, *The Image Empire*, pages 160–170.

[58] See Schlesinger, *Thousand Days*, pages 150–152; and Dallek, *Kennedy*, pages 308–309.

[59] See Robert McNamara, *In Retrospect*, pages 13–25; and Errol Morris, *The Fog of War*.

president – kept the government team intact.[60] Although their new leader lacked Kennedy's modern image, the Cold War Left was equally enthusiastic about Johnson. During his five years in power, his administration dedicated itself to the implementation of the movement's twin-pronged programme of social reforms at home and imperial expansion overseas. At Johnson's side at the most critical moments of his time in office was his personal choice as national security advisor, Walt Rostow.[61] This former Marxist had been given his chance to prove that the American empire could act as a modernising and progressive force in the world.

> It is out of the intermediate and higher ranges of abstraction that new ways of looking at things emerge which embrace but transcend what is already known; and it is from new ways of looking at things that new paths of action emerge. To help define these paths, the intellectual must be prepared to enter ... into the world of operational choice.[62]

Both the Kennedy and Johnson administrations were convinced that state interventionism could dramatically increase the rate of economic growth if the correct Keynesian policies were adopted. Under their Republican predecessor, a respect for the dogmas of laissez-faire liberalism had constrained the ambitions of the US government. After the Cold War Left came to power, these inhibitions disappeared. As Rostow and Galbraith had demonstrated in their celebrated books, the US state had a duty to ensure that effective demand kept pace with the growth in the productive potential of the economy. Best of all, this public spending would pay for itself by pump-priming a faster growth rate. Determined to win support from both sides of the class divide, the new Democratic administration shared its budgetary munificence between capital and labour. McNamara's purchases of hi-tech weaponry were soon filling the order books of the defence contractors. For those companies which hadn't directly gained from this stimulation of the private sector, the Democrats also reduced taxes on profits and dividends. Under the Cold War Left, the business community would have no reason to complain.

---

[60] See Irving Bernstein, *Guns or Butter*, pages 15–26.
[61] See David Halberstam, *The Best and the Brightest*, pages 635–636.
[62] Rostow, *United States*, page 490.

At the same time, the Kennedy administration also began a rapid expansion in welfare spending to raise the living standards of those people who had missed out on the economic boom of the previous decade: the 'war on poverty'. After he won the 1964 presidential election, Johnson built upon this initiative with an ambitious programme of improvements in public health care, pension provision, social housing and environmental protection.[63] Under third-way management, the US economy was easily capable of producing both more guns and more butter. As poverty was abolished and prosperity was extended to all, the Cold War Left were convinced that America was becoming the most advanced welfare democracy on the planet. In 1964, President Johnson prophesised to a university audience that:

> The challenge of the next half century is whether we have the wisdom to use ... [our] wealth to enrich and elevate our national life, and to advance the quality of our American civilisation ... we have the opportunity to move not only toward the rich society and the powerful society, but upward to the Great Society. ... It is a place where the city of man serves not only the needs of the body and the demands of commerce but [also] the desire for beauty and the hunger for community.[64]

During the early 1960s, the Cold War Left acted to remove the most intractable problem in America: legalised racism. Despite its self-image as the bastion of democracy, the United States was still not a fully-fledged democracy when Kennedy was elected president. In the south of the country, millions of its African-American citizens were denied the right to vote. For the Cold War Left, the failure of the previous Republican administration to deal decisively with this outrage wasn't only morally reprehensible, but also strategically dangerous. In the propaganda battle with the Russian enemy within the global village, television coverage of racist police beating unarmed demonstrators in the US South severely weakened the American cause.[65] Yet, once they were in power,

---

[63] See Dallek, *Kennedy*, pages 575–606; and Bernstein, *Guns or Butter*, pages 27–42, 82–113, 156–306.

[64] Lyndon Johnson, 'Remarks at the University of Michigan', pages 1–2.

[65] See Benjamin Mays, 'Race in America'; and W.W. Rostow, *The Diffusion of Power*, pages 64–67.

the new Democrat government also initially hesitated. Political compromise was difficult to achieve when the most vocal opponents of universal suffrage were the leaders of the southern wing of its own party. The overwhelming victory of Johnson in the 1964 presidential and legislative elections headed off this split within the Democratic Party. A century after the abolition of slavery, the US government finally extended the franchise to all Americans.[66] In its Vital Centre redefinition, liberalism really did mean freedom for all of the people.

What had begun as an international embarrassment had ended as a Cold War propaganda victory. Contrary to the predictions of its critics, America had demonstrated the capacity to reform itself. The excluded had been included. In the battle to win over global public opinion, the granting of the vote to all Americans contrasted strongly with the absence of any meaningful form of electoral democracy in Russia. Under the leadership of the Cold War Left, the USA was remedying its last remaining political and economic problems. The American system had proved itself to be the social model for the whole of humanity. Nowhere else did ordinary people enjoy so much freedom and prosperity. No other nation was so successful in turning esoteric new technologies into everyday household items. There could be no doubt which superpower represented progress and modernity. The long and arduous process of social evolution had culminated in the most advanced and sophisticated civilisation in human history: the Great Society of the USA.

---

[66] See Schlesinger, *Thousand Days*, pages 924–977; Bernstein, *Guns or Butter*, pages 43–81; and Dallek, *Kennedy*, pages 380–388, 492–495.

10

THE PROPHETS OF POST-INDUSTRIALISM

By the early 1960s, the Cold War Left had acquired a pivotal role within the US elite. The movement provided ideological leadership for the propaganda struggle against the Russian enemy. Its intellectuals had created a sophisticated American version of historical materialism. Cybernetics without Wiener had been successfully combined with Marxism without Marx. By subcontracting the task of thinking about society to the Cold War Left, the American ruling class had allowed this movement to exert a decisive influence over the political agenda. From the early 1950s onwards, this group of intellectuals had promoted their programme of political consensus, economic compromise and efficient administration by producing evidence that these principles were already shaping American society. By the time that Kennedy became president, the Cold War Left's research projects had helped to restore the intellectual hegemony of the Democratic Party. Impartial social science had proved the case for introducing a wide range of political, social and economic reforms. Above all, American voters could now have confidence that the policies of the US government had been devised by the best minds in the country.

With the Democrats in power, the Cold War Left believed that the remaining serious domestic problems in their country were in the process of being resolved. Compared to its Russian opponent, the United States already had the more advanced social system. After the Democrats' reforms were implemented, it would become obvious to the whole world that only America could create the good society. Yet, at the same time, the Cold War Left realised that this achievement wouldn't deliver the decisive victory in the global propaganda struggle. It was relatively easy to prove that the American present was superior to the Russian present. What was much more difficult was prevailing in the ideological contest over which superpower owned the future. Unfortunately for the Cold War Left, their programme only offered improvements to the existing system of welfare Fordism. In its Vital Centre remix, the reformist strategy of Social Democracy had been deprived of its revolutionary goal: the transcendence of capitalism. On the other side of the superpower confrontation, propagandists weren't faced with this problem. On the contrary, the ideologues of Stalinism were convinced that the Russian regime was building the entirely new civilisation of socialism. From the 1917 Revolution onwards, its apologists had argued that any imperfections in its social system – such as mass murder and class exploitation – were temporary expedients adopted to speed up the arrival of the earthly paradise. Communism with a capital C was the precursor of communism with a small c. However inferior the Russian present might be compared to the American present, Stalinism still had ownership of the future. Spatial comparisons had been trumped by temporal prophecies.[1]

As the ideological champions of the US elite, the Cold War Left had the responsibility for neutralising this ideological threat. Having been Marxists in their youth, the founders of the movement understood the emotional appeal of the promise of the socialist future. Emphasising the superiority of the American present alone would not be enough to discredit the libertarian prophecies of their nation's enemies. Whether from instinct or experience, they knew that the pragmatism of the third way only offered a timid substitute for Marx and Engels' visionary synthesis of liberalism and socialism. Instead of cherry picking from two incompatible ideologies to propose a better present, these two leftists had explained that modern capitalism was an unavoidable historical epoch which was leading towards proletarian emancipation. Far from being the opposite of socialism, liberalism was its necessary precondition. Free trade between nations was uniting the workers of the world.[2] The joint-stock company was pioneering the collective ownership of capital.[3] The extension of the franchise created the conditions for socialists to intervene within the political process.[4] Cuts in the working week were freeing time for people to learn how to run their own lives.[5] After a long incubation inside capitalism, socialism would finally emerge as a fully-fledged and distinct civilisation. Only then would bourgeois liberalism have fulfilled its historical mission: the triumph of proletarian communism.

> The monopoly of capital becomes a fetter upon the mode of production which has flourished alongside and under it. The

[1] See Susan Buck-Morss, *Dreamworld and Catastrophe*, pages 2–39.

[2] See Karl Marx and Friedrich Engels, *The Communist Manifesto*, pages 12–34.

[3] See Karl Marx, *Capital*, Volume 3, pages 567–573; and Friedrich Engels, *Socialism: Scientific and Utopian*, pages 74–101.

[4] See Friedrich Engels, 'The Prussian Military Question and the German Workers' Party'.

[5] See Karl Marx, *Capital*, Volume 1, pages 389–416; *Grundrisse*, pages 707–711.

centralisation of capital and the socialisation of labour reach a point when they become incompatible with their capitalist integument. ... The death knell of capitalist private property sounds. The expropriators are expropriated.[6]

Back in the late nineteenth century, Marx and Engels had been convinced that the American working class was at the forefront of the worldwide struggle to create the new society of freedom, equality and prosperity. As the most liberal nation on earth, the United States must also be the furthest advanced along the path towards socialism. Surpassing their British rivals, American magnates were already leading the transformation of global capitalism from an economy of small businesses into one dominated by giant corporations. With the overwhelming majority of males having the vote, the USA was one of the few countries in the world where the labour movement could seize state power by electoral means.[7] It was only a matter of time before the American proletariat took its rightful place as the pre-eminent contingent of the international socialist movement. The working class of the most economically and politically developed nation on the planet would be among the first to reach the revolutionary goal of libertarian communism.

During the 1950s, the gurus of the Cold War Left revisited Marx's prognosis to discredit the Stalinist claim that Russia was the paradise of the proletariat. If living standards in the two superpowers were compared, it was obvious that communism was much closer to being realised in Fordist America than in Communist Russia.[8] Although they enjoyed this political paradox among themselves, the Cold War Left's intellectuals had no intention of publicly disputing the Stalinists' ideological monopoly over Marxism. On the contrary, they had invented their own versions of the materialist conception of history to refute this dangerous theory in all of its competing interpretations. In particular, the advocates of the Vital Centre wanted to avoid any discussion of Marx and Engels' admiration for the more radical aspects of American democracy. Politicised in the struggle against the authoritarian regimes of continental Europe,

[6] Marx, *Capital, Volume 1*, page 929.
[7] See Karl Marx, 'Letter to Nicolai Danielson'; 'Speech to the Hague Conference', page 322; and Friedrich Engels, 'Letter to Eduard Bernstein'.
[8] See W.W. Rostow, *The Process of Economic Growth*, pages 328–331.

these thinkers had been passionately opposed to the ascendancy of big government. Just like the marketplace, the state was a fetishised structure which oppressed the many in the interests of the few.[9] Universal suffrage was only the first step in taming this bureaucratic monster. As long as politics remained a specialised profession, the majority of the population would only have a limited influence over the decisions which shaped their lives. According to Marx and Engels, representative democracy had to be deepened into participatory democracy. When everyone took part in government, the division between the rulers and the ruled could be overcome. Citizens, not bureaucrats, should be in control of the collective interests of society.[10]

In *Capital, Volume 3*, Marx also identified participatory democracy as the organisational principle of proletarian economics. Just like the state, capitalist firms had imposed the domination of a small elite over the majority of the population. But, by electing the directors of their enterprises in the same way as they did with the leaders of the republic, members of industrial cooperatives were pioneering the democratisation of the factory system.[11] Only when every worker was also a manager would the differences between capitalists and proletarians finally disappear. In complete contrast to their Social Democratic and Communist disciples in the next century, Marx and Engels denounced the nationalisation of industry, education and the media. For them, cooperative communism was the antithesis of state capitalism.[12] Far from advocating the fusion of big government with big business, Marx and Engels looked forward to the victory of participatory democracy over all forms of bureaucratic fetishism. The market and the plan were symbiotic aspects of the same oppressive system. As the heroic example of the 1871 Paris Commune had proved, the people who produced the wealth upon which human

[9] See Karl Marx and Friedrich Engels, *The German Ideology*, pages 51–54; and Karl Marx, *Critique of Hegel's Philosophy of Right*, pages 5–19. Also see Richard Hunt, *The Political Ideas of Marx and Engels, Volume 1*; pages 17–175.

[10] See Marx, *Critique of Hegel's Philosophy of Right*, pages 54–127; *The Civil War in France*, pages 37–48. Also see Hunt, *Marx and Engels, Volume 2*, pages 212–265.

[11] See Marx, *Capital, Volume 3*, pages 511–514.

[12] See Karl Marx, 'Debates on Freedom of the Press'; 'Critique of the Gotha Programme', pages 354–357; and Engels, *Socialism: Scientific and Utopian*, pages 90–94.

civilisation was founded must become masters of their own collective destiny: the 'dictatorship of the proletariat'.[13]

Looking for other prototypes of this self-managing society, Marx and Engels found inspiration across the Atlantic. In the frontier states of America, grassroots democracy was already up and running. All public officials were elected. Citizens enforced the law themselves by forming posses, serving on juries and appointing judges. In this liberal republic, there was no state church, no press censorship and no government monopoly over education. Compared to the bureaucratic leviathans of continental Europe, its professional army and civil service were tiny.[14] Marx and Engels saw the labour movement as the modern champion of the democratic gains of the American Revolution. In 1871, the Paris Commune had opted to fight rather than surrender its cannon to the central government. The Marxist Left fervently believed in every word of the Second Amendment of the US Constitution's Bill of Rights: 'A well regulated militia, being necessary to the security of a free state, the right of the people to keep and bear arms, shall not be infringed.'[15]

For Marx and Engels, this French prototype of the dictatorship of the proletariat had embodied all of the most radical democratic ideals of the 1776 Revolution: the federal republic; town hall meetings, mandated delegates and a citizen army. Crucially, its most important constitutional innovation was outlawing the worst flaw in the American system: the professionalisation of politics. By setting the wages of both assembly members and public officials at those of a skilled worker, the Paris Commune had made sure that serving the state could no longer be turned into a lucrative career.[16] Within a participatory democracy, amateurs should carry out the bulk of the administrative work of the republic. In his valedictory appreciation of this proletarian political experiment, Marx highlighted one of its greatest achievements: 'The [Paris] Commune made that catchword

[13] For the republican inspiration for this revolutionary slogan, see Hunt, *Marx and Engels, Volume 1*, pages 284–336.

[14] See Karl Marx. 'On the Jewish Question', pages 216–218; and Friedrich Engels, *The Origins of the Family, Private Property and the State*, pages 194–195. Also see Alexis de Tocqueville, *Democracy in America, Volume 1*, pages 61–101, 206–263; *Democracy in America, Volume 2*, pages 99–132.

[15] US Constitution, 'The Bill of Rights'. Also see Marx, *Civil War*, pages 30–37.

[16] See Marx, *Civil War*, pages 40–41; and Friedrich Engels, 'The Civil War in France – Introduction', pages 17–18.

of bourgeois revolutions, cheap government, a reality by destroying the two greatest sources of expenditure – the standing army and State functionarism.'[17]

From the late nineteenth century onwards, the different currents of American Marxism identified socialism as the modern incarnation of their nation's proud tradition of radical politics. In the same way that their forebears had fought for independence from the British crown and to abolish chattel slavery, the activists of the labour movement were struggling against the unaccountable power of the 'robber barons' who ruled over monopoly capitalism like absolutist monarchs or plantation owners. From the Populists to the Wobblies, the American Left championed the most communal and levelling aspirations of the 1776 Revolution. During the 1920s and 1930s, both Social Democrats and Communists argued that the long battle for political freedom would soon culminate in the victory of economic emancipation. Marxism was an all-American creed.[18]

The founders of the Cold War Left had grown up within this socialist milieu. Having shed their youthful revolutionary utopianism, they were now the prophets of pragmatic reformism. In a smart move, these intellectuals had redefined the meaning of liberalism. By emphasising its pluralist and consensual principles, this political philosophy was stripped of its most subversive concept: minimal government. Instead of citizens administrating the republic themselves, voters were now given the choice of which of the competing party elites would control the state. With this new version of liberalism, Marxism could be condemned as an un-American ideology. Far from being the inheritor of the 1776 Revolution, socialism was an exotic foreign import. In contrast with its peers in the less developed countries of Europe, the American working class had never had any need for a powerful labour movement. As a consequence, neither the Social Democrats nor the Communists had been able to supplant the Democratic Party as the leading organisation of the US Left. Marxism had no relevance in the new world across the Atlantic: 'American exceptionalism'.[19]

[17] Marx, Civil War, page 43.

[18] See Howard Zinn, A People's History of the United States, pages 211–295, 321–357, 377–406.

[19] See Seymour Martin Lipset, American Exceptionalism; and Seymour Martin Lipset and Gary Marks, It Didn't Happen Here.

Paradoxically, by celebrating its parochial origins, the Cold War Left proclaimed their global ambitions for US-style planned capitalism. In their version of historical materialism, America today was everywhere else tomorrow. Even if the marginalisation of Marxism was confined to the United States in the present, the universal hegemony of Anti-Communism was inevitable in the long term. Marx and Engels' admiration of the proto-socialist democracy of the Wild West had disappeared from the textbooks. Just like their Stalinist opponents, the boosters of the third way affirmed that there was only one form of communism: Russian-style Communism with a big C. When socialism was indistinguishable from totalitarianism, American planned capitalism was obviously the most advanced socio-economic system on the planet.

More than anything else, the Cold War Left's grand narrative of human progress was designed to prove from the American experience that the class struggles analysed by Marx were now over. In the laissez-faire past, US workers had been forced to fight for political emancipation and economic justice against fierce conservative opposition. But, in modern America, demanding democracy and prosperity for all was no longer controversial. Under welfare Fordism, social conflicts had become disputes over group status rather than fights for class power. According to the Cold War Left, the decline of economic liberalism was also responsible for another welcome paradox: the growth of political liberalism. Unlike Russian totalitarianism, American democracy had been founded upon the principles of free speech, social tolerance and ideological pluralism. Yet, for most of US history, the exercise of these rights had been restricted to a minority of the population. Fortunately, the advent of welfare Fordism had finally created the conditions for all Americans to enjoy the benefits of these constitutional principles. The democratic ideals of the 1776 Revolution were no longer the privilege of a few. In the land of the free, everyone now had the right to vote, express their opinions and lobby their representatives.[20]

In the same way that it had appropriated useful concepts from socialism, the Cold War Left had also separated the virtues of political liberalism from the vices of laissez-faire economics. However impressive, this theoretical legerdemain still remained trapped

[20] See W.W. Rostow, 'The National Style', pages 272–295.

within a perpetual present. Welfare Fordism might be improved, but never superseded. In this form, the ideology of the Vital Centre was incapable of depriving the Russian enemy of ownership of the future. If the geopolitical threat posed by the Marxist prophecy of communism was to be overcome, the leaders of the USA had to commit the resources and skills needed to construct a plausible alternative vision of the shape of things to come. After the Democrats came to power, the Cold War Left was finally able to raise the money for this priority project. In 1964, the American Academy of Arts and Sciences was given a large grant to set up a multi-disciplinary team of intellectuals dedicated to inventing the Anti-Communist vision of the non-communist future: *The Commission on the Year 2000*.[21]

Daniel Bell – the intellectual doyen of the Cold War Left – was placed in charge of this top-level assignment. Like the chair, the majority of the commission's 42 members were also recruited from elite universities. Following the multi-disciplinary model pioneered by the Macy conferences, the project drew upon a wide range of expertise. Among its members were not only economists, sociologists and political scientists, but also geographers, biologists and even a professor of biblical studies. Joining these academics on the project team were colleagues from the Democratic administration, career civil servants, corporate scientists and the sages of military think-tanks.[22] By recruiting intellectuals representing different disciplines and interest groups, the sponsors of the Bell commission had ensured that every section of the US elite would be involved in inventing the new imaginary future of the American empire.

Between 1964 and 1968, these Cold War Left experts wrote papers and participated in seminars on a common theme: what would US society look like in 30 to 40 years time? Sharing their knowledge and debating their hypotheses, they slowly but surely reached a consensus on their predictions for the year 2000. As at the 1964 New York World's Fair, technological innovation provided the starting point for the commission's enquiry into the shape of things to come. What existed in the mid 1960s could be easily extrapolated

[21] For the background history of the project, see Daniel Bell, *Towards the Year 2000*, pages 1–13.
[22] For the members of the Bell commission, see Bell, *Towards the Year 2000*, pages 382–386.

forward to the first decade of the next century. NASA rockets, atomic power stations and IBM mainframes were already being promoted as the precursors of space tourism, unmetered electricity and artificial intelligence. Following the same approach, Herman Kahn and Anthony Wiener from the military-funded Hudson Institute compiled an audacious list of 100 imminent inventions for the Bell commission.[23] Over the next 40 years, American scientists would not only develop space liners, free energy and sentient computers, but also discover – among other things – how to control the weather, put human beings into hibernation, make holographic movies, programme people's dreams, build individual flying platforms and use nuclear bombs for construction projects. Looking at the impressive achievements of the previous 20 years, the Bell commission was convinced that these technological fantasies would become everyday realities over the next four decades.[24]

> [T]he world of the year 2000 has already arrived, for the decisions which we make now, in the way we shape our environment and thus sketch the lines of constraints, the future is committed. ... The future is not an overarching leap into the distance; it begins in the present.[25]

In Rostow's *Stages of Economic Growth*, the past evolution of capitalism had been presented as a process without a subject. Although each nation's origins were different, their paths of development after take-off became increasingly identical. In the same way that this economic determinism explained the history of modernity, the Bell commission argued that technological innovation had become the impersonal force driving humanity towards the future. As in earlier stages of growth, people were spectators of an evolutionary movement outside of their control. Crucially, Bell and his colleagues had made an important modification to Rostow's canonical theory. In their futurist version, the process of modernity now had a highly visible object as its subject: the

---

[23] Kahn first achieved notoriety in the 1950s for his work at the US Air Force's RAND think-tank, which claimed that America could win a nuclear war against Russia. See Herman Kahn, *On Thermonuclear War*.

[24] See Bell, *Towards the Year 2000*, pages 79–84; and Herman Kahn and Anthony Wiener, *The Year 2000*, pages 66–117.

[25] Bell, *Towards the Year 2000*, page 1.

machine. Rather than humans deciding their own destiny, new technologies determined what was going to happen. Commodity fetishism had inspired sci-fi social prophecy. By 2000 at the latest, the self-expansion of fixed capital would have recreated humanity in its own hi-tech image.

The final step in the Bell commission's construction of a new imaginary future was devising a post-Fordist social utopia for the American empire. What the Cold War Left required was a third way replacement for Marx's prognosis of proletarian liberation. Fortunately for the Bell commission, they were able to find exactly what they were looking for in Marshall McLuhan's *Understanding Media*. Just like Marx, this prophet had also foreseen that the next stage of modernity would sweep away the most disagreeable manifestations of capitalism: national rivalries, industrial exploitation and social alienation. As in proletarian communism, peace, prosperity and harmony would reign in the global village. What made McLuhan so much more attractive than Marx for the Cold War Left was that the message of this oracle was technological determinism. Confirming the insights of the Bell commission, he dismissed the role of human decision making within social evolution. Technological fetishism had elevated the machine into the subject of history. For the Cold War Left's purposes, McLuhan's prophecy – especially when stripped of its caveats – was perfect. At one and the same time, it promised all of the rewards of socialism without any of the dangers of working-class activism. Best of all, this revelation celebrated 1960s America as the prototype of the imaginary future of the information society in the present. The Bell commission had successfully completed its mission to find a credible alternative to Marx's vision of communism. The American empire now had its own futurist ideology: McLuhanism.

Taking their cue from *Understanding Media*, the Bell commission identified the three key technologies which would determine the future of humanity: computing, media and telecommunications. In their list of 100 inventions of the year 2000, Kahn and his colleague had foreseen that amazing discoveries would be made by every discipline within the natural sciences. Yet, at the same time, the gurus of the Hudson Institute were convinced that only information technologies could act as the demiurges of the new social order.

The ideological prioritisation of these specific machines was a new phenomenon. For over a decade, along with space rockets and atomic power stations, computers had been promoted to the general public as one of the iconic technologies of modernity. Ever since the Macy conferences, cybernetics had provided the theoretical paradigm for multi-disciplinary academic research. Inspired by von Neumann and Shannon, university and corporate scientists had long anticipated the advent of artificial intelligence. But, up to the mid 1960s, the gurus of computing had focused the public's attention upon the possibility of replacing fallible humans with robot slaves. Now, for the first time in a US government report, Kahn and Wiener were claiming that the primary impact of the advances in information technology would be the transformation of the whole of society. Instead of making solitary super-beings, the new goal was to build a collective utopia. The imaginary future of artificial intelligence had morphed into the imaginary future of the information society.

Inspired by McLuhan's anticipation of the transforming power of the Net, the Bell commission eulogised the demiurgic role of cybernetic technologies. In their opinion, the full impact of electronic media upon humanity would only be felt when television had fused with computing and telecommunications. Believing that the synthesis of these three types of machines had become the subject of history, every advance in information technology was heralded as another step towards the information society. The Cold War Left was now convinced that – as the process of convergence was implemented – humanity was moving towards its utopian destiny: the Net. Like many of their peers in the US elite, the majority of the Bell commission never doubted that computers would one day evolve into sentient beings.[26] But, in contrast with Simon and Minsky, its members were much more pessimistic about the timeframe needed to achieve this technological miracle. Tellingly, Kahn and his colleague excluded the advent of 'true' artificial intelligence from their list of likely 100 inventions by the year 2000.[27] Relegating the creation of electronic brains to a long-term aspiration, the Bell

---

[26] See Kahn and Wiener, *The Year 2000*, pages 52, 91–94; and Bell, *Towards the Year 2000*, pages 31, 80, 308, 353.
[27] See Kahn and Wiener, *The Year 2000*, page 55.

commission instead emphasised the McLuhanist path of development for information technologies: computer-mediated communications. According to the gurus of artificial intelligence, the machine would replace the individual. Moving beyond this prophecy, the Bell commission argued that the machine now had a new – and more important – goal: the remodelling of the social system. Technological fetishism was creating a cyborg civilisation.

In 1966, three years before scientists at UCLA, Stanford Research Institute, UCSB and Utah University connected its first four hosts together, the Bell commission had convinced itself that the arrival of the Net utopia was imminent.[28] They confidently predicted that the majority of Americans would have access to on-line databases, shops and libraries within the next decade.[29] This technological advance would not only radically transform the workplace, but also have profound social and cultural effects. In place of homogenised mass media, people would be informed and entertained by 'electronic newspapers' which were tailored to their personal preferences. Instead of education being confined inside schools and universities, individuals would improve their minds with 'on-line learning' courses. As well as choosing political leaders in elections, citizens would be able to express their opinions through 'instant referendums' held on the Net.[30] Just as McLuhan had foreseen, the limitations of industrialism were about to be overcome by the wondrous technologies of the information society. Best of all, as Bell stressed in his chairman's summary of the commission's findings, 1960s America was already entering into this post-capitalist future. 'To put the matter most baldly – domestically the United States is becoming a *communal* society rather than a *contractual* one.'[31]

A decade earlier, this master thinker of the Cold War Left had announced that the age of social utopias was over. Modern politics was about improving capitalism not overthrowing it. Suddenly, in

[28] The original kernel of the Net went live in September 1969. See Janet Abbate, *Inventing the Internet*, pages 56–64; and Arthur Norberg, Jody O'Neill and Kerry Freedman, *Transforming Computer Technology*, pages 171–172.

[29] See Bell, *Towards the Year 2000*, page 4; and Kahn and Wiener, *The Year 2000*, page 83.

[30] See Bell, *Towards the Year 2000*, pages 52, 145, 260–262, 303–304, 352.

[31] Bell, *Towards the Year 2000*, pages 303–304.

the mid 1960s, Bell started preaching what he had only recently denounced. The sceptical pundit of the end of ideology had become the confident prophet of the post-Fordist information society. Instead of occluding the libertarian ideals of the 1776 Revolution, Bell was now predicting that the Net would realise its most radical demands: participatory democracy, universal enlightenment and media freedom. By embracing McLuhanism, he had returned to the utopianism of his Trotskyist youth in a new hi-tech form. When everyone was on-line, big bureaucracies would lose their potency. Taking their place, network communities would become the pre-eminent form of social organisation. In 1964, echoing Wiener and Vonnegut, the socialist authors of *The Manifesto of the Triple Revolution* had warned the Johnson administration that the 'cybernation' of the American economy was slowly but surely destroying the foundations of the Keynesian compromise: easily obtainable, high-waged factory jobs. The US Left needed radical solutions to tackle the new problems of the emerging post-Fordist epoch. Third way policies could no longer prevent the looming crises of mass unemployment and social exclusion.[32] Far from pouring scorn on what he would have once characterised as apocalyptic Marxism, Bell's response was to outflank this analysis from the left. While *The Manifesto of the Triple Revolution* argued for sensible reformist measures like providing a basic income for all citizens, this guru of the Vital Centre proclaimed the imminent arrival of the all-transforming social revolution. Humanity would soon be living within a hi-tech post-industrial utopia: the global village.

Ironically, the motivation for Bell's dramatic theoretical about-turn was entirely pragmatic. This leader of the Cold War Left had changed his stance on social millenarianism to counter a new – and highly dangerous – upgrade of the ideological threat from the East. In 1964, at the same time as Bell's commission was being set up, the American Cybernetics Society had organised a conference on the geopolitical implications of new information technologies. John F. Ford – the CIA's leading expert in this field – was a keynote speaker at this event. For a number of years, this analyst had been raising the alarm about the 'cybernetics gap' which was opening up

---

32 See Triple Revolution, 'Manifesto of the Triple Revolution'.

between the two superpowers.[33] Despite their slow start and fewer resources, Russian computer scientists had been steadily catching up on their American rivals. In both hardware and software, their machines were beginning to match – and even surpass – the US opposition. More worryingly, in 1956, the Russians had built one of the world's first fully functioning computer networks to provide a command and control system for Moscow's air defences.[34] By the early 1960s, Ford and his CIA colleagues had convinced themselves that the USA was in the process of being overtaken by its superpower rival. In his presentation for the American Cybernetics Society conference, he issued a stark warning: Russian scientists were now at the cutting edge of research into computer-mediated communications. According to Ford, the race to invent the Net would become 'a new kind of international competition during the next 15 years'.[35] America ignored this dangerous turn of events at its peril. Decisive action was needed to reverse the cybernetics gap with the Russians.

Back in 1957, America had suffered a major setback in the propaganda struggle in the global village when its Cold War enemy succeeded in launching the first satellite into space. Determined to prevent any repetition of this humiliation, the US government had quickly set up ARPA: the Advanced Research Projects Agency. Under its leadership, the talent and resources of America could be mobilised to ensure that the Russian enemy didn't pull off any further potentially embarrassing scientific breakthroughs.[36] When, in the early 1960s, the CIA alerted the US government to the danger of falling behind its rival in the race to build the Net, ARPA was given the responsibility for fighting this new battle on the technological front of the Cold War. Bringing together the top scientists in the field, the agency created, coordinated and funded an ambitious programme of research into computer-

[33] See John F. Ford, 'Soviet Cybernetics and International Development', pages 185–190. Ford's 'cybernetics gap' phrase echoed Kennedy's false claims about a growing 'missile gap' between America and Russia during the 1960 US presidential elections. See Robert Dallek, John F. Kennedy, pages 288–290.

[34] See Igor Apokin, 'The Development of Electronic Computers in the USSR'; and V.P. Shirikov, 'Scientific Computer Networks in the Soviet Union', pages 168–169.

[35] Ford, 'Soviet Cybernetics', page 189.

[36] See Norberg, O'Neill and Freedman, Transforming Computer Technology, pages 1–23.

mediated communications. This time, the United States was going to win the hi-tech race.[37]

At the 1964 American Cybernetics Society conference, Ford emphasised that the competition to invent the Net was much more than a test of scientific virility. The Russians weren't just forging ahead in the race to develop new technologies, but also, more importantly, in the competition to decide which side had the most advanced social system. Ford informed his American audience that their rivals were convinced that 'cybernetics ... [is] a science ... regulating ... the building of communism'.[38] Armed with this knowledge, the Russians believed that the Net would provide the technological infrastructure for a post-Stalinist utopia. By identifying itself with this hi-tech cornucopia, America's superpower enemy hoped to achieve a decisive victory in the global propaganda war. Communism, not Fordism, would be the prototype of the cybernetic future.[39] ARPA was already engaged in the task of seizing the technological lead in computer-mediated communications. The Bell commission's top-priority mission was countering the ideological aspect of this new threat to the USA's soft power. The building of the Net had to be disassociated from the emergence of a cybernetic form of communism. America must own the future.

A decade earlier, the USA had enjoyed a monopoly over cybernetics. In Russia, the media and the academy had poured scorn upon the meta-theory of the Cold War enemy. Wiener was denounced as the philosopher of US imperialism and corporate capitalism.[40] But, after Stalin's death in 1953, this condemnation was quickly replaced with admiration. Nikita Khrushchev – the new ruler of Russia – slowly began to open up the totalitarian system. Led by Axel Berg, a group of reformers within the Communist Party realised that cybernetics provided a superb metaphorical framework for talking about formerly taboo subjects such as economics, genetics, psychology and sociology. As Khrushchev relaxed ideological

---

[37] See Abbate, *Inventing the Internet*, pages 76–81; and Norberg, O'Neill and Freedman, *Transforming Computer Technology*, pages 24–118, 153–196.

[38] Ford, 'Soviet Cybernetics', pages 166–167.

[39] See Ford, 'Soviet Cybernetics' pages 171–190; and Maxim Mikulak, 'Cybernetics and Marxism–Leninism', pages 137–140, 153–154.

[40] See Arnost Kolman, 'The Adventure of Cybernetics in the Soviet Union'; and Slava Gerovitch, *From Newspeak to Cyberspeak*, pages 115–131.

controls, Russian intellectuals applied their new master theory across the academic disciplines. Just like Marxism, cybernetics was also a materialist methodology.[41] For the Communist reformers, Wiener was much more than the scientific champion of academic freedom. Heralded as the philosophy of the computer age, cybernetics became the theoretical justification of their progressive political and economic programme. Wiener was now praised as an engaged intellectual who had courageously criticised American militarism and class exploitation.[42] When he visited Moscow in 1960, the founder of cybernetics was treated like a rock star. Appealing to the best instincts of his Communist reformer hosts, Wiener emphasised the democratic message of his master theory. Positive feedback was the antidote to bureaucratic mismanagement on both sides of the Cold War. Marginalised at home, Wiener had become a hero in Russia.[43]

Ever since the Macy conferences, the new theory of cybernetics had been identified with the new technology of computing. Because of this connection, it was argued that the discovery of feedback and information were portents of revolutionary changes within society. However, in both superpowers, the conservative institutions of the military dominated the computer industry. Fortunately, like their American peers, Russian managers also discovered in the early 1950s that war-fighting computers had many peaceful applications. Just like private corporations, nationalised industries benefited from the mechanisation of clerical labour.[44] Yet, despite working within similar bureaucratic hierarchies, the gurus of Russian cybernetics had a very different concept of the imaginary future of computing from that of their American peers. Unlike von Neumann, Simon and Minsky, they dismissed artificial intelligence as a sci-fi fantasy.[45]

[41] See D.A. Pospelov, 'The Establishment of "Informatics" in Russia', pages 231–249; Gotthard Günther, 'Cybernetics and the Dialectical Materialism of Marx and Lenin'; and Gerovitch, *From Newspeak to Cyberspeak*, pages 200–214, 253–64.

[42] See Arnost Kolman, 'What is Cybernetics?' and Gerovitch, *From Newspeak to Cyberspeak*, pages 154–251.

[43] See Flo Conway and Jim Siegelman, *Dark Hero of the Information Age*, pages 315–316.

[44] See Igor Apokin, 'The Development of Electronic Computers in the USSR'; and A.Y. Nitussov and B.N. Malinovskiy, 'Economic Changes in the Sixties and the Internationalisation of Soviet Computing', pages 163–164.

[45] See Kolman, 'What is Cybernetics?', pages 141–142; and Loren Grahem, *Science, Philosophy and Human Behaviour in the Soviet Union*, pages 277–280.

Instead, their research was focused on making a machine-like society more human rather than on creating a human-like machine. For Berg's cybernetics group, the computer was the hi-tech saviour of the frustrated hopes of the 1917 Russian Revolution.

By the late 1950s, leading members of the Communist elite had realised that their tried-and-trusted methods of top-down management were losing their effectiveness. The growth rate was slowing. Living standards were still low. Worker unrest in Eastern Europe was a portent of what would happen at home if the Russian economy didn't deliver the goods.[46] Ironically, the biggest obstacles to changing the totalitarian system were its impressive achievements. During the 1930s and 1940s, the Stalinist regime had succeeded in not only organising the take-off of industrialisation, but also defeating Nazi Germany. Abandoning Bukharin's mixed-economy strategy, the totalitarian state had concentrated the ownership of almost all capital under its own control. Ignoring the feedback model in *Capital, Volume 2*, Stalin's planners had conceived of the national economy as a giant Fordist factory.[47] Breaking with their Social Democratic predecessors' reliance upon financial incentives, they issued direct orders down the chain of command to the managers of each and every firm and farm in Russia. Production targets were set from above – and those who failed to meet them risked imprisonment or worse.[48] In 1951, at the height of his power, Stalin exulted that central planning guaranteed the rapid and uninterrupted growth of the Russian economy. Showing its historical superiority over market capitalism, state management had abolished the boom-and-bust cycle. Totalitarian Communism was the fastest route to proletarian communism. 'The ... basic law of socialism ... [is] the maximum satisfaction of the constantly rising material and cultural requirements of the whole of society through the continuous expansion and perfection of socialist production on the basis of higher techniques.'[49]

[46] See Stanislaw Gomulka, *Growth, Innovation and Reform in Eastern Europe*, pages 93–149; and Moshe Lewin, *Political Undercurrents in Soviet Economic Debates*, pages 127–188.

[47] See Lewin, *Political Undercurrents*, pages 97–124; and Stephen Kotkin, *Magnetic Mountain*, pages 355–366.

[48] For Stalin's militarisation of the Russian state bureaucracy, see Peter Holquist, 'State Violence as Technique'.

[49] Joseph Stalin, *Economic Problems of Socialism in the USSR*, page 45.

During the 1930s, Stalinist planning was widely admired for having emancipated the industrial system from its laissez-faire past. As Marx had explained, market competition was a chaotic and wasteful method of regulating a modern economy. According to the promoters of Stalinism, when a capitalist society was reorganised into a nation factory, these problems disappeared. Applying the precepts of Lenin and Taylor, scientific managers knew how to optimise the production of goods and services. Unfortunately for its admirers, this Stalinist theory didn't match the Russian experience. The planned economy was as crisis-ridden as the market economy. Just like prices, targets also created boom-and-bust cycles. Shortages of vital goods and services were coupled with excesses of others. Rushing to meet one economic target led to the neglect of many more equally pressing needs.[50] This mismanagement of the workplace was coupled with structural instability within the national economy. Founded to modernise an agrarian society, Stalinist planning was designed to prioritise investments in heavy industry over raising living standards. When the plan's targets were set, the totalitarian state strove to limit any improvement in workers' wages and peasant incomes. The overproduction of industrial goods was dependent upon the underproduction of consumer goods.[51] Under Stalinism, the factory system was barred from evolving into the affluent society: Ford without Fordism.

For the Communist reformers in the late 1950s, this gathering crisis was an opportunity. If the Stalinist elite wanted to stay in power, it would have to abandon Stalinist planning. The tasks of primitive accumulation had been largely accomplished. Russia was now an advanced industrial nation which was already moving into the next stage of growth. As Hobson, Kalecki and Keynes had pointed out, raising living standards was the most effective method of ensuring the uninterrupted expansion of this more advanced Fordist economy. The workers must become consumers. According to the Communist reformers, Stalinist planning was structurally incapable of carrying out this essential task. Arbitrarily decided top-

---

[50] For a shop-floor view of the failings of this factory system, see Miklós Haraszti, *Worker in a Worker's State.*

[51] See Jacek Kuron and Karol Modzelewski, 'Open Letter to the Polish United Workers Party', pages 18–51.

down targets blocked all feedback from below. Waste and shortages were the inevitable result.[52] Back in the 1920s, Ludwig von Mises – a founding father of neo-liberal economics – had argued that the deficiencies of Russian state planning proved that physical measures of output couldn't be used to decide between the relative merits of different goods and services. Market prices were the only mathematically rational method of harmonising the ambitions of producers with the desires of consumers.[53] Looking for a third way between totalitarian Stalinism and its laissez-faire antithesis, the Communist reformers revived the centrist strategy of Bukharin and his followers from the 1920s. The economy could be decentralised without abandoning the state's monopoly over capital. Competitive pricing would encourage a more balanced development of the heavy industry, consumer goods and agricultural sectors. State-owned firms would no longer waste capital and labour if their investments had to generate a minimum rate of profit. Crucially, the detailed planning of these complex financial flows had become much easier than it had been 30 years earlier. The Communist Party now possessed the technology which would transform the East into an affluent society: the computer.[54]

Like Galbraith, these cybernetic reformers also envisioned the national economy as a programmable machine. With the correct mixture of indirect incentives and direct orders, the state was now able to deal with the two-sided structural crisis of Stalinist planning. Rational pricing corrected the target-driven boom-and-bust cycles which afflicted most areas of the economy. Feedback from below discouraged overinvestment in heavy industry at the expense of the consumer goods sector.[55] Inspired by Wiener's leftist concept of cybernetics, Berg's group believed that Russia now had the opportunity to build the technological infrastructure for the most sophisticated – and democratic – economic system in human history. Computers would be placed in every factory, office, shop and

52 See Lewin, *Political Undercurrents*, pages 127–157.
53 See Ludwig von Mises, *Planned Chaos*. The founding text of games theory provided the mathematical proof of this theoretical assertion: John von Neumann and Oskar Morgenstern, *Theory of Games and Economic Behaviour*.
54 See Leonid Kantorovich, 'My Journey in Science', pages 27–38; Lewin, *Political Undercurrents*, pages 158–188; and A.Y. Nitussov, 'Leonid Vitalyevich Kantorovich'.
55 See D.A. Pospelov, 'The Establishment of "Informatics" in Russia', pages 243–253; and Lewin, *Political Undercurrents*, pages 158–188.

educational institution over the next decade. In this Russian vision of the Net, two-way feedback between producers and consumers would calculate the correct distribution of labour and resources which most efficiently satisfied all of the different needs of society. In early 1960s Russia, like market competition three decades earlier, top-down Taylorism was becoming an anachronism. Computers and telecommunications were creating a new cybernetic form of economic management: the 'Unified Information Network'.[56]

> Mathematical programming assisted by electronic computers becomes the fundamental instrument of long-term planning, as well as solving dynamic economic problems of a more limited scope. Here, the electronic computer does not replace the market. It fulfils tasks which the market never was able to perform.[57]

Ever since the 1917 Revolution, the Communist Party had drawn ideological sustenance from its self-proclaimed role as the vanguard of proletarian communism. For four decades, wondrous visions of this imaginary future had been the rewards for submitting to its oppressive rule in the present. Under Stalin, the horrors of forced industrialisation were sold to the Russian population as premonitions of the promised land of socialism. Collective suffering was the precursor of cooperative prosperity.[58] Ironically, it was the successful completion of primary industrialisation which posed a potentially fatal existential dilemma for the Communist Party. Taylorist discipline had lost its allure of organisational modernity. According to the reformers, the ruling party required a new vision of the socialist future if it wanted to rule over this new paradigm. Having fulfilled Stalin's goal of industrialising the Russian economy, the vanguard had to move on to tackling the tasks of the next stage of its world-historical mission. Under its leadership, the country's best scientists and engineers should focus their energies upon prototyping the cybernetic future. Russia's factory society must be upgraded into the Unified Information Network. By replacing

---

[56] See B.N. Malinovskiy, 'Viktor Mikhaylovich Glushkov', pages 141–145; and Gerovitch, *From Newspeak to Cyberspeak*, pages 253–279.

[57] Oskar Lange, 'The Computer and the Market', page 161. Lange was a Polish economist who worked with the Russian cybernetics movement.

[58] For the cultural project of Stalinism, see Jeffrey Brooks, *Thank You, Comrade Stalin!* and Kotkin, *Magnetic Mountain*.

Stalin with Wiener, bureaucratic Communism would be able to preserve its ideological hegemony over the imaginary future of proletarian communism.

Like their conservative opponents, the reformers saw themselves as the rightful inheritors of the 1917 Russian Revolution. The building of the Unified Information Network was the rediscovery of the managerial elite's world-historical mission. In 1961, at the 22nd Communist Party Congress, Khrushchev assured the Russian people that the construction of socialism would be completed within the lifetimes of most of his audience. After decades of purges, wars, corruption and austerity, the promised land was within sight. By the 1980s at the latest, the inhabitants of Russia, Central Asia and Eastern Europe would be enjoying all the wonders of proletarian communism.[59] As the successor of Lenin and Stalin, Khrushchev's political legitimacy was founded upon the credibility of this prophetic promise. For over four decades, the Communist Party had been trapped within an ideological contradiction of its own making. During the upheavals of 1917, Lenin had shown his mastery over the Russian revolutionary movement by identifying himself with the simultaneous realisation of its two founding – and incompatible – political ideals: participatory democracy and the vanguard party. In his speeches and writings, this Marxist intellectual celebrated the determination of the Russian workers and peasants to take responsibility for their own lives. Like the Paris Commune, popular assemblies, factory collectives and soldiers' committees were modernising democratic institutions. Mass participation was the revolutionary antidote to monarchical despotism.[60]

As well as embodying the hopes of the industrialised future, the 1917 Revolution's experiments in self-management were also the application of the equalitarian traditions of the peasantry in an urban setting. From the mid nineteenth century onwards, Russian radicals had dreamt of sparking off a spontaneous rural uprising against the absolutist system. Mikhail Bakunin – their master philosopher – had foreseen that this peasant insurgency would culminate in the total

---

59 See Nikita Khrushchev, *Report on the Programme of the Communist Party of the Soviet Union*, pages 22–23.
60 See V.I. Lenin, *State and Revolution*, pages 37–40, 67–79; and Oskar Anweiler, *The Soviets*, pages 144–207.

destruction of the Russian state: 'anarchy'. Once freed of central controls, village communes would be quite capable of running their own affairs and working together to meet their collective needs.[61] By 1917, these anarchic attitudes had been imported into the cities. With a large proportion of the working class coming from the countryside, Russian socialists found eager listeners when they argued that mass meetings should be used to manage the factories just like in the villages. Agrarian backwardness was − paradoxically − politically more advanced than industrial modernity.[62] On the eve of his party's seizure of power, Lenin promised that revolutionary Russia would build the world's first fully participatory democracy:

> From the moment when all members of society, or even only an overwhelming majority, have learned how to govern the state themselves, have taken this business into their own hands ... from this moment the need for any government begins to disappear.[63]

Back in the early 1870s, Bakunin had challenged Marx's intellectual leadership of the international labour movement. Anticipating the rise of state socialism in the next century, this first patriarch of anarchism had denounced his rival as the apologist of industrial despotism. Looking to Russia rather than England for his revolutionary model, Bakunin publicly positioned himself as the champion of spontaneous rebellion and direct democracy.[64] Yet, simultaneously, this enemy of authority was also a devotee of conspiratorial politics. When the Russian people finally rose up against their oppressors, their struggle would require firm direction from a self-selected elite: the 'invisible dictatorship'.[65] At the time, Bakunin's fascination with revolutionary conspiracies lost him his battle with Marx. Ironically, it would also make him into the unacknowledged prophet of the dominant current of twentieth-century Marxism: Communism with a capital C. In the 1900s, Lenin's concept of the vanguard party had initially been a rationalisation of

[61] See Mikhail Bakunin, 'The Programme of the Slav Section'; Franco Venturi, Roots of Revolution, pages 36–62, 429–506; and Aileen Kelly, Mikhail Bakunin, pages 151–226
[62] See Jacques Camatte, Community and Communism in Russia; Anweiler, The Soviets, pages 20–143; and Venturi, Roots of Revolution, pages 507–557.
[63] Lenin, State and Revolution, pages 78–79.
[64] See Mikhail Bakunin, 'On Marx and Marxism'; and Kelly, Bakunin, pages 151–226.
[65] See Mikhail Bakunin, 'Letter to Albert Richard'; Venturi, Roots of Revolution, pages 354–388; and Kelly, Bakunin, pages 227–288.

the secrecy and discipline required for any political organisation to carry out subversive activities under an absolutist monarchy.[66] But, by the 1917 Revolution, he had succeeded in synthesising the two opposing sides of Bakunin's politics into one master theory. Lenin had discovered that dictatorship was the anticipation of anarchy. The old Marxist programme of parliamentary democracy and free trade unions was obsolete. The Communist elite was the embodiment of the imaginary future of proletarian communism in the present.

At each defining moment in its history, the rival factions of Lenin's party had fought for ownership of this world-historical mission. In the 1930s, Stalin had prevailed and his industrialisation programme was declared the only route to the imaginary future. After the death of the tyrant, the Communist reformers were given their chance to challenge this ideological settlement. The Stalinists were stuck in the industrial past. Building the Net was the task of the rising generation of hi-tech reformers. The new vanguard of computerised Communists with a capital C would lead the building of a McLuhanist form of communism with a small c: *cybernetic communism*. From the late 1950s onwards, Berg's group had proselytised this reformist programme within the inner circles of the Russian elite. In 1961, at its 22nd Congress, the Communist Party formally adopted the goal of spreading the benefits of computerisation across the whole economy. Within two decades, as Khrushchev promised in his leader's speech, the Russian people would be living in the post-industrial paradise of cybernetic communism.

This official approval from Moscow emboldened other reformist movements in Eastern Europe. In 1967, the new leadership of the Czechoslovak Communist Party set up a multi-disciplinary group of experts to provide a theoretical rationale for its decision to break with the Stalinist past. Given the apt title *Civilisation at the Crossroads*, Radovan Richta and his team produced the best-selling Marxist–McLuhanist manifesto of the 1968 Prague Spring.[67] They explained that top-down orders and arbitrary targets might have

---

66 See V.I. Lenin, *What Is to Be Done?* and Marcel Liebman, *Leninism under Lenin*, pages 25–96.
67 For the membership and mission statement of this reformist group, see Radovan Richta, *Civilisation at the Crossroads*, pages x–xx. Also see Z.A.B. Zeman, *Prague Spring*, pages 87–90

been needed to manage the semi-educated factory proletariat, but, with the spread of computerisation, these Taylorist controls were losing their effectiveness. The social structure of the economy was already changing rapidly. Technicians and scientists were forerunners of a new working class: skilled, educated and informed.[68] If these post-industrial proletarians were to work effectively within the emerging knowledge economy, the Communist Party would have to loosen its political monopoly. The two-way feedback of information was incompatible with censorship and intimidation. Top-down management had to be supplemented with worker participation.[69] Absolved of its Stalinist crimes, the Leninist party could now be reconnected with the libertarian ideals of the Russian Revolution. Workers' councils and peasant communes were premonitions of the computerised participatory democracy to come. Embracing the Richta report with enthusiasm, the Czechoslovak Communist Party dedicated itself to realising the new utopia: *the imaginary future of cybernetic communism*.

> By its inner logic, the scientific and technological revolution points to the possibility of superseding the old industrial division of labour and replacing it by a conscious organisation of human cooperation, where ... the split between the intellectual forces of production and labour, between physical and mental work, disappears – where, in short, one and all can affirm themselves through creative activity, whatever form it may assume.[70]

[68] See Richta, *Crossroads*, pages 1–124.
[69] See Richta, *Crossroads*, pages 177–251.
[70] Richta, *Crossroads*, page 98.

11

THE AMERICAN ROAD TO THE GLOBAL VILLAGE

Across the Atlantic, the CIA had watched the rise to power of the post-industrial reformers in the East with growing concern. Embracing his opponents' analysis, John F. Ford argued that the technological race to develop the Net had become the key contest which would decide whether America or Russia would lead humanity into the information society. The superpower that owned this imaginary future had hegemony over the entire planet. Responding to these CIA briefings, the Kennedy administration sent ARPA into battle against the cybernetic Communist enemy. In 1962, the head of the agency recruited the brightest of the best to lead this vital mission: J.C.R. Licklider. During the 1950s, this mathematician–psychologist had participated in the Macy conferences and later worked with the MIT team building the networked control systems of the SAGE missile defence scheme. Adding to his Keynesian credentials, he had subsequently transferred his knowledge into the private sector as vice-president of the cutting-edge BBN computing company. By the time that he was appointed ARPA's director for Net research, Licklider was the exemplar of the third way intellectual: warrior–academic–entrepreneur–bureaucrat.[1]

The US government laid down the primary goal of his mission: America must invent the Net first. It was Licklider's job to make sure that the Russians lost the technology race this time. Flush with taxpayers' money, he sought out the small band of computer scientists who had expertise in this area. Both superpowers had built specialised military command and control systems, but neither side had attempted anything as ambitious and complex as constructing the Unified Information Network. When, in 1960, Paul Baran had put forward a proposal for writing software which allowed people in different locations to 'time-share' mainframes, his bosses at the RAND think-tank had not surprisingly been highly sceptical. According to his paper, a network of expensive and flaky computers would provide a more robust communications infrastructure in the aftermath of a nuclear war than the existing ones made out of cheap and reliable switches. Yet, within a few years, the US Air Force's research institute was prioritising work on this unlikely project.[2]

---

[1] See Arthur Norberg, Jody O'Neill and Kerry Freedman, *Transforming Computer Technology*, pages 26–30, 68–74; and Leo Beranek, 'BBN's Earliest Days', pages 9–12.
[2] See Paul Baran, 'On Distributed Communications'; and Katie Hafner and Matthew Lyon, *Where Wizards Stay up Late*, pages 52–67.

With a generous grant from ARPA, Baran and his colleagues played a leading role in the development of a new method of transmitting data between computers over telephone lines: packet-switching. Pulling ahead of the Russian opposition, they helped to create a universal interface which allowed all makes of machine to communicate with one another. When the UCLA, Stanford Research Institute, UCSB and Utah University hosts were linked together in 1969, the RAND team's software provided the technical architecture for the appropriately named first ever iteration of the Net: ARPANET.[3]

From the outset, Licklider was well aware that the primary purpose of his project wasn't to investigate the potential military applications of time-sharing mainframes. On Baran's funding application, his research was justified as an efficiency measure which would enable ARPA's laboratories to share their computer resources. In the medium term, there was the promise that packet-switching would improve the reliability of battlefield communications.[4] But, for Licklider, this military rationale was only a means to a higher end. Back in the late 1950s, the US Air Force had funded his psychological study of the staff operating the SAGE missile control system. From this pioneering research into human–computer interaction, he had concluded that the mainframe was much more than a calculating machine. Among his peers, Licklider soon became well known for his premonitions of the Net. Like his counterparts in Russia, he believed that the fusion of computing, media and telecommunications was imminent.[5] When he became an ARPA director, Licklider was given the chance to fulfil his own predictions. With money diverted from the US defence budget, he set out to realise his dream of building a computer-mediated communications system accessible to everyone: the 'intergalactic network'.[6]

Heavily influenced by his MIT colleague Wiener, Licklider's vision of the wired future closely resembled that of the Russian proponents

[3] See Janet Abbate, *Inventing the Internet*, pages 56–64; and Norberg, O'Neill and Freedman, *Transforming Computer Technology*, pages 171–172.

[4] See Norberg, O'Neill and Freedman, *Transforming Computer Technology*, pages 171–172

[5] For his manifesto on the social implications of network computing, see J.C.R. Licklider, 'The Computer as a Communications Device'.

[6] This nickname for the Net was a remix of McLuhan's electric global network.

of cybernetic communism. This ARPA director was convinced that – within a decade at most – typewriters would be transformed into terminals connected to a global network of mainframes. When every office, factory and educational institution was hooked up to the Net, people would be able to access information from on-line data banks regardless of their geographical location. Once computer consoles were combined with interactive television broadcasting, citizens would begin directly participating in the democratic decision-making process. Using their terminals, individuals would form virtual communities with like-minded people from across the world. Above all, like his friend Wiener, Licklider believed that the Net would also radically transform the workplace. The factory and the market were no longer the most efficient and productive methods of running the economy. Over the superior feedback system of the Net, people could work together at a much higher level of collaboration and intelligence: 'cooperative creativity'.[7]

During his brief stint as its first director, Licklider succeeded in hard-wiring his social vision of computing into ARPA's research project. As a precondition of funding, he insisted that all of his grant recipients participated in a computer time-sharing experiment. From these initially reluctant recruits, Licklider mentored the Net's formative virtual community. Putting his own ideas into practice, he encouraged the ARPA-funded scientists to cooperate creatively over the technological system which they were in the process of constructing. Academics were expected to build the Net in their own image.[8] For Licklider, the primary purpose of computer-mediated communications was facilitating the idiosyncratic working methods of the scientific community. Instead of trading information with each other like the overwhelming majority of cultural producers, academics collaborated by sharing knowledge. Promotion and prestige depended upon contributing articles to journals, presenting papers at conferences and distributing findings for peer review.[9] Although deeply enmeshed within the state and corporate hierarchies, American universities nonetheless privileged

[7] See J.C.R. Licklider, 'Man–Computer Symbiosis'; 'The Computer as a Communications Device'; and Hafner and Lyon, *Wizards*, pages 34–35.

[8] See Abbate, *Inventing the Internet*, pages 54–60; and Norberg, O'Neill and Freedman, *Transforming Computer Technology*, pages 88–112, 153–179.

[9] See Warren Hagstrom, 'Gift Giving as an Organisational Principle in Science'.

this academic gift economy. From nuclear weapons to the end-of-ideology thesis, this communistic method of advancing knowledge had proved its worth in both the natural and social sciences. As a third-way ARPA director, Licklider had no qualms about working with the private sector. Under a successor, BBN – his former employer – was given the hardware contract for ARPANET.[10] Yet, at the same time, Licklider also carefully nurtured the non-commercial kernel of the Net. By stressing its focus on pure research, ARPA was able to recruit leading scientists who otherwise would have had moral qualms about working for the US military.[11] Insulated from outside pressures and distractions, Licklider's researchers could concentrate all of their efforts on their main task: inventing the Net in the quickest possible time.

In the early 1960s, British scientists at the National Physics Laboratory had been at the forefront of the development of computer networking. Unfortunately for them, their Labour government's vision of 'the white hot heat of the technological revolution' was much more limited than that of Licklider. For this cash-strapped administration, the primary purpose of state-funded research was producing quick commercial applications.[12] In contrast, Licklider was able to avoid this sort of short-term thinking. Thanks to the US military, he had the money to sponsor the emergence of a social space emancipated from both the market and the factory. Inside this hi-tech gift economy, proprietary hardware and software were technical obstacles to the most efficient ways of working. Sharing knowledge was much more productive than trading information. Like the cooperatives described by Marx in *Capital, Volume 3*, the ARPANET developers were encouraged to behave as a self-governing community. The people who built the Net were the ones who ran it. In an ironic twist, at the height of the Cold War, the US military was funding the invention of cybernetic communism.

In 1966, at its 'Future of Technology' seminar, Licklider gave a progress report to the Bell commission on the US government's project to build the Net.[13] Through ARPA's efforts, America

[10] See Beranek, 'BBN's Earliest Days', page 12; and Norberg, O'Neill and Freedman, *Transforming Computer Technology*, pages 167–168.
[11] See Steven Levy, *Hackers*, pages 130–132.
[12] See Abbate, *Inventing the Internet*, pages 21–41.
[13] See Daniel Bell, *Towards the Year 2000*, page 368.

had now taken the lead in the race to build the cybernetic future. While the Russians' Unified Information Network remained at the conceptual stage, Licklider's scientists were already beta-testing the new technological structures and social mores of the information society. From its own experience, the ARPANET team was proving that common protocols and cooperative creativity were the driving forces of the convergence of media, telecommunications and computing. After listening to Licklider's presentation, the Bell commission could have had no doubts that the McLuhanist prophecy was on the verge of being realised. Even if the Canadian guru's claims that television was already transforming humanity were exaggerated, the preliminary results of ARPA's research programme demonstrated that the convergence of computing, media and telecommunications was going to be the catalyst for 'important sociological changes'.[14] Licklider had created the premonition of the imaginary future in the present: hacker democracy.

> As I talked to these digital explorers ... I found a common element ... It was a philosophy of sharing, openness, decentralisation, and getting your hands on machines at all costs − to improve the machine, to improve the world. This Hacker Ethic is their gift to us: something with value even to those of us with no interest at all in computers.[15]

Ironically, it was the Russian elite which lacked the self-confidence to sponsor even small-scale ARPA-style experiments in cybernetic communism. The reformers had offered a rejuvenation of the world-historic mission of the vanguard party. However, for their conservative opponents, the advantages of owning the imaginary future were by far outweighed by the threat which the Net posed to their power and authority. If the Berg group's proposals were taken seriously, the workers and peasants would no longer be subjugated under Taylorist discipline. Instead, they would be able to organise their own lives over the Unified Information Network.[16] Even when it was an oppositional movement, the Communist elite had equated

---

14 Bell, *Towards the Year 2000*, page 379.
15 Levy, *Hackers*, page 7.
16 One reformer recalled being asked a revealing question by a top bureaucrat: 'Where is the leading role of the [Communist] Party in your [cybernetic] machine?' Igor Poletaev in Slava Gerovitch, *From Newspeak to Cyberspeak*, page 167.

knowledge with power. Before the 1917 Revolution, Lenin had combined the political role of party leader with the ideological role of newspaper editor. Like Bakunin, he insisted that the dictatorship of intellectuals had the task of directing the anarchic struggles of the masses against the monarchy.

When Lenin's party seized power in October 1917, the new government's first decree asserted its claim to ideological supremacy: the reimposition of press censorship.[17] The tactics of the underground now justified the revival of the absolutist state in a new form. In backward Russia, the Communist elite was the educator of the ignorant and illiterate majority. The scientific truth was at war with 'false consciousness'.[18] As its most powerful weapon in this ideological struggle, the vanguard party possessed the correct interpretation of the only theory which revealed the path to modernity: Marxism. After Lenin's death, the political contest for the succession was conducted in public through a bitter quarrel over his ideological legacy. By the time that Trotsky and Bukharin were finally vanquished, Stalin had silenced any debate about the meaning of Marxism in Russia. The quoting of approved texts replaced the studying of the canonical books. The dictator decided the orthodoxy in not only politics and economics, but also the arts and sciences. Hard power strictly policed all manifestations of soft power. In this paranoid world, even questioning the official line on abstract painting or genetic biology became a treasonable activity. Under Stalin, artists and scientists were rewarded for not only their technical abilities, but also their political loyalties. Both admired and feared, intellectuals were the cultural elite of the Russian factory society: the 'engineers of the human soul'.[19]

Following the death of Stalin, Communist conservatives stayed faithful to their master's teachings. Allowing intellectuals to debate freely among themselves was the first step towards dismantling the ruling party's political monopoly. If artists and scientists could escape from factory discipline, then the rest of the population would

[17] See John Reed, *Ten Days That Shook the World*, page 166.
[18] See V.I. Lenin, *What Is to Be Done?* pages 34–65; George Lukács, *History and Class Consciousness*, pages 46–222, 295–342; and Richard Barbrook, *Media Freedom*, pages 38–42.
[19] For the political implications of Stalin's infamous slogan, see A.A. Zhdanov, *On Literature, Music and Philosophy*.

inevitably want to follow them. In 1956, the relaxation of ideological controls in Hungary had sparked off a popular uprising against Russian rule which had to be crushed by military force.[20] For Communist conservatives, Berg's cybernetic reforms were the hi-tech iteration of this political blunder. Feedback from below introduced chaos into the bureaucratic order. When Khrushchev was ousted in 1964, the cybernetic Communist movement lost its most important patron. Abandoning the construction of the Unified Information Network, Leonid Brezhnev's new government made sure that computing was kept under strict political control.[21] When the Czechoslovak reformers' theoretical manifesto celebrated the Net as the demiurge of participatory democracy, the subversive image of this cybernetic technology was confirmed for these conservative bureaucrats. In 1968, the Russian government sent in its tanks to put an end to the Prague Spring.[22] The perpetuation of totalitarian Communism depended upon the prevention of cybernetic communism.

In complete contrast, Licklider's experiments in networked creativity could be generously funded in third-way America. Under military Keynesianism, the academic gift economy was appreciated for its small but vital role within the mixed economy of Fordism. Sharing information was simply the most efficient method of conducting scientific research. Despite its pragmatic advantages, the Stalinists in Russia were deeply suspicious of the academic gift economy. Peer review was far too close to proletarian democracy for their liking. Under the Brezhnev regime, Russia's experimental academic and commercial networks were barred from acquiring the common protocols which would allow them to fuse together into the Net.[23] Research was focused upon developing specialist machines for the military rather than producing cheap computers for the masses. The theoretical knowledge of Russia's scientists was never matched by the entrepreneurial skills of its industrial managers. Instead of solving its problems, cybernetic technologies had fallen victim to the shortcomings of the Stalinist planning system. Further

---

20 See François Fejtö, *A History of the People's Democracies*, pages 29–123; and Andy Anderson, *Hungary '56*.

21 See Gerovitch, *From Newspeak to Cyberspeak*, pages 279–292.

22 See Z.A.B. Zeman, *Prague Spring*.

23 See V.P. Shirikov. 'Scientific Computer Networks in the Soviet Union'; and Gerovitch, *From Newspeak to Cyberspeak*, pages 279–284.

limiting the political influence of the domestic computer lobby, the Brezhnev regime in the late 1960s decided to manufacture IBM System/360 clones for their industrial and educational customers. Fear of the imaginary future had discouraged any serious investment in its precursors in the present.[24]

At the 1964 American Cybernetics Society conference, Ford had argued that the race to invent the Net was both a technological and an ideological contest. Over the next five years, team USA surged ahead of its Russian rival. By the time that the Stalinists dropped out of this competition, the building of the Net had acquired a momentum of its own in America. ARPA money had directed computer science research towards achieving this technical and political goal. The Bell commission focused the attention of social science departments upon the transition to the information society. Crucially, by entering into this technological contest, the Democratic administration had discovered a powerful propaganda weapon. The Cold War Left became convinced that ownership of the imaginary future of the Net was essential to achieving intellectual hegemony in the present. By abandoning the prophecy of cybernetic communism, the Russians were conceding defeat in this crucial ideological battlefield. ARPANET was Version 1.0 of the post-industrial future. The American remix had become the original.

The Bell commission was set up to complete the task begun at the ARPANET development labs. Like Marxism, cybernetic communism must be transformed into an American ideology. Before the Bell Commission started work, the Cold War Left's speculations about the information society were still speculative and tentative compared to those of the Russian prophets of the Net. At the 1964 American Cybernetics Society conference, McLuhan – who like Wiener was also a friend of Licklider's – was the only participant at the conference who was convinced that he possessed the Anti-Communist theory which deciphered this new imaginary future: technological determinism.[25] Unfortunately for his US admirers, this Canadian intellectual was a mystical Catholic trickster rather

---

[24] See A.Y. Nitussov and B.N. Malinovskiy, 'Economic Changes in the Sixties and the Internationalisation of Soviet Computing'.
[25] See Marshall McLuhan, 'Cybernation and Culture'.

than a politically reliable member of the Cold War Left. The Bell commission's task was domesticating the new master theory of McLuhanism. The tricky questions posed by its founder were to remain unanswered. The close resemblance between the information society and cybernetic communism must be obscured. Above all, McLuhanism had to prove that the networked future was made-in-the-USA.

Back in the 1950s, Rostow and Galbraith had asserted that America was pioneering the new mass-consumption stage of growth. A decade later, these two master thinkers now believed that the Johnson administration was on the verge of completing the transformation of the USA into an advanced welfare democracy. Both Rostow and Galbraith argued that the satisfaction of material wants would soon lead to the emergence of a new political agenda: post-scarcity desires.[26] In its Great Society programme, the Democratic government anticipated this shift in public opinion by introducing limited measures for environmental protection and community development.[27] The task of the Bell commission was much more ambitious. Its members had been charged with planning the transition from the mass-consumption stage of growth to the new epoch of post-industrialism. In two interim reports, the Bell commission confidently predicted the social changes which would take place over the next 40 years. The production of goods would be supplanted by the production of services. The nation state would be subsumed within the global village. These dramatic economic and political changes would lead to the emergence of a new post-industrial culture.[28] The lesson of the Cold War Left's version of the materialist conception of history was clear. The affluent society was inexorably evolving into the information society. Above all, it was America that was the prototype of this marvellous future. Licklider's ARPANET experiment was the premonition of cooperative creativity for all. The utopian dreams of Russian-style cybernetic communism could only be turned into everyday reality within the made-in-the-USA global village.

26 See W.W. Rostow, *The Process of Economic Growth*, pages 326–328; *The Diffusion of Power*, 528; and John Kenneth Galbraith, *The New Industrial State*, pages 323, 367–368.
27 See Irving Bernstein, *Guns or Butter*, pages 261–306.
28 See Bell, *Towards the Year 2000*, pages 5–6, 95–96, 323; and Herman Kahn and Anthony Wiener, *The Year 2000*, pages 185–193, 198–202.

No more would man have to live by the sweat of his brow. The promise of automation and technology could be fulfilled throughout the world, and all would share in the fruits of modern science – all who choose to could soon live in a post-industrial culture.[29]

Between 1967 and 1968, the Bell commission presented their initial findings in two hefty books: Herman Kahn and Anthony Wiener, *The Year 2000: a framework for speculation*; and Daniel Bell, *Towards the Year 2000: work in progress*. In the former, the doyens of the Hudson Institute published the report which had been used as the starting point for discussions among members of the project. In the latter, the chair of the commission provided an edited version of his team's papers and seminars. Despite the importance of their subject, neither of these books made any significant impact outside the inner circle of the Cold War Left. The Hudson Institute's report was written in a tortuous bureaucratic style. Belying its striking cover, Bell's book was a confusing hodgepodge of transcripts and interventions with no single authorial voice. These were publications for the committed few rather than for the general reader.

While the Bell commission was carrying out its research work, this exclusivity wasn't a problem. But, once the project team had agreed upon the new imaginary future for the American empire, their findings had to be presented in a more accessible form. If it was to complete its mission successfully, the Bell commission had to produce a canonical text of Anti-Communist theory: the definitive codification of the information society prophecy. Ironically, even though it had provided the first iteration of this imaginary future, *Understanding Media* couldn't fulfil this vital role. In his writings, McLuhan had not only demonstrated his political unreliability, but also taken delight in promiscuously combining insights from modernist literature, mass culture and Catholic theology with ideas taken from cybernetics, behavioural psychology, positivist sociology and quantum physics. Despite being extremely popular with the general public, this exuberant style appalled the Cold War Left. McLuhan's intuitive thought probes offended against the accepted methodology of intellectual labour. In academic texts and government reports, the proper way of doing things involved carefully collecting evidence

---

[29] Kahn and Wiener, *The Year 2000*, page 378.

and diligently referencing sources. In order for McLuhanism to become the new dogma of American hegemony, the Cold War Left had to reconcile McLuhan's idiosyncratic technique with these professional requirements. Literary musings about society had to be turned into hardnosed social science. Oracular pronouncements had to be backed up with value-free research. Only after making these corrections would the Cold War Left's intellectuals have completed the construction of their new intellectual orthodoxy: *McLuhanism without McLuhan*.[30]

Zbigniew Brzezinski – an up-and-coming Polish émigré geopolitical analyst at Columbia University – was the first member of the Bell commission to take on the task of rewriting *Understanding Media*. In 1968, he published an article promoting his new interpretation of the information society prophecy which was then followed in 1970 by his big book: *Between Two Ages: America's role in the technetronic era*. In contrast with McLuhan, Brzezinski meticulously observed the pieties of his profession by including statistics, footnotes and a bibliography in his publications. Just as importantly, he replaced the wacky catchphrases of *Understanding Media* with his own more sober neologisms. The paradoxical image of the global village was replaced by the more credible concept of the 'global city'.[31] Above all, *Between Two Ages* was focused upon the analysis of the shift from Fordism to the 'technetronic' society.[32] By toning down the populist style of *Understanding Media*, Brzezinski was able to endow its visionary prediction of the information society with an aura of academic respectability. Even better, by incorporating Rostow's stages of growth into the analysis, he had added some theoretical rigour to McLuhan's impressionistic overview of the historical process. In the Brzezinski remix of *Understanding Media*, the imminent arrival of post-industrialism was proved by objective analysis rather than by subjective assertion. Prophesising the future had become impartial social science.

---

30 Despite their very obvious theoretical debt to McLuhan, Kahn and Wiener never mentioned his writings in their book, while the chair's collection of essays and seminars only contained three passing references to the first prophet of post-industrialism.

31 See Zbigniew Brzezinski, *Between Two Ages*, page 19.

32 Brzezinski invented his 'technetronics' neologism by combining the words 'technology' and 'electronics' together. See Brzezinski, *Between Two Ages*, page xiv.

Yet, this image of value-free theoretical knowledge derived from careful empirical research was a sham. In his article and book, Brzezinski acted as a booster for the McLuhanist catechism. The electronic global network might have been renamed the 'global information grid', but the prophecy was exactly the same.[33] Technology was the driving force of human history. The convergence of computing, media and telecommunications into the Net was creating a new social system. The production of goods was being supplanted by the provision of services. Representative democracy would soon be supplemented by on-line voting. The nation state was being integrated into the process of world unification. The linear thought patterns of literacy were being replaced by the fragmented consciousness of audio-visual communications.[34] Even when these assertions were justified by statistics, graphs and references, Brzezinski's advocacy of McLuhanism was founded upon faith, not reason. Facts proved what had already been agreed upon as the transcendent goal of human history: the information society.

> In the course of the work [of writing the book], I have expressed my own opinions and exposed my prejudices. This effort is, therefore, more in the nature of a 'think-piece' backed by evidence, than of a systematic exercise in social-science methodology.[35]

As the subtitle of his book suggested, Brzezinski's firm belief in the information society prophecy came from a deep patriotism for his adopted country. The Bell commission had been set up to seize the future for the American empire from its Russian rival. Like most of its members, Brzezinski believed that the project team had successfully completed their vital mission. The USA now possessed its own imaginary future for the Cold War propaganda struggle. When the Russians proclaimed the inevitable triumph of cybernetic communism, the Americans would be able to counter them by predicting the imminent arrival of the technetronic society. Crucially, having entered into this media war over which superpower represented the hi-tech destiny of humanity, the USA had to convince the peoples of the world that its imaginary future was more modern

---

[33] See Brzezinski, *Between Two Ages*, page 299.
[34] See Zbigniew Brzezinski, 'America in the Technetronic Age', pages 16–18, 26; *Between Two Ages*, pages 3–5, 9–23, 59–60, 117.
[35] Brzezinski, *Between Two Ages*, page xvi.

than that of the Russian empire. In his book, Brzezinski devoted many pages to proving that Stalinist Communism was an obsolete ideology from the steam age.[36] It was America – not Russia – that was leading humanity towards the post-industrial utopia.

By admitting Marxism's important contribution in the past to the social sciences while carefully avoiding any serious discussion of *Capital*, Brzezinski was able to dismiss this theory as a relic from the industrial past. In its place, McLuhanism was heralded as the up-to-date method for understanding the transition to the information society.[37] This technological determinist approach foretold the direction of social, political and economic changes. Like Licklider, Brzezinski confidently predicted that the global information grid would be fully operational by the mid 1970s.[38] Because of this technological marvel, the treasured policies of the Cold War Left would rapidly spread across the whole world. Echoing Schlesinger, Bell, Rostow and Galbraith, he foresaw rigid ideologies being supplanted by pragmatic solutions. Monolithic parties would be replaced by pressure groups. Class confrontation would give way to partnership between the public and private sectors. Since the USA was the most technologically advanced country on the planet, the rest of the world would inevitably have to imitate what was already happening there. The information society future was an improved and globalised version of the American present.[39]

Despite his best efforts, Brzezinski's attempt to create the master theory of McLuhanism was only partially successful. As Bell pointed out, his writings placed too much emphasis on technological determinism. Excited by the geopolitical significance of the global information grid, Brzezinski had failed to provide a detailed analysis of what the social structure of post-industrialism would look like.[40] More seriously, his appropriation of McLuhan's imaginary future was primarily a celebration of contemporary America. If the USA was to win the propaganda struggle against Russia, its boosters had to offer a much more utopian vision of post-industrialism. Brzezinski's

36 See Brzezinski, *Between Two Ages*, pages 72–75, 77–84, 123–193.
37 See Brzezinski, *Between Two Ages*, pages 72–84, 115–125.
38 See Brzezinski, *Between Two Ages*, pages 32, 59, 299.
39 See Brzezinski, 'America in the Technetronic Age', pages 25–26; *Between Two Ages*, pages 258–265, 274–309.
40 See Daniel Bell, *The Coming of Post-Industrial Society*, pages 38–39.

downplaying of the revolutionary impact of cooperative creativity meant that his limited upgrade of the programme of the Vital Centre was insufficiently futurist to provide an attractive alternative to the prophecy of cybernetic communism. Fortunately for the Cold War Left, Bell had also begun work on his own interpretation of McLuhanism. Beginning with a couple of articles in 1967 and 1968, he devoted himself to writing the important book which would codify the findings of his commission.[41] He would crown his career by becoming the intellectual who had provided the definitive Anti-Communist theory for analysing the social implications of technological convergence. Like Brzezinski, Bell devoted himself to translating the Canadian oracle's inspired hunches into the rational discourse and footnoted evidence of social science. After years of effort, the job was finally finished. In 1973, Bell published the canonical text of the Cold War Left's imaginary future: *The Coming of Post-Industrial Society*.

As soon as it was published, this classic book became the leading academic justification of the McLuhanist prophecy. First and foremost, Bell remained faithful to the theoretical core of *Understanding Media*: information technologies were making the information society. Like McLuhan and Brzezinski, he also claimed that the manufacture of goods was being replaced by the provision of services, national independence was giving way to global interdependence and the new forms of media were creating a new culture.[42] From Licklider's participation in the discussions of his commission, Bell knew that the convergence of computing, media and telecommunications was about to transform the whole of society. By the end of the 1970s at the latest, most American homes and businesses would be connected to the Net and have access to its incredible variety of on-line services. In the same way that the steam engine had produced the industrial era, the computer was building the post-industrial future.

The major social revolution of the latter half of the twentieth century is the attempt to master [the] 'scale' [of political and economic institutions] by new technological devices, whether it

---

[41] See Daniel Bell, 'Notes on the Post-Industrial Society (I)'; 'Notes on the Post-Industrial Society (II)'.

[42] See Bell, 'Notes (I)', pages 27–28; 'Notes (II)', pages 109–111; *The Coming of Post-Industrial Society*, pages 14–15, 126–128, 483–486.

be 'real-time' computer information or new kinds of quantitative programming.[43]

According to Brzezinski, McLuhanism was hard-line technological determinism. The machine was the subject of history. In contrast, Bell wanted to fuse this new orthodoxy with the more familiar theory of economic determinism. Social evolution was a process without a subject. As a leading member of the Cold War Left in the 1950s, Bell had helped to invent the American version of the materialist conception of history. In his iconic book, he applied this Anti-Communist theory to the analysis of post-industrialism. While Brzezinski had identified the technetronic society by its innovative machinery, Bell argued that the new social system should also be identified by its novel economic goals.[44] In his interpretation of McLuhanism, the shift from the production of goods to the provision of services was elevated into the defining feature of the post-industrial future. Under capitalism, both employers and workers were focused upon the accumulation of material wealth. In contrast, the principle activity of the information society would be the creation of knowledge. Scientists in their research laboratories were prefiguring the communal and democratic methods of working of the future. Like its predecessors, this new stage of growth would be built by the class of the new.[45]

In Bell's opinion, there was plenty of evidence that this social transformation was already under way within the United States. In 1962, Fritz Machlup – a German émigré economist – had published detailed statistics showing that the industrial working class was fast disappearing. In its place, bureaucrats and technicians were becoming the most important members of the economy.[46] In his 1967 update of the affluent society thesis, Galbraith had also argued that increased automation and better education led to factory labour being replaced with office jobs. In the same year, Peter Drucker – the founding father of modern management theory – explained that economic development was leading to the rise of a new post-Taylorist producing

---

43 Bell, *Post-Industrial Society*, page 42.
44 See Bell, *Post-Industrial Society*, page 127.
45 See Bell, *Post-Industrial Society*, pages 167–265, 343–345, 378–386. For the precursors of Bell's analysis, see Richard Barbrook, *The Class of the New*.
46 See Fritz Machlup, *The Production and Distribution of Knowledge in the United States*.

class: the 'knowledge workers'.[47] Building on this research, Bell created pages of tables for his great tome proving that manual labour was giving way to mental labour, the production of things was being superseded by the provision of services and an increasing proportion of the wages bill was devoted to scientific research.[48] As Burnham, Galbraith, Rostow and Drucker had explained, this shift in employment patterns had begun with the rise of Fordism. Bell now claimed that this transformation was accelerating as the US economy moved into the next stage of growth. The computerisation of production would soon remove the need for most forms of physical labour. By extrapolating from recent history, it was obvious that the white-collar employees of Fordism were the precursors of the paramount social group of post-industrialism: the *knowledge class*.[49] 'If the dominant figures of the past hundred years have been the entrepreneur, the businessman and the industrial executive, the "new men" are the scientists, the mathematicians, the economists and the engineers of the new intellectual technology.'[50]

In their remixes of *Understanding Media*, Brzezinski and Bell had transformed McLuhan's flights of imagination into sober academic analysis. Inspired by Licklider, they had proved that the Net was the demiurgic machine. Drawing on the latest research, they had examined the social and economic impact of post-industrialism in much greater depth. Yet, their pages of theoretical discussions, detailed statistics and meticulous footnotes were just the background detail for their initial leap of faith: new information technologies were creating a new social system. Despite Brzezinski and Bell's refusal to acknowledge their mentor, both of them remained completely dependent upon McLuhan's oracular pronouncements. The Cold War Left had lacked an imaginary future of its own so it had been forced to borrow one from somebody else. Although McLuhan's ecstatic visions had provided the Anti-Communist alternative to cybernetic communism, the credibility of his speculations was undermined by the unorthodox methodology which had allowed

---

[47] See Galbraith, *New Industrial State*, pages 238–250; and Peter Drucker, *The Effective Executive*, pages 3–4.

[48] See Bell, *Post-Industrial Society*, pages 16–19, 130–142, 212–265.

[49] See Bell, *Post-Industrial Society*, pages 27–33, 167–265. Also see Barbrook, *Class of the New*.

[50] Bell, *Post-Industrial Society*, page 344.

him to foresee the shape of things to come. Remixing *Understanding Media* was essential to ensuring that the flaky intellectual origins of the information society prophecy were kept well hidden. Thanks to Brzezinski and Bell, it was now possible to be a McLuhanist without having to quote McLuhan.

For the Cold War Left, *Understanding Media* had endowed the American empire with a transcendental goal: post-industrialism. The greatest blessing of McLuhanism was that the class struggle played no part in the creation of this utopian future. Because the new society would be made in the image of the new media, social emancipation could arrive without any conscious human intervention. By elevating Bell's remix of McLuhan into the canonical text for analysing the transition to the future, American academics were also able to recuperate Marx's historical materialism. The dangerous ideas had been dismissed as anachronisms from the steam-powered industrial past. The harmless concepts had been repackaged for the computerised post-industrial future. Above all, there was no longer any need to read subversive books like *Capital*, as the founders of the Cold War Left had done in their youth. McLuhanism without McLuhan explained why Marx had been removed from Marxism. What was worth saving from his ideas had been incorporated within Bell's theoretical masterpiece. For patriotic American intellectuals, everything that they needed to know about the future evolution of humanity could be found in the learned sentences and detailed diagrams of *The Coming of Post-Industrial Society*.

By the early 1970s, the Cold War Left's reworking of McLuhan had spawned its own academic discipline: futurology. Equipped with their canonical texts as a theoretical guide, Brzezinski and Bell's disciples confidently wrote articles, spoke at conferences and taught courses about what had not yet happened.[51] This self-assurance was founded upon their gurus' clear vision of the information society. In *Understanding Media*, McLuhan had only given a vague idea of what the global village would look like. In contrast, the Bell commission had promoted a positive description of the post-industrial future. The promises of cybernetic communism could only be countered by turning them into creations of the information society. Above all,

---

51 See Irving Louis Horowitz, *Ideology and Utopia in the United States*, pages 113–130; and William Kuhns, *The Post-Industrial Prophets*, pages 247–261.

as one of their key arguments, the team's publications emphasised that – if you looked carefully enough – the shape of things to come could already be discerned within contemporary America. In *The Coming of Post-Industrial Society*, Bell argued that the managerial and academic employees of Fordism were already working within a post-industrial economy. What was ultra-modern in 1960s America was a premonition of what life would be like in the 2000s.

More than any other institution, the Bell commission believed that the university was the forerunner of the information society. Ever since the 1940s, higher education had been a boom sector of the US economy. For the Cold War Left, the university had long been the epitome of the third way. With their income coming from a variety of public and private sources, American campuses combined the best features of the state and the market.[52] According to Brzezinski and Bell, these universities were also precursors of the future information society in the present. Their students were acquiring the skills needed to join the knowledge class. Their social scientists were using computers to analyse current problems and predict future developments. Their research labs were inventing most of the new information technologies.[53] Above all, academics were the quintessential members of the emerging knowledge class: makers of ideas not things. When the futurologists wanted to know what post-industrialism would be like, they just had to look out of their office windows and envisage the whole of society remodelled as a giant campus.

> Perhaps it is not too much to say that if the business firm was the key institution of the past hundred years, because of its role in organising production for the mass creation of products, the university will become the central institution of the next hundred years because of its role as the new source of innovation and knowledge.[54]

This imaginary future appealed to an influential and appreciative audience within Cold War America. As well as the large numbers

[52] See Galbraith, *New Industrial State*, pages 367–368, 372–378; and Clark Kerr, *The Uses of the University*, pages 29–41.
[53] See Bell, *Towards the Year 2000*, page 6, 32, 342–344; *The Coming of Post-Industrial Society*, pages 116–117, 212–265, 409–411, 423; and Brzezinski, *Between Two Ages*, pages 200–205.
[54] Bell, 'Notes (I)', page 30.

of people who were studying or working at universities, a growing proportion of the population were graduates from these institutions. As Machlup and Bell emphasised in their studies, a degree had become the prerequisite of advancement within the managerial hierarchies of big business and big government.[55] It was very flattering for white-collar workers to be told that they were the hope of the future rather than the factory labourers. Within the rapidly expanding media, telecommunications and computing sectors, the prophecy of post-industrialism had even more resonance. Their employees were delighted when they were praised as builders of the hi-tech future. Just as the factory had been the icon of industrialism for their grandparents, the university was the symbol of post-industrialism for these modern Americans.

The Cold War Left's prophets were eager to lead the emerging knowledge class into the computer paradise. Contradicting their own theoretical assertion that technology was the subject of history, these intellectuals saw themselves as the moving spirits of the transition to the utopian future. Echoing the Communist reformers in the East, they believed that only their select band possessed the social knowledge which could successfully guide humanity during the 20 years that it would take to reach the promised land. Like inspirational entrepreneurs in the early days of capitalism, they were the leaders of the new class which was inventing the new methods of working and new ways of living. Their multi-disciplinary research teams were already showing how ideas would be produced in the post-industrial future. Their colleagues were directing the academic institutions which would become the powerhouses of the information society. Their tastes and aspirations would inspire the culture of post-industrialism. Like the Fabians in late-Victorian England, the Cold War Left was developing new government policies for successfully managing the transition into the next stage of modernity. Above all, the gurus of the movement were writing the canonical texts that defined the shape of things to come. Like the theorists of the Leninist vanguard party, their unique understanding of the grand narrative of modernity had given them leadership over the social group which embodied the promise of universal emancipation.

---

55 See Machlup, *The Production and Distribution of Knowledge in the United States*, pages 77–100; and Bell, *Post-Industrial Society*, pages 213–242.

Under the firm direction of the Cold War Left, the knowledge class would spend the next two decades building the imaginary future of post-industrialism.

In 1930s Russian propaganda, the dedicated party militant had been celebrated as the Nietzschean 'New Man' of the Stalinist utopia.[56] Thirty years later, the thinkers of the Cold War Left now proclaimed themselves as the ideal citizens of America's global village. Cosmopolitan and sophisticated, the members of this movement combined the liberal virtues of education, tolerance and enquiry with the modern advantages of jet aeroplanes, colour television, long-distance telephony and mainframe computers. Although only a few intellectuals enjoyed this privileged existence in the present, everyone would be able to live like them in the post-industrial future. The gurus of the Cold War Left had discovered the embryo of the new society in their own academic workplaces. They themselves were already living in the imaginary future of post-industrialism. They were the cybernetic vanguard of the class of the new. Having seen the prototype of the American hi-tech utopia, it was now their mission to preach the good news to the expectant peoples of the world: the First Coming of the Net Messiah.

[56] See Bernice Rosenthal, *New Myth, New World*, pages 233–350; and Henri Lefebvre, *Introduction to Modernity*, pages 84–85.

12

THE LEADER OF THE FREE WORLD

During the 1950s, the Cold War Left became the mentors of a new generation of ambitious young American scholars. Encouraged by government subsidies, the top US universities had embarked upon a rapid expansion of their social science departments. For go-getting academics and students in these institutions, the third way philosophy of the Cold War Left provided an up-to-date and sophisticated replacement for the tired old ideologies of laissez-faire liberalism and Stalinist socialism. This intellectual ascendancy at home was the movement's reward for its outstanding services to the US state in Western Europe. The mentors of the new generation of American social scientists had won their prominent positions within the nation's ruling class by winning a decisive round in the ideological struggle against Stalinism on the partitioned continent. Inside its sphere of influence, the American empire had encountered few problems in winning the loyalty of local elites and conservative voters. Looking at what was happening in Eastern Europe, it was obvious that Stalinism threatened the greatest achievements of bourgeois civilisation: civil rights, the rule of law and political pluralism. More importantly, the US military and the CIA were defending the property of the privileged against expropriation by either Russian invaders or home-grown radicals.

What was much more difficult to achieve was persuading the Left to collaborate with American hegemony over Western Europe. For any self-respecting socialist in the late 1940s, the USA was still – despite its major contribution to the defeat of fascism – the imperialist enforcer of capitalist exploitation. Yet, within a few years, this negative image of America had been successfully overturned. Funded by the CIA, the Cold War Left had organised a propaganda campaign to re-brand the United States as the friend of progressive causes: the Congress for Cultural Freedom (CCF). Like many other aspects of the movement, this initiative had its origins in American Trotskyism. Back in the late 1930s, a group of New York activists had set up the prototype of the CCF to protest against the Stalinist persecution of modern art.[1] In solidarity with this new organisation, Leon Trotsky himself had helped André Breton – the

---

[1] This first iteration of the CCF was called the *Committee* for Cultural Freedom. See Judy Kutulas, *The Long War*, pages 154–163; and Alan Wald, *The New York Intellectuals*, pages 139–147.

French 'pope' of Surrealism – and Diego Rivera – the Mexican Communist muralist – to write an impassioned defence of the role of avant-garde experimentation in the revolutionary struggle.[2] However, by the mid 1940s, the founders of the CCF had become disillusioned with Trotskyism. As had happened with Burnham, their opposition to Russian totalitarianism soon reconciled them with American capitalism. In an opening move of the Cold War, these ex-Trotskyists worked with the US intelligence services to disrupt a cultural conference held by Stalinist sympathisers in New York. Emboldened by this success, they decided to revive the CCF with money provided by the newly founded CIA. The Trotskyist Left had evolved into the Cold War Left.[3]

While its predecessor had been designed to attack domestic apologists of the Russian regime, this new iteration of the CCF was – right from the outset – focused upon the propaganda struggle inside Western Europe. In stark contrast with the political situation in America, Stalinism had emerged from the Second World War as the dominant force on the Left across most of the continent. The Russian army had won the military victory over Nazi Germany. Communists had led the most effective resistance movements in occupied Europe. Well before most of the US elite, the organisers of the CCF had – as ex-Trotskyists – realised that this mass support for the Stalinist Left threatened American hegemony over Western Europe. In those countries where their Social Democratic rivals had been severely weakened by war and fascism, the Communists now provided the only credible alternative to the traditional order.[4] Among both workers and intellectuals, the Stalinist movement had come to embody the imaginary future of proletarian communism in the present. In 1948, the Czechoslovak Communist Party had been able to destroy parliamentary democracy because it had won the most seats in the 1946 parliamentary elections. Backed by the well-organised support of a large section of the population, Russian sympathisers were also in a position to seize control of countries like

[2] For their 'Manifesto: Towards a Free Revolutionary Art', see Leon Trotsky, *Art and Revolution*, pages 115–121.
[3] See Frances Stonor Saunders, *Who Paid the Piper?* pages 45–56; and S.A. Longstaff, 'The New York Intellectuals and the Cultural Cold War 1945–1950'.
[4] The Communist Party won 26 per cent of the popular vote in the 1945 French elections. See Serge Halimi, *Sisyphus est Fatigué*, page 251.

France and Italy without any need for direct intervention by their superpower sponsor. If the US government didn't act quickly, the Cold War would be lost in Europe almost before it had started. Soft power was about to trump hard power.[5]

In the late 1940s, the American empire formed military alliances and provided economic subsidies to consolidate its control over the western half of the continent. As the partition lines hardened, the propaganda battle between the superpower rivals became ever more intense. Despite its economic and military superiority, the USA's favourable position on the continent was endangered by the suspicion of American intentions among the European Left. At this moment of crisis, the former Marxists of the CCF came to the rescue. Unlike conservative Americans, they possessed the skills to persuade left-wing Europeans to reject Stalinism. With CIA money and advice from US media companies, the CCF embarked on an ambitious programme of publishing books, setting up magazines, making radio broadcasts, hosting conferences and sponsoring art exhibitions. Just like its 1930s Communist antecedents, this front organisation was devoted to the promotion of a single idea. But, instead of praising Stalinism, the CCF used Stalinist techniques to expose the hypocrisy of Stalinism.[6] 'The United States, as against the Communists, has a peculiar potential advantage in mass propaganda. ... United States propaganda could be, and would benefit by being, for the most part true, or close to the truth.'[7]

In the same way that Stalinist parties had created their own cultural milieu, the CCF also set out to build its own space within the minds of the West European Left. Ideology had to become common sense. European radicals must become convinced that American capitalism was much more equalitarian, progressive and democratic than Russian socialism. Not surprisingly, the stars of the CCF were the American founders of the Cold War Left. As the conduit for CIA funds, Burnham politically dominated the organisation until he stormed out in a rage in the early 1950s. Schlesinger's *The*

5 See James Burnham, *The Coming Defeat of Communism*, pages 182–195; and Wald, *New York Intellectuals*, pages 267–280. For the tragedy of the Stalinist takeover of Czechoslovakia, see John Bloomfield, *Passive Revolution*.

6 See Burnham, *Defeat of Communism*, pages 165–181; Saunders, *Who Paid the Piper?* pages 85–278; and Giles Scott-Smith, 'The Organising of Intellectual Consensus (Part 1)'.

7 James Burnham, *The Struggle for the World*, page 178.

Vital Center became the manifesto of its propaganda offensive. Bell promoted his end-of-ideology thesis at CCF conferences and in its media outlets during the late 1950s.[8] Although almost openly funded by the CIA, the CCF kept up the pretence that it was an independent initiative of concerned American intellectuals. In the looking-glass world of the Cold War, the Left and the Right had become almost indistinguishable.

As in other CIA missions, the best proof of success was the turning of enemy agents. In CCF-sponsored books such as *I Chose Freedom* and *The God That Failed*, former believers in the false Russian utopia publicly repented the sins of their Leninist past.[9] From such celebrated texts, the Cold War Left created an Anti-Communist catechism. Modern socialists knew – if Social Democracy in Western Europe had to choose between socialism and democracy – that Fordist democracy was preferable to Stalinist socialism. Given what was happening in the Russian half of the continent, the success of the CCF's propaganda offensive was almost inevitable. Needing liberal freedoms to protect socialist and trade union activism, the majority of the Left in Western Europe had good reason to fear the Stalinist enemy in the East. At the outbreak of the Cold War in 1948, George Orwell – who later, once he was safely dead, became the CCF's favourite socialist novelist – explained the predicament of the British Labour Party:

> From the point of view of the Russians and the Communists, Social Democracy is a deadly enemy ... The reason is clear enough. Social Democracy, unlike capitalism, offers an alternative to Communism. ... It will not do to give the usual quibbling answer, 'I refuse to choose [between Russia and America].' ... We are no longer strong enough to stand alone, and, if we fail to bring a western European union into being, we shall be obliged, in the long run, to subordinate our policy to one Great Power or the other. And ... everyone [on the left-wing of the Labour Party] knows in his [or her] heart that we should choose America. The great mass of [the British] people ... would make this choice almost instinctively.[10]

---

[8] See Saunders, *Who Paid the Piper?* page 63; and Scott-Smith, 'Intellectual Consensus (Part 2)', pages 19–20.

[9] See Victor Kravchenko, *I Chose Freedom*; and Richard Crossman, *The God That Failed*.

[10] George Orwell, 'In Defence of Comrade Zilliacus', pages 451, 453.

The CCF helped to transform this short-term tactical alliance into a long-term strategic dependency. The Cold War Left shared the same intellectual and political background as the West European Left. Under its guidance, open-minded socialists soon discovered the American third way to modernity beyond tooth-and-claw capitalism and Leninist totalitarianism. After three disastrous decades of wars, genocide and economic collapse, the ideology of the end of ideology seemed very attractive to large numbers of people within the West European Left. In 1956, Tony Crosland – a former admirer of Stalinist Russia – produced the key text which explained how the consensual politics of the Vital Centre could be successfully adapted for the other side of the Atlantic: *The Future of Socialism*. First and foremost, this prominent member of the British Labour Party dismissed Russian Marxism as an anachronism. In its place, American third-way theorising was praised as the up-to-date analysis of society.[11] The political implications of his switch in doctrinal loyalties were clear. Class struggle and ideological extremism were no longer relevant. Social partnership and status politics were the only ways forward.[12] Since the Russian system had lost its allure, the West European Left must instead imitate the modernity of America: consumer prosperity, class mobility, mass education and economic efficiency.[13] By setting this new goal, Crosland transformed the political purpose of Social Democratic reforms. Far from being a transitory stage on the route towards proletarian communism, the building of a cultured and tolerant version of US-style welfare Fordism was now an end in itself. Not surprisingly, the CCF enthusiastically promoted Crosland's flattering analysis at its events and in its publications. By the end of the decade, his European remix of the third way had become the new orthodoxy of parliamentary socialism. At its 1959 Bad Godesberg conference, the German Social Democratic Party – the party founded by Marx's inner circle – publicly renounced its allegiance to Marxism.[14] The West European Left had been a diligent student of its American teacher.

11 See Anthony Crosland, *The Future of Socialism*, pages 2–7, 23–26, 60–69, 104–133, 325–327.
12 See Crosland, *Future of Socialism*, pages 29–42, 76–80, 111–122, 328–340.
13 See Crosland, *Future of Socialism*, pages 151, 155–159, 179–187, 195–207, 248–251.
14 See Social Democratic Party, 'Basic Programme of the Social Democratic Party of Germany'.

Any Social Democrats who doubted their party's allegiance to the USA only had to look at the fate of their comrades in the Stalinist East. Like the colonies of the old European empires, the nations inside the Russian sphere of influence were in thrall to a foreign despotism. Dissident socialists and trade union activists were murdered, tortured and imprisoned. Even the leaders of the East European satellites who were too independent-minded ran the risk of becoming victims of show trials.[15] The death of Stalin in 1953 eased conditions, but it didn't end the repression. When Hungarian workers and students rose in revolt in 1956 against their Stalinist oppressors, the Russian army ruthlessly crushed their revolution. The blatant contradiction between this authoritarian reality and the libertarian promises of proletarian communism was a propaganda gift for the CCF. Far from being the workers' state, the Stalinist system had proved itself to be the dictatorship against the proletariat.

By exposing the crimes of Russia in the East, the CCF emphasised the advantages for the Left of collaborating with the American rulers of the West. Socialists inside the US sphere of influence could not only campaign openly, but also, in some countries, form the government. The USA even publicly supported some of the most cherished dreams of the European Left. During the Time of Troubles of the mid twentieth century, both Social Democrats and Communists had advocated the unification of the continent as the progressive alternative to the belligerent rivalry of autarchic nationalisms. When the Cold War started in the late 1940s, the American empire proclaimed itself as the new champion of this Left arcadia. Under its sponsorship, the nations inside the US sphere of influence were already being bound together through military alliances and economic agreements: NATO and the Common Market. Promoting Rostow's analysis of this process, CCF propaganda emphasised that America provided the most progressive model for the eventual political unification of Europe. The future of socialism lay to the West not in the East.[16]

Following the example of its first incarnation, the Cold War Left's CCF also advanced its political cause by championing artistic

---

[15] See François Fejtö, *A History of the People's Democracies*, pages 7–25.

[16] For the CIA's funding of the European federalist movement, see Richard Aldrich, *The Hidden Hand*, pages 342–370.

modernism. As its name suggested, denouncing the absence of cultural freedom was an effective method of exposing the political failings of Stalinism. This strategy had originally been developed in the late 1930s to discredit the apologists of Russian totalitarianism within New York's intellectual community. When the first CCF was founded, both Trotskyist militants and modernist artists in America had been convinced that political radicalism and cultural experimentation were inseparable. But, by the time that its second iteration was set up, this assumption was no longer valid. Like their Trotskyist comrades, the cultural bohemians were now also part of the establishment. During the early 1940s, the advocates of modernism had become the arbiters of the New York art world. Backed by important public and private patrons, they had founded the first authentically American avant-garde movement: Abstract Expressionism.[17] When the CCF was reborn, these artistic modernists had once again joined forces with their left-wing political friends to protest against the iniquities of Stalinist censorship. Despite the similarity of its rhetoric, the second version of this cultural campaign had a very different political goal. In its exhibitions and publications, the CCF celebrated Jackson Pollock, Mark Rothko and the other stars of Abstract Expressionism as symbols of the US elite's devotion to individual freedom. Instead of serving the socialist revolution, the avant-garde was now working for American imperialism.[18]

In their Trotskyist youth, the founders of the Cold War Left had – correctly – identified artistic modernism with the moment of utopian creativity unleashed by the 1917 Russian Revolution. Yet, by the end of the 1940s, they had succeeded in breaking the historical link between Communist politics and avant-garde aesthetics. Ironically, it was the cultural policies of the Russian state which had created the opportunity for the recuperation of modernism by its superpower rival. In the late 1920s and early 1930s, the Stalinist dictatorship had ruthlessly crushed the artistic avant-garde and revived the aesthetics of the old regime with a new message: Socialist Realism.[19] Since the Russians had been foolish enough to abandon

17 See Clement Greenberg, *Art and Culture;* and Serge Guilbaut, *How New York Stole the Idea of Modern Art,* pages 49–124.
18 See Saunders, *Who Paid the Piper?* pages 213–278; and Guilbaut, *Modern Art,* pages 139–194.
19 See John Bowlt, *Russian Art of the Avant-Garde,* pages 265–297.

modernism, the Cold War Left gleefully seized its democratic hi-tech imagery for the West. When the first CCF championed this avant-garde aesthetic, the new style had only appealed to a select few. But, by the time that this organisation was revived, these former Trotskyists had become important players within the US elite. Aided by their powerful patrons, they repackaged modernist aesthetics as the celebration of American modernity. Stripped of its subversive politics, the iconography of this avant-garde was popularised by the dream factories of New York and Hollywood. From architecture to furniture, Communist modernism became the house style of American Fordism.

For the CCF, the image of a vibrant and innovative culture across the Atlantic was a powerful weapon in its ideological struggle against Stalinism in Western Europe. America was no longer a nation of philistines. Instead it had become the spiritual home of the emerging knowledge class. New York had replaced Paris as the capital of the art world. Even the cultural rebels were made-in-the-USA. However oppositional, cool jazz and beat poetry proved that artistic creativity was flourishing in America. The CCF's propaganda hammered home the political message of this cultural renaissance: modernity came from the West not the East. Far from threatening its core values, American hegemony was beneficial for European civilisation. The best of the old was being combined with the best of the new.

The CCF's emphasis on high culture was designed to impress the educated minority among the West European Left. Even when they had been Trotskyists, the Cold War Left had distrusted the tastes of the majority of the working class. As the leaders of the new knowledge class, this avant-garde elite fought against not only the crudities of Stalinist totalitarianism, but also the banality of popular culture.[20] Yet, at the same time, the CCF itself was a beneficiary of the mass media whose social effects were so strongly deplored in its publications. During the 1950s, it was Hollywood movies and rock 'n' roll music that made by far the greatest contribution in securing American hegemony over Western Europe. Crucially, these populist art forms appealed to the rank and file supporters of the Left. As working-class incomes rose, increasing numbers of

[20] See Michael Wreszin, *A Rebel in Defence of Tradition*, pages 325–326.

people imitated the fashions and lifestyles of the world's first affluent society across the Atlantic. Nowhere were the ambiguities of this democratic popular culture more pronounced than in the impact of rock 'n' roll upon the youth of 1950s Europe. On the one hand, its American stars symbolised libertarian rebellion against patriarchal authority and moral conformity. On the other hand, its musicians encouraged admiration of the conformist consumer lifestyle of the Cold War master. Elvis Presley – the 'king of rock 'n' roll' – not only shocked the old folks with his sexy hip movements, but also loyally did a highly publicised tour of duty with the US Army in West Germany.[21]

The CCF thrived in a historical moment when pop stars were in the frontline of global geopolitics. At the end of earlier Times of Troubles, the new Universal State had restored peace and prosperity by conquering the known world. For Burnham, the lesson of Toynbee's historical analysis had been clear: America should liberate all of Europe and Asia from Russian totalitarianism.[22] Yet, ironically, his impassioned Anti-Communist writings soon became the founding texts of a very different world system: the armed peace of the Cold War. This new global order began as a diplomatic compromise designed to put an end to the imperial rivalries which had – for three traumatic decades – inflicted misery and destruction upon the peoples of the planet. In the closing months of the Second World War, US President Franklin Roosevelt and the Russian dictator Joseph Stalin had met at the Ukrainian seaside resort of Yalta to finalise the succession to the defunct British empire. As their first task, the non-European superpowers had to resolve the fate of Europe.[23]

The two wartime allies quickly decided to divide the troublesome continent between them: the Yalta Agreement. Almost by accident, they had discovered a mutually beneficial solution. Under American and Russian occupation, the fratricidal Europeans were prevented from starting any more wars. What proved to be more difficult was agreeing on the exact demarcation of the truce line between

21 See George Melly, *Revolt into Style*, pages 36–47; and Jeff Nuttall, *Bomb Culture*, pages 11–36.
22 See Burnham, *Struggle for the World*, pages 42–55, 181–199, 242–248; *Defeat of Communism*, pages 135–148, 208–221, 272–278.
23 See Jeremy Isaacs and Taylor Dowling, *Cold War*, pages 11–19.

their two spheres of influence. Soon both sides were claiming that the other had failed to respect the terms of the Yalta Agreement.[24] However, neither America nor Russia had any intention of escalating their quarrel into a shooting war in Europe. Beginning in Germany, the two superpowers turned the temporary borders of the Yalta Agreement into a permanent frontier: the 'Iron Curtain'. In place of the British empire, two Universal States now shared the task of policing the planet. Permanent confrontation was the precondition of mutual collaboration. War was Peace.

> In the past, the ruling groups of all countries ... did fight against one another, and the victor plundered the vanquished. In our own day, they are not fighting against each other at all. The war is waged by each ruling group against its own subjects, and the object is not to make or prevent conquests of territory, but to keep the structure of society intact.[25]

As was tragically demonstrated during the 1945–50 Greek Civil War and the 1956 Hungarian Revolution, America and Russia had no compunction about using extreme violence when it was the most effective method for advancing their imperial interests in Europe. Yet, at the same time, both superpowers benefited from the maintenance of political and social stability within their spheres of influence. As the Cold War became everyday normality, military violence was transubstantiated into a media spectacle. Hard power had become soft power. Avoiding an all-or-nothing confrontation in Europe now depended upon the masses believing in the nightmare of atomic Armageddon. At the same time, because the nuclear arms race was – as a military strategy – literally MAD, America and Russia also had to prevent this irrational form of realpolitik from inspiring rebellious thoughts of pacifism and defeatism among the citizens of their satellites.[26] In Cold War propaganda, the superpower confrontation was endowed with the highest aspirations of humanity: democracy, justice and equality. The survival of the species wasn't being put at risk over a petty territorial dispute between two greedy empires. On the contrary, America and Russia were engaged in

[24] See W.W. Rostow, *The United States in the World Arena*, pages 101–118, 128–131, 177–188.

[25] George Orwell, *Nineteen Eighty-Four*, page 161.

[26] See Nuttall, *Bomb Culture*, pages 42–65.

a world-historical struggle to decide the destiny of humanity. According to the doublethink logic of the Cold War, the essence of freedom was voluntary submission to an imperialist superpower.

In the early 1950s, the Congress for Cultural Freedom was a pioneering institution of this new world order in the American half of Europe. Over on the other side of the Iron Curtain, a monolithic ideology was indoctrinated – with mixed results – into the minds of the masses. Totalitarian Communism was proclaimed as the one and only path to proletarian communism. In contrast with this insistence on political and ideological uniformity, American hegemony thrived amongst heterogeneity and pluralism. The US-led Free World in Europe included Imperial Britain, Social Democratic Scandinavia, Catholic Italy, heterodox Stalinist Yugoslavia and Fascist Spain. The CCF provided the American grand narrative of modernity which united these satellites in their diversity. After terrifying them with nuclear nightmares, their citizens were seduced with promises of consumer prosperity and hi-tech futures. Political consensus, class compromise and efficient management at home would guarantee international cooperation and global peace. Under benevolent US guidance, the nations of Western Europe were steadily progressing through the stages of growth towards mass consumption and continental unity. Their long-term destiny was to become prosperous suburbs of the global city of the information society. The future of Europe was America.

13

THE GREAT GAME

The Cold War Left was convinced that the information-society prophecy had dramatically shifted the international balance of power in America's favour. Marxism had been exposed as a defunct steam-age ideology. This meant that – for the first time since the 1917 Revolution – Russia had lost ownership of the future. In the new computer age, the United States was the vanguard of human progress. With its well-funded universities, it was the homeland of the emerging knowledge class. With its scientific expertise, it was building the prototype of the Net. There was no doubt that America was the only nation capable of leading humanity towards the post-industrial global village. Within Western Europe, the USA no longer had to rely solely upon military might and economic supremacy to protect its interests. The majority of West Europeans had happily succumbed to American cultural hegemony: 'coca-colonisation'. Hard power had been upgraded into soft power. Not surprisingly, the CCF – and their CIA backers – believed that their psychological operations had played the decisive role in winning the hearts and minds of the peoples within the US sphere of influence. As former Leninists, the leaders of the Cold War Left were convinced that a vanguard of committed intellectuals had the power to shape the minds of the masses. The CCF had taken on the Stalinists on this all-important ideological battlefield – and decisively defeated them. But, at the same time, their Marxist training also told them that cultural hegemony was founded upon the USA's political and economic ascendancy. In Western Europe, Social Democrats benefited from the popularising of the CCF's geopolitical message: the dilution of national independence was a progressive step. Pragmatic self-interest had been endowed with world-historical significance.[1]

By the mid 1950s, the leaders of parliamentary socialism had realised that American rule also delivered full employment and rising living standards for their voters. As its decisive opening move in the Cold War, the US government had kick-started the revival of the Western European economy with a Keynesian programme of generous subsidies and cheap credit. America's half of the continent

[1] One historian of the CCF stressed that 'it is important to recognise that the CIA involvement was centred on the promotion and manipulation of existing viewpoints on the Left [in Western Europe] ... and not the creation of them out of thin air'. Giles Scott-Smith, 'The Organising of Intellectual Consensus (Part 1)', page 8.

was once again open for business.² Within a few years, US companies and banks had taken a leading role within the various economies of Western Europe. From then onwards, their subsidiaries – and their local imitators – led the transition to welfare Fordism.³ Economic prosperity had a dramatic social impact. For millennia, the rich had been the principle arbiters of taste within Europe. In contrast, the icons of US-style Fordism were mass-produced commodities for sale to everyone: motor cars, T-shirts, jeans, hamburgers, cigarettes, fridges, washing machines and rock 'n' roll records. Not surprisingly, a growing proportion of the electorate of the West European socialist parties became enthralled by American popular culture. Across the Atlantic, workers enjoyed high wages, secure jobs, good education and class mobility. When the dream of the West European proletariat was to live the American dream, Social Democratic politicians welcomed the third way ideology which explained why the Left could manage welfare Fordism in the interests of the voters better than the Right.

During the 1950s, one commodity above all others symbolised the arrival of the US-style affluent society: the TV set. Like the radio in the 1920s, this new media technology very quickly went from being a luxury to a necessity. Watching television soon became the most important activity after working and sleeping. Being a member of the TV audience was the primary collective experience. National politics and international rivalries were now played out on the television screen. Production and consumption were harmonised through TV advertising campaigns. The latest fads and technological breakthroughs were hyped. Modern lifestyles were praised. Above all, television provided entertainment for a mass audience. After a hard day's labour, the reward was sitting down to watch the box. Even if they weren't as well paid as Americans, West European workers still experienced the same fantasy world of glamour, prosperity, adventure and celebrity for a few hours each evening. Fordism had democratised capitalism.⁴

²See W.W. Rostow, *The United States in the World Arena*, pages 214–217; and Kees van der Pilj, *The Making of an Atlantic Ruling Class*, pages 138–177.
³See Jean-Jacques Servan-Schreiber, *The American Challenge*, pages 17–67; and van der Pilj, *Atlantic Ruling Class*, pages 178–195.
⁴See Guy Debord, *Society of the Spectacle*, theses 1–54; and Raymond Williams, *Television*, pages 19–31, 44–118.

When the CCF had launched their propaganda offensive against Stalinism in late-1940s Western Europe, their task seemed daunting. Far from being identified with affluence and democracy, capitalism was held responsible for the sufferings of the previous three decades: war, fascism, genocide, poverty and mass unemployment. However, as the West European economies successfully moved from laissez-faire liberalism to welfare Fordism, public attitudes gradually began to change. By the mid 1950s, the programme of the Vital Centre had been vindicated. American capitalism had proved itself to be politically and economically superior to Russian socialism. In the late 1940s and early 1950s, the CIA had engaged in 'dirty tricks' to prevent the French and Italian Communist Parties winning elections. By splitting the Left vote, the CIA succeeded in not only stopping the Stalinists from taking power, but also closing off the neutralist option. At this moment of crisis at the outbreak of the Cold War, covert operations had played a decisive role in stabilising America's rule over its half of the continent.[5] However, what turned this short-term victory into long-term ascendancy was the economic revival of the region. The CIA might have financed the CCF to manipulate the West European Left in the interests of the American empire, but the parliamentary socialist parties embraced the new faith because they wanted to win votes from an increasingly prosperous electorate. In place of its own interpretation of Marxism, Social Democracy now had the ideology of the end of ideology to distinguish itself from Communism.

By the early 1960s, the leading nations of Western Europe had almost completed the transition to Fordism. Building on its success in the previous decade, the Cold War Left began promoting post-industrialism as the next made-in-the-USA stage of growth for these satellites to imitate. When they watched television, West Europeans were already living partially within the information society. When the TV news bulletins covered superpower summits and United Nations meetings, the continent's electronic media were prefiguring the global village in the present. Thanks to McLuhanism, the Bell commission was now able to project the social impact of television in the 1960s forward into the imaginary future. The accelerating

5 See William Blum, *Killing Hope*, pages 27–39, 61–64 104–108; and Rhodri Jeffreys-Jones, *The CIA and American Democracy*, pages 49–53.

convergence of media, telecommunications and computing would unleash changes as important in human history as the industrial revolution. The demiurge of the Net was going to liberate humanity without any need for class struggles. Camouflaged by Anti-Communist theory, the information society prophecy had become the American substitute for cybernetic communism. In place of the Leninist vanguard party, the McLuhanist knowledge class was now leading humanity towards the glittering future of participatory democracy and cooperative creativity. As the owner of time, the USA had maintained its control over the space of Western Europe.

In his classic 1916 pamphlet *Imperialism*, Lenin had warned that the twentieth century was the epoch of endless war and economic stagnation.[6] Yet, with remarkable speed, the US elite had succeeded in constructing a new – and more advanced – imperial system on the ruins of the old one. In the 1945 Yalta Agreement, America and Russia had divided the defeated continent between them. Under their joint hegemony, peace and prosperity finally returned to Europe after 30 years of chaos. At the Yalta conference, the two superpowers had also inadvertently created a framework for global governance. Because Western Europe and Japan had fallen inside its sphere of influence, the US elite was convinced that it had inherited responsibility for their defunct colonial empires. However, as the heir of the 1776 Revolution, the American government had no desire to repeat the mistakes of these failed imperialists. Occupying other people's countries wasn't only immoral, but also, even worse, extremely expensive.[7] Back in the early nineteenth century, the British had proved that the world system could be successfully run along more liberal lines. When the Royal Navy had policed the oceans and the City of London had regulated the global financial system, free trade created 'perpetual peace' between the peoples of the world. Instead of fighting against each other, nations traded with each other.[8] By specialising within the global marketplace, every region on the planet became more prosperous.[9] As scientific

---

[6] See V.I. Lenin, *Imperialism*, page 147.
[7] See Andrew Bacevich, *American Empire*, pages 7–31.
[8] See Immanuel Kant, 'To Perpetual Peace'.
[9] See David Ricardo, *The Principles of Political Economy*, pages 77–93.

knowledge advanced, new technologies like railways, steamships and telegraphy brought the citizens of the world together. Best of all for its American admirers, England had been the dominant power in this liberal global system without the expense and traumas of running a vast colonial empire: *the imperialism of free trade.*[10]

At the end of the Second World War, the consensus among the US elite blamed the breakdown of the British-run system of global liberalism for precipitating three decades of death and destruction.[11] Crucially, the Truman administration was convinced that this disaster could have been avoided. Lenin's and Toynbee's analyses of imperialism were far too pessimistic. At the end of the First World War, US President Woodrow Wilson had tried to rebuild the shattered global economy on more democratic principles, but he had been thwarted by short-sighted opposition at home and abroad.[12] Thirty years later, the Truman administration knew that it could succeed where its predecessor had failed. After another global conflagration, the Republican Party had finally realised that America couldn't shirk its international responsibilities. More importantly, the USA's imperial rivals had all been severely weakened by the war. With the only undamaged industrial base and the largest armed forces in the world, the dominant superpower was able to reorder the globe in its own interests.[13] Rejecting old-style European colonialism, American hegemony was founded upon global institutions which indirectly limited the independence of their member states. On the one hand, there were the economic organisations binding the US sphere of influence together: the IMF, the World Bank, GATT, OECD and the European Common Market. On the other hand, there were the military alliances protecting the boundaries of the new empire: NATO, ANZUS, SEATO and the Baghdad pact.[14] Overarching these bodies was the United Nations which – at one and the same time – acted as an embryonic world government and

10 See Ellen Meiksins Wood, *Empire of Capital*, pages 73–101; P.J. Cain and A.G. Hopkins, *British Imperialism*, pages 53–104; and Ronald Hyam, *Britain's Imperial Century*, pages 1–73.
11 See W.W. Rostow, *The Diffusion of Power*, pages 133–134.
12 See Rostow, *United States*, pages 23–25.
13 See Rostow, *United States*, pages 43–88, 165–171; and Stephen Ambrose, *Rise to Globalism*; pages 27–28, 100–101.
14 See van der Pilj, *Atlantic Ruling Class*, pages 107–177; and Donald White, *The American Century*, pages 161–210.

a public platform for superpower rivalry. Just to remind everyone who was boss, the headquarters of the UN were in New York.

Like their former oppressors in Western Europe and Japan, the newly independent nations of the South soon found themselves conscripted into the US side in the Cold War. Having freed themselves from colonialism, they were now expected to join the military and economic institutions of the new world system. As the recent Time of Troubles had tragically proved, autarchic nationalism created war and poverty. Global liberalism was the sole guarantor of peace and prosperity.[15] However, in stark contrast with Western Europe, embracing the American model wasn't clearly the preferable option out in the periphery of the world system. Imposed by the hated colonial master, capitalism had blocked the development of the indigenous economy for generations. In contrast, the Stalinist dictatorship had – in less than three decades – transformed an impoverished and defeated peasant nation into a victorious nuclear-armed industrial superpower. For radicals in the new nations of the South, the Russian model represented the hope of turning formal independence into full sovereignty. 'Politically, there must be a complete break with world capitalism ... during the period of reconstruction ... [the] Marxist–Leninist strategy ... [is the] transition to a self-reliant, self-sustaining economy.'[16]

In 1950, the Cold War suddenly flared up into a shooting war in East Asia. Blamed at home by their Republican opponents for failing to prevent the 1949 Chinese Revolution, the Truman administration sent a US expeditionary force to protect the pro-American nationalists in Korea against their pro-Russian rivals. For the next three years, the two superpowers fought each other over whose dictator was going to oppress the Korean people.[17] Contrary to expectations of the Democratic leadership, their decisive move against the advance of Communism in the South was unpopular at home. In 1952, the Republican candidate won the US presidential elections for the first time since the late 1920s. Despite all the propaganda emphasising the vital necessity of resisting the Red Menace, American voters

[15] See W.W. Rostow, *The Stages of Economic Growth*, pages 108–121, 139–144; *United States*, pages 250–258.

[16] Mohamed Babu, 'Development Strategy – Revolutionary-Style', pages 63–64.

[17] See Jeremy Isaacs and Taylor Dowling, *Cold War*, pages 83–105; and Blum, *Killing Hope*, pages 45–55.

were unhappy that their nation's armed forces were fighting an Anti-Communist land war in faraway East Asia.[18]

For the rest of the decade, the Democratic Party found itself out of power. Traumatised by its defeat, its leadership desperately needed a new strategy for solving crises in the South like the Korean confrontation. Unfortunately for the Democrats, the Eisenhower administration carefully avoided making the same mistake as its predecessor. The United States didn't need military force to punish insufficiently subservient satellites. When the British and French invaded Egypt without American permission in 1956, a combination of political pressure and economic sanctions quickly forced them back into line.[19] Applying the lessons learnt in its covert operations against the West European Communist Parties, the CIA successfully removed unfriendly governments in Iran, Guatemala, Congo and other 'hotspots'.[20] Under the Republicans, the American public could enjoy the material and psychic benefits of global hegemony without having to suffer the human and material costs of foreign wars.

In the late 1950s, Kennedy – as he prepared his bid for the US presidency – was well aware that victory over his Republican opponent depended upon the Democrats regaining their reputation as the champions of America's interests in the South. Fortunately, he knew exactly where to find the intellectuals who could help him to win the forthcoming election: the CENIS think-tank at MIT.[21] Building upon its successes in Western Europe, the CIA had funded Rostow and his colleagues to hone their Anti-Communist grand narrative of history in research work on the emerging nations of the South. As the 1950s progressed, the Cold War Left became increasingly frustrated with the failings of the Eisenhower administration. Like its European predecessors, the American empire was becoming identified with the authoritarian rule of the privileged minority who had done well out of the old colonial system: landowners, bureaucrats and merchants. Fearing social unrest, these members of the traditional elite were eager to cooperate with the new American overlord who protected their wealth and power.

18 See Rostow, *United States*, page 242.
19 See Ambrose, *Rise to Globalism*, page 253.
20 See Blum, *Killing Hope*, pages 64–83, 156–163; and Jeffreys-Jones, *The CIA and American Democracy*, pages 81–117.
21 See W.W. Rostow, *Concept and Controversy*, pages 188–253; and Robert Dallek, *John F. Kennedy*, pages 220–226.

Unfortunately, they also had a vested interest in delaying economic modernisation. In the short-term, the Republican Party's policy of sharing power with traditional elites might be cheap and easy. But, as the Cold War Left emphasised, this strategy was leading to disaster in the long-term. If America didn't quickly lose its reputation as the 'lover of dictators', all struggles for political democracy and economic justice in the South would develop into Communist-led nationalist rebellions against Yankee imperialism.[22] In the looking-glass logic of the Cold War, a totalitarian police state was becoming the champion of progress and freedom across most of the developing world.

The 1949 Chinese Revolution was a stark warning of what could happen elsewhere in the South. Defeated in the cities in the late 1920s, the Communists had instead – as Bakunin had recommended – focused their energies on organising the peasantry. During the next two decades, this vanguard party had developed a strategy of rural guerrilla warfare which finally delivered victory over its US-backed opponents.[23] As the paramount leader of Chinese Communism, Mao Zedong supervised the transformation of this revolutionary experience into an eponymous theory: Maoism. His new form of Marxism–Leninism took its inspiration from one fundamental insight: it was impossible for the South to modernise without a violent social upheaval in the countryside. The traditional elite was responsible not only for keeping the peasantry in poverty and ignorance, but also for helping foreign powers to dominate the economies of the underdeveloped world.[24] By politically organising the oppressed rural population, the Chinese Communist Party could combine the struggles for social justice and national independence. Among the Maoists, self-reliance was more than just a survival technique for guerrilla fighters. Economic autarchy was the essential precondition for beginning the process of modernisation in the South.[25]

---

[22] See Eleanor Roosevelt and Huston Smith, 'What Are We For?' pages 10–12. Eleanor Roosevelt was an icon of the left of the Democratic Party and the influential wife of the 1933–45 US president.

[23] See Mao Zedong, *Six Essays on Military Affairs*; and Geoffrey Fairbairn, *Revolutionary Guerrilla Warfare*, pages 65–124.

[24] See Mao Zedong, 'Analysis of the Classes of Chinese Society'; 'Report on an Investigation of the Peasant Movement in Hunan'.

[25] See Mao Zedong, 'We Must Learn to do Economic Work'; Edgar Snow, *Red Star over China*, pages 211–244; and Bill Brugger, *China: Liberation and Transformation*, pages 29–38.

During the 1930s, Stalin had ruthlessly exploited the Russian peasantry to pay for his ambitious industrialisation programme. The movement of the population from the countryside to the cities had measured progress towards the communist utopia. Leading a rural guerrilla army, Mao not surprisingly rejected this Stalinist version of primitive accumulation. Instead, like Bakunin and his admirers, the chief theoretician of Chinese Communism believed that peasant communes were the harbingers of the communist future in the present. In Stalin's Russia, the factory had been idealised as the epitome of rational modernity. But, in Maoist China, this fascination with Taylorist hierarchies was denounced as ideological pessimism. Unlike its proletarian antecedent, peasant communism could be created in the here and now. Participatory democracy and cooperative creativity already existed in prefigurative forms within the villages of China.[26] There was no need for the country to pass through the industrial stage of growth to reach the promised land. With a combination of mass mobilisation and ideological fervour, Maoist China could jump directly into the imaginary future of peasant communism: the 'Great Leap Forward'.[27]

The Cold War Left identified this new mutation of Stalinism as the greatest threat to American hegemony over the South.[28] In the year before the US presidential elections, their worst fears were confirmed. Because it offered no hope for political freedom and economic development in the South, the Eisenhower administration had allowed the Communists to hijack the 1959 Cuban Revolution.[29] Emboldened by this victory, rural guerrilla movements were emerging to challenge pro-American regimes across the South. Drawing the lessons of the Cuban Revolution, Che Guevara explained how a small group of radicals could launch an armed uprising which would inspire the impoverished peasantry to

26 See William Hinton, *Fanshen*, pages 319–416. Before he joined the Communist Party, Mao had been involved in the peasant cooperative movement; see Philip Short, *Mao*, pages 101–102.
27 'In the future, everything will be called a commune, [including] factories ... and cities.' Mao Zedong in Short, *Mao*, page 485. See also Brugger, *China*, pages 109–129, 174–206.
28 The CENIS experts diligently studied their Maoist opponents' critique of imperialism: W.W. Rostow, *The Prospects for Communist China*, pages 18–45.
29 See Rostow, *Diffusion of Power*, pages 49–52; and Arthur Schlesinger, Jr., *A Thousand Days*, 215–220.

rise in rebellion against their US-backed oppressors.[30] The Russians might win the Cold War – without even having to risk a military showdown in Europe – by leading a worldwide anti-imperialist insurrection against the American empire. In a global rerun of the 1949 Chinese Revolution, the heroic peasants of the South would overthrow the corrupt capitalists of the North.

> Since the Second World War, the proletarian revolutionary movement has for various reasons been temporarily held back in the North American and West European capitalist countries, while the people's revolutionary movement in Asia, Africa and Latin America has been growing vigorously. In a sense, the contemporary world revolution ... presents a picture of the encirclement of cities by the rural areas. In the final analysis, the whole cause of world revolution hinges on the revolutionary struggles of Asian, African and Latin American peoples who make up the overwhelming majority of the world's population.[31]

Aided by the CIA, Rostow and his colleagues developed the up-to-date Anti-Communist response to the revolutionary crisis in the South: MIT modernisation theory. First and foremost, they dismissed Lenin and Mao's geopolitical analysis as a relic from the long-gone epoch of European imperialism. In contrast with its European and Japanese predecessors, the prosperity of the American empire wasn't founded upon the exploitation of overseas colonies.[32] Locked in a global competition with Russia, the USA's priority was preserving political stability within its sphere of influence. As in Western Europe, social discontent in the South would eventually diminish as living standards rose. Contrary to the claims of the Maoists, it was in the United States' self-interest to speed up the urbanisation and industrialisation of the developing world.[33] Under the benevolent protection of the American empire, impoverished peasant nations were now able to begin the arduous process of building prosperous and pluralistic societies. With generous financial aid from the US government and guidance from multi-disciplinary

---

[30] See Che Guevara, *Guerrilla Warfare*; and Regis Debray, *Revolution in the Revolution?*
[31] Lin Biao, 'People's War', page 84. Lin Biao was the 1959–71 Chinese minister of defence.
[32] See W.W. Rostow, *View from the Seventh Floor*, page 115.
[33] See Max Millikan and Donald Blackmer, *The Emerging Nations*, pages 144–145; and Rostow, *Seventh Floor*, pages 106–111.

teams of MIT-trained experts, the nations of the South could progress faster through the stages of growth towards the goal of welfare Fordism. Like the Fabians, the Cold War Left believed that successful imperialism required a civilising mission.

Inspired by the success of the CCF in Western Europe, the CENIS academics were convinced that America could win the support of the impoverished masses in the developing world. The USA should openly aid the modernising elites in their struggle against both feudal reactionaries and totalitarian revolutionaries. Having overcome their rivals, this 'Third Force' vanguard would lead the urban poor and the peasantry towards democracy and plenty. As in Western Europe, America's protégés in the developing world were encouraged to imitate the centrist policies of the Cold War Left: political consensus, economic compromise and managerial efficiency. At a global level, free trade might be necessary to prevent the revival of autarchic imperialist blocs. But, at a national level, laissez-faire liberalism was as anachronistic in the South as in the North. The Third Force must follow the third way of planned capitalism to prosperity.[34]

The CENIS think-tank believed that the media played a key role in preparing the preconditions for take-off and speeding up the process of industrialisation. In agrarian societies, there were many irrational psychological barriers which discouraged the adoption of modern attitudes and lifestyles.[35] Echoing McLuhan, these MIT theorists were convinced that the spread of new media would inevitably change people's consciousness and, in turn, lead to the emergence of a new society. With US money and guidance, the modernising elites in the South were now able to set up newspapers and radio stations in their countries. They were also extending their telephone systems and starting television broadcasting. For the first time, peasants in these developing countries were learning about the world outside their villages. Over time, traditional prejudices and fears would be eroded away. Modernist ideologies would give a common identity to the new nation being built by people from different social and

34 See W.W. Rostow, *Essays on a Half-Century*, pages x-xi, 8–11, 65–67, 85–118; and Millikan and Blackmer, *Emerging Nations*, pages 55–67.
35 See Millikan and Blackmer, *Emerging Nations*, pages 5–6, 23–26, 43–48; David McLelland, 'The Impulse to Modernisation'; and Alex Inkeles, 'The Modernisation of Man'.

cultural backgrounds.[36] Thanks to the media, the masses would be eager to embrace US-style industrialisation. Rejecting the false utopia of totalitarian Communism, they could now look forward to becoming full members of the global information society.

CENIS believed that the new class which was needed to lead the process of industrialisation already existed in most countries in the South. But, in some unfortunate countries, the indigenous modernising elite was missing. In such cases, the Cold War Left argued that America should intervene to force the traditional ruling class to take on this role. Sometimes, as had happened in 1920s Turkey, the army could provide the decisive leadership needed to make the painful break with the past. When supervised by CENIS graduates, authoritarian regimes were able to create the socio-economic preconditions for representative democracy and welfare Fordism to flourish in the future.[37] Like the CIA covert operations in late-1940s Western Europe, political repression within the American sphere of influence in the South was a temporary inconvenience in the unfolding of the grand narrative of social progress.

> [I]t seems ... to be the greater evil [in pre-modern nations] to develop 'popular government' at the expense of a viable administration capable of carrying out an amalgam of elite and mass wills. ... while efficient administration may actually depress some aspects of politicisation, such sedation may be beneficial in the long-run.[38]

Rostow and his colleagues believed that MIT modernisation theory would become the accepted orthodoxy across the South as soon as economic growth began to accelerate. There was only one major obstacle preventing this happy outcome. Across the developing world, there existed a small minority of revolutionary fanatics determined to sabotage the take-off of their countries. In their research studies, CENIS academics had discovered that the slow pace of modernisation was causing psychological neuroses among a key social group: the intellectuals. Alienated and frustrated, many members of the embryonic knowledge class in the South succumbed

[36] See Ithiel de Sola Pool, 'Communications and Development'; and Leonard Binder, 'Ideology and Development'.
[37] See Millikan and Blackmer, Emerging Nations, pages 31–34; and Myron Weiner, 'Modernisation of Politics and Government', pages 213–218.
[38] Ralph Braibanti, 'Administrative Modernisation', page 167.

to the temptations of revolutionary romanticism and ideological extremism.[39] In Rostow's oft-repeated phrase, Communism was a psychological disease of the transition to modernity. With aid from Russia and China, these intellectual malcontents were now leading peasant guerrilla movements across the South. Instead of developing their economies, pro-American governments were forced to concentrate their meagre resources on defeating this intransigent enemy.[40]

Because the Russian and Chinese dictatorships ruthlessly persecuted their internal enemies, the Cold War Left accepted that it was sometimes necessary – if regrettable – for US-backed regimes to murder, torture and imprison Communist subversives and their sympathisers. However, these MIT experts feared that a policy of indiscriminate repression would polarise political debate in the South into the choice between two unpleasant extremes: the traditional oligarchy and the revolutionary vanguard.[41] If the Third Force was to prevail, its American sponsors needed a more intelligent strategy for defeating rural insurrections. Learning from the writings of Mao and Guevara on guerrilla warfare, the CIA and CENIS believed that US special forces and their local allies could adapt the techniques of their revolutionary enemy to win the struggle in the countryside: *counter-insurgency*.[42]

According to MIT modernisation theory, every nation had its own unique path of development. Yet, at the same time, every economy had to move through the same predetermined sequence of stages of growth. For the CENIS team, this duality explained the stark dichotomy in living conditions between the North and the South. The admirers of Lenin and Mao had placed the blame upon American imperialism for perpetuating the 'underdevelopment' of the developing world.[43] Rejecting this analysis, Rostow and his colleagues argued that each nation was at a different moment in time within a single historical process. From their various starting points,

39 See Millikan and Blackmer, *Emerging Nations*, pages 22, 36–37, 69–70, 95–96, 102–104; and Harold Lasswell, 'The World Revolution of our Time', pages 88–94.

40 See Rostow, *Seventh Floor*, pages 113–114; *Essays*, pages 99–103.

41 See Millikan and Blackmer, *Emerging Nations*, pages 97–98.

42 See Millikan and Blackmer, *Emerging Nations*, pages 110–114; and Rostow, *United States*, pages 319–323.

43 See Andre Gunder Frank, *Capitalism and Underdevelopment in Latin America*.

the countries of the world were all converging into the US-led global village. Sooner or later, the poor South would enjoy the same living standards as the rich North.[44] The recent shift in the ideological meaning of liberalism within American political theory turned this Anti-Communist grand narrative into the historical justification for US global leadership. Within a world economy composed of nations at very different stages of growth, free trade remained the only credible alternative to autarchic nationalism. Fortunately, as their economies developed within the global market, every nation would slowly adopt more modern concepts of liberalism. At a world level, market competition was already being supplemented with international financial institutions and regional planning. The global village needed a global government.

As in Western Europe, America – the first continental nation – provided the best model for this emerging world federation. For Rostow and other CENIS members, the experience of the 1776 Revolution proved that economic unity could be combined with political democracy on a global level.[45] The international popularity of Hollywood movies and rock 'n' roll music showed how America was already acting as the prototype of a united world. As a nation of immigrants and descendents of immigrants, the USA was the first country with a truly international outlook. The Cold War Left enthused that America's 'melting pot' culture must be the forerunner of the global village culture to come. When everyone on the planet had access to the new information technologies, national and ethnic peculiarities would blend into a US-style universal identity. As in the sci-fi future of the *Star Trek* TV series, the diversity of humanity would soon be working together for a common purpose under an American captain. Even aliens would want to be on the team.[46] America today was the premonition of everywhere else tomorrow.

> The pace at which means of communications are now under development argues ... that the present nations of the world will move into relations of increasing intimacy and interaction. Between

---

[44] The CENIS essay collection entitled *Modernisation* opened with the proposition that 'many countries in the developing world are today experiencing a comprehensive process of change which Europe and America once experienced'. Myron Weiner, 'Preface', page v.

[45] See W.W. Rostow, 'The National Style'; *Essays*, pages 29–30.

[46] See Startrek.com, 'Star Trek – the original series'; and Melancholic Troglodytes, 'The Star Trek Myth'.

them, the urgent imperative to tame military force and the need to deal with people everywhere on the basis of the accelerating proximity argue strongly for movement in the direction of federalised world organisation under effective international law.[47]

In the 1960 US presidential campaign, Kennedy's enthusiasm for MIT modernisation theory reinforced his public image as the most modern candidate. After his victory, the new administration immediately adopted the dual strategy of CENIS: development and repression. In news reports, President Kennedy identified himself with the elite US military units trained for counter-insurgency warfare.[48] As their first covert operation, the Democrats approved the previous administration's plan for a CIA-led invasion of Cuba. With US help, the Third Force would defeat totalitarianism without restoring the old oligarchy.[49] When this adventure ended in disaster, Kennedy quickly launched an ambitious programme of subsidies and advice to accelerate economic growth in Latin America: the Alliance for Progress. To ensure its success, Rostow was appointed to oversee the project.[50] If military force couldn't remove Communism from its Caribbean base, political and economic modernisation would prevent the revolutionary contagion from spreading to other countries in the region. In a highly publicised initiative, the Kennedy government sent idealistic young Americans to work with US-funded aid projects in the South: the Peace Corps. By helping those in distress, these volunteers demonstrated that the Number One superpower supported social progress in the less fortunate parts of the world.[51] At a 1961 meeting of a regional economic forum in Uruguay, the Latin American delegates didn't know which left-wing politician was the greater threat to the old order on the continent: Che Guevara – the representative of revolutionary Cuba – or Douglas Dillon – the US proponent of MIT modernisation theory.[52]

By the time that Kennedy came to power in 1961, the partition of Europe had solidified. Although the nuclear arms race continued

47 Rostow, *United States*, page 549.

48 See Dallek, *Kennedy*, page 350.

49 See Schlesinger, *Thousand Days*, pages 233–297; and Rostow, *Diffusion of Power*, pages 208–215.

50 See Rostow, *Diffusion of Power*, pages 216–221; and Schlesinger, *Thousand Days*, pages 186–205.

51 See Schlesinger, *Thousand Days*, pages 604–609.

52 See Schlesinger, *Thousand Days*, pages 761–765.

unchecked, an all-out war between America and Russia now seemed very unlikely. Yet, only a year later, a series of miscalculations on both sides nearly triggered the atomic Armageddon. In 1962, the competition between the two superpowers for control of Cuba had escalated into the most dangerous crisis of the Cold War. Fearful of another CIA-sponsored invasion, the revolutionary regime agreed to the Russians stationing nuclear missiles on their island. When US aerial surveillance discovered their bases, the Kennedy regime threatened war if these weapons weren't removed from Cuba. In a terrifying stand off, both sides – in a moment of insanity – had decided to risk losing everything over who controlled a small Caribbean island.[53]

Back in 1916, Lenin had argued that imperialism was the struggle over who owned the riches of the world. Incessant war was the inevitable result. Yet, in wealthy Europe, the American and Russian empires had faithfully respected the terms of the Yalta Agreement for nearly two decades. Military posturing and propaganda rhetoric had never been allowed to escalate into an all-out confrontation. Even when they had fought each other for control of Korea, the two superpowers had successfully localised their armed confrontation to the peninsula.[54] By the beginning of the 1960s, living with the Cold War had become normality. Crises had come and gone, but nothing had fundamentally changed. Few people had foreseen the Cuban crisis that threatened the survival of humanity. Above all, they were surprised that the final showdown between the superpowers was taking place in the South rather than in Europe.

Paradoxically, the Yalta Agreement was responsible for this spasm of irrationality. By partitioning Europe, America and Russia had imposed peace on the continent. But, as both superpowers established order within their spheres of influence, the opportunities for competition between them became ever scarcer. As a result, imperial rivalries were increasingly diverted to the South. In this extension of the Yalta Agreement, the dangerous nuclear confrontation in Europe was sublimated into a 'great game' of diplomacy, espionage,

---

[53] See Errol Morris, *The Fog of War*; Schlesinger, *Thousand Days*, pages 794–841; and Dallek, *Kennedy*, pages 535–574.
[54] See Rostow, *United States*, pages 231–232; and Isaacs and Dowling, *Cold War*, pages 101–102.

conspiracies, propaganda campaigns and covert operations played out in exotic lands. Russian and American agents experienced the thrill of fighting for dominance over the internal politics of other people's countries. In this Cold War game, the nations of the South became the pieces on the board which were lost or won when loyalties shifted from one bloc to another. Every country in the developing world had symbolic importance as a counter in the superpower confrontation. Soft power was now the measure of hard power.

Although both sides played to win, the aim of the Cold War game was to continue playing without ever winning.[55] In a world system founded upon the cooperative rivalry of two blocs, the outright victory for one side was a disastrous defeat for both sides. The Cold War game didn't – and couldn't – have a final score. By moving the battlefield to the South, Russia and America were now able to compete for mastery of the world without ever fundamentally altering the geopolitical balance of power. Losing or winning a contest over a country inhabited by impoverished peasants would never be important enough to trigger a nuclear showdown. Best of all, by counting the number of client states in each bloc, it was now possible to measure which side was ahead at any particular moment in the 'zero sum' game of the Cold War. Russia and America had preserved stability in the rich North by exporting instability to the poor South.[56] '[Game theory] projects symmetrical models onto an asymmetrical political climate, and rules-of-the-game comprehension into a context of social disorganisation and political disequilibrium.'[57]

The cult of the computer encouraged this cybernetic ritualisation of the Cold War. Both Turing and von Neumann had identified playing games as a key marker of intelligence. When processed through a computer, the irrational could be made to appear rational. In Kahn's simulations, it was even possible to calculate which side had won a nuclear war. For the Vital Centre gurus, games theory offered a value-free analysis of the superpower contest in the South.

55 Anatol Rapoport – a guru of games theory – emphasised that '[t]he opponent speaks the same language; he is seen as ... a mirror-image of self'. Anatol Rapoport, *Fights, Games and Debates*, page 9.
56 For the mathematical theorisation of this new form of geopolitical competition, see Rapoport, *Fights, Games and Debates*, pages 105–242.
57 Irving Louis Horowitz, *The War Game*, page 21.

Chaotic struggles for class justice and national independence were played according to certain rules. By replicating them in software, the US side could discover how to come out on top in these contests. Like the economy, the Cold War was a programmable machine. In the early 1960s, MIT modernisation theory was the most advanced American strategy for playing this geopolitical game in the South. With ARPA grants, social scientists had created computer simulations which devised the best tactics for each locality.[58] At the beginning of the Cold War game, the USA had controlled most of the pieces on the board. But, by allying itself with the old elites from colonial times, the new empire had slowly but surely alienated the majority of the population in the South. Invigorated by the 1959 Cuban Revolution, Stalinism was now the pre-eminent ideology of political emancipation and social justice in Asia, Africa and Latin America. When it came to power, the Democratic Party was determined to prove that its progressive policies were not only morally preferable, but also the most effective strategy for crushing the Communist threat in the developing world. Crucially, winning victories overseas helped to win elections at home. Patriotic Americans wanted to see the US team being in the lead in the great game of the South. The new Democratic administration had no intention of disappointing them.

The Cuban missile crisis was the first time the two superpowers forgot that the Cold War game was only a game. Compared to the wealthy industrial regions of Europe, a small sugar-producing tourist island in the Caribbean was an expendable pawn. Ignoring this geopolitical reality, the leaders of Russia and America in the early 1960s made a series of foolhardy decisions that came close to destroying human civilisation. The symbolic soft power of a Communist revolution in America's 'backyard' had persuaded both players to escalate to the brink of catastrophe to secure a single piece on the board. After looking into the abyss, the two brother enemies came to their senses and struck a deal. Cuba secured its independence from America by submitting to Russian hegemony. There was no neutralist third option in the zero sum game in the South. Although disaster had been averted, the Kennedy administration feared that the loss of any more pieces on the board could further weaken

[58] See Andrew Wilson, *The Bomb and the Computer*, pages 66–76.

the US playing position by detonating a chain reaction of anti-American uprisings across the South. In the aptly named 'domino theory', Mao became the master strategist of the Cold War game. The CENIS computers predicted that a Communist victory in one country could set off a negative feedback cycle which would destabilise the entire South.[59]

By inverting Mao's revolutionary prophecy, these MIT analysts became convinced that – after the US defeat in Cuba – every pro-American regime in the developing world had acquired immense ideological significance. Even nations of little strategic or economic value were now important pieces on the board. If guerrilla revolutionaries were allowed to seize power in another country in the developing world, the Maoist enemy would have proved that there were alternative paths to modernity. After winning the first contest in Western Europe, the USA would have lost the second round in the South. Instead of America leading humanity towards the information society, Communism would – once again – be the wave of the future. The Cold War Left insisted that this geopolitical analysis inexorably led to one conclusion: America had to inflict a humiliating defeat on the peasant revolution in the South. Hard power must be used to magnify soft power. Controlling a small piece of space would demonstrate to the peoples of the world that America still owned the vast immensities of time.

---

[59] See Rostow, *United States*, pages 293–294; and Robert McNamara, *In Retrospect*, pages 214–215.

14

THE AMERICAN INVASION OF VIETNAM

At the 1964 New York World's Fair, the Unisphere was flanked on one side by the international area. When touring its pavilions, visitors to the exposition were presented with a vision of global harmony. From all corners of the world, representatives of many different nations had travelled to New York to put on a show for their American friends. Close allies like France and South Korea showed their gratitude for US help in the past by enthusiastically participating in the event. Former enemies of America like Japan and Spain had built impressive pavilions for the exposition. Even Israel and its Arab neighbours peacefully coexisted within the international area. The McLuhanist message of the Unisphere had been confirmed. In one corner of the World's Fair, the globe already was a village.[1]

Back in 1939, the Russian pavilion had been one of the stars of the show.[2] However, at the 1964 World's Fair, there was no exhibit from the Number Two superpower. This omission wasn't an accident. By snubbing the UN's Bureau of International Expositions, the organisers were able to host a World's Fair which excluded most of the world's population. This time, the Communist enemy wasn't invited.[3] More than any other exhibit at the 1964 World's Fair, the massive red–gold pagoda situated in a prime spot right next to the Unisphere symbolised the geopolitical surreality of the US elite's concept of the global village.[4] Inside this building, visitors saw displays of 'ancient and modern Chinese culture ... and ... of the evolution of Chinese money'. A restaurant served Chinese food and concerts of Chinese music were staged. From outward appearances, visitors to the World's Fair might have been forgiven for thinking that China – a very large country in East Asia – had sponsored this impressive pavilion. In the guidebook of the World's Fair, the red–gold pagoda was clearly listed as the entry of the 'Republic of China'. Yet, these innocent visitors would have been mistaken. Bizarrely, it was Taiwan – an island off the mainland of China

---

1 See Editors of Time–Life Books, *Official Guide*, pages 118–171.
2 See New York World's Fair 1939, *Official Guide Book*, page 148; and Jeffrey Hart, 'Yesterday's America of Tomorrow', page 65.
3 See Robert A. M. Stern, Thomas Mellins and David Fishman, *New York 1960*, pages 1028, 1039.
4 This building can be seen in the background on the left-hand side of the Barbrook family photo.

– that had been responsible for organising the Chinese pavilion at the World's Fair.[5]

This geopolitical charade commemorated the traumatic moment of America's first major defeat in the Cold War. In 1949, China – a long-standing US ally – had unexpectedly transferred its loyalties to the Russian enemy. Traumatised by the loss of such an important piece in the opening moves of the great game, successive American administrations had stubbornly refused to recognise the new Maoist government on the mainland. In its place, Taiwan – the refuge of the former regime – became their symbolic substitute for 'Red China'.[6] Organised by leading members of the US elite, the World's Fair materialised this Cold War doublethink in the form of the red–gold pagoda of the self-styled Republic of China. Even if some important countries were absent, the US elite still had a sufficient number of overseas pavilions at their exposition to celebrate American hegemony over the planet. At a World's Fair held in mid-1960s New York, it was easy to conceive of the globe as a village. For over a century, this city had been the gateway for the millions of people from Europe and Russia who came looking for a better life across the Atlantic.[7] The US elite was convinced that – just like these immigrants – almost all foreigners were wannabe Americans. As the Cold War Left kept emphasising, the destiny of every nation in the world was assimilation within the US-dominated global village.

In Latin America in the early 1960s, the Democratic administration promoted the Alliance for Progress as the quickest route to the American version of hi-tech modernity. Guided by MIT-trained experts, the Third Force would deliver rapid economic development without sacrificing political pluralism. Back in the late 1940s, the US elite had made similar promises to the West Europeans and, within a decade, it had made them come true. The Cold War Left claimed that the Alliance for Progress was now extending the benefits of welfare Fordism to the workers and peasants of Latin America. As long as they firmly resisted the temptations of Cuban Maoism, the long-oppressed masses would soon be enjoying both prosperity and

---

[5] See Editors of Time–Life Books, *Official Guide*, pages 112, 120, 166.
[6] See David Halberstam, *The Best and the Brightest*, pages 106–120; and Stephen Ambrose, *Rise to Globalism*, pages 192–193.
[7] See Ric Burns and James Sanders with Lisa Ades, *New York*, pages 220–230.

democracy. The Alliance for Progress was designed to symbolise the Democrats' break with the failed policies of the past. Before they came to power, Rostow and his CENIS colleagues had fiercely condemned the Republican strategy of allying with the traditional rulers of Latin America. Instead, the USA must become the champion of the progressive forces in the South. But, once they were in office, these MIT experts soon began to doubt the wisdom of their own analysis. Like its predecessor, the new Democratic administration quickly learnt to distrust the nationalist reformers on the southern continent. In Western Europe, the advocates of third-way socialism were devoted admirers of the USA. In contrast, the leaders of the Third Force in Latin America were much more attracted by the unacceptable option in the zero-sum Cold War game: neutrality.

When the Alliance for Progress was unable to recruit these urban intellectuals for the US cause, the gurus of MIT modernisation theory realised that – much to their horror – the modernising elite in this part of the developing world wanted to follow its own path to modernity. Since the Third Force had demonstrated its political unreliability, the Democrats decided to return to the policies of the past in a new guise. Soft power had to be reinvigorated with hard power. As recommended by the CENIS textbooks, they would persuade the military to take on the role of the modernising vanguard. Financed, trained and organised by the US government, the enforcer of the old oligarchy would be transformed into the builder of the new social order in Latin America. Democrats with a capital D had decided that democracy with a small d was an optional extra.[8]

Back in the early nineteenth century, the Monroe Doctrine had first asserted US hegemony over the entire continent. Having patiently waited until the mid twentieth century to displace the British, the American empire had no intention of letting its southern neighbours escape from its grasp.[9] In 1954, the Eisenhower administration had ordered the CIA to restore the traditional elite to power in Guatemala when the policies of its democratically elected government threatened US business interests. Now that

---

8 See John Gerassi, *The Great Fear in Latin America*, pages 305–316.
9 See James Monroe, 'Monroe Doctrine'; and Maurice Lemoine, 'Uncle Sam's Manifest Destiny'.

they were in charge, the Cold War Left became equally determined to prevent radical nationalists from disturbing the established order in Latin America. Following the CIA's assassination of the dictator of the Dominican Republic in 1962, the Kennedy administration invaded this Caribbean island to ensure that its protégés kept political control.[10]

After this victory, the next target was Brazil. In 1964, the CIA organised a military coup to overthrow the reformist government of João Goulart. Much to the delight of his supporters, this Brazilian president had adopted a more independent foreign policy.[11] According to Rostow, his pandering to popular sentiment had proved that elected politicians lacked the maturity needed to run the most important country in Latin America. In their place, US-trained generals would have to provide the much-needed leadership for the Brazilian modernising elite.[12] By destroying political pluralism, this military substitute for the Third Force was – paradoxically – better able to implement the economic and managerial programme of the third way. Dictatorship in the present guaranteed the future of democracy in Brazil. Repudiating its own programme for the Alliance for Progress, the Cold War Left had become convinced that the traditional elite was the USA's only reliable ally in Latin America. Just like its Republican predecessor, the Democratic administration now denounced economic nationalism as the path to Stalinist tyranny. As in the previous decade, Anti-Communism transformed fascist torturers and corrupt oligarchs into heroes of the US-led Free World. Instead of being the up-to-date American strategy for the South, MIT modernisation theory had become the new name for old-fashioned imperialism of free trade. 'As to the efficacy of the policy recommended by Rostow, it speaks for itself: no country, once underdeveloped, ever managed to develop by Rostow's stages [of growth to US-style Fordism].'[13]

Across Latin America in the mid 1960s, the Democratic administration won victory after victory in its counter-insurgency campaign against left-wing nationalist groups inspired by the Cuban

[10] See William Blum, *Killing Hope*, pages 175–184; and Gerassi, *Latin America*, pages 194–202.

[11] See Blum, *Killing Hope*, pages 163–172; and Gerassi, *Latin America*, pages 82–99.

[12] See W.W. Rostow, *The Diffusion of Power*, pages 310, 411, 419–420, 425.

[13] Andre Gunder Frank, *Sociology of Development*, page 26.

Revolution. In 1967, CIA-led forces in Bolivia even succeeded in capturing and killing Che Guevara: the celebrated theorist of rural guerrilla warfare.[14] But, for the Cold War Left, the disciplining of the disobedient peoples of Latin America was only a partial success. Although the Cuban path to modernity had been closed off in Brazil and Bolivia, defeating this divided and disorganised opponent had little impact upon the rest of the developing world. If it wanted to discredit the Maoist prophecy of global peasant revolution, then the American empire must take on – and humiliate – the toughest rural guerrilla movement in the South. Winning this vital piece on the board would ensure that America retained its dominant position in the Cold War game. Above all, by beating its enemy's champion fighter, the Democratic administration would have proved beyond doubt that the USA owned the imaginary future.

Around the same time that the Bell commission was beginning its deliberations, the US elite became convinced that it had found the perfect location for staging its world-historical confrontation with the Maoist peasant revolution: Vietnam. Back in the late 1940s and early 1950s, Communist-led guerrillas had outmanoeuvred and outfought the numerically stronger and better equipped French army of occupation. Even massive amounts of US aid had failed to reverse the situation.[15] When the old imperial power finally admitted defeat in 1954, the new American empire intervened to split Vietnam into two. While the victorious Communists came to power in the north, a US-sponsored Anti-Communist dictatorship was imposed upon the south.[16] By the early 1960s, this artificial division of Vietnam was no longer sustainable. Corrupt and repressive, the regime in the south was incapable of defending itself against the resurgent revolutionary movement. The Democratic administration realised that – if the USA didn't act decisively – the Maoist north would soon seize control of the whole country.[17] According to the domino theory, a Communist victory in Vietnam would quickly be followed by the Communist takeover of the whole of South-East Asia and, in the

---

14 See Che Guevara, *Bolivian Diary*; and Blum, *Killing Hope*, pages 221–229.
15 See Robert Taber, *The War of the Flea*, pages 59–72.
16 See Neil Sheehan, Hedrick Smith, E.W. Kenworthy and Fox Butterfield, *The Pentagon Papers*, pages 1–13, 26–40; and Neil Sheehan, *A Bright Shining Lie*, pages 145–172.
17 See Sheehan, Smith, Kenworthy and Butterfield, *Pentagon Papers*, pages 13–25, 41–78; and Gabriel Kolko, *Anatomy of a War*, pages 80–108.

worst-case scenario, the implosion of the entire American empire. In 1964, US President Johnson explained the case for war:

> Why are we in ... Vietnam? ... Across the globe, from Berlin to Thailand, [there] are people whose well-being rests ... on the belief that they can count on us if they are attacked. To leave Vietnam to its fate would shake the confidence of all these people in the value of an American commitment ... The result would be increased unrest and instability, and even wider war.[18]

The Democratic administration was supremely confident of victory. While America was the richest and most powerful nation on the planet, Vietnam was a backward peasant country with few natural resources.[19] As in the past, economic and technological superiority meant military invincibility. Led by the Cold War Left, America now also had the ideological advantage. Possessing a more sophisticated understanding of the grand narrative of modernity, the Cold War Left knew how to defeat Stalinism in the developing world.[20] Under the supervision of MIT-trained advisers, a nation called South Vietnam would be built on the American model. As had already happened in Western Europe, the Anti-Communist half of the country would become a prosperous and democratic mass-consumption society. Within a few decades, South Vietnam would be fully integrated within the global village. In contrast, just like its Russian and Chinese allies, the Communist north was condemned to stagnation at the stage of growth of its steam-age ideology. MIT modernisation theory would prove its superiority over the Maoist peasant revolution.

In the early stages of the conflict, the Kennedy administration placed the CIA in charge of the struggle against Vietnamese Communism.[21] Flush with money and weaponry, its CENIS-trained counter-insurgency experts and economic development advisers set to work on modernising the military and bureaucratic structures of the southern state. As its top priority, the CIA wanted to win the

---

[18] Lyndon Johnson, 'Peace Without Conquest', page 2.

[19] President Johnson contemptuously dismissed Vietnam as a 'damn little piss-ant country'. Irving Bernstein, *Guns or Butter*, page 329.

[20] In the Bell commission's list of 100 imminent inventions, number 37 was the discovery of 'new and relatively effective counter-insurgency techniques'. Herman Kahn and Anthony Wiener, *The Year 2000*, page 53.

[21] See John Kennedy, 'Special Message to Congress on Urgent Needs'; and Robert Dallek, *John F. Kennedy*, pages 442–461, 664–669.

hearts and minds of the majority of the Vietnamese population, the peasantry. Imitating the Maoist enemy, its propaganda promised that the corruption and brutality of the old feudal order would soon be swept away. Following the precepts of MIT modernisation theory, the CIA launched a programme of 'Revolutionary Development' in the Vietnamese countryside. Land reform, universal education, health care, free speech and honest government would secure the loyalty of the peasantry.[22] Funded by ARPA, academic experts invented a computer game to develop war-winning tactics for the CIA-led forces in the field.[23] Unlike the defeated French colonial regime, the American-sponsored modernising elite knew how to defeat the Chinese-inspired revolutionary vanguard.

By the time that Johnson became US president, the CIA's counter-insurgency strategy for pacifying the Vietnamese countryside had stalled. Paramilitary operatives and MIT-trained advisers couldn't make an army fight which didn't want to fight or eliminate corruption in a political system founded upon corruption.[24] The shoddily built nation of South Vietnam was on the brink of collapse. Determined to win this round in the Cold War game, the Johnson administration decided in 1964 to send the US Air Force into battle. Rostow – the presidential security advisor – and McNamara – the minister of defence – organised intensive – and ever more destructive – attacks against Communist-controlled areas of the south, the liberated north and guerrilla supply routes in neighbouring countries. Guided by IBM mainframes, B-52 bombers were able to locate and destroy any enemy target. According to the ARPA-funded computer simulations, the success of this air offensive was guaranteed.[25] When their losses in people and property reached the critical breaking point, the Communists would be forced to admit defeat and agree to abandon their struggle against the pro-American southern regime. In 1965, Rostow assured his government colleagues that 'the Vietcong [guerrillas] are already

22 See Rostow, *Diffusion of Power*, pages 451–459; and Halberstam, *Best and Brightest*, pages 121–129.

23 See Andrew Wilson, *The Bomb and the Computer*, pages 118–126.

24 See Daniel Ellsberg, *Secrets*, pages 114–115, 129–131, 169; and Mary McCarthy, *Vietnam*, pages 69–97.

25 See Wilson, *Bomb and Computer*, pages 168–169.

coming apart under the bombing. They're going to collapse in weeks. Not months, weeks.'[26]

Within a short period of time, it became clear that the US Air Force – like the CIA – couldn't deliver victory. In a decade of conflict, the Americans dropped more explosives on Vietnam – and on neighbouring Cambodia and Laos – than in its early-1940s campaigns against Germany and Japan.[27] Yet, despite all this death and destruction inflicted upon them, the Communists never reached their breaking point. Early on, President Johnson had reluctantly accepted that bombing on its own couldn't defeat the Vietnamese resistance. In 1965, he decided to send in the army to finish off the job. America had become the new colonial ruler of Vietnam. Like their air force colleagues, US generals were also convinced that a combination of massive firepower and hi-tech weaponry would quickly win the war. Back in the 1950s, Vietnamese guerrillas had taken over the countryside by concentrating their forces in surprise hit and run attacks against the widely dispersed and sluggish French army. A decade later, Rostow argued that advances in weapons technology had completely changed the balance of forces on the Asian battlefield.[28] Transported by helicopters, American soldiers were now able to take the war to the enemy in the villages. Directed by computer planning, the US military's 'search and destroy' missions would flush out and eliminate the Communist guerrillas. With the Johnson administration committing ever more troops and resources to the conflict, the generals confidently predicted that victory was close: 'the light at the end of the tunnel'.[29]

In its struggle against Vietnamese Communism, the US military faced an unexpected problem: measuring its achievements on the battlefield. When fighting a conventional war, winning meant conquering the opponent's territory. But, in the late 1940s and early 1950s, the Vietnamese Maoists had beaten the French army by winning over the peasantry to their cause. Once the colonial regime had lost control of the countryside, its fate was sealed. Without

[26] Walt Rostow, in Ellsberg, *Secrets*, page 184.
[27] See Michael Maclear, *Vietnam*, page 249.
[28] See Rostow, *Diffusion of Power*, page 450; and Halberstam, *Best and Brightest*, pages 122–124, 542–543.
[29] See Sheehan, Smith, Kenworthy and Butterfield, *Pentagon Papers*, pages 382–417, 459–485; and Robert McNamara, *In Retrospect*, pages 209–214.

taking a single city, rural guerrillas had overcome a modern army. Learning from this defeat, the US military knew that controlling the peasantry was the key to victory. The conundrum was how to assess the results of American offensives in the countryside. Unable to measure territorial gains, the US military decided instead to focus instead upon the number of enemy combatants killed in each operation: the 'body count'. From this data, its analysts could programme computers to calculate which side had inflicted the most damage on its opponent: the 'kill ratio'. The US military now had the mathematical measure of victory.[30]

This statistical solution delighted the politicians back home. When he had worked for Ford in the 1950s, McNamara had dramatically improved managerial efficiency by using computers to produce detailed statistics about the company's different activities: 'cost–benefit analysis'. In his new job as defence minister, he urged the US military to apply this hi-tech method of making cars to the task of fighting wars.[31] Happy to oblige, the generals became computer-age managers. In Vietnam, the US military would kill Communists as efficiently as the Ford motor company manufactured cars back home. Just as in the private sector, the generals carefully measured whether their subordinates were fulfilling their production quotas. By processing data from battlefields across the country on high-speed mainframes, analysts produced detailed statistics proving that the Americans were winning the war. According to the body count score, the US military now had the kill ratio advantage. The Vietnamese resistance was losing fighters more quickly than it could recruit them. American collaborators would soon outnumber Communist militants in the countryside. Just as when he was at Ford, McNamara now had the facts and figures to beat the competition. By 1967, Rostow had found a new justification for his optimistic prognosis: 'The other side is near collapse. ... The charts are very good ... Victory is very near.'[32]

30 'Body counts are like football games. They keep a score and as long as the other side has more dead then it's got to be a success.' Moderator of panel in Winter Soldier Investigation, 'Third Marine Division, Part 2', page 3. Also see McNamara, *In Retrospect*, pages 48, 237–238; and Maclear, *Vietnam*, pages 224–227.

31 See McNamara, *In Retrospect*, pages 10–25; and Halberstam, *Best and Brightest*, pages 215–247.

32 Walt Rostow, in Ellsberg, *Secrets*, page 184.

As the conflict dragged on, the US government desperately searched for the wonder weapon which could win the war. In this sellers' market, university research labs and military contractors seized the opportunity to test their cutting-edge military technologies in battlefield conditions. Everything was tried, but nothing delivered the decisive blow against the Vietnamese resistance. In 1967, the Johnson government believed that it had finally found its magic bullet. Appropriately named in honour of the US defence secretary, a multi-disciplinary team of America's leading scientists devised a plan to build an impenetrable hi-tech barrier to separate the two halves of Vietnam: the McNamara Line. In this military version of the information Panopticon, millions of electronic sensors – interspersed with mines and booby-traps – would be installed along the frontiers of the southern state. Robot drones would patrol the skies overhead. Computers would collate and sort the data from the barrier's surveillance devices. When Communist guerrillas were detected crossing the McNamara Line to infiltrate the south, US planes and helicopter-borne troops would be scrambled to repel them. As it was improved and expanded, this system would – in a few years time – be able to control combat operations over the entire South-East Asian war zone: the 'electronic battlefield'. Sooner or later, post-industrial technologies would deliver the knockout blow against the peasant revolution.[33]

Over the next five years, the US government funded a lavish development programme to put this new military strategy into practice. Since the information society was the next stage in human development, the convergence of media, telecommunications and computing must be able to provide the technological fix for anti-imperialist nationalism in Vietnam. During the late 1960s and early 1970s, the US military made strenuous efforts to construct an electronic barrier blocking the supply routes between the liberated north and the occupied south. Within minutes of enemy forces being detected by its ADSID sensors, IBM System/360 mainframes calculated their location and dispatched B-52 bombers to destroy

---

[33] See Sheehan, Smith, Kenworthy and Butterfield, *Pentagon Papers*, pages 507–509; Berkeley SESPA, *Science against the People*, pages 1–6, 17–18; and Paul Dickson, *The Electronic Battlefield*, pages 20–31.

them.[34] It was inevitable that computer-age McLuhanism would emerge victorious from its struggle with steam-age Maoism in the jungles of Vietnam. 'I foresee ... battlefields ... that are under 24 hour ... real-time surveillance ... on which we can destroy anything we can locate through instant communications and the almost instantaneous application of highly lethal firepower.'[35]

Like all the other sophisticated strategies for winning the war, the electronic battlefield also didn't deliver on its promises. In 1972, even after five years of testing and refining, the McNamara Line failed to detect large numbers of noisy Vietnamese tanks and other heavy equipment moving down the supply routes from the north to launch an offensive in the south. Maoist ingenuity had outwitted McLuhanist machinery.[36] Long before this embarrassing fiasco took place, the costs of the occupation had become unbearable for the American empire. From a minor part of US state expenditure under Kennedy, spending on the war exploded under the Johnson administration.[37] More troublingly, in the years immediately after the 1965 invasion, the size of the American expeditionary force increased exponentially. By 1967, the Johnson government had committed over 500,000 US troops to the struggle.[38] For the first time since Korea in the early 1950s, America was fighting a major – and very expensive – land war.

Back in 1954, as the French colonial regime collapsed, the US Joint Chiefs of Staff had told their political masters that South-East Asia was 'devoid of decisive military objectives'.[39] This conclusion wasn't a surprise. Unlike the French colonialists, the new American empire had much more lucrative ways of making money than exploiting the impoverished peasants of the region. Located far away from both the USA and Europe, Vietnam's geopolitical orientation also had minimal impact upon the superpower balance of power.

---

34 See Berkeley SESPA, *Science against the People*, pages 8–9; and Dickson, *Electronic Battlefield*, pages 32–54, 67–75.

35 W.C. Westmoreland, 'Address to the Association of the United States Army', page 221. Westmoreland was commander-in-chief of the US military in Vietnam from 1964 to 1968.

36 See Berkeley SESPA, *Science against the People*, page 14; and Dickson, *Electronic Battlefield*, pages 78–80.

37 By 1967, the cost of the occupation of Vietnam had risen to over a third of the American military budget. See McNamara, *In Retrospect*, page 265.

38 See Maclear, *Vietnam*, pages 178–179.

39 See Sheehan, Smith, Kenworthy and Butterfield, *Pentagon Papers*, pages 44–45.

Even if the Communists did unify the country, America had little to fear. Having fought against Chinese domination since medieval times, the Vietnamese might well prefer an alliance with far-away capitalist America to being dominated by a more powerful neighbour which happened to be an ideological soul mate. History was on the side of the optimists. As part of the common struggle against Japan in the early 1940s, the forerunner of the CIA had armed and trained the Vietnamese resistance. Twenty years later, it would have been much easier and cheaper for the Americans to renew their alliance with the Communists than to fight them for possession of an insignificant agricultural country. If – as the Democrats claimed at the time – the Johnson administration had formulated its foreign policy through rational cost–benefit analyses calculated on computers, then the USA's loss-making subsidiary in South-East Asia would have been immediately closed down.

During the 1960s, the Cold War Left provided the intellectual leadership for those within the US elite opposed to making a mutually beneficial deal with the Communist leaders of Vietnam. Under both the Kennedy and Johnson administrations, Rostow was one of the prime movers behind the American invasion of South-East Asia. As each military strategy failed, he was always the most enthusiastic advocate of further escalation. Another big push would reach the breaking point of the Vietnamese resistance. When accused of being an old-style imperialist, Rostow angrily refuted this charge. In contrast with the villainous European empires in Lenin's pamphlet, the USA had no desire to steal Vietnam's meagre resources or rack-rent its peasantry.[40] America was fighting for a much more valuable prize: 'credibility'. Despite Vietnam itself being economically and strategically unimportant, defeating its Maoist guerrilla movement had immense symbolic value. In the Cold War game, America would have taken on and humiliated a battle-hardened revolutionary movement. Across the South, the message would be clear. The revolutionary road to modernity was discredited. There was no alternative to US hegemony.

The Americans needed to fight a serious opponent like the Vietnamese for their victory over Communism to have any credibility within the developing world. But, if no one outside South-East Asia

40 W.W. Rostow, *View from the Seventh Floor*, pages 112–120.

witnessed the drama of its titanic contest with the heavyweight champion of the peasant revolution, the ideological impact of this triumph would be minimal. People had to be spectators of this military struggle for its outcome to have any symbolic significance. Luckily, in the emerging global village, an increasing proportion of the world's population had access to the new technology of television. Even those who didn't own a set would hear about the dramatic story unfolding on the TV screens from other media or their friends. For this vital psychological operation, the US military ensured that American and foreign news crews in Vietnam were able to provide dramatic images – along with sympathetic commentary – for the audiences watching in their front rooms across the world.[41] Filmed from the occupying power's viewpoint on the battlefield, these reports presented a one-sided experience of the ebb and flow of the distant war. Heroic journalists went on search and destroy missions with US troops. TV pundits explained the latest American strategy for winning the war. US embassy press officers talked about favourable kill ratios and rising body counts. Above all, the viewers saw – with their own eyes – the awesome destructive power of American hi-tech weaponry.[42] Hard power was creating the special effects for soft power. In the most literal sense of the phrase, the American invasion of Vietnam was a show of force: a spectacular display of imperial might.

> In the end, victory was ours ... a very important point was made – that US infantrymen using established techniques, impromptu ingenuity and plenty of support in the air can seek out and destroy the best guerrilla army in the world.[43]

In January 1968, the Vietnamese resistance launched an urban uprising against the American occupation: the Tet Offensive. Convinced by studying Mao and Guevara that the war would be decided in the countryside, the US military was initially taken by surprise by this sudden switch in strategy. Their opponent had broken the rules of the counter-insurgency computer game. In the first week of the Tet Offensive, Vietnamese guerrillas seized

41 See Michael Mandelbaum, 'Vietnam: the television war'; and Michael Herr, Dispatches, pages 214–219.
42 See CBS, The Vietnam War: courage under fire; The Vietnam War: the end of the road; and Mandelbaum, 'Vietnam', pages 158–160.
43 Morley Safer – a CBS TV news correspondent – in CBS, Vietnam War.

control of major cities in the provinces and large areas of Saigon – the capital of the southern state. But, once it had recovered from the momentary shock, the US military's massive firepower ruthlessly put down the uprising. When the final body count was made, the Americans were the clear winners of the Tet Offensive. The Communists had lost almost half their army in a suicidal frontal assault against a far superior force. Crucially, the overwhelming majority of the urban population of the south had refused to join the uprising against the American army and its local collaborators.[44] Rostow and his colleagues were jubilant. The CENIS academics knew that the Vietnamese had ignored the basic principles of Maoist peasant guerrilla war by attacking in the cities. According to their computer calculations, the US army had finally inflicted the decisive blow on their Communist enemy. After the Tet Offensive, an American victory was certain.[45]

Unfortunately for the Johnson administration, the US military's computers had badly miscalculated. As subsequent events would prove, Vietnam – a nation without television – had just won the war on television. On the first day of the Tet Offensive, people around the world had watched in amazement as the US Army fought Communist guerrillas in the grounds of the American embassy in Saigon. Having seized the lead item in the daily news bulletins, the Vietnamese resistance held the attention of the international TV audience for as long as possible. Week after week, their guerrillas stubbornly held their ground against far superior American forces. By the time that the Communists were defeated on the Asian battlefield, they had emerged victorious in the global village. By putting on their own spectacular show of force, the Vietnamese had won the television war. Hard power had been sacrificed to create irresistible soft power.[46] When the Tet Offensive was finally over, Walter Cronkite – the well-loved presenter of the top-rated US television news show – gave a sombre analysis of its long-term impact upon the conflict. For the first time, an authority

---

[44] See Sheehan, Smith, Kenworthy and Butterfield, *Pentagon Papers*, pages 589–601, 613–621; and Maclear, *Vietnam*, pages 274–300.

[45] See Rostow, *Diffusion of Power*, 459–470; and Sheehan, Smith, Kenworthy and Butterfield, *Pentagon Papers*, pages 615–621.

[46] The *Washington Post* journalist who covered this crisis was convinced that 'the Tet Offensive was America's first television superbattle'. Don Oberdorfer, *Tet!*, page 159.

figure publicly expressed what many Americans were thinking after watching three months of dramatic TV coverage of vicious urban fighting: victory wasn't certain.

> We have been too often disappointed by the optimism of American leaders ... to have any faith in the silver linings they find in the darkest clouds. ... For it seems now more certain than ever that the bloody experience of Vietnam is to end in stalemate. ... To say that we are closer to victory is to believe ... the optimists who have been wrong in the past.[47]

During the rapid escalation of the war after the 1965 invasion, the overwhelming majority of Americans had patriotically backed the Johnson administration's firm action to halt the spread of global Communism in Vietnam.[48] Night after night, the evening news bulletins had told them that US troops were on the verge of beating their guerrilla opponents. With the government being led by the best minds in the country, they had no reason to doubt the predictions of their political leaders. The Tet Offensive changed everything. In the three years before 1968, the Johnson administration had repackaged the failure of its military offensives in the countryside as great victories. But, when Communist guerrillas fighting in the cities dominated the news bulletins every night, this carefully constructed hyper-reality suddenly imploded. The Vietnamese resistance's intelligent use of information technologies had inflicted a crushing defeat upon the American ideologues of the information society. Fighting for credibility in the South, the Democratic government had lost it at home. Public support for the war fell dramatically and never recovered.[49] During the six months following the uprising, Johnson announced his resignation from the presidency, the commander of American forces in Vietnam was removed and a committee of the inner circle of the US elite concluded that the occupation was unsustainable. After trying everything else, the only remaining option was withdrawal with the minimum of symbolic damage: 'peace with honour'.[50]

---

47 Walter Cronkite in CBS, *The Vietnam War: the end of the road*.

48 See Rostow, *Diffusion of Power*, 478–481.

49 See Oberdorfer, *Tet!*, pages 238–345; and Halberstam, *Best and Brightest*, pages 647–648.

50 See Bernstein, *Guns or Butter*, pages 473–521; and Halberstam, *Best and Brightest*, pages 647–658.

The collapse of public support at home was fatal in an occupation army made up overwhelmingly of conscripts. Like its Vietnamese client regime, the American government discovered that it was impossible to persuade soldiers to fight if they were determined not to fight. Gung-ho officers were murdered by their own troops. Disaffected soldiers published anti-war newspapers. Drug-taking became widespread within the armed forces.[51] For seven agonising years after the Tet Offensive, the American empire refused to concede defeat. As the mutinous infantry went home, US bombers continued to inflict pain and misery upon the unfortunate inhabitants of South-East Asia. America – as media communicators kept reminding their viewers – was stuck in a quagmire. In 1975, the agony was finally over. A political scandal at home allowed opponents of the war in the legislature to cut off financial and military support for the made-in-the-USA puppet state. Deprived of its American patron, the never-built nation of South Vietnam quickly collapsed.

In the last scene of the final episode of the long-running television series, Communist troops seized control of the US client regime's presidential palace in Saigon. After more than three decades of war, Vietnam was finally liberated from foreign occupation. Unfortunately, the international TV news crews had arrived too late for the dramatic moment when the Vietnamese tank had driven straight through the front gates of the palace. Determined to capture this world-historical image for the viewers in the global village, the victors quickly repaired the gate and took their positions. When the camera crews were ready, the tank drove through the gates for a second time and Vietnamese soldiers once again liberated the palace. Evening news bulletins across the world now had the iconic image to accompany their lead story. The war won on television had ended on television.[52]

Confounding the CENIS experts' dire predictions, the liberation of Saigon didn't lead to American dominos toppling across the South. On the contrary, the victorious Maoists quickly turned on each other. In the late 1970s, Vietnam was first attacked by Cambodia and then, after defeating this erstwhile ally, by its former

---

[51] For an account of the conscripts' revolt against their officers, see Kolko, *Anatomy of a War*, pages 359–367; and Jonathan Neale, *The American War*, pages 117–146.
[52] See Maclear, *Vietnam*, pages 465–466; and CBS, *Vietnam War*.

sponsor China.[53] When peace finally came, the country – belatedly – began to modernise its economy. With the Communists securely in power, Vietnam was able to focus its energies on moving towards industrialisation and urbanisation. In the 1960s, Rostow had predicted that the unification of the two halves of the country would lead to Maoist-style economic autarchy. Instead, Vietnam – like China itself – decided to imitate its East Asian neighbours which had successfully industrialised within the US sphere of influence during the 1960s and 1970s. By the mid 2000s, American companies were making substantial investments in the Vietnamese economy. With the arrival of the Net, this once-isolated country was joining the global village. Back home, US business magazines reported that free trade was succeeding where military force had failed.[54] Soft power had proved its superiority over hard power. In the last years of his life, Rostow felt confident enough to claim that the grand narrative of history had – three decades after 1975 – vindicated the mistakes of the past:

> [T]he American people ... held the line [in Vietnam] so that a free Asia could survive and grow; for, in the end, the war ... [was] about who would control the balance of power in Asia ... Those [Americans] who died or were wounded or are veterans of that conflict were not involved in a pointless war.[55]

Like most Hollywood movies about the Vietnam conflict, Rostow's article tried to repackage America's most humiliating defeat as a retrospective victory.[56] However, it was far too late for him to rescue a public reputation which had been ruined by the media spectacle of the Tet Offensive. At the very beginning of 1968, Rostow had stood at the peak of his career. This Cold War Left intellectual was the closest adviser to the most powerful political leader on the planet. Using his deep understanding of the materialist conception of history, he was devising wise and rational policies for the Modern Prince. But, before the year was over, Rostow was out of office and openly reviled. His downfall began when the weeks

---

53 See Grant Evans and Kelvin Rowley, *Red Brotherhood at War*, pages 34–62, 84–164.
54 See Frederick Balfour, 'Vietnam Toddles into a Capitalist Future'; 'Vietnam's Time is Running Out'.
55 W.W. Rostow, 'The Case for the Vietnam War', page 6.
56 In a 1985 film fantasy, its Vietnam veteran hero plaintively asked: 'Sir? Do we get to win this time?' George Cosmatos, *Rambo: First Blood Part 2*.

of dramatic television coverage of the Tet Offensive shattered the credibility of the Johnson administration's optimistic predictions of imminent victory. Worst of all, the Democrats' disastrous imperial adventure in Vietnam had completely overshadowed its impressive political and social achievements at home. At the end of 1968, the Republicans were able to win a narrow majority in the presidential elections. By failing to deliver a quick and easy victory in Vietnam, the Cold War Left had lost political power in America.[57]

When Rostow asked to return to his old job at MIT, his request was politely refused. Too closely identified with the American debacle in Vietnam, the founder of the world-famous CENIS research centre had become a political embarrassment. Turned down by every other elite educational institution, Rostow was forced to take an academic post at Austin University that was in the gift of his former employer: Lyndon Johnson.[58] As well as publicly shaming him as an individual, the exiling of the author of *The Stages of Economic Growth* to Texas also marked the end of the collective hegemony of the Cold War Left over intellectual life in America. Back in 1960, when Rostow departed from MIT to join the Kennedy administration, this movement had defined its common identity through its consensual third-way politics. But, by 1968, the American war against the Vietnamese had shattered this image of ideological unity. Instead of speaking with one voice, the master thinkers of the Cold War Left were now angrily arguing with each other. Rostow was the bellicose architect of the invasion. Galbraith had always opposed US intervention in the region. Kahn claimed that a more sophisticated counter-insurgency strategy would bring victory. Schlesinger published a book advocating a negotiated settlement with the Communist resistance.[59] Just like the rest of the American public, the Vital Centre had been forced to choose between two incompatible positions: patriotic imperialism or anti-war activism. There was no third-way solution to this crisis.

Like political consensus, economic compromise was another treasured principle of the Cold War Left which became a casualty

---

[57] See Bernstein, *Guns or Butter*, pages 471–542.

[58] See Geoffrey Hodgson, 'Walt Rostow'.

[59] See Dallek, *Kennedy*, pages 355, 451, 460–461; Herman Kahn, 'Toward a Program of Victory'; and Arthur Schlesinger, Jr., *The Bitter Heritage*.

of the conflict. Inspired by Keynesian theory, both the Kennedy and Johnson administrations simultaneously cut taxes and increased expenditure. At first, this expansionary policy was highly successful. The growth rate went up and so did employment, wages and profits.[60] Unfortunately, as the costs of the occupation of Vietnam escalated out of control, this expansion of effective demand outpaced the productive powers of the US economy. Even worse, the stimulation of output was increasingly diverted from solving pressing social needs at home into financing imperial expansion overseas. Contrary to the Cold War Left's expectations, the USA did have to choose between guns and butter. By the late 1960s, American military spending was beginning to destabilise the global financial system. As the inflationary spiral took off, governments across the North struggled to control the economic crisis.[61] Back in the 1950s, the Cold War Left had argued that state intervention was essential to correct the boom-and-bust cycle of the market. Enlightened regulation was the guarantor of prosperity. Yet, when the Democratic administration put this Keynesian policy into practice in the mid 1960s, its expansionist policies had instead destabilised the market. Confounding the expectations of Galbraith and the CENIS researchers, the US economy couldn't be programmed like an IBM System/360 mainframe. The Vital Centre's software had crashed.

In the 1950s, the founders of the Cold War Left had been convinced that – by objectively analysing the empirical evidence with value-free theory – the US government would be able to formulate policies in an informed and intelligent manner. Using computer games, academic experts could dispassionately calculate the winning moves in the contest for global hegemony. Yet, when the Kennedy and Johnson administrations had made the key decisions about American intervention in Vietnam, ideology had always taken precedence over rationality. In the great game between the superpowers, struggles in the impoverished South were no longer the harmless sublimation of dangerous rivalries in the rich North. By the early 1960s, the Cold War Left had convinced itself that the

---

[60] See Dallek, Kennedy, pages 333–335, 506–509, 583–589; and Bernstein, Guns or Butter, pages 27–42, 82–113.
[61] See Bernstein, Guns or Butter, pages 358–378; and Alain Lipietz, L'Audace ou l'enlisement, pages 37–64.

security of the American empire depended upon securing a symbolic victory over Vietnamese Communism. As it committed more and more resources to winning this unwinnable war, the Democratic administration inadvertently turned an impoverished rice-growing region into the most valuable piece of real estate on the planet. The war had become an end in itself.

> At each decision point, we have gambled; at each point to avoid the damage to our effectiveness of defaulting on our commitment, we have upped the ante. ... We have not defaulted, and the ante (and our commitment) is now very high.[62]

As the military situation deteriorated after the 1965 invasion, President Johnson and his advisers became increasingly incapable of distinguishing their own wishful thinking from the reality on the ground in Vietnam. Paradoxically, the availability of the latest information technologies encouraged their delusions about the war. Thanks to advances in computing and telecommunications, politicians in America believed that they were able to direct military operations over on the other side of the world. Mesmerised by their virtual proximity to the fighting, they placed their trust in the mediated interpretation of the war provided by information technologies. Crucially, the civilians never seriously questioned the reliability of the data provided by the US military. As long as the daily body count kept rising, Johnson – encouraged by Rostow – persuaded himself that victory was close. Every time that information from the battlefield was inputted into the IBM mainframes, the CENIS software calculated that the Americans were winning the war. Ironically, far from helping the Democratic leadership to understand what was happening in South-East Asia, these computerised statistics had created an ideological hyper-reality. Like the subjects of the Turing test, the Johnson administration could no longer distinguish between the imitation and the original. Technological fetishism had deceived its greatest admirers.[63]

Nowhere was this contradiction between theory and practice clearer than in the social background of the Vietnamese who

---

[62] John McNaughton – a junior US defence minister – in Sheehan, Smith, Kenworthy and Butterfield, *Pentagon Papers*, page 492.

[63] See Oberdorfer, *Tet!*, pages 98–100; and Halberstam, *Best and Brightest*, pages 637–639.

welcomed the American occupation of their country. According to the CENIS textbooks, the US should have supported the Third Force modernising elite. Instead, the Democratic administration had become the new protector of the minority who had prospered under French rule: absentee landlords, foreign merchants, nepotistic bureaucrats and greedy generals. As in Brazil, the MIT experts picked the military forces of this corrupt oligarchy as its replacement for the missing modernising elite. Not surprisingly, the Vietnamese peasantry failed to appreciate their good fortune when steam-age European colonialism was replaced by computer-age American imperialism. All that happened was that their oppressors had transferred their loyalties to another foreign power. The Democratic administration's decision to ally itself with the traditional elite doomed the American cause in Vietnam. Hard power couldn't replace soft power. For the peasantry, expelling the imperialists who protected the old regime meant victory over the parasitical landowners and merchants who had exploited them for centuries. Confounding Rostow's prognosis, the majority of the Vietnamese population saw Maoism as much more modern than MIT modernisation theory. The US promise of democracy and plenty within the global village in times to come was no substitute for the immediate benefits of national independence and land reform. In 1960s Vietnam, Communism was still the wave of the future.[64] When the conflict was finally over, Vo Nguyen Giap – the military leader of the resistance – celebrated Maoist mobilisation as a higher stage of modernity than McLuhanist technology: '... our people ... have succeeded ... in ... making civilisation triumph over brute force and overcoming our enemy's superior armaments with our absolute political and moral superiority'.[65]

The weakness of the American position in Vietnam had inexorably led to the decision in 1965 to crush the peasant insurgency with overwhelming force. Lacking any other solution to the crisis, the Johnson administration rapidly lost control over the US military in its desperation for a quick victory. Unable to win the hearts and minds of the Vietnamese peasantry, the American armed forces declared all-out war on the entire countryside. Needing high scores

64 See Taber, The War of the Flea, pages 73–89; and Kolko, Anatomy of a War, pages 107–108, 208–222.
65 Vo Nguyen Giap, National Liberation War in Vietnam, page 28.

in the body count to please their commanders, soldiers began to massacre civilians and then record their deaths as Communist losses.[66] What started as spontaneous atrocities quickly evolved into a policy of deliberate genocide. In 1930s China, the Maoists had poetically described their guerrilla army as fish swimming in the sea of the peasantry.[67] Having failed to find the fish, the US military decided that it would drain the sea. More and more of the Vietnamese countryside was turned into a 'free-fire zone' to terrify the population into the cities. When there were no more peasants, the peasant revolution would be finished.[68]

In 1968, Samuel Huntington – a political scientist at Harvard University – claimed that the US military had finally found the antidote to the Maoist threat in the South.[69] By destroying the peasantry as a class, the Americans were depriving the revolutionary movement in Vietnam of its social base. As added bonus, the refugees in the southern cities were now available as a pool of cheap labour. The Vietnamese economy was about to take off into the industrial stage of growth. Echoing Stalin in the 1930s, Huntington praised state violence for its alchemic ability to accelerate the process of modernisation. In this noble cause, the US military's indiscriminate slaughter of Vietnamese civilians was excused as a regrettable necessity. Back in the 1950s, the CCF had successfully defined the superpower confrontation in Europe as the choice between American democracy and Russian dictatorship. But, in 1960s Vietnam, this favourable comparison couldn't be made. As the US military's offensives in the countryside demonstrated, the Cold War Left had become more totalitarian than its Stalinist opponents. Worst of all, unlike in 1930s Russia, the destruction of the peasantry in Vietnam didn't even lead – as Huntington had promised – to the rapid industrialisation of the country. On the contrary, like the old

---

[66] See Halberstam, *Best and Brightest*, pages 616–618; and Noam Chomsky, *For Reasons of State*, pages 83–84.

[67] See Geoffrey Fairbairn, *Revolutionary Guerrilla Warfare*, pages 98–100; and Mao Zedong, *Six Essays on Military Affairs*, pages 268–271.

[68] In 1971, an American soldier informed a US Congressional committee that '[t]he military doesn't distinguish between North Vietnamese, South Vietnamese, Vietcong [guerrilla], civilian – all of them are gooks, all of them are considered subhuman ... And all of them can be killed and all of them are killed'. Jamie Henry in Winter Soldier Investigation, 'Third Marine Division, Part 3', page 4.

[69] See Samuel Huntington, 'The Bases of Accommodation'.

ruling class, these new proletarians also ended up living off the US taxpayer. MIT modernisation theory put into practice had created the squalid slums of Saigon.[70]

As the war in Vietnam intensified in the mid 1960s, Rostow spent many hours arguing the Johnson administration's case at university meetings and with delegations of students.[71] However, all of his efforts were in vain. Within the universities, the gurus of the Cold War Left were becoming the targets of the increasingly militant student anti-war movement. Instead of being credited for its major political and social achievements at home, the Johnson administration was identified with the brutal imagery of the Vietnamese battlefield dominating the TV news bulletins. The audience who had once listened in awe was now openly contemptuous. Student radicals denounced their Anti-Communist professors as perpetrators of genocide. Inside the institutional icon of the information society, the knowledge class was joining the anti-imperialist revolution. If about nothing else, the militants of the New Left were united in their contempt for the guilty intellectuals of the Cold War Left.

At the very moment when the Bell commission began preaching the prophecy of post-industrialism to the peoples of the world, the Tet Offensive had suddenly exposed the limitations of American technological superiority. As the leaders of the Vietnamese resistance emphasised, humanity – not machinery – was the subject of history. Even worse, as the Cold War Left realised to its dismay, American imperial hegemony was now threatened by two key components of the emerging information society: the knowledge class and the electronic media. Student protests were demoralising the troops in Vietnam. The TV news bulletins were responsible for undermining support for the war at home. Traumatised by their fall from power, Rostow and other hawks of the Cold War Left needed scapegoats for their own disastrous misjudgements. Like the Nazis blaming Marxists and Jews for Germany's defeat in the First World War, they claimed that the US military had been betrayed by a 'stab in the back' by infantile hippies and irresponsible journalists.[72] These two

---

70 See Kolko, *Anatomy of a War*, pages 465–469, 489–491.

71 See Rostow, *Diffusion of Power*, pages 497–498.

72 See Rostow, *Diffusion of Power*, pages 484–503; and C. Dale Walton, *The Myth of Inevitable U.S. Defeat in Vietnam*, pages 33–47.

privileged sectors of the nascent information society had inexplicably turned on their generous benefactors.

In the late 1960s, the New Left forged its identity through a rejection of the Cold War Left credo. The murderous reality of Vietnam had exposed the hypocrisy of the consensual rhetoric of the third way. Democrats with a capital D had proved themselves to be the enemies of democracy with a small d. Not surprisingly, these young activists wanted to be everything that that their elders weren't: revolutionary, upfront and passionate. Admiration for the heroism of the Vietnamese freedom fighters soon led them to the rejection of all Cold War orthodoxies. American opponents of US imperialism must be Anti-Anti-Communists. Forgetting his crimes in Stalinist Cuba, the New Left idolised Che Guevara as a Christ-like revolutionary martyr who had sacrificed his life for the poor.[73] More seriously, ignoring the brutal reality of Maoist China, the leaders of the anti-war movement embraced the ideology of America's Vietnamese enemy: Maoism.[74] In a form of reverse colonisation, the revolutionary vanguard of the South now had a detachment in the North.

Back in the 1930s, Stalinists and Trotskyists in the USA had looked to Russia for their model of the socialist imaginary future. Three decades on, the New Left had found a new Communist homeland: the South. Inverting Rostow's stages of growth, these hippy radicals argued – like Giap – that peasant China stood at a more advanced point in the grand narrative of history than Fordist America. Each evening on the TV news bulletin, the Vietnamese resistance proved that solidarity, not technology, was the measure of human progress. By launching the 'Great Proletarian Cultural Revolution' in 1966, Mao was ridding China of the last vestiges of capitalist hierarchy. Inside the factory society of Russia, the experts still ruled over the masses just as they did in America. Fortunately, thanks to Mao, the Chinese were already living according to the principles of the Paris Commune. In the South, participatory democracy and cooperative creativity weren't postponed to the

---

[73] A hippy leader exulted: 'Che is a bigger hero to Amerikan youth than ... Kennedy. ... You gotta be born a Kennedy. Anybody can become Che. Revolutionaries have eternal life – because we live on in each other.' Jerry Rubin, Do It! page 130.

[74] See A. Belden Fields, Trotskyism and Maoism, pages 184–229; and Kirkpatrick Sale, SDS, pages 369–556.

imaginary future of the information society. Peasant communism existed in the here and now. As the vanguard of the South in the North, American revolutionaries had the task of remaking their country in the image of China. On his return from the Maoist wonderland, Huey P. Newton – the leader of the Black Panther Party – reported:

> Everything I saw in China demonstrated that the People's Republic is a free and liberated territory with a socialist government. The way is open for people to gain their freedom and determine their own destiny. ... Here, Marx's dictum – from each according to his abilities to each according to his needs – is in operation.[75]

At the 1939 New York World's Fair, living in a suburb and owning a car had symbolised the wonders of the imaginary future. However, three decades on, hippy radicals who had grown up within this Fordist utopia were much more aware of the downsides of the affluent society. Boxed into their prosperous suburbs, many Americans were enduring unfulfilled and frustrated lives. For all tendencies of the New Left, the horrors of the Vietnam War were the most extreme manifestation of this deeper social malaise. In the late 1960s, the struggle against the system was as much cultural as political. Hippy fashions and psychedelic drugs symbolised the rejection of the warped values of their parents' generation.[76] Living in a collective household and owning a record player were the new symbols of the imaginary future. Among a committed minority, dropping out of the consumer society altogether was the ultimate declaration of independence from the Cold War Left's grand narrative of modernity. Rather than waiting patiently for the arrival of the information society, the New Left would prefigure participatory democracy and cooperative creativity within its own organisations.[77] If Chinese peasants could run their own lives, then the rebels of affluent America could also liberate themselves from big government and big business. Crucially, by looking to the South, the New Left had rediscovered the founding principles of their own nation. Before the advent of Fordism, the USA had been the land of town hall

75 Huey P. Newton, *Revolutionary Suicide*, page 326.
76 See Charles Reich, *The Greening of America*; and Rubin, *Do It!*
77 Bob Avakian – a leading American Maoist – argued that these hippy collectives were already 'halfway communist' in their organisational structure. See Bob Avakian, *From Ike to Mao*, page 218.

meetings, protest movements and grassroots activism. After a long detour through Europe, Russia and China, the libertarian ideals of the 1776 Revolution had returned to America in a Maoist guise. The past had become the future. Che was a sexier version of Jefferson.

In *Understanding Media*, the younger generation found another kindred spirit who shared their antipathy towards the soullessness of modern capitalism. Like them, McLuhan also favoured an imaginary future which promised a return to the intimacy of village life. Best of all, this Canadian guru celebrated the emancipatory potential of new media. For the New Left, rock concerts, psychedelic happenings, beat poetry, underground newspapers, alternative films, community radio stations and video screenings were an integral part of making the revolution. Young people were creating their own forms of expression to combat the repressive ideologies promoted by the commercial media of straight society.[78] Like Mao, McLuhan provided these radicals with theoretical confirmation of what they were already doing. Being participatory, collective and intuitive, the hippy counter-culture was the embodiment of the imaginary future of the global village in the present. The New Left had rejected all of the Cold War Left's ideologies except its most seductive product: McLuhanism.

By the late 1960s, counter-cultural activists had turned the prophecy of the information society into the theory of their own rebellion. Devised to replace the imaginary future of cybernetic communism, McLuhanism now became its intellectual rationale. In this remix, the New Left's own media experiments were praised as the precursors of the participatory utopia of the Net: the electronic agora. The monologue of capitalist propaganda was turning into the dialogue of hippy communities. Across the Atlantic, the Situationists had pioneered this theoretical fusion of Marxism and McLuhanism. In contrast with their Maoist comrades, these New Left thinkers had found their revolutionary inspiration in the heartland of global capitalism. The inhabitants of America and Western Europe may have been temporarily pacified by welfare democracy, consumer goods and television fantasies: the 'society of the spectacle'.[79] But,

[78] See David Armstrong, *A Trumpet to Arms*; and Theodore Roszak, *The Making of a Counter Culture*.
[79] See Guy Debord, *The Society of the Spectacle*; and Raoul Vaneigem, *The Revolution of Everyday Life*.

by building this technological infrastructure, Fordism had also summoned into being its own nemesis. Anticipating the arrival of the Net, the Situationists believed that the one-way flow of information from the few to the many was already in the process of being transformed into two-way interactive communications amongst the entire population. The party politics and bureaucratic hierarchies of the newspaper and television age would soon be obsolete. In their place, the Paris Commune would be reborn as the electronic agora. As the fetishised institutions of the market and the state withered away, the Fordist society of the spectacle would be superseded by the cybernetic society of the Net.[80] Following the May '68 Revolution in France, this Situationist analysis was popularised across the North as the cutting-edge theory of Marxism–McLuhanism. Technological determinism now became the proof of inevitable victory in the class struggle. As media, telecommunications and computing converged, humanity was re-emerging as the subject of history. The affluent society was the immediate precursor of cybernetic communism.[81]

> Like almost everyone in the [US] left, I have a genuine suspicion about the mass media, especially television. [However] ... some day real soon most families in [the American] PIG NATION will be able through their TV sets to have a computer at their disposal ... the most revolutionary means of communications since language itself was invented.[82]

On the libertarian left of the New Left, the building of the electronic agora promised the completion of the grand narrative of history. According to Marx and Engels, premonitions of hi-tech communism could be found in tribal societies: 'primitive communism'.[83] Before the European invasions, Native Americans had successfully run their own lives without any need for either the state or the market. For the more radical members of the New

---

80 See Raoul Vaneigem, 'Notice to the Civilised Concerning Generalised Self-Management'; and Daniel Cohn-Bendit and Gabriel Cohn-Bendit, Obsolete Communism, pages 103–112.
81 See Richard Barbrook, Media Freedom, pages 96–113.
82 Abbie Hoffman, Woodstock Nation, page 105. This hippy McLuhanist prophecy was made in 1969.
83 See Friedrich Engels, The Origins of the Family, Private Property and the State; and Franklin Rosemont, 'Karl Marx and the Iroquois'.

Left, these indigenous peoples, compared to the Stalinist factory or the Maoist village, seemed to offer a much more equalitarian and democratic model for the post-capitalist utopia.[84] With the advent of the Net imminent, the peoples of the North now had the opportunity to recreate this participatory society at a much higher technological level. In the universities, academic research was already organised like a tribal gift economy. From their 'Red Bases' in higher education, the New Left would sally out to remake the whole of US society in the image of the campus. Since cybernation was going to abolish most factory jobs, everyone should live like a student. With a growing surfeit of consumer goods, everything would soon be available for free. After centuries of suffering, the path of modernisation had reached its final destination: the socialist–feminist utopia of cybernetic communism.[85]

Focused upon the ideological threat from overseas, the Cold War Left had inadvertently provided political inspiration for its New Left opponents at home. By the early 1970s, many young Americans equated the global village with cybernetic communism. Enthused by a mixture of Marxism and McLuhanism, radical members of the knowledge class had become convinced that the academic gift economy was the precursor of the social revolution. Yet, despite its increasingly subversive image, the US government never abandoned this disruptive method of organising intellectual labour. In Russia, political controls over information distribution were slowing down the pace of scientific research. If America was going to win the Cold War technology race, its academic institutions required more sophisticated methods of working. While at ARPA, Licklider began the process of constructing the Net by creating a self-governing community of computer scientists. When cleverly managed, the practitioners of cybernetic communism could be persuaded to serve the interests of the US military. In return, the builders of the Net were allowed to hard-wire the academic gift economy into its social mores and technical architecture. Insulated from the state and the market, the university became the prototype of the post-capitalist information society. Over in the East, communism still remained

---

[84] The Situationists discovered an attractive description of this tribal gift economy in Marcel Mauss, The Gift.
[85] See Shulamith Firestone, The Dialectic of Sex, pages 183–195, 210–224.

a distant imaginary future. Ironically, it was in the West that the hi-tech gift economy existed in embryo. Within a small group of computer scientists, the participatory democracy and cooperative creativity of the Net had already arrived. Before a select gathering of American and European decision makers at the 1969 meeting of the conspiratorial Bilderberg Group, McLuhan mischievously highlighted this ideological conundrum by asking the never-to-be-asked-in-public question: 'What are we fighting Communism for? We are the most Communist people in world history.'[86]

While American campuses were engulfed in revolutionary turmoil, Daniel Bell continued working on the canonical text of the Cold War Left's imaginary future. McLuhan's impressionistic thought probes were slowly translated into scholarly McLuhanist theory and carefully provided with empirical evidence. In 1973, the great work was finally published. During the years since the Bell commission had first met, excessive optimism in hi-tech solutions had led America into disaster at home and abroad. Like other thinkers of the Cold War Left, its chairman was disorientated by the sudden implosion of the movement. The advocate of the ideology of the end of ideology had been confronted by the choice between two incompatible – and undesirable – ideologies. On the one hand, Bell refused to join his hawkish friends who would soon become the stalwarts of the neo-conservative faction of the Republican Party.[87] On the other hand, he despaired when the student revolutionaries made the same mistakes as he had in his youth. Just like Trotskyism, Maoism was totalitarian ideology from an earlier stage of growth.

In *The Coming of the Post-Industrial Society*, Bell stressed that the knowledge class was the new vanguard of the future. During its libertarian moments, the New Left had believed that participatory democracy and cooperative creativity could be prefigured within its own organisations. But, for Bell, the only sure road to human emancipation was completing the convergence of media, telecommunications and computing into the Net. Until this imaginary future arrived in the 2000s, the knowledge class would

---

86 Marshall McLuhan, 'Letter to Prince Bernhard of the Netherlands', page 373. Also see Mike Peters, 'Bilderberg and the Origins of the EU'.
87 See Alan Wald, New York Intellectuals, pages 344–365.

remain a privileged minority. Far from being a Red Base, the university was the hi-tech home of intellectual elitism. By publishing his canonical text, Bell reasserted the Cold War Left's claim of ownership over the McLuhanist prophecy. With both Maoists and Situationists fascinated by the demiurgic power of information technologies, this codification of his commission's research had ideological potency. The Vital Centre was seizing modernity back from the New Left. McLuhanism was the replacement for Marxism, not its reinvigoration. Technology was – once again – the maker of history. The next stage of growth would be made-in-the-USA. The Cold War Left was dead – and the global village was still the imaginary future. 'In a cybernetic culture, power grows from computer print-outs, not the barrel of the gun'.[88]

---

[88] Michael Shamberg and Raindance Corporation, *Guerrilla Television*, page 30. This insight is a New Left remix of Mao's famous slogan: 'Political power grows out of the barrel of a gun.' Mao Zedong, *Quotations of Chairman Mao Zedong*, page 61.

15

THOSE WHO FORGET THE FUTURE ARE CONDEMNED TO REPEAT IT

On 30 April 2005, the anchor of the ABC evening news bulletin introduced – in a sombre and thoughtful voice – a short piece about the thirtieth anniversary of the 'fall of Saigon'. The pictures taken earlier in the day of the Vietnamese victory celebrations were followed by longer coverage of American veterans mourning their dead buddies. Archive material reminded viewers about the New Left's political and cultural rebellion against the war at home. Sound bites from experts proved that this conflict still divided the nation. On this particular anniversary, reporting on the Vietnam War commemorations wasn't just about marking a historical turning point. Only minutes before, the ABC evening bulletin had covered the latest grim news from Iraq. For many Americans, the parallels with Vietnam were obvious. Three decades on, US soldiers were once again fighting against guerrillas in a faraway country. In 2005, Middle Eastern current affairs bore a disturbing resemblance to South-East Asian history.

What had changed dramatically in the intervening 30 years was the ideological credo of America's enemies. When the Johnson administration had launched its war against the Vietnamese, the US military's task was halting the spread of Communism: the autarchic path of modernisation in the South. Thirty years on, this American dream had been realised. Far from being the wave of the future, Communism was now history. China and Vietnam had abandoned Maoism for the market economy. The authoritarian regimes of Eastern Europe had collapsed. Above all, Communism had lost its Russian heartland. In 1968, by crushing the Czechoslovak reform movement, the Brezhnev government had institutionalised bureaucratic conservatism within the Eastern bloc. Like social change, technological innovation became mistrusted as a disruptive and subversive force.[1] Back in the 1930s, Stalinist state planning had been at the cutting edge of economic modernity. But, as the theorists of the Prague Spring had pointed out, this was no longer the case in the computer age. By holding on to its ideological monopoly, the Communist Party had deprived itself of the information which it needed to deliver the goods.

In 1980, the Polish workers rebelled when they were once again called upon to pay for the mistakes of the economic planners.[2]

---

[1] See Stanislaw Gomulka, *Growth, Innovation and Reform in Eastern Europe*, pages 42–61.
[2] See Stanislaw Starski, *Class Struggle in Classless Poland*; and Jean-Yves Potel, *The Summer Before the Frost*.

Like an inverted version of the domino theory, the disintegration of Communism in one country started a chain reaction of events which within a decade brought down the entire Communist empire. When he became Russian leader in 1985, Mikhail Gorbachev attempted – too late – to open up the Stalinist system to feedback from below. Having long forgotten its world-historical mission, the vanguard party was much more interested in becoming fully-fledged members of the Western bourgeoisie. As the ruling elite rushed to enrich itself by privatising state assets, the cybernetic planners were among the last believers in non-market solutions. In an ironic twist, the arrival of the Net in Russia had coincided with the disappearance of the communist imaginary future. The new generation of reformers had decided that only free markets could accomplish what state planning was incapable of doing: optimising the distribution of labour and resources across the economy.[3] In 1991, the ousting of Gorbachev marked the final end of the Communist era. Live on television, Stalinist statues were toppled and the red flag lowered over the Kremlin. The transition to capitalism could now be accelerated. Communism was the future which had failed.

In his 1992 neo-conservative best-seller, Francis Fukuyama proudly announced that – at the end of the grand narrative of history – the whole world had become American.[4] The experience of the twentieth century proved that there was no alternative to the US model of democratic capitalism. By winning the Cold War, America had healed the divisions created by the fall of the British empire. With autarchy discredited, economic liberalism was – once again – uniting humanity. The only Stalinist holdouts were the maverick regimes of North Korea and Cuba. Like Rostow, Fukuyama and his admirers were convinced that Russia, China and the other 'post-communist' countries were all capable of imitating the American way of doing things. With all alternatives now discredited, there was only one path to modernity. Under the tutelage of the US-led international institutions, free markets and free media were spreading the benefits of American capitalism to everyone on the planet. Global brands were creating a globalised

---

[3] For a perceptive eyewitness account of this transition, see Jonathan Steele, *Eternal Russia*.
[4] See Francis Fukuyama, *The End of History and the Last Man*.

humanity. When they appeared together at UN meetings and G8 summits, the leaders of the major powers formed the executive of this new Universal State. Guided by the US elite, the global village was the universalisation of the constitutional settlement of the 1776 American Revolution.[5] A single market required a single model of government.

Between 1948 and 1991, the Cold War standoff had underpinned US domination of the world system. When its Russian opponent had folded, America was proclaimed the winner of the great game. Capitalism had beaten Communism. Unfortunately for the US elite, this victory also came at the cost of losing the geopolitical benefits of the Yalta Agreement. With no external threat to discipline its satellites, America's hold over its sphere of influence was seriously weakened.[6] At this moment of ideological crisis, Huntington – the apologist of genocide in Vietnam – provided a new geopolitical rationale for US hegemony: the 'clash of civilisations'.[7] The victory of American democracy over Russian totalitarianism had misled the advocates of globalisation. During the 1990s, instead of uniting around common values, the peoples of the world had become even more divided by their different – and competing – cultural identities. Not surprisingly, in this remake of the Cold War, America again had the starring role as the champion of Western civilisation against the barbarian menace from the East. Replacing the Russians and Chinese, Muslims were identified as the new enemy. Updating Rostow's condemnation of Communism as the mental disease of underdeveloped countries, Huntington blamed *jihadi* fanaticism on the pathologies of Islamic culture. Because of these deep psychological roots, this confessional clash of civilisations between West and East was going to dominate global politics for generations.

For over two decades, the memory of defeat – the 'Vietnam syndrome' – limited the imperial ambitions of the US elite. American voters would punish the party which got too involved in costly wars in the South. After the 2001 al-Qa'ida attacks on New York and Washington, Republican neo-conservatives seized the opportunity

---

5 See Fukuyama, *End of History*, pages 153–161.

6 In 1987, a leading Russian geopolitical analyst joked: 'We are going to do the worst thing we possibly can to America – we are going to take away their enemy.' Georgi Arbatov, in Martin Walker, *The Cold War*, page 340.

7 See Samuel Huntington, *The Clash of Civilisations and the Remaking of World Order*.

to mobilise public support for a more unashamedly aggressive foreign policy.[8] In a rerun of the Cold War victory over Communism, the USA would defeat its new enemy by reshaping the Muslim world in its own image. Military victories in Afghanistan and Iraq would be catalysts for a wider political and economic transformation of the whole region. Under American leadership, the inhabitants of the Middle East would discover the benefits of electoral democracy and competitive markets. When the local media were reformed on the US model, people would learn to appreciate political and cultural pluralism. The Republican Party's propagandists argued that the majority of Muslims could easily be won over to the American side in the 'War on Terror'. For inhabitants of the Middle East and Central Asia, the choice was between the poverty of the Islamist past and the prosperity of the American future.[9] In 2002, US President George Bush explained:

> Today, the United States enjoys a position of unparalleled military strength and great economic and political influence. In keeping with our heritage and principles, we ... seek ... to create a [global] balance of power ... in which all nations and all societies can choose for themselves the rewards of political and economic liberty. ... Throughout history, freedom has been threatened by war and terror ... and it has been tested by widespread poverty and disease. Today, humanity holds in its hands the opportunity to further freedom's triumph over all these foes. The United States welcomes our responsibility to lead in this great mission.[10]

It was no accident that the Bush administration's geopolitical analysis was Rostow remixed for the early twenty-first century. After the Cold War Left split over Vietnam, some of its more hawkish members had reinvented themselves in the 1970s as the neo-conservative gurus of the Republican think-tanks. Despite this switch in party allegiances, they claimed that their political goals were unchanged: social reform at home and imperial expansion

---

[8] For the anticipation of this new strategy, see William Kristol and Robert Kagan, 'National Interest and Global Responsibility' and the report by the revealingly named Project for a New American Century, *Rebuilding America's Defenses*.

[9] See Shafeeq Ghabra, 'Democracy for the Arab World'; and Richard Hass, 'Towards Greater Democracy in the Muslim World'.

[10] George W. Bush, 'The National Security Strategy of the United States of America', pages 1, 2.

overseas.[11] For these neo-conservatives, Huntington's conclusions were far too pessimistic. Like Communists, Muslims could also be converted to the American political and economic model. According to the McLuhanist creed, all civilisations were converging into the US-dominated global village. Echoing Huntington himself in his infamous 1968 article, they argued that military force should be used to speed up this process. Whatever had gone wrong last time, the awe-inspiring advances in information technologies since the 1970s had changed everything.[12] In its new 'shock and awe' strategy, the US military foresaw that the power and precision of its hi-tech weaponry would terrify the enemy into submission.[13] This time around, sophisticated computer games would be able to devise the winning strategy.[14]

For the Bush administration, hard power was soft power. The Iraq War was not only a war for oil, but also, more importantly, a war for media. When the US military's hi-tech victories were covered live and in full colour on the global TV news bulletins, the whole world would understand that the United States was the most advanced nation on the planet. Like the hawks who had advocated the invasion of Vietnam, Donald Rumsfeld – the US defence secretary – believed that the conquest of Iraq would be a spectacular 'demonstration of American power'.[15] Controlling space meant ownership of time – and owning time was control over space. Proving his point, as if it was still the 1950s, the British, Spanish, Italian and Japanese prime ministers in the early 2000s enthusiastically rallied to the US cause. In its struggle against the Islamist menace, America had the edge in both territory and time.

Like its Cold War Left antecedent, the neo-conservative Right honoured the memory of the 1776 Revolution while repudiating its more libertarian aspirations. Plato rather than Jefferson was the

---

11 See Irving Kristol, 'Forty Good Years'; and Nathan Glazer, 'Neoconservative from the Start'.

12 See Chris Hables Gray, 'Perpetual Revolution in Military Affairs, International Security and Information'.

13 See Harlan Ullman and James Wade, 'Shock and Awe'; and Michael Gordon and Bernard Trainor, Cobra II, pages 4–9, 33–35.

14 See Gordon and Trainor, Cobra II, pages 87–88, 140–141; and Timothy Lenoir, 'Programming Theatres of War'.

15 See Gordon and Trainor, Cobra II, pages 18–19, 80–81, 168–169; and Retort, Afflicted Powers, pages 30–31.

philosopher of their oligarchic vision of the republic.[16] For those who refused to conform, the Bush administration now possessed the machinery to deal with them. Far from weakening the nation state, the development of computer-mediated communications was increasing the power of its repressive institutions. From CCTV systems to e-mail monitoring software, the US government and its allies were systematically acquiring the tools for constant surveillance of the entire global population.[17] In the private sector, information technologies had similarly revitalised Taylorist hierarchies. With barcodes and RFID tags, corporations could now track the manufacture and sale of every product. With audits and targets, they could also check the performance of every employee. Rather than disappearing, Fordist hierarchies still ruled over the post-Fordist economy.[18] When production was outsourced to their artisanal enterprises, the knowledge class wasn't liberated from the authority of the factory. On the contrary, thanks to the networked Panopticon, the corporate elite was now able to control their lives in much greater detail than in the Fordist past. The techno-collectivism of McLuhanism had morphed into the techno-authoritarianism of the McKinsey management consultancy.[19]

At the beginning of the twenty-first century, American hegemony appeared to be unassailable. In politics, culture and economics, there was no other way of doing things. But what had never been envisaged in these neo-conservative reveries was that the US military would once again be fighting an unwinnable war in the South. American officials in Iraq, just like their predecessors in Vietnam 30 years earlier, talked about body counts, nation building and the 'light at the end of the tunnel'.[20] Repeating Johnson's error, Bush had placed too much confidence in hi-tech weaponry.[21] The shock-and-awe strategy had been inspired by the same flawed assumptions as the McNamara Line. In a reload of the Tet Offensive debacle, the

[16] See Anne Norton, *Leo Strauss and the Politics of American Empire*, pages 109–140.

[17] See Susan Landau, 'The Transformation of Global Surveillance'; and Duncan Campbell, 'Echelon and its role in COMINT'; 'COMINT Impact on International Trade'; 'COMINT, Privacy and Human Rights'.

[18] See Shoshana Zuboff, *In the Age of the Smart Machine*, pages 315–361.

[19] For the McKinsey credo, see Tom Peters and Robert Waterman, *In Search of Excellence*. Also see Richard Barbrook, *The Class of the New*, pages 34–36.

[20] See Tom Engelhardt, 'The Return of the Body Count'.

[21] See Gordon and Trainor, *Cobra II*, pages 499–500.

US military's computer war games had failed to predict the reality of the Iraqi battlefield.[22] Worst of all, as in its South-East Asian adventure, the master of the media had also lost the media war. Instead of the coverage of the toppling of the tyrant's statue, Iraqi prisoners being tortured by their American jailers had become the iconic images of the conflict.[23] The sectarianism and brutality of the *jihadis* in the resistance didn't change the verdict. The US military was stuck in another Southern quagmire. Among the sceptics, the analysis was damning: 'Iraq is Vietnam on speed'.[24]

Whatever its fallibility as a foreign policy, America's War on Terror was good news for US businesses. Like that of every administration since the 1940s, the Bush government's economic policy was founded upon military Keynesianism. After its mid-1970s defeat in Vietnam, the US Department of Defense had quickly rediscovered its appetite for hi-tech weaponry. When faced with a choice between guns and butter, the Reagan administration in the 1980s had prioritised the rebuilding of the nation's armed forces. When the Cold War finally ended in 1991, the 'peace dividend' did lead to some fall-off of orders from the US military. This decade of relative dearth was ended by the discovery of the new Islamist enemy. In the early 2000s, the Bush government was able to revive the conservative version of military Keynesianism with great success. While Iraq and Afghanistan collapsed into civil war, the American economy kept on growing.[25]

During the 1970s and 1980s, the multiplier effect of military spending had powered the emergence of Silicon Valley in northern California as the global hub of the post-industrial economy. With the profits from defence contracts, its businesses were able to fund the development of world-beating products for the civilian market. Thanks to government grants, academics at Stanford, Berkeley and other local universities had the time and resources to invent

---

22 As the Iraqi insurgency grew, a top American military planner reluctantly admitted: 'The enemy we're fighting ... is a bit different than the one we war-gamed against, because of these paramilitary forces.' William Wallace, in Gordon and Trainor, *Cobra II*, page 311.

23 See Antiwar.com, 'The Abu Ghraib Prison Photos'; and Retort, *Afflicted Powers*, pages 35–36.

24 Roger Burbach and Jim Tarbell, *Imperial Overstretch*, page 192.

25 See Brian Waddell, 'Limiting National Interventionism in the United States', pages 133–136.

the cutting-edge information technologies which Silicon Valley's companies became so adept at commercialising.[26] As Rostow, Galbraith and Bell had argued, the private and public sectors acting in synergy was the recipe for economic success. From personal computers to telecommunications networks, the most advanced machines were made-in-the-USA. By the 1980s, the gurus of Silicon Valley McLuhanism were assuring American business leaders that Fordist manufacturing was history. The pioneer of the post-industrial society no longer needed a large industrial base.

Back in the mid 1960s, McLuhanism had been invented as a credo of the Vital Centre. Two decades later, the meaning of this master theory among the US elite had moved rightwards. With the Cold War Left discredited, many of its members had found ideological solace in the 1970s revival of free-market liberalism: neo-liberalism. Despite this shift in political position, these new converts emphasised that they had nothing in common with old-style conservatives who mourned the loss of the traditional way of life. On the contrary, they identified their new laissez-faire ideology, just like its third-way predecessor, with the imaginary future of the information society. In 1983, Ithiel de Sola Pool – a former CENIS academic and Bell commission member – codified this neo-liberal appropriation of McLuhanism in his masterpiece, *Technologies of Freedom*. Instead of building the electronic agora, the convergence of media, telecommunications and computing was creating the electronic marketplace. From software to soap operas, all forms of information would soon be traded as commodities over the Net. For the first time, everybody could be a media entrepreneur.[27] Far from being a return to the past, free-market policies were the fastest route to the hi-tech future. Jefferson, not Mao, was the prophet of the cybernetic revolution.

> The easy access, low cost and distributed intelligence of modern means of communications are a prime reason for hope. ... The commitment of the American culture to pluralism and individual rights is reason for optimism, as is the pliancy and profusion of electronic technology.[28]

---

[26] See Dennis Hayes, 'Sil.Val'; and Stuart Leslie, 'The Biggest "Angel" of Them All'.

[27] See Ithiel de Sola Pool, *Technologies of Freedom*, pages 151–251.

[28] De Sola Pool, *Technologies of Freedom*, page 251.

By the end of the 1980s, this conservative remix had become the dominant form of American McLuhanism. George Gilder – a Republican Party activist – proclaimed the computer companies of northern California as the harbingers of a free-market paradise. Every sector of the US economy would soon be reorganised in imitation of these pioneers of post-Fordist neo-liberalism: the Silicon Valley model. In early-1960s Russia, the cybernetic Communists had looked forward to computers calculating the optimal distribution of labour and resources. More than two decades later in America, Gilder was arguing that only deregulated markets could provide the economic kernel of this two-way feedback system. Silicon Valley's venture capitalists, yuppie entrepreneurs and geeky engineers were the new makers of the networked future. State controls and corporate leviathans were now obsolete. Both Social Democratic reforms and Stalinist planning were relics from the Fordist past. Supplanting cybernetic communism, the free-enterprise model of Silicon Valley had become the new vision of the future.[29] In his great work, Bell had predicted that the factory would be superseded by the campus. However, in 1980s America, post-industrialism had taken a very different form. Looking at Silicon Valley, the neo-liberal prophets were convinced that the factory and the campus were synergising into a superior entity: the hi-tech entrepreneurial firm.[30]

In 1993, the editors of *Wired* announced in the opening pages of its first issue that their new cyber-culture magazine was dedicated to the patron saint of the Net: Marshall McLuhan.[31] After three decades of anticipation, this Canadian guru's prophecy was on the verge of being fulfilled. At a federal level, Al Gore – the US vice-president – was advocating the wiring up of every American office and home to a fibre-optic broadband network, the 'information superhighway'.[32] More importantly, at a grassroots level, computer hackers and community activists were already exploring the social and artistic applications of these new media technologies.[33] Based in San Francisco, *Wired* promoted this emerging Net scene as the

29 See George Gilder, *Life After Television*; *Wealth and Poverty*.

30 See George Gilder, *The Spirit of Enterprise*.

31 See *Wired*, 1.1, page 14.

32 See Al Gore, 'Speech delivered at Information Superhighway Summit at UCLA'.

33 See Howard Rheingold, *The Virtual Community*; and Bruce Sterling, *The Hacker Crackdown*, pages 43–152.

inheritor of the hippy counter-culture. Its founding editors included local celebrities from the baby-boomer generation: Stewart Brand, Kevin Kelly, Howard Rheingold and John Perry Barlow. The magazine's graphic style mimicked the psychedelic aesthetics of late-1960s Haight-Ashbury. Its editorial line shared the Berkeley New Left's suspicion of government and corporate bureaucracies. Above all, like their hippy predecessors, the writers of *Wired* identified themselves as the champions of the libertarian principles of the 1776 American Revolution. At the 1996 Davos summit of world political and economic leaders, John Perry Barlow – casting himself as the Thomas Jefferson of the Net – issued the magazine's political manifesto: 'A Declaration of Independence of Cyberspace'. In the US Congress, moral conservatives were trying to impose TV-style controls over the content of websites. Appealing to the McLuhanist teleology, Barlow explained that these authoritarian methods of Fordism no longer had any relevance within the participatory democracy of the Net.

> Governments of the Industrial World ... I come from Cyberspace, the new home of Mind. On behalf of the future, I ask you of the past to leave us alone. ... You have not engaged in our great and gathering conversation, nor did you create the wealth of our marketplaces. You do not know our ... unwritten codes that already provide our society more order than could be obtained by any of your impositions.[34]

For his *Wired* colleague Howard Rheingold, the Net was also the healer of social alienation. In his early-1990s upgrade of New Left McLuhanism, bulletin board systems, MUDs, real-time chat services and e-mail listservs represented the principles of the electronic agora put into practice: 'virtual communities'.[35] Founded upon the sharing of information and knowledge, the Net was one of the 'tools for thought' which would liberate humanity from the Fordist factory society.[36] Rheingold's analysis drew its inspiration from over two decades of digital activism in northern California. In the early 1970s, Berkeley had been the home of the world's first open-access network, Community Memory. Like the New Left's media

---

[34] John Perry Barlow, 'A Declaration of Independence of Cyberspace'.

[35] See Rheingold, *Virtual Community*.

[36] See Howard Rheingold, *Tools for Thought*.

experiments, this project tried to break down the division between producers and consumers within computing.[37] A decade later, drawing on their experience in hippy communes, Rheingold's fellow *Wired* editors Stewart Brand and Kevin Kelly had played a leading role in establishing San Francisco's late-1980s pioneering virtual community, the WELL. Like Minitel in France five years earlier, this Californian proto-Net had confirmed the McLuhanist prognosis. Within the virtual communities of cyberspace, the old hierarchies of race, class, age and gender mattered much less. Connected through cooperative creativity, the members of the WELL had been able to express themselves freely, define their own identities and work together in more equalitarian ways.[38] Where San Francisco led, the rest of the world would surely follow. The central node of the hippy global village was still located in northern California.

In the mid 1990s, *Wired* set out to appropriate this New Left utopia for the neo-liberal cause: the 'Californian ideology'.[39] Ignoring the collective freedoms sought by the hippy radicals, its contributors instead identified the Net with the liberty of individuals within the marketplace. These restyled McLuhanists vigorously argued that big government should stay off the backs of the cool and resourceful new media entrepreneurs who were advertising in the pages of *Wired*. In 1999, Kevin Kelly published one of the canonical texts of the dotcom boom, *New Rules for the New Economy*. Combining cybernetic communism with networked neo-liberalism, this hippy ecologist favoured both the sharing and trading of information. The history of the personal computer and the Net had provided an important lesson for US businesses: 'follow the free'. Technologies which were prototyped within the hi-tech gift economy could be successfully spun off into commercial products.[40] By following this development path, dotcom entrepreneurs were already successfully transforming virtual communities into profitable enterprises. In the pages of *Wired*, the bitter political divisions of late-1960s and early-1970s America had disappeared. Vietnam was now an unimportant

37 See Lee Felsenstein, 'How Community Memory Came to Be'; and Steven Levy, *Hackers*, pages 155–180.
38 See Rheingold, *Virtual Community*, pages 17–37.
39 See Richard Barbrook and Andy Cameron, 'The Californian Ideology'.
40 See Kevin Kelly, *New Rules for the New Economy*, pages 50–64; *Out of Control*, pages 214–296.

backwater in which conservative Stalinist bureaucrats were vainly trying to hold back the democratising force of the Net.[41] Alongside the musings of former hippy activists, *Wired* was also running hagiographic interviews with Newt Gingrich – the Republican leader in the House of Representatives – and the Tofflers – the ex-Communist husband-and-wife team who were his close advisers.[42] Echoing Gilder, these conservative ideologues told the magazine's readers that America was blessed with a winning combination of rugged individualists, genius inventors, risk-taking financiers and competitive markets. Gingrich and the Tofflers had discovered the neo-liberal trajectory of the grand narrative of networked modernity: 'In cyberspace... market after market is being transformed by technological progress from a "natural monopoly" to one in which competition is the rule.'[43]

Three years before *Wired* was launched, Barlow and other members of the WELL had set up the Electronic Frontier Foundation, EFF.[44] As its name suggested, this civil liberties organisation identified the futuristic information society with the rough-and-ready democracy of the old Wild West. But, unlike Marx and the New Left, the EFF's hippy capitalists could see no socialist possibilities in this historical experience. For them, the liberal constitutional settlement of the 1776 Revolution was to be admired for nurturing the self-sufficient and independently minded pioneers who had built the American nation out of a wilderness. In the 1990s, respecting the US Constitution's Bill of Rights was still the best way of guaranteeing these personal liberties. On the new electronic frontier, a new generation of freebooting individualists was creating a virtual version of the Wild West. Freed from the hierarchies of big government and big business, entrepreneurs, techies and artists were making a networked society in which all Americans would be free to express their ideas and turn their creativity into money: 'Jeffersonian democracy'.[45]

According to this dotcom orthodoxy, both the Cold War Left's and the New Left's prophecies of the information society

[41] See David Case, 'Big Brother Is Alive and Well in Vietnam'.
[42] See Esther Dyson, 'Friend and Foe'; and Peter Schwartz, 'Shock Wave (Anti) Warrior'. Also, for the couple's best-selling books, see Alvin Toffler, *Future Shock; The Third Wave*.
[43] Progress and Freedom Foundation, *Cyberspace and the American Dream*, page 5.
[44] See Sterling, *Hacker Crackdown*, pages 239–313.
[45] See Mitch Kapor, 'Where is the Digital Highway Really Heading?' and Barlow, 'Declaration'.

were mistaken. Far from transcending the market, the Net was its apotheosis. Clever managers knew how to make cybernetic communism serve establishment goals. At the turn of the millennium, the Global Business Network proudly announced that the Net was reshaping the entire world along American lines.[46] Updating Rostow and Bell, these adepts of the *Wired* editorial line insisted that the meaning of McLuhanism was Gilder-style neo-liberalism. The knowledge class was no longer the vanguard of the collectivist imaginary future. Instead, in late-1990s America, the makers of new media were symbolic analysts, digerati, swarm capitalists and bobos: individualistic members of the new multiply named ruling class.[47] The dotcom company had superseded both the campus and the commune. Picking up on this theme, Thomas Friedman – globalisation's cheerleader at the *Wall Street Journal* – exulted in the geopolitical implications of this new business paradigm: 'It's a post-industrial world, and America today is good at everything that is post-industrial. In a winner-take-all world, America ... certainly has the winner-take-a-lot [socio-economic] system.'[48]

The *Wired* revival of upbeat McLuhanism captured the post-Cold War zeitgeist. With the Vietnam debacle forgotten, the imaginary futures of the 1964 New York World's Fair were coming back into fashion. By the early 2000s, serious money was being committed to their realisation. American entrepreneurs were developing rocket planes which one day would take tourists into outer space.[49] A global consortium had been formed to construct an experimental fusion reactor as the first step towards creating a limitless source of cheap energy.[50] Even the most embarrassing failures of prophecy had been erased from the collective memory. In the 1970s, the followers of Turing and von Neumann had been reluctantly forced to accept that IBM mainframes would never be able to think. Despite this setback, the US military's enthusiasm for the sci-fi dream of robot warriors had kept the research labs in business. Combining two imaginary futures, some acolytes of artificial intelligence became

---

[46] See Peter Leyden, Peter Schwartz and Joel Hyatt, *The Long Boom*, pages 63–89.

[47] See Barbrook, *Class of the New*, pages 15–48. Also see Robert Reich, *The Work of Nations*; John Brockman, *Digerati*; Kelly, *New Rules*; and David Brooks, *Bobos in Paradise*.

[48] Thomas Friedman, *The Lexus and the Olive Tree*, pages 303–304.

[49] See Space Adventures, 'DSE Lunar Orbital'.

[50] See ITER, 'Cadarache'.

convinced that what was impossible on room-sized computers must be achievable on PCs connected to the Net. Others like Kurzweil and Vinge kept on hoping that the rapid advances in hardware and software would eventually culminate in the achievement of the Singularity.[51] Within the pages of *Wired*, these proponents of artificial intelligence were welcomed, along with the other advocates of the 1964 World's Fair futures.[52] In the Californian ideology, McLuhanist technological determinism was embraced as a full-blown social philosophy. By reading its articles on the shape of things to come, the fans of *Wired* could learn how to reap the benefits of 'out of control' neo-liberal capitalism. Illuminated by McLuhanism, they were engaged in spontaneously constructing a future which was inevitable.

During the run-up to the 2003 American invasion of Iraq, the close alliance of the British prime minister, Tony Blair, with US President George Bush puzzled many of his Labour Party supporters.[53] Unlike its Democratic predecessor, this Republican administration took pride in its reactionary stance on social, cultural and environmental issues. But, despite all of the evidence to the contrary, Blair and his coterie never faltered in their belief in the American future. Long before he came to power, this British prime minister had convinced himself that modernity was made-in-the-USA. During the 1980s and 1990s, the US elite had cultivated its links with right-wing factions of the Labour Party. Like its CCF antecedent, BAP – the British–American Project for the Successor Generation – brought together politicians, intellectuals, journalists and activists from both sides of the Atlantic.[54] In 1997, Blair modelled his successful election campaign on those of US President Bill Clinton.[55] Updating Crosland, Tony Giddens – the prime minister's favourite theorist – explained that the Democrats' centrist strategy was the epitome of postmodern politics. As in the 1950s, the British Labour Party had to follow the American path to the future, the 'Third Way'.[56]

---

[51] See H.P. Newquist, *The Brain Makers*, pages 135–449.

[52] See Michael Gruber, 'In Search of the Electronic Brain'; and Paul Boutin, 'Kurzweil's Law'.

[53] See John Kampfner, *Blair's Wars*, pages 255–284.

[54] See Tom Easton, 'The British–American Project for the Successor Generation'; and Andy Beckett, 'Friends in High Places'.

[55] See Andrew Rawnsley, *Servants of the People*, pages 5–6.

[56] See Anthony Giddens, *The Third Way*; and Rawnsley, *Servants of the People*, pages 308–315.

'Five years before I joined BAP, I thought that wealth creation and progressive politics were completely incompatible. BAP was one of the things that made me think that was absurd.'[57]

Four decades earlier, the leaders of West European parliamentary socialism had enthusiastically embraced the precepts of the Vital Centre because they had made electoral sense. From the 1950s to the 1970s, promises of a more equitable and tolerant model of welfare Fordism were vote-winners. Unfortunately, by the 1980s, this Social Democratic programme had lost much of its credibility. During the previous decade, Keynesian demand management had failed to cure the twin crises of Fordism: high inflation and mass unemployment. Much to the surprise of the third-way Left, the neo-liberal Right now had the up-to-date vote-winning economic policies: tax cuts, deregulation and privatisation.[58] But, unlike their more radical comrades, these respectable parliamentary socialists weren't willing to search for an explanation of this unsettling detour in the grand narrative of history within the canonical texts of Trotskyism, Maoism or Situationism. On the contrary, as in the 1950s, they looked across the Atlantic for ideological sustenance. Thanks to de Sola Pool's and Gilder's interpretations of McLuhanism, they were able to understand why Social Democracy had lost its electoral appeal. Bureaucratic regulation and state ownership were the outdated policies of the defunct economic model of industrial autarchy. For running a national government in the new epoch of globalisation, the European Left must commit itself to a post-industrial strategy which combined social justice with technological innovation. The third way had to be upgraded into the Third Way.

In 1983, while visiting Silicon Valley, François Mitterrand – the Socialist president of France – announced his party's conversion to this version of McLuhanism. Since its previous strategy of nationalisation and central planning had failed to revive the French economy, his government would instead focus its attention upon helping entrepreneurial firms, especially within the media, computing and telecommunications sectors.[59] Minitel – the state-run proto-Net

57 Trevor Phillips – a 1980s community activist turned 2000s Blairite manager – in Beckett, 'Friends', page 42.
58 See Alain Lipietz, L'Audace ou l'enlisement, pages 5–110.
59 See Serge Halimi, Sisyphe est fatigué, pages 351–455; and Lipietz, L'Audace, pages 165–300. Also see Richard Barbrook, Media Freedom, pages 148–189.

launched in 1981 – would be transformed over the next decade into a fully-fledged electronic marketplace.[60] Within a few years, progressive politicians across the world were identifying themselves with Californian-style McLuhanism. Reforming governments would implement policies which accelerated the transition of their nations into the information society. In the late 1980s and early 1990s, the decline and fall of Communism provided irrefutable proof that all statist alternatives had failed. Even when carried out by Social Democrats, economic planning and public ownership were anachronisms. In the age of the Net, the path of progress had a new destination: the global electronic marketplace. By the mid 1990s, the parties of Left and Right in postmodern Europe were competing over who had the best strategy for implementing the Silicon Valley model in their own country. Whatever their ideological differences, all sides now agreed that the next stage of growth was US-style post-industrialism. Like their Democratic Party colleagues, the European Left's task was proving that only their politicians knew the fastest route to the imaginary future of the information society.

During the 1990s, the Clinton administration saw itself as the global champion of this revived third-way McLuhanism. In cooperation with its allies, America would spread political consensus, multicultural understanding and market competition to the furthest corners of the earth. Emboldened by the dotcom boom, the US government declared that the benefits of the Net would soon be made available to the inhabitants of the South: the 'Global Information Infrastructure'.[61] Best of all, the Clinton administration was able to succeed where the Cold War Left had failed. Back in the 1960s, the US Air Force had been sent into battle against the Vietnamese resistance. Three decades later, things were very different. In the 1999 Kosova War, American pilots found themselves fighting on the same side as a Maoist-led national liberation movement. Under Clinton, the bad guys were rebranded as the good guys. Victory had replaced defeat.[62] 'The Third Way is ... an attempt to minimise the

---

[60] For the history of this forerunner of the Net, see Michel Marchand, *The Minitel Saga*.
[61] See Ronald Brown, Larry Irving, Arati Prabhakar and Sally Katzen, 'The Global Information Infrastructure'.
[62] See Tim Judah, *Kosovo*; and Kampfner, *Blair's Wars*, pages 36–61.

human costs of the global capitalist machinery without disturbing its operation.'[63]

When Bush became US president in 2001, Blair kept faith with this McLuhanist credo. The nation which had created the Net must be the prototype of the new information society.[64] For pro-American politicians like Blair, adopting an independent foreign policy implied much more than the dangerous reordering of geopolitical space. Above all, this shift threatened their certainties about time. It was almost unthinkable that the future might not be American. During the previous three decades, the intellectual hegemony of McLuhanism over the academy had confirmed this political–temporal assumption. Although claiming to represent rival classes, the master thinkers of both Left and Right had shared a common obsession with this made-in-the-USA imaginary future. According to radical postmodernists, psychosexual 'semiotic machines' were sweeping away the repressive hierarchies of industrialism.[65] In the view of Californian neo-liberals, the emergent properties of the Net were upgrading humanity for the new dotcom age.[66] For both variants of McLuhanism, history was a process without a living subject. As with von Neumann's computers, bits of information acted as self-reproducing automata. As in Darwinian evolution, technological improvements were self-generated responses to environmental pressures. Despite heated arguments over the political meaning of the Net, postmodernists and neo-liberals had come to a consensus over the theoretical doctrines of McLuhanism. The fetishised ideology of the information society had spawned the intellectual fetishisation of information.

Within the academy, there were both conservatives and radicals who stubbornly resisted the ascendancy of McLuhanism. Outraged by this deluge of hi-tech utopianism, sceptics took delight in highlighting the repeated failures of its predictions. At various times, offset printing, FM radio, VCRs, cable television and bulletin board systems had been celebrated as liberating technologies, but, in the end,

63 Slavoj Žižek, *NATO as the Left Hand of God?* page 59.
64 For the Blairite remix of the Californian ideology, see Charles Leadbetter, *Living on Thin Air*; and Geoff Mulgan, *Connexity*.
65 See Gilles Deleuze and Félix Guattari, *A Thousand Plateaus*, pages 75–148, 351–473. For the application of this theory to analysing the Net, see Richard Barbrook, 'The Holy Fools'; and Rob Shields, *Cultures of Internet*.
66 See Kelly, *Out of Control*, pages 6–36, 89–142, 454–540.

all of them had disappointed these hopes.[67] As the heirs of Hilferding
and Stalin, old-style leftists stressed that the cultural industries
couldn't escape the processes of monopolisation and centralisation
which shaped every sector of the capitalist economy.[68] More
sensationally, other academic doom-mongers blamed the electronic
media and computers for exacerbating a wide variety of social evils:
elitism, paedophilia, terrorism, poor education and loneliness.[69]
Gilles Deleuze – a veteran New Left philosopher – warned that
new information technologies were providing the surveillance and
monitoring infrastructure of the emerging authoritarian 'society of
control'. Instead of emancipating the masses, the advent of the Net
threatened to reinforce the power of their oppressors. 'Compared
to the approaching forms of continuous control in open sites, we
may come to see the harshest confinement as part of a wonderfully
happy past. The quest for "universals of communication" ought to
make us shudder.'[70]

By the early 1990s, its opponents were satisfied that McLuhanism
had been exposed as a mishmash of wild assumptions, theoretical
simplifications and political naivety. When the dotcom boom
took off a few years later, these sceptical academics took pride in
their refusal to succumb to the libertarian hype of the Californian
ideology. Big business would inevitably swallow up the hi-tech gift
economy just as it had done with all earlier forms of community
media.[71] Paradoxically, some of the most virulent critics of
McLuhanism were themselves – often unwittingly – also disciples
of McLuhanism. In the same way that the Cold War Left had
remixed Marxism while denouncing Marx, these techno-phobic
intellectuals had simultaneously embraced the theory of technological
determinism while castigating its futurist utopianism. Despite the
heat of the debate, all sides were now in agreement about their
most important discovery: the Net was the subject of history. The
theory of technological determinism had become a self-reproducing

---

[67] See Brian Winston, *Media, Technology and Society*.
[68] See Nicholas Garnham, 'Contribution to a Political Economy of Mass Communication';
and Bernard Miège, *The Capitalisation of Cultural Production*.
[69] See Theodore Roszak, *The Cult of Information*; and Clifford Stoll, *Silicon Snake Oil*.
[70] Gilles Deleuze, 'Control and Becoming', pages 174–175.
[71] See Gerald Sussman, *Communication, Technology and Politics in the Information Age*;
and Nicholas Garnham, 'Information Society: Myth or Reality?'.

abstraction. Anti-McLuhanism was another form of McLuhanism without McLuhan.

In 2006, the British prime minister, Tony Blair, told a conference of News International executives that his support for the Bush administration's War on Terror represented the choice of the open society of modernity over the closed world of tradition.[72] McLuhanism meant that the future was found in the USA. Ironically, by the same logic, America's *jihadi* enemies also had a strong claim to ownership of this post-industrial utopia. Just like dotcom businesses, al-Qa'ida terrorist cells were organised as autonomous franchises coordinated over the Net by a charismatic leader. As in other virtual communities, the Islamist movement was a social network formed through websites, listservs, e-mails and on-line chat rooms. Moving towards the post-industrial global village was the quickest way of returning to the medieval Caliphate: 'cyber-jihad'.[73] This bizarre political phenomenon demonstrated the ideological potency of commodity fetishism. Fragmented by money into self-directing individuals, the modern social collective is reconstituted by the impersonal forces of the market and the state. Under capitalism, humans are both free and dependent. Subjectivity is a class issue. As members of the elite, neo-liberal entrepreneurs, dotcom inventors, McLuhanist gurus, third-way politicians and Islamist emirs were all fascinated by their own 'will to power'.[74] Yet, at the same time, their dominance over others was credited to autonomous powers: economics, technology and ideology. During the late twentieth century, these fetishised identities were upgraded for the computer age. Free markets were feedback mechanisms. Scientific innovation was a self-generating process. Intellectual debate was a cybernetic sign system. Politics was an interactive network. True believers met in cyberspace. Enthused by these theories, the Nietzchean masters embraced their destiny as slaves of the hi-tech subject of history: the Net. In its most fantastic form, McLuhanism was melded with New Age mysticism. As the inhabitants of spaceship Earth went on-line, mortal humans were fusing into a single spiritual entity. 'Cyberspace now presents the possibility of providing a universal mind to all.

[72] See Tony Blair, 'Speech to News Corp'.
[73] See Abdel Bari Atwan, *The Secret History of al-Qa'ida*, pages 120–149.
[74] See Friedrich Nietzsche, *The Will to Power*, pages 457–550.

... [The] ability to computerise has now generated a World Wide Web where the consciousness of one person can respond to the consciousness of many.'[75]

Across the ideological spectrum, possessing the prophecy of the Net had become a claim to political power. When the owner of the future controlled the present, geopolitical rivalries and class conflicts were focused upon the struggle between opposing definitions of the global village. At various times from the 1950s to the 2000s, the information society has been identified as a state plan, a military machine, a mixed economy, a university campus, a hippy commune, a free market, a medieval community or a dotcom firm. During these five decades, these rival definitions came in and out of fashion as the fortunes of their promoters waxed and waned. Only one principle remained constant throughout. If about nothing else, the rival ideologues agreed that building the Net was making the future society. Above all, whatever their political positions, these competing proponents of McLuhanism saw themselves as the vanguard of this hi-tech utopia. Humanity required the guidance of the cybernetic elite to reach the promised land. When everyone had access to the Net, participatory democracy and cooperative creativity would be the order of the day. But, until this happy moment arrived, the old Fordist hierarchies hadn't lost their efficacy. As the representatives of the imaginary future in the present, the knowledge class had the task of ruling over the rest of the population during this period of transition into the information society. Just like their Leninist predecessors, the McLuhanists had convinced themselves that domination prefigured liberation. What would be in the future, justified what was in the present.

For the baby-boomer generation, McLuhanism in all of its different variants offered hope of better times to come. Back in the late 1960s, radicalised by the Vietnam War, many members of the American and European New Left had decided that the Chinese Cultural Revolution was the participatory democracy of the Paris Commune put into practice in the South. Thankfully, by the end of the next decade, most of these hippy Maoists had eventually realised that reading Mao was very different from living under Mao.[76] In

[75] Narayana Gurukula, 'Contemplation Gaia Mind'. Also see Erik Davis, TechGnosis, pages 289–318.

[76] See A. Belden Fields, Trotskyism and Maoism, pages 213–218, 269–284.

both America and Europe, veterans of the New Left discovered that McLuhanism provided a theoretical rationale for their ideological reconciliation with mainstream society. Technological change was a more effective motor of social change than the class struggle. The hippy commune would be reborn as the virtual community. Proving its superiority over Maoist Communism, Jeffersonian democracy protected the rights of the individual and defended the autonomy of dissident minorities. By the late 1990s, vanguard parties seemed like a leftover from the industrial stage of growth. According to the Californian ideology, formal organisations of disciplined cadres had been superseded by spontaneous swarms of self-directed entrepreneurs. In the neo-liberal epoch, financial speculation was the leitmotif of innovation and invention.[77] As Louis Rossetto – the editor-in-chief of *Wired* – explained:

> This new world [of the Net] is characterised by a new global economy that is inherently anti-hierarchical and decentralist, and that disrespects national boundaries or the control of politicians and bureaucrats ... and by a global, networked consciousness ... that is turning ... bankrupt electoral politics ... into a dead end.[78]

Ironically, it was the cult of Jefferson which revealed the elitist reality underpinning this democratic rhetoric. Like Lenin and Mao, this American hero was not only a courageous revolutionary, but also a vicious reactionary. In 1776, when he wrote the inspiring call for democracy and liberty in the US Declaration of Independence, Jefferson had owned nearly 200 human beings as his slaves. As a politician, this freedom fighter had championed the right of American farmers and artisans to determine their own destinies without being subject to the restrictions of feudal Europe. By protecting their property in land and businesses, liberalism ensured that all Americans had the economic resources to enable them to participate as full citizens within the democratic institutions of the new republic. Yet, at the same time, as a Virginian planter, Jefferson's economic prosperity had depended upon the brutal and humiliating system of slave labour. Although the South's 'peculiar institution' had troubled his conscience, this liberal revolutionary believed that the rights of

---

77 See Robert Brenner, *The Boom and the Bubble*, pages 16–93, 128–153, 188–264.

78 Louis Rossetto, in David Hudson, 'There's No Government Like No Government' page 30.

the individual included his right to own other human beings as his private property. In the original version of Jeffersonian democracy, freedom for white folks meant slavery for black people.[79]

For late-1990s Californian McLuhanists, the sordid history of America was much less important than its glorious future. These heirs of the Cold War Left looked on the past – like the present – as just an anticipation of the wonders to come. Echoing de Sola Pool and Gilder, they stressed that the full flowering of Jeffersonian democracy could only take place when humanity was living within the information society. As the dotcom boom gathered momentum, the rapid growth of the Net proved that the pace of this grand narrative of history was accelerating. With each new hardware and software release, the utopian future came ever closer. Human societies were now evolving at warp speed: 'Internet time'.[80] Within the lifetimes of most readers of *Wired*, sophisticated information technologies would have cured many of the political, economic, cultural, ecological and even spiritual downsides of modernity. Like the Cold War Left, the Californian-inspired digerati saw themselves as the all-American vanguard of the US-led global village. As the early adopters and beta-testers of the dotcom future, this privileged group was prefiguring today what the general public would be doing tomorrow.[81] Very soon, when the Net was ubiquitous, everyone would be equal within cyberspace. The rule of the few over the many was only a temporary condition. In 1996, Rossetto proclaimed his creed: 'Not haves and have-nots – [but have-nows and] have-laters.'[82]

In 1961, Khrushchev had made a similar promise to the Russian people. Over the next two decades, the computer technologies being developed within the vanguard party's research laboratories were going to create a socialist paradise. The Unified Information Network would not only optimise the distribution of labour and resources across the economy, but also democratise an undemocratic society. The Paris Commune would be realised as an electronic agora. In response, the Bell commission had countered with its own

---

[79] See John Miller, *The Wolf by the Ears*.
[80] For the dotcom boom origins of this phrase, see Michael Cusamo and David Yoffie, *Competing on Internet Time*, pages 1–16, 298–328.
[81] See Brockman, *Digerati*.
[82] Louis Rossetto, '19th Century Nostrums Are Not Solutions to 21st Century Problems'.

utopian prophecy. By the 1970s, a decade before their Russian rivals, American scientists and entrepreneurs would be ready to go public with the Net. Over the next three decades, the knowledge class would lead the building of the information society. By the time the 2000s were reached, the USA would have completed its transition into the next stage of growth. Thanks to the Net, Americans would be enjoying all the benefits of participatory democracy and cooperative creativity. Three decades on from Khrushchev's speech and the Bell commission, the proponents of the Californian ideology weren't perturbed by the delays in realising this McLuhanist prophecy. The rigidities of the planned economy and the mixed economy had been responsible for slowing down the pace of progress. Fortunately, the free-market economy was now in the ascendancy. Replacing the industrial age elites, the diffuse vanguard of the digerati had become the new class of the new.

In 1930s Russia, the promise of proletarian communism had acted as the justification of the horrors of totalitarian Communism. Suffering in the present would be rewarded in the better times to come. Ironically, it was the completion of the first stage of industrialisation which had discredited this ideological ruse rather than its inherent implausibility. Having successfully identified Communism with the factory, the Communist Party was now making itself obsolete. If it wanted to continue its world-historical mission, the vanguard would have to upgrade to the new cybernetic vision of the communist future. But, by vetoing the Unified Information Network, the Brezhnev government instead opted to resist the grand narrative of modernity. The survival of conservative Communism depended upon the prevention of cybernetic communism. In contrast, the US elite decided to go with the flow. All the dreams of participatory democracy and cooperative creativity would be realised within the global village to come. In earlier stages of modernity, these libertarian principles had only been partially realised. Fortunately, when they were connected to the Net, everyone – including the descendents of slaves – would enjoy the benefits of hi-tech Jeffersonian democracy. Unlike its Russian rival, the American vanguard was able to complete the upgrade of its ideological system.

When the year 2000 finally arrived, the boosters of the information society – like the Stalinists before them – were unexpectedly faced with the problem of living within their own future. In its formative years, access to the Net had been a privilege of an extremely small minority of the world's population: scientists and hackers. Nurtured within university research labs, its technical architecture and social mores were – as Licklider intended – designed to facilitate the idiosyncratic working methods of this miniscule academic gift economy. However, over time, the charmed circle of the Net's users slowly grew from scientists through hobbyists to the general public. Each new member had not just to learn the software of the system, but also to adhere to certain behaviour patterns: 'netiquette'.[83] Quite spontaneously, non-academics began to adopt the Net's academic ways of working. Without even thinking about it, people shared information with each other for free. Crucially, self-interest dictated this preference for cybernetic communism. Within a market economy, buyers and sellers tend to exchange commodities of equivalent worth. In contrast, within this hi-tech gift economy, everyone was able to download far more information than they could ever possibly upload.[84] By adding their own ideas, the Net's users were able to contribute to the collective knowledge which was shared among all of them. As academics had discovered long ago, giving was receiving within the information society.[85] Not surprisingly, there was no popular clamour for imposing the equal exchange of the marketplace upon the Net. Confirming Bell's prediction, the knowledge class had successfully pioneered the new ways of working which everyone else was copying in the post-industrial age.

During the late-1990s dotcom boom, Richard Stallman – an MIT computer scientist and guru of the Free Software Foundation – stood firm against the rush to commercialise the Net. Remaining faithful to Licklider's vision, he championed the hacker ethic of collective endeavour and open enquiry. From the perspective of the university research lab, proprietary software had an in-built design fault: copyright restrictions. Within the academic gift economy, programmers were encouraged to share, appropriate and improve

---

[83] See the 1992 definition of this concept in Brendan Kehoe, *Zen and the Art of the Internet*.
[84] See Richard Barbrook, 'The Hi-tech Gift Economy'; and Rishab Ghosh, 'Cooking-Pot Markets'.
[85] See Tim Berners-Lee, *Weaving the Web*, pages 8–72; and Richard Barbrook, 'Giving is Receiving'.

each other's work. In contrast, Microsoft and other commercial companies jealously guarded the secrets of their source code. The computer user was prevented from being a producer of programs as well as their consumer.[86] In the mid 1980s, Stallman and his colleagues began work on the development of a non-proprietary operating system: GNU. No longer confined to the university, hacker democracy was capable of taking on the Microsoft monopoly. Within a decade, Stallman's dream had evolved into a global community of user–developers making their own operating system: Linux.[87] Because its source code was not protected by copyright, this program could be modified, amended and improved by anyone with the appropriate programming skills. Linus Torvalds – the founder of the project – and a small group of techie experts did most of the work and directed the Linux community. What distinguished this hacker elite from a Microsoft development team was its openness. The construction of their virtual machine was a do-it-yourself effort. All users of Linux were encouraged to make their own tweaks to the source code. As within the scientific community, when someone contributed an improvement to this software project, the gift of their labour was rewarded by recognition within the Linux community. For the first time, especially within the South, Microsoft had a serious competitor.[88]

The self-confidence of the open-source software movement appeared to be well founded. The Net – the icon of the dotcom boom – was the creation of the campus, not the corporation. Its protocols were designed to overcome proprietary barriers to computer-mediated communications. Most of its servers were running Apache: an open-source program.[89] Despite having started his business career with a denunciation of shareware, Bill Gates – the owner of Microsoft – had been forced to give away his web browser as a free download.[90] Within the open architecture of the Net, copyright

86 See Richard Stallman, 'Why Software Should Not Have Owners'.

87 See Free Software Foundation, 'The Free Software Definition'; and Eric S. Raymond, 'Homesteading the Noosphere'.

88 See Eric S. Raymond, 'The Cathedral and the Bazaar'; and Julian Dibbell, 'We Pledge Allegiance to the Penguin'.

89 See Keith W. Porterfield, 'Information Wants to Be Valuable', page 2.

90 This give-away was only one part of Microsoft's strategy to monopolise Net software – see Ken Auletta, World War 3.0; and James Wallace, Overdrive. Also see Bill Gates, 'An Open Letter to the Hobbyists'.

restrictions were becoming an anachronism. Although producers should still be able to prevent their work from being claimed by others, everyone must be allowed to copy and alter information for their own purposes. In the mid 1990s, Stallman launched a campaign for the US intellectual property laws to be reformed according to this university-style method of working: 'copyleft'.[91] According to this hippy interpretation of Jeffersonian democracy, free speech was freedom from compulsory commodification. Crucially, as Tim Berners-Lee – the inventor of the World Wide Web – stressed, this collectivist vision of shared information was already hard-wired into the technical structure of the Net itself. Inside the communications system of the global village, cybernetic communism was displacing monopoly capitalism.

> In an information space, we can consider the authorship of materials, and their perception; but ... there is a need for the underlying infrastructure to be able to make copies simply for reasons of efficiency and reliability. The concept of 'copyright' as expressed in terms of copies made makes little sense.[92]

Designing for their own use, computer scientists from the early 1960s onwards had built the Net as a virtual space for sharing knowledge among themselves: the 'intellectual commons'.[93] For three decades, as long as it remained confined within the academy, this technological subversion of the copyright regime was ignored by the corporate giants which dominated the American media. The neo-liberal McLuhanists had reassured them that all that would change when the information superhighway went live would be that books, newspapers, music, films, games, radio broadcasts and TV programmes would be commercialised as digital files as well as physical products and over the airwaves. In the late 1990s, much to the surprise of the US media majors, this Gilder-style vision of an all-encompassing electronic marketplace turned out to be a flawed prophecy. Among the new generation of young Net users, the hacker ethic was a much more attractive option. For them, Licklider's dream of ubiquitous peer-to-peer computing was a reality. Talented

[91] See Free Software Foundation, 'The Free Software Definition'. Also see the 1998 interview with Stallman in Andrew Leonard, 'The Saint of Free Software'.

[92] Tim Berners-Lee, 'The World Wide Web: Past, Present and Future', page 11.

[93] See Lawrence Lessig, Code, page 141.

school kids and university students were making websites, hosting chat rooms, writing code and creating virtual communities which helped their peers to share interesting stuff with each other. As bandwidth increased, these netizens quickly discovered the pleasures of swapping MP3 copies of their record, tape and CD collections. Having successfully coopted the 1960s hippy counter-culture, the music business had long prided itself in its skill at making money out of the most subversive forms of youth rebellion. Suddenly, for the first time, it was confronted with an impossible demand. Compared to its predecessors, the ambitions of this apparently apolitical youth subculture seemed much more modest: sharing cool tunes over the Net. But, for the music industry, this hacker utopia was a business disaster. Preaching revolution, taking drugs and sexual perversity could all be tolerated within this hip capitalist enterprise. Everything was permitted within the wonderful world of pop, with just one exception: free music.

In 1999, Shawn Fanning released the first version of Napster. Written by an MP3 collector, this program created a virtual meeting-place where people into swapping music files could find each other. From the moment of its release, the popularity of Napster grew exponentially. Early adopters recommended the program to their friends who, in turn, passed on the good news to their mates. What had begun as a cult quickly crossed over into the mainstream. For the first time, rebellious youth were identifying themselves, not by following particular bands, but by using a specific Net service: Napster.[94] A new generation gap had emerged. Each youth subculture had achieved notoriety by antagonising its elders. Just like hippies smoking dope, the users of Napster were also united through a minor form of civil disobedience: breaking the copyright laws. As in the 1960s, their youthful cool was confirmed when out-of-touch oldies tried to stop them from misbehaving. What was different this time around was that the music industry was leading the persecution of the new subculture. Rock 'n' roll had declared war on the Net.

In 2001, the US courts closed down Napster for violating federal copyright laws. Like other companies, media corporations needed

94 For an account of the rise of Napster, see John Alderman, *Sonic Boom*. Also see Richard Barbrook, 'The Napsterisation of Everything'.

a secure legal framework for conducting e-commerce with their customers. As in the old Wild West, business could only prosper once law and order was established on the new electronic frontier. Anyone who distributed unauthorised copies of copyright material over the Net must be punished. Anyone who invented software potentially useful for on-line piracy should be criminalised. The courts and police had to stop consenting adults from sharing information with each other without permission.[95] In a series of high-profile cases, corporate lawyers sued the parents of file-swapping teenagers and the writers of encryption-breaking code.[96] Through a successful lobbying campaign, the media multinationals persuaded both American and European law-makers to strengthen the legislation protecting their intellectual property: the 1998 US Digital Millennium Copyright Act and the 2001 EU Copyright Directive.[97] Unlike the *Wired* editors, big business welcomed the authority of big government being extended into the Net. For the copyright owners, the prevention of cybernetic communism was now the state's primary duty.[98] As Jack Valenti — the head of the Motion Picture Association of America — explained: 'If you can't protect that which you own, then you don't own anything'.[99]

During the late 1990s, the music industry's failure to create a virtual marketplace for selling their products opened the way for Napster and other file-sharing systems. Deprived of a legal method of obtaining tunes over the Net, people learnt how to swap MP3 copies of their CDs, tapes and vinyl collections — and copies of these copies — with each other. As connection speeds got faster, the users of peer-to-peer programs quickly realised that they could now do the same thing with their DVDs and videos as well. In the wake of Napster's demise, a new wave of sophisticated file-sharing programs emerged: Gnutella, Freenet, Kazaa, Bit Torrent.

[95] See the Recording Industry Association of America, 'RIAA Lawsuit Against Napster'; and Richard Barbrook, 'The Regulation of Liberty'.

[96] See the Motion Picture Association of America, 'DVD-deCSS'; and Barbrook, 'Regulation of Liberty'.

[97] See US Government, 'Digital Millennium Copyright Act'; and European Union, 'Directive 2001/29/EC'.

[98] For a wider application of this insight, see David Binns and William Dixon, 'The Decay of Capitalism, the Prevention of Communism and the Need for Planning'.

[99] Jack Valenti, in Motion Picture Association of America, 'Film Studios Bring Claim Against DVD Hackers'.

Instead of turning all information into commodities, post-industrial technologies were facilitating the decommodification of information within important sections of the media. For decades, a small minority of techies had been hacking the copyright laws. Now, for the first time, millions of otherwise respectable people were ignoring the capitalist rules of the economic game. If you knew where to look, most commercially made films, TV programmes, music, games and software programs were available for free. With their lawyers, the owners of copyrights attempted to hold back this unabashed piracy of their intellectual property. Through legal download services, the media multinationals tried to provide customers with more reliable and convenient methods of obtaining their products on the Net. Apple's i-Tunes service and the providers of mobile ringtones proved that there was still lots of money to be made out of selling music in the global electronic marketplace. In 2006, going one stage further, Vivendi Universal decided that giving away their artists' recordings made good business sense. According to the chief sales officer of its new SpiralFrog service, only one out of 40 tracks downloaded from the Net was paid for anyway. Instead of trying – and failing – to replicate this bricks-and-mortar model in the virtual world, music downloads should instead be funded – like TV and radio – by advertising.[100] The big brands would flock to any service which successfully attracted the all-important youth demographic. Where the music industry led, the rest of the media would eventually have to follow. Under dotcom capitalism, information was – at one and the same time – free and profitable.

From its earliest days under Licklider, the Net had been built in cooperation with the private sector. In the 2000s as in the 1960s, cybernetic communism operated with hardware and software bought from capitalist companies. As Kelly had explained, the dotcom entrepreneur's task was discovering new ways of making money out of this hi-tech gift economy. The music majors had found out to their cost that it was futile trying to resist the onrush of the McLuhanist future. Long before the invention of Napster, sampling, DJ-ing and remixing had already blurred property rights

---

100 See Bobbie Johnson and Andrew Clark, 'Free Music Download Service Wants a Bite Out of Apple'. Also see SpiralFrog.

within the reggae, rap and dance scenes.[101] Not surprisingly, these hip musicians felt at home with the Net's hacker ethic. As soon as they were completed, their new tracks could now be made available to a worldwide audience. If someone liked the tune, they could play it out in a DJ set, download it for personal listening, use it as a sample or make their own remix. Through their websites, mailing lists, chat rooms, blogs and on-line radio stations, musicians formed friendships, played together and inspired each other's work. Within this virtual community, the gift economy was in ascendancy over the market economy.[102]

Three decades earlier, New Left activists had been inspired by the Situationist dream of breaking down the division between the producers of media and its consumers. In 1977, Félix Guattari proudly announced that the Italian free radio stations had succeeded in creating the first electronic agora: 'the immense permanent meeting of the airwaves'.[103] The listeners were now broadcasters. By the early 1980s, this French psychoanalyst–philosopher was also celebrating the subversive possibilities of the Minitel system. Like community radio stations, computer networks were inherently participatory and equalitarian.[104] In *A Thousand Plateaus*, Guattari – and his New Left colleague Deleuze – predicted that the top-down hierarchies of the state and the market would find it increasingly difficult to subjugate these fluid and autonomous 'rhizomes' which were emerging in opposition to the cybernetic society of control.[105] Among radical intellectuals, this update ensured that hippy-style McLuhanism kept its position as the cutting edge of theory. When the Net became a mass phenomenon, Deleuze and Guattari's writings seemed truly prophetic. The most important technological achievement of the hacker ethic had put the principles of the New Left into practice. In the mid 1990s, Hakim Bey – an American populist of this libertarian theory – identified the Net's virtual communities with the subversive subcultures of the rave, squatting and festival

[101] For an account of music piracy before the arrival of the Net, see John Chesterman and Andy Lipman, *The Electronic Pirates*.
[102] See Barbrook, 'Hi-Tech Gift Economy'; 'Napsterisation of Everything'.
[103] Félix Guattari 'Les Radios libres populaires'. Also see John Downing, *Radical Media*, pages 215–301.
[104] See Félix Guattari, 'Three Ecologies', pages 142–3.
[105] See Deleuze and Guattari, *A Thousand Plateaus*, pages 3–25.

scenes: 'Temporary Autonomous Zones'.[106] As the New Left had predicted three decades earlier, the future was anarcho-communist. By the turn of the millennium, Toni Negri – the prophet of Italian Autonomism – and Michael Hardt – his American comrade – were declaring that the Net was preparing the way for the victory of the oppressed 'multitudes' of humanity over the 'empire' of corporate capitalism.[107] Backing them up, Maurizio Lazzarato foresaw the imminent overthrow of the factory system. Dotcom companies were already dispensing with Fordist hierarchies. Within the emerging information economy, the producers were their own managers.

> The workers ... become 'active subjects' in the coordination of the different functions of production, instead of being subjected to it as simple command. Collective learning becomes the heart of productivity, because it is not a matter of composing differently, or organising competences which are already codified, but of looking for new ones.[108]

This remix of New Left McLuhanism emphasised the sharp distinction between the participatory and spectacular applications of the Net. Many of the coolest people within alternative scenes weren't members of the new knowledge elite. The majority of the population who earned their living outside the information economy were also capable of being cultural producers. For them, creativity was what happened when they were playing outside work. In the late 1990s, the rapid spread of the Net amplified the social impact of this do-it-yourself attitude. Echoing Wiener and Licklider, Berners-Lee explained that this technological breakthrough was transforming the passive consumption of fixed information products into a fluid process of 'interactive creativity'.[109] Within the Net, everybody could be an artist, writer or coder. During the late 1990s, radical McLuhanists argued that dotcom capitalism was acting as a brake on the emergence of this self-managed cyber-culture. Yet, within less than a decade, it was big business that was leading the rush to build a global participatory media system. Becoming a popular host for 'user generated content' sold lots of advertising. Helping amateurs to

106 See Hakim Bey, TAZ.
107 See Toni Negri and Michael Hardt, Empire, pages 280–303, 353–369, 393–413. During his 1983–97 exile in Paris, Negri had worked with Guattari.
108 Maurizio Lazzarato, 'General Intellect'.
109 Tim Berners-Lee, 'Realising the Full Potential of the Web', page 5.

make their own media could be as profitable as selling professionally made media products. The phenomenal growth of MySpace, Bebo, Flickr and YouTube demonstrated that successful businesses could be built upon Kelly's dictum of following the free. Confounding the hopes of the radical Left, dotcom capitalists were learning how to make money out of cybernetic communism. However, in return, the media moguls had been forced to relinquish direct control over the content of their media. Unlike his reporters at the US-based Fox News channel or the *Sun* newspaper in Britain, Rupert Murdoch couldn't impose an editorial line upon the myriad contributors to his corporation's MySpace site. As its founding principle, dotcom capitalism accepted that the spectacle had been broken.

Over the decades, the different schools of McLuhanism correctly predicted many important aspects of the early-twenty-first-century information society. The cybernetic Communists had foreseen a computerised economy where barcodes and RFID tags were tracking every product. The Bell commission had identified the managers and employees of post-industrial workplaces as the up-and-coming social group. The New Left had anticipated that everyone would be able to make media within their own virtual communities. The Californian ideologues had foretold the withering away of copyright restrictions inside the Net. Yet, at the same time, the central prophecy of McLuhanism remained unfulfilled. In the late 2000s, the Net was ubiquitous, but it was still business as usual. The global village hadn't healed the divisions of nation, class and culture which had plagued the industrial era. Confounding the McLuhanist credo, the advent of the Net hadn't marked the birth of a new humanistic and equalitarian civilisation. When the promises of artificial intelligence were disappointed time after time, its promoters just kept on postponing the arrival of their imaginary future. In 2000, after failing to meet Turing's goal of inventing a thinking machine by that date, British Telecom scientists simply announced that this technological miracle wouldn't happen for another 15 years.[110] Unfortunately for the McLuhanists, this ideological legerdemain was no longer an option. For more than four decades, the knowledge elite had asserted its control over space through ownership of time. Now, in the early twenty-first century,

[110] See BT, 'A Glimpse of Future Life'.

the imaginary future of the information society was materialising in the present. What the McLuhanists had to explain is why this technological revolution hadn't caused a social revolution. For some reason, utopia had been delayed.

Back in the 1960s, the Bell commission had embraced McLuhanism as an ideology of fetishism: technological determinism. For its members, their theoretical work had a clear political purpose. As these apologists of the US elite were well aware, the intellectual achievements of the most influential master thinkers were all too often marred by their unsound opinions and unorthodox lifestyles. In their ideological project, the Bell commission had to deal with an acute version of this problem. All of the founders of their key theories were serious weirdos. Marx was a bohemian communist. Wiener refused to develop Cold War weaponry for the US military. McLuhan was a mystic and a trickster. But, by writing new canonical texts, Bell and his colleagues were able to appropriate Marxism, cybernetics and McLuhanism without acknowledging their intellectual debts to Marx, Wiener and McLuhan. The theoretical differences between these master thinkers could then be smoothed over. Best of all, their intellectual creations were no longer contaminated by their unconventional politics and personal eccentricities. The labour of inventing the meta-theories of Marxism, cybernetics and McLuhanism had apparently disappeared. Like commodities in the market, intellectual abstractions had been separated from their human creators. The ideology of fetishism was a fetishised ideology.

By the early 1970s, McLuhanism had become institutionalised. Successive generations of academics and students kept alive the prophecy of the information society. Across the decades, this immutable imaginary future needed continual modification to reflect the ever-changing circumstances of the present. With regular infusions of living human labour, the verities of the fetishised ideology were successfully perpetuated. Because of its political flexibility, the new orthodoxy of McLuhanism was quickly overshadowed by its heretical offspring. With the historical origins of post-industrial theory obscured, its vision of the networked utopia was able to take many forms. A fetishised ideology had no political loyalties. Within the education factories of America and Europe, the information-society prophecy became the essential raw material for academic production in the social sciences, humanities, arts and philosophy. Praising or criticising McLuhanism provided an intellectual identity. Remixes and neologisms sold books. Updating the prophecy attracted research funding. Courses were taught, conferences were held and articles were written. By continually labouring on McLuhanism, academics succeeded in freezing the imaginary future for four decades. As long as the details of the theory were constantly changing, its core concepts could stay the same. Like other pop-culture products, a successful version of McLuhanism had to be both familiar and innovative. Even the humblest journalist could benefit from this cybernetic theory. By sampling its latest iteration, ephemeral events were given a world-historical meaning.

From the mid 1960s onwards, the McLuhanists lauded the knowledge elite as the precursor in the present of the wonders to come. It would be many decades before everyone in the world gained access to the global village. But, by embedding cooperative creativity within its architecture, Licklider and his colleagues had subverted this Cold War logic. It was America – not Russia – that was building cybernetic communism. When the Net became a mass phenomenon in the mid 1990s, this McLuhanist structure proved its flexibility and scalability as millions of new users went on-line. Although much of the world's population was still living in poverty, large numbers of people – especially in the North – had both the disposable income and the spare time to participate in this new participatory media phenomenon. Over the next decade, the users of the Net started turning the Marxist–McLuhanist prophecy of the electronic agora into reality. Like 1960s underground newspapers, the nettime and rhizome listservs provided a space for artists and intellectuals to publish their articles and discuss their ideas. As in 1970s community radio stations, IndyMedia and OhMyNews not only provided a more radical slant on the day's political events, but also encouraged their supporters to contribute their own reports and comments. Like a 1980s free software project, Wikipedia was written by its own users. Within the emerging information society, do-it-yourself was often preferable to professional production.

In the late 1990s, the global justice movement organised itself in the image of the Net. Rejecting the top-down discipline of the vanguard party, the disparate tribes of anti-capitalist activism were united through their virtual communities. Replacing ideological orthodoxy, open-source software inspired a new open-source form of politics. Unlike their neo-liberal opponents, these anti-globalisers could bring together North and South within the global village.[111] In 2003, the American invasion of Iraq amplified this dissent into the largest and most extensive protest movement in human history. Millions of people across the world quickly discovered the truth behind the spin of the war party from dissident websites and blogs. They expressed their outrage and scepticism in chat rooms and on discussion boards. They used e-mails, instant messaging and web postings to organise anti-war marches and protest meetings. Through the cybernetic extension of the Net, isolated individuals had become a powerful new political force: 'mass critical intelligence'.[112]

Not surprisingly, from the mid 1990s onwards, authoritarian regimes tried to slow down the emergence of the electronic agora. Yet, at the same time, these governments found it impossible to resist the hype of the dotcom boosters. In China, the Communist elite adopted a confused strategy of simultaneously constraining and enhancing the Net.[113] Founded by Leninists, this vanguard party wanted to control the making and distribution of information. As in Iran and other authoritarian countries, the regime's secret police blocked access to disapproved websites, monitored chat room discussions and jailed people whose postings were too subversive. But, being modernisers, the rulers of China also knew that it was impossible to build a post-industrial economy without mobile phones, PCs, printers, cameras and, above all, the Net. Within the information society, the monopolisation of information was over. Fortunately for the Chinese and other elites, cooperative creativity wasn't inherently subversive. Far from being a hi-tech revival of the Paris Commune, virtual communities were – for the most part – apolitical. In the founding texts of New Left McLuhanism, the inhabitants of the electronic agora were revolutionaries, artists, dropouts and visionaries. Four decades on, things were very different. The overwhelming majority of the contributors to the most popular

111 See Armin Medosch, 'Piratology'; and Nick Dyer-Witheford, *Cyber-Marx*, pages 145–164.
112 See John Barker, *Frankenstein and the Chickenhawks*, page 46.
113 See Amnesty International, 'State Control of the Internet in China'; and John Gittings, *The Changing Face of China*, pages 8–9, 266–267.

social-networking sites led much more ordinary lives. Rather than debating the pressing political issues of the day, their time on-line was usually taken up with gossiping about their personal experiences, friends, celebrities, sport, cool websites, pop music, TV shows and holiday trips. Within this MySpace version of the electronic agora, cybernetic communism was mainstream and unexceptional. What once had been a revolutionary dream was now an enjoyable part of everyday life.

Ironically, the vindication of the Bell commission's technological prediction had disproved its social prophecy. The imaginary future of the Net was here – and humanity was still waiting for the McLuhanist utopia. In part, the disappointment of this prophecy can be explained by its origins. At the height of the Cold War, the master theory of McLuhanism was invented as the hi-tech synthesis of American liberalism and Russian socialism. Elite rule was the fastest route to participatory democracy and comparative creativity. Knowing who invented the information society prophecy is the precondition for understanding the ideological meaning of its intellectual concepts. First and foremost, this historical analysis of McLuhanism reveals that abstract theory is a human creation. Far from being self-generating entities, its canonical texts were the products of many hours of mental labour. In recent history, humans made the theory that denies humans are making their own history.

Through this insight, the ideas of McLuhan, Wiener and Marx are no longer subsumed within the ideology of McLuhanism. Back in the mid 1960s, the Bell commission separated the master theories from the master thinkers. Defetishisation reverses this process. McLuhan's idiosyncratic texts are restored to the reading lists. Wiener is recognised as the founding father of cybernetics. Marx's books are studied before those of the Marxist–Leninists. Their political beliefs and personal eccentricities are no longer covered up. Their intellectual ideas are connected with their historical experiences. Their theoretical differences aren't glossed over. In a moment of exasperation, Marx once declared: 'As for me, I am no Marxist'.[114] This joke had a serious side. His more obtuse followers were already fetishising his ideas. They had failed to understand one of his most important concepts: labour is the source of all theory.

114 See Friedrich Engels, 'Letter to Conrad Schmidt'.

In their writings, McLuhan, Wiener and Marx have provided us with a starting point for a modern understanding of the Net. Reading their books is discovering a cornucopia of perceptive ideas. In *Understanding Media*, McLuhan argued that new technologies are 'extensions' of the human body. With access to the Net, people are now able to converse, work and play together on a global scale. The physical restrictions of locality have been partially overcome. In *The Human Use of Human Beings*, Wiener explained that the most efficient form of cybernetic feedback was two-way communications in a non-hierarchical system. Using the Net, people are now able to share ideas, work cooperatively and decide things collectively. In *Capital* and *Grundrisse*, Marx emphasised that different social groups struggle with each other to shape the technologies in their own interest. Over the past decade, entrepreneurs and hackers have fought over whether the Net should be the home of e-commerce or the gift economy. As a fetishised theory, McLuhanist technological determinism has downplayed the primacy of human creativity in this historical process. In contrast, for the majority of the population, their social position is always a temptation to break the rules and discover new ways of doing things – as the music business discovered to its cost in the late 1990s. Long ago, in *The Eighteenth Brumaire*, Marx pointed out that people may be constrained by their historical circumstances and personal experiences, but they were still capable of making their own history.[115] To be intelligent, early twenty-first century Marxism-McLuhanism must become humanist.

Since the mid 1990s, the cultural and political possibilities opened up by the Net have become symbolised by new icons: socialist–feminist cyborgs, anarcho-communist hackers and social democratic digital artisans.[116] Over the past four decades, their do-it-yourself attitude has successfully transformed the machines of war fighting and money making into the tools of sociability and self-expression. In the early twenty-first century, the users of the Net are now both consumers and producers of media. The vanguard has lost its ideological monopoly. The spectacle has been broken. Within the Net, cybernetic communism is here and now. Yet, at the same time,

---

115 See Karl Marx, 'The Eighteenth Brumaire of Louis Bonaparte', pages 146–150.
116 See Donna Haraway, 'A Cyborg Manifesto; McKenzie Wark, A Hacker Manifesto; and Richard Barbrook and Pit Schultz, 'The Digital Artisans Manifesto'.

the arrival of the information society hasn't precipitated a wider social transformation. Post-Fordism is almost indistinguishable from Fordism. Cybernetic communism is quite compatible with dotcom capitalism. Contrary to the tenets of McLuhanism, the convergence of media, telecommunications and computing has not liberated – and never will liberate – humanity. The Net is a useful tool, not a redemptive technology. In defetishised theory, it is humans who are the heroes of the grand narrative of history. In the late 2000s, ordinary people have taken control of sophisticated information technologies to improve their everyday lives and their social conditions. Freed from the preordained futures of McLuhanism, this emancipatory achievement can provide inspiration for new anticipations of the shape of things to come. Cooperative creativity and participatory democracy should be extended from the virtual world into all areas of life. This time, the new stage of growth must be a new civilisation. Rather than disciplining the present, these new futurist visions can be open-ended and flexible. We are the inventors of our own technologies. We can master our own machines. We are the makers of the shape of things to come. We can intervene in history to realise our own interests. Our utopias provide the direction for the path of human progress. Let's be hopeful and courageous when we imagine the better futures of libertarian social democracy.

REFERENCES

16

Abbate, Janet, *Inventing the Internet*, MIT Press, Cambridge, Mass., 2000.

Agar, Jon, *The Government Machine: a revolutionary history of the computer*, MIT Press, Cambridge, Mass., 2003.

Agar, Jon, *Turing and the Universal Machine: the making of the modern computer*, Icon, Cambridge, 2001.

Aglietta, Michel, *A Theory of Capitalist Regulation: the US experience*, Verso, London, 1979.

Alderman, John, *Sonic Boom: Napster, P2P and the battle for the future of music*, Fourth Estate, London, 2001.

Aldrich, Richard, *The Hidden Hand: Britain, America and Cold War secret intelligence*, John Murray, London, 2001.

Ambrose, Stephen, *Rise to Globalism: American foreign policy 1938–1970*, Penguin, London, 1971.

American Society for Cybernetics, 'Summary: The Macy Conferences', <www.asc-cybernetics.org/foundations/history/MacySummary.htm>, accessed 14 September 2006.

Amnesty International, 'State Control of the Internet in China', 26 November 2002, <web.amnesty.org/library/Index/engasa170072002?OpenDocument&of=COUNTRIES%5CCHINA>, accessed 14 September 2006.

Anderson, Andy, *Hungary '56*, Solidarity, London, 1964.

Antiwar.com, 'The Abu Ghraib Prison Photos', <www.antiwar.com/news/?articleid=2444>, accessed 14 September 2006.

Anweiler, Oskar, *The Soviets: the Russian workers, peasants and soldiers councils 1905–1921*, Pantheon, New York, 1974.

Apokin, Igor, 'The Development of Electronic Computers in the USSR', in Georg Trogemann, Alexander Nitussov and Wolfgang Ernst (editors), *Computing in Russia: the history of computer devices and information technology revealed*, Vieweg, Braunschweig/Wiesbaden, 2001, pages 76–104.

Aristotle, *The Politics*, Penguin, London, 1962.

Armstrong, David, *A Trumpet to Arms: alternative media in America*, South End Press, Boston, Mass., 1981.

Asimov, Isaac, *I, Robot*, Panther, London, 1968.

Asimov, Isaac, *The Rest of the Robots*, Panther, London, 1968.

Atwan, Abdel Bari, *The Secret History of al-Qa'ida*, Saqi, London, 2006.

Auerbach, Jeffrey, *The Great Exhibition of 1851: a nation on display*, Yale University Press, New Haven, 1999.

Auletta, Ken, *World War 3.0: Microsoft and its enemies*, Profile, London, 2001.

Avakian, Bob, *From Ike to Mao: my journey from mainstream America to revolutionary communist*, Insight, Chicago, 2005.

Babu, Mohamed, 'Development Strategy – Revolutionary-Style', *Journal of African Marxists*, Number 1, November 1981, pages 44–64.

Bacevich, Andrew, *American Empire: the realities and consequences of U.S. diplomacy*, Harvard University Press, Cambridge, Mass., 2002.

Bagehot, Walter, *The English Constitution*, Fontana, London, 1963.

Bakunin, Mikhail, 'Letter to Albert Richard, 1st April 1870', *Selected Writings*, Jonathan Cape, London, 1973, pages 178–182.

Bakunin, Mikhail, 'On Marx and Marxism', *Selected Writings*, Jonathan Cape, London, 1973, pages 232–270.

Bakunin, Mikhail, 'The Programme of the Slav Section', *Selected Writings*, Jonathan Cape, London, 1973, pages 175–177.

Balfour, Frederick, 'Vietnam's Time is Running Out', *Business Week*, 1 December 2003, <www.businessweek.com/print/magazine/content/03_48/b3860054. htm?chan=mz&>, accessed 30 September 2005.

Balfour, Frederick, 'Vietnam Toddles into a Capitalist Future', *Business Week*, 25 July 2000, <www.businessweek.com/print/dnflash/jul2000/nf00725b.htm?chan=db&>, accessed 4 September 2006.

Baran, Paul, 'On Distributed Communications', *Rand Corporation*, <www.rand.org/pubs/research_memoranda/RM3420>, accessed 14 September 2006.

Barbrook, Alec, *God Save the Commonwealth: an electoral history of Massachusetts*, University of Massachusetts Press, Amerhurst, 1973.

Barbrook, Richard, *The Class of the New*, Open Mute, London, 2006.

Barbrook, Richard, 'Giving is Receiving: the gift economy of the Internet', *Passages/Passagen*, Number 23, Winter 2002, pages 25–26, <www.nettime.org/Lists-Archives/nettime-l-0210/msg00033.html>, accessed 14 September 2006.

Barbrook, Richard, 'The Hi-Tech Gift Economy', in nettime (editor), *Readme! ASCII culture and the revenge of knowledge*, Autonomedia, New York, 1998, pages 132–139; and *First Monday*, Volume 3, Number 12, 7 December 1998, <www.firstmonday.dk/issues/issue3_12/barbrook/index.html>, accessed 14 September 2006.

Barbrook, Richard, 'The Holy Fools: revolutionary elitism in cyberspace', in Patricia Pisters (editor), *The Micropolitics of Media Culture: reading the rhizomes of Deleuze and Guattari*, Amsterdam University Press, Amsterdam, 2001, pages 159–175, <www.hrc.wmin.ac.uk/theory-holyfools.html>, accessed 14 September 2006.

Barbrook, Richard, *Media Freedom: the contradictions of communications in the age of modernity*, Pluto Press, London, 1995.

Barbrook, Richard, 'The Napsterisation of Everything', *Science as Culture*, Volume 11, Number 2, 2002, pages 277–285, <www.commoner.org.uk/revbarb1.htm>, accessed 14 September 2006.

Barbrook, Richard, 'The Regulation of Liberty: free speech, free trade and free gifts on the Net', *Science as Culture*, Volume 11, Number 2, 2002, pages 155–170, <www.heise.de/tp/english/inhalt/co/8726/1.html>, accessed 14 September 2006.

Barbrook, Richard and Andy Cameron, 'The Californian Ideology', in Peter Ludlow (editor), *Crypto Anarchy, Cyberstates and Pirate Utopias*, MIT Press, Cambridge, Mass., 2001, pages 363–387; and *Science as Culture*, Volume 6, Number 26, Part 1, 1996, pages 44–72, <www.hrc.wmin.ac.uk/theory-californianideology.html>, accessed 14 September 2006.

Barbrook, Richard and Pit Schultz, 'The Digital Artisans Manifesto', *ZKP 4*, nettime, Ljubljana, 1997, pages 52–53, <www.ljudmila.org/nettime/zkp4/72.htm>, accessed 14 September 2006.

Barker, John, *Frankenstein and the Chickenhawks*, Christie Books, Hastings, 2003.

Barlow, John Perry, 'A Declaration of Independence of Cyberspace', *Electronic Frontier Foundation*, <homes.eff.org/~barlow/Declaration-Final.html>, accessed 14 September 2006.

Barnouw, Erik, *The Image Empire: a history of broadcasting in the United States, Volume 3 – from 1953*, Oxford University Press, New York, 1970.

Barnouw, Erik, *A Tower in Babel: a history of broadcasting in the United States, Volume 1 – to 1933*, Oxford University Press, New York, 1966.

Baudrillard, Jean, *The Ecstasy of Communication*, Semiotext(e), New York, 1987.

Baudrillard, Jean, *Simulations*, Semiotext(e), New York, 1983.

Beckett, Andy, 'Friends in High Places', *Guardian*, Weekend, 6 November 2004, pages 36–45.

Bell, Daniel, *The Coming of Post-Industrial Society: a venture in social forecasting*, Basic Books, New York, 1973.

Bell, Daniel, *The End of Ideology: on the exhaustion of political ideas in the fifties*, Free Press, New York, 1962.

Bell, Daniel, 'Notes on the Post-Industrial Society (I)', *Public Interest*, Number 6, Winter 1967, pages 24–35.

Bell, Daniel, 'Notes on the Post-Industrial Society (II)', *Public Interest*, Number 7, Spring 1968, pages 102–118.

Bell, Daniel (editor), *The Radical Right*, Doubleday, New York, 1963.

Bell, Daniel, *Sociological Journeys: essays 1960–1980*, Heinemann, London, 1980.

Bell, Daniel (editor), *Towards the Year 2000: work in progress*, Houghton Mifflin, Boston, Mass., 1968.

Bell, Daniel and Henry David Aiken, 'Ideology – a Debate', in Chaim Waxman (editor), *The End of Ideology Debate*, Simon & Schuster, New York, 1968, pages 259–280.

Bell, James, 'Exploring the "Singularity"', <www.kurzweilai.net/meme/frame.html?main=/articles/art0584.html?m%3D1>, accessed 14 September 2006.

Beniger, James, *The Control Revolution: technological and economic origins of the information society*, Harvard University Press, Cambridge, Mass., 1986.

Benjamin, Walter, *The Arcades Project*, Harvard University Press, Cambridge, Mass., 1999.

Beranek, Leo, 'BBN's Earliest Days: founding a culture of engineering creativity', *IEEE Annals of the History of Computing*, Volume 27, Number 2, April–June 2005, pages 6–14.

Berkeley, Edmund, *The Computer Revolution*, Doubleday, New York, 1962.

Berkeley SESPA, *Science against the People*, Berkeley SESPA, Berkeley, 1972.

Berle, Adolf and Gardiner Means, *The Modern Corporation and Private Property*, Transaction, New Brunswick, 1991.

Berman, Marshall, *All That Is Solid Melts into Air: the experience of modernity*, Verso, London, 1983.

Berners-Lee, Tim, 'Realising the Full Potential of the Web', *W3C: World Wide Web Consortium*, 3 December 1997, <www.w3.org/1998/02/Potential.html>, accessed 14 September 2006.

Berners-Lee, Tim, 'The World Wide Web: Past, Present and Future', *W3C: World Wide Web Consortium*, August 1996, <www.w3.org/People/Berners-Lee/1996/ppf.html>, accessed 14 September 2006.

Berners-Lee, Tim, with Mark Fischetti, *Weaving the Web: the past, present and future of the World Wide Web by its inventor*, Orion Business, London, 1999.

Bernstein, Irving, *Guns or Butter: the presidency of Lyndon Johnson*, Oxford University Press, Oxford, 1996.

Berry, Christopher, *Social Theory of the Scottish Enlightenment*, Edinburgh University Press, Edinburgh, 1997.

Bey, Hakim, *TAZ – the temporary autonomous zone, ontological anarchy, poetic terrorism*, Green Anarchist Books, Camberley, 1996.

Binder, Leonard, 'Ideology and Development', in Myron Weiner (editor), *Modernisation: the dynamics of growth*, Basic Books, New York, 1966, pages 192–204.

Binns, David and William Dixon, 'The Decay of Capitalism, the Prevention of Communism and the Need for Planning', *Radical Chains*, Volume 1, Number 1, Winter 1989–90, pages 4–11.

Blair, Tony, 'Speech to News Corp', 10 Downing Street Website, 30 July 2006, <www.number10.gov.uk/output/Page9937.asp>, accessed 14 September 2006.

Bloomfield, John, *Passive Revolution: politics and the Czechoslovak working class 1945–48*, Allison & Busby, London, 1979.

Blum, Léon, 'Exercise et Conquête du Pouvoir', *L'Oeuvre de Léon Blum, Volume 6: 1945-47*, Éditions Albin Michel, Paris, 1958, pages 427–437.

Blum, William, *Killing Hope: US military and CIA interventions since World War II*, Zed Books, London, 2003.

Böhm-Bawerk, Eugen, *Karl Marx and the Close of his System*, Orion, Philadelphia, 1984.

Boutin, Paul, 'Kurzweil's Law', *Wired*, 9.04, April 2001, <www.wired.com/wired/archive/9.04/kurzweil.html>, accessed 14 September 2006.

Bowlt, John E. (editor), *Russian Art of the Avant-Garde: theory and criticism*, Thames & Hudson, London, 1976.

Braibanti, Ralph, 'Administrative Modernisation', in Myron Weiner (editor), *Modernisation: the dynamics of growth*, Basic Books, New York, 1966, pages 166–180.

Brain, Robert, *Going to the Fair: readings in the culture of nineteenth-century exhibitions*, Whipple Museum of the History of Science, Cambridge, 1993.

Brenner, Robert, *The Boom and the Bubble: the US in the world economy*, Verso, London, 2002.

Brockman, John, *Digerati: encounters with the cyber elite*, Hardwired, San Francisco, 1996.

Brook, Jeffrey, *Thank You, Comrade Stalin! Soviet public culture from revolution to Cold War*, Princeton University Press, Princeton, 2000.

Brooks, David, *Bobos in Paradise: the new upper class and how they got there*, Simon & Schuster, New York, 2000.

Brown, Ronald, Larry Irving, Arati Prabhakar and Sally Katzen, 'The Global Information Infrastructure: agenda for cooperation', *US Department of Commerce*, 1994, <www.ntia.doc.gov/reports/giiagend.html#New%20World>, accessed 14 September 2006.

Brugger, Bill, *China: Liberation and Transformation 1942–1962*, Croom Helm, London, 1981.

Brzezinski, Zbigniew, 'America in the Technetronic Age: new questions of our time', *Encounter*, January 1968, pages 16–26.

Brzezinski, Zbigniew, *Between Two Ages: America's role in the technetronic era*, Viking Press, New York, 1970.

Buck-Morss, Susan, *Dreamworld and Catastrophe: the passing of mass utopia in East and West*, MIT Press, Cambridge, Mass., 2000.

Bukharin, Nikolai, *Imperialism and World Economy*, Merlin, London, 1972.

Bukharin, Nikolai and Eugeni Preobrazhensky, *The ABC of Communism*, Penguin, London, 1969.

Burbach, Roger and Jim Tarbell, *Imperial Overstretch: George W. Bush and the hubris of empire*, Zed Books, London, 2004.

Burnham, James, *The Coming Defeat of Communism*, John Day, New York, 1949.

Burnham, James, 'Letter of Resignation of James Burnham from the Workers' Party', in Leon Trotsky, *In Defence of Marxism*, New Park, London, 1975, pages 257–263.

Burnham, James, *The Machiavellians: defenders of freedom*, Putnam, London, 1943.

Burnham, James, *The Managerial Revolution*, Penguin, London, 1945.

Burnham, James, *The Struggle for the World*, John Day, New York, 1947.

Burns, Ric and James Sanders, with Lisa Ades, *New York: an illustrated history*, Alfred A. Knopf, New York, 1999.

Bush, George W., 'The National Security Strategy of the United States of America', 17 September 2002, <www.whitehouse.gov/nsc/nssall.html>, accessed 14 September 2006.

BT, 'A Glimpse of Future Life', advertising promotion, *Observer Technology Magazine*, Number 1, July 2005, pages 26–27.

Cain, P.J. and A.G. Hopkins, *British Imperialism: innovation and expansion 1688–1914*, Longman, London, 1993.

Camatte, Jacques, *Communism and Community in Russia*, David Brown, London, 1978.

Cameron, James (director), *The Terminator*, MGM/United Artists, 1984.

Campbell, Duncan, 'COMINT Impact on International Trade', *Telepolis*, 27 May 2001, <www.heise.de/tp/r4/html/result.xhtml?url=/tp/r4/artikel/7/7752/1.html>, accessed 14 September 2006.

Campbell, Duncan, 'COMINT, Privacy and Human Rights', *Telepolis*, 27 May 2001, <www.heise.de/tp/r4/html/result.xhtml?url=/tp/r4/artikel/7/7748/1.html>, accessed 14 September 2006.

Campbell, Duncan, 'Echelon and its role in COMINT', *Telepolis*, 27 May 2001, <www.heise.de/tp/r4/html/result.xhtml?url=/tp/r4/artikel/7/7747/1.html>, accessed 14 September 2006.

Cannon, James, *The History of American Trotskyism 1928–1938: report of a participant*, Pathfinder, New York, 1944.

Carr, E.H., *The Bolshevik Revolution 1917–1923, Volume 2: a history of Soviet Russia*, Penguin, London, 1966.

Carroll, Lewis, *Through the Looking Glass*, Pan Books, London, 1947.

Carson, Michael, 'David Dellinger' (obituary), *Guardian*, 28 May 2004, page 29.

Case, David, 'Big Brother Is Alive and Well in Vietnam – and he really hates the web', *Wired*, 5.11, November 1997, <www.wired.com/wired/archive/5.11/es_vietnam.html>, accessed 14 September 2006.

Castells, Manuel, *End of Millennium: the information age – economy, society and culture, Volume 3*, Blackwell, Oxford, 1998.

Castells, Manuel, *The Power of Identity: the information age – economy, society and culture, Volume 2*, Blackwell, Oxford, 1997.

Castells, Manuel, *The Rise of the Network Society: the information age – economy, society and culture, Volume 1*, Blackwell, Oxford, 1996.

CBS, *The Vietnam War: courage under fire*, DD Video, Harrow, 2000.

CBS, *The Vietnam War: the end of the road*, DD Video, Harrow, 2000.

Ceruzzi, Paul, *A History of Modern Computing*, MIT Press, Cambridge, Mass., 2003.

Chappell, Urso, 'Expomuseum: World's Fair history, architecture and memorabilia', <expomuseum.com>, accessed 14 September 2006.

Chesterman, John and Andy Lipman, *The Electronic Pirates: DIY crime of the century*, Comedia, London, 1988.

Chomsky, Noam, *For Reasons of State*, New Press, New York, 2003.

Coase, R.H., 'The Nature of the Firm', *The Firm, the Market and the Law*, University of Chicago Press, Chicago, 1988, pages 33–55.

Cohn-Bendit, Daniel and Gabriel Cohn-Bendit, *Obsolete Communism: the left-wing alternative*, Penguin, London, 1969.

Commission of the European Communities, 'Commission Launches Five-Year Strategy to Boost the Digital Economy', 1 June 2005, <europa.eu.int/rapid/pressReleasesAction.do?reference=IP/05/643&format=HTML&aged=0&language=EN&guiLanguage=en>, accessed 14 September 2006.

Conway, Flo and Jim Siegelman, *Dark Hero of the Information Age: in search of Norbert Wiener father of cybernetics*, Basic Books, New York, 2005.

Copeland, B. Jack, 'Computable Numbers: a guide', in Alan Turing, *The Essential Turing: seminal writings in computing, logic, philosophy, artificial intelligence and artificial life plus the secrets of the Enigma*, Oxford University Press, Oxford, 2004, pages 5–57.

Copeland, B. Jack, 'Enigma', in Alan Turing, *The Essential Turing: seminal writings in computing, logic, philosophy, artificial intelligence and artificial life plus the secrets of the Enigma*, Oxford University Press, Oxford, 2004, pages 217–264.

Cosmatos, George (director), *Rambo: First Blood Part 2*, Tri-Star Pictures, 1985.

Crosland, Anthony, *The Future of Socialism*, Jonathan Cape, London, 1956.

Crossman, Richard (editor), *The God That Failed: six studies in communism*, Hamish Hamilton, London, 1950.

Cusamo, Michael and David Yoffie, *Competing on Internet Time: lessons from Netscape and its battle with Microsoft*, Free Press, New York, 1998.

Dallek, Robert, *John F. Kennedy: an unfinished life 1917–1963*, Penguin Books, London, 2003.

Davis, Erik, *TechGnosis: myth, magic and mysticism in the age of information*, Serpent's Tail, London, 1999.

Davis, Lance, J.R.T. Hughes and Stanley Reiter, 'Econometrics', in Edward Saveth (editor), *American History and the Social Sciences*, Free Press, New York, 1964, pages 449–457.

Davis, Mike, *Prisoners of the American Dream*, Verso, London, 1986.

Debord, Guy, *Society of the Spectacle*, Black & Red, Detroit, 1983.

Debray, Regis, *Revolution in the Revolution? armed struggle and political struggle in Latin America*, Penguin, London, 1968.

Tyson, Neil deGrasse, 'Unisphere', *Natural History Magazine*, <www.naturalhistorymag. com/city_of_stars/05_unisphere.html>, accessed 14 September 2006.

DeLamarter, Richard Thomas, *Big Blue: IBM's use and abuse of power*, Pan, London, 1986.

Deleuze, Gilles, 'Control and Becoming', *Negotiations: 1972–1990*, Columbia University Press, New York, 1995, pages 169–176.

Deleuze, Gilles, *Difference and Repetition*, Athlone Press, London, 1994.

Deleuze, Gilles and Félix Guattari, *A Thousand Plateaus: capitalism and schizophrenia*, Athlone, London, 1988.

Desai, Meghnad, *Marx's Revenge: the resurgence of capitalism and the death of statist socialism*, Verso, London, 2002.

Deutscher, Isaac and David King, *The Great Purges*, Basil Blackwell, Oxford, 1984.

Dibbell, Julian, 'We Pledge Allegiance to the Penguin', *Wired*, 12.11, November 2004, <www.wired.com/wired/archive/12.11/linux.html>, accessed 14 September 2006.

Dickson, Paul, *The Electronic Battlefield*, Marion Boyars, London, 1977.

Donner, Frank, *The Un-Americans*, Ballantine Books, New York, 1961.

Drucker, Peter, *The Effective Executive*, Pan, London, 1970.

Downing, John, *Radical Media: the political experience of alternative communication*, South End Press, New York, 1984.

Dyer-Witheford, Nick, *Cyber-Marx: cycles and circuits of struggle in high-technology capitalism*, University of Illinois Press, Urbana, 1999.

Dyson, Esther, 'Friend and Foe', *Wired*, 3.08, August 1995, pages 106–112, 160–162.

Eames, Charles and Ray, *A Computer Perspective: a sequence of 20th century ideas, events and artefacts from the history of the information machine*, Harvard University Press, Cambridge, Mass., 1973.

Eames, Charles and Ray (directors), *IBM at the Fair*, in *The Films of Charles and Ray Eames, Volume 5*, Pyramid, Chatsworth, Calif., 1997.

Easton, Tom, 'The British–American Project for the Successor Generation', *Lobster*, Number 33, pages 10–14.

Editors of Time–Life Books, *Official Guide: New York World's Fair 1964/5*, Time–Life Books, New York, 1964.

Edwards, Paul, *The Closed World: computers and the politics of discourse in Cold War America*, MIT Press, Cambridge, Mass., 1996.

Ellsberg, Daniel, *Secrets: a memoir of Vietnam and the Pentagon Papers*, Penguin, London, 2003.

Engelhardt, Tom, 'Ambush at Kamikaze Pass', in Donald Lazere (editor), *American Media and Mass Culture: Left perspectives*, University of California Press, Berkeley and Los Angeles, 1987, pages 480–498.

Engelhardt, Tom, 'The Return of the Body Count', *Mother Jones*, 23 May 2005, <motherjones.com/commentary/columns/2005/05/body-count.html>, accessed 30 September 2005.

Engels, Friedrich, 'The Civil War in France – Introduction', in Karl Marx, *The Civil War in France*, Martin Lawrence, London, 1933, pages 17–19.

Engels, Friedrich, 'Letter to Eduard Bernstein, 24 March 1884', in Karl Marx and Friedrich Engels, *Selected Correspondence*, Progress, Moscow, 1975, page 350.

Engels, Friedrich, 'Letter to Conrad Schmidt, 5 August 1890', in Karl Marx and Friedrich Engels, *Selected Correspondence*, Progress, Moscow, 1975, page 393.

Engels, Friedrich, *The Origins of the Family, Private Property and the State*, Lawrence & Wishart, London, 1940.

Engels, Friedrich, 'The Prussian Military Question and the German Workers' Party', in Karl Marx, *The First International and After*, Penguin, London, 1974, pages 121–146.

Engels, Friedrich, *Socialism: Scientific and Utopian*, Foreign Languages Press, Beijing, 1975.

European Union, 'Directive 2001/29/EC of the European Parliament and of the Council of 22 May 2001 on the harmonisation of certain aspects of copyright and related rights in the information society', *EurLex*, <europa.eu.int/smartapi/cgi/sga_doc?smartapi!celexapi!prod!CELEXnumdoc&lg=EN&numdoc=32001L0029&model=guichett>, accessed 14 September 2006.

Evans, Grant and Kelvin Rowley, *Red Brotherhood at War: Indochina since the fall of Saigon*, Verso, London, 1984.

Evans, Richard, *The Third Reich in Power, 1933–1939*, Allen Lane, London, 2005.

Fairbairn, Geoffrey, *Revolutionary Guerrilla Warfare: the countryside version*, Penguin, London, 1974.

Fejtö, François, *A History of the People's Democracies: Eastern Europe since Stalin*, Penguin, London, 1974.

Felsenstein, Lee, 'How Community Memory Came to Be', *Internaut*, 18 January 1994, <oldeee.see.ed.ac.uk/online/internaut/internaut-01/comm.html>, accessed 14 September 2006.

Ferguson, Adam, *An Essay on the History of Civil Society*, Edinburgh University Press, Edinburgh, 1966.

Fields, A. Belden, *Trotskyism and Maoism: theory and practice in France and the United States*, Autonomedia, 1988.

Firestone, Shulamith, *The Dialectic of Sex: the case for feminist revolution*, Paladin, London, 1971.

Ford, John F., 'Soviet Cybernetics and International Development', in Charles Dechert (editor), *The Social Impact of Cybernetics*, University of Notre Dame Press, Notre Dame, 1966, pages 161–192.

Ford, Henry, in collaboration with Samuel Crowther, *My Life and Work*, William Heinemann, London, 1922.

Foucault, Michel, *Discipline and Punish: the birth of the prison*, Penguin, London, 1977.

Frank, Andre Gundar, *Capitalism and Underdevelopment in Latin America: historical studies of Chile and Brazil*, Monthly Review, New York, 1969.

Frank, Andre Gundar, *Sociology of Development and Underdevelopment of Sociology*, Pluto Press, London, 1971.

Free Software Foundation, 'The Free Software Definition', *Free Software Foundation*, 12 February 2005, <www.fsf.org/licensing/essays/free-sw.html>, accessed 14 September 2006.

Friedman, Thomas, *The Lexus and the Olive Tree: understanding globalisation*, Farrar Straus Giroux, New York, 1999.

Fukuyama, Francis, *The End of History and the Last Man*, Penguin, London, 1992.

Galbraith, John Kenneth, *The Affluent Society*, Penguin, London, 1970.

Galbraith, John Kenneth, *The New Industrial State*, Penguin, London, 1969.

Garnham, Nicholas, 'Contribution to a Political Economy of Mass Communication', *Media, Culture and Society*, Number 1, 1979, pages 123–146.

Garnham, Nicholas, 'Information Society: Myth or Reality?', Bugs, Globalism and Pluralism Conference, 19–22 September 2001, Montreal, <www.er.uqam.ca/nobel/gricis/actes/bogues/Garnham.pdf#search=%22NICHOLAS%20GARNHAM%22>, accessed 14 September 2006.

Gates, Bill, 'An Open Letter to the Hobbyists', 3 February 1976, <www.blinkenlights.com/classiccmp/gateswhine.html>, accessed 14 September 2006.

Gelernter, David, *1939: the lost world of the fair*, Free Press, New York, 1995.

Gerassi, John, *The Great Fear in Latin America*, Collier, New York, 1965.

Gerovitch, Slava, *From Newspeak to Cyberspeak: a history of Soviet cybernetics*, MIT Press, Cambridge, Mass., 2002.

Ghabra, Shafeeq, 'Democracy for the Arab World', *American Enterprise Institute for Public Policy Research*, 21 October 2002, <www.aei.org/eventsummary835>, accessed 30 September 2005.

Ghosh, Rishab, 'Cooking-Pot Markets: an economic model for the trade in free goods and services on the Internet', *First Monday*, Volume 3, Number 3, 2 March 1998, <www.firstmonday.org/issues/issue3_3/ghosh>, accessed 14 September 2006.

Giap, Vo Nguyen, *National Liberation War in Vietnam*, Foreign Languages Publishing House, Hanoi, 1971.

Gibson, William, 'The Gernsback Continuum', in Bruce Sterling (editor), *Mirrorshades: the cyberpunk anthology*, Paladin, London, 1986, pages 1–11.

Giddens, Anthony, *The Third Way: the renewal of social democracy*, Polity, Cambridge, 1998.

Gilder, George, *Life After Television: the coming transformation of media and American life*, W.W. Norton, New York, 1992.

Gilder, George, *The Spirit of Enterprise*, Penguin, London, 1986.

Gilder, George, *Wealth and Poverty*, Institute for Contemporary Studies, San Francisco, 1993.

Gitlin, Todd, 'Television's Screens: hegemony in transition', in Donald Lazere (editor), *American Media and Mass Culture: Left perspectives*, University of California Press, Berkeley and Los Angeles, 1987, pages 240–265.

Gittings, John, *The Changing Face of China: from Mao to market*, Oxford University Press, Oxford, 2006.

Glazer, Nathan, 'Neoconservative from the Start', *The Public Interest*, Spring 2005, <www.thepublicinterest.com/current/article2.html>, accessed 30 September 2005.

Glover, Daniel, 'Telstar', *NASA Experimental Communications Satellites*, <roland.lerc.nasa.gov/~dglover/sat/telstar.htm>, accessed 30 September 2005.

Golby, J.M. and A.W. Purdue, *The Civilisation of the Crowd: popular culture in England 1750–1900*, Batsford, London, 1984.

Gomulka, Stanislaw, *Growth, Innovation and Reform in Eastern Europe*, Harvester, London, 1986.

Gordon, Michael and Bernard Trainor, *Cobra II: the inside story of the invasion and occupation of Iraq*, Atlantic, London, 2006.

Gore, Al, 'Speech delivered at Information Superhighway Summit at UCLA', 11 January 1994, <www.uibk.ac.at/sci-org/voeb/texte/vor9401.html>, accessed 14 September 2006.

Gornick, Vivian, *The Romance of American Communism*, Basic Books, New York, 1977.

Grahem, Loren, *Science, Philosophy and Human Behaviour in the Soviet Union*, Columbia University Press, New York, 1987.

Gramsci, Antonio, *Selections from the Prison Notebooks*, edited by Quintin Hoare and Geoffrey Nowell-Smith, Lawrence & Wishart, London, 1973.

Gray, Chris Hables, 'Perpetual Revolution in Military Affairs, International Security and Information', in Robert Latham (editor), *Bombs and Bandwidth: the emerging relationship between information technology and security*, New Press, New York, 2003, pages 199–212.

Greenberg, Clement, *Art and Culture: critical essays*, Beacon Press, Boston, Mass., 2004.

Gruber, Helmut, *Red Vienna: experiment in working-class culture 1919–1934*, Oxford University Press, Oxford, 1991.

Gruber, Michael, 'In Search of the Electronic Brain', *Wired*, 5.05, May 1997, <www.wired.com/wired/archive/5.05/es_evolutionary.html>, accessed 14 September 2006.

Guattari, Félix, 'Les Radios libres populaires', in P. Defrance (editor), *De la Nécessité socio-culturelle de l'existence de radios libres*, IUT Carriéres Sociales Animateurs Socio-culturels Université de Lille, Lille, 1979, pages 159–160.

Guattari, Félix, 'Three Ecologies', *New Formations*, Number 8, Summer 1989, pages 131–147.

Guevara, Che, *Bolivian Diary*, Jonathan Cape/Lorrimer, London, 1968.

Guevara, Che, *Guerrilla Warfare*, Penguin, London, 1969.

Guilbaut, Serge, *How New York Stole the Idea of Modern Art: Abstract Expressionism, freedom and the Cold War*, University of Chicago Press, Chicago, 1983.

Günther, Gotthard, 'Cybernetics and the Dialectical Materialism of Marx and Lenin', in Georg Trogemann, Alexander Nitussov and Wolfgang Ernst (editors), *Computing in Russia: the history of computer devices and information technology revealed*, Vieweg, Braunschweig/Wiesbaden, 2001, pages 317–332.

Hafner, Katie and Matthew Lyon, *Where Wizards Stay up Late: the origins of the Internet*, Touchstone, New York, 1996.

Halberstam, David, *The Best and the Brightest*, Random House, New York, 1969.

Hagstrom, Warren O., 'Gift Giving as an Organisational Principle in Science', in Barry Barnes and David Edge (editors), *Science in Context: readings in the sociology of science*, Open University Press, Milton Keynes, 1982, pages 21–34.

Halimi, Serge, *Sisyphe est fatigué: les échecs de la gauche au pouvoir*, Robert Laffont, Paris, 1993.

Hally, Mike, *Electronic Brains: stories from the dawn of the computer age*, Granta, London, 2005.

Hamilton, Alexander, James Madison and John Jay, *The Federalist*, Wesleyan University Press, Middletown, 1961.

Haraway, Donna, 'A Cyborg Manifesto: science, technology and socialist-feminism in the late twentieth century', in *Simians, Cyborgs and Women: the reinvention of nature*, Free Association Books, London, 1991, pages 149–181.

Haraszti, Miklós, *Worker in a Worker's State: piece rates in Hungary*, Penguin, London, 1977.

Hart, Jeffrey, 'Yesterday's America of Tomorrow', *Commentary*, Number 80, July 1985, pages 62–65.

Hass, Richard, 'Towards Greater Democracy in the Muslim World', *Council on Foreign Relations*, 4 December 2002, <www.cfr.org/publication.html?id=5283>, accessed 14 September 2006

Hauben, Michael and Ronda Hauben, *Netizens: on the history and impact of Usenet and the Internet*, IEEE Computer Society Press, Los Alamitos, 1997.

Hayes, Dennis, 'Sil.Val: the chips of our lives', in Chris Carlsson (editor), with Mark Leger, *Bad Attitude: the Processed World anthology*, Verso, London, 1990, pages 149–158.

Heims, Steve, *The Cybernetics Group*, MIT Press, Cambridge, Mass., 1991.

Heims, Steve, *John von Neumann and Norbert Wiener: from mathematics to the technologies of life and death*, MIT Press, Cambridge, Mass., 1980.

Herr, Michael, *Dispatches*, Picador, London, 1978.

Hilferding, Rudolf, 'Böhm-Bawerk's Criticism of Marx', in Eugen von Böhm-Bawerk, *Karl Marx and the Close of his System*, Orion, Philadelphia, 1984, pages 119–221.

Hilferding, Rudolf, *Finance Capital: a study of the latest phase of capitalist development*, Routledge & Kegan Paul, London, 1981.

Hilferding, Rudolf, 'State Capitalism or Totalitarian State Economy?', *Modern Review*, Volume 1, Number 4, 1947, pages 266–271.

Hinckle, Warren, 'Marshall McLuhan: the kind of guy he was', *Rolling Stone*, 5 March 1981, pages 9, 13.

Hinton, William, *Fanshen: a documentary of revolution in a Chinese village*, Vintage, New York, 1966.

Hobsbawm, Eric, *Age of Extremes: the short twentieth century 1914–1991*, Abacus, London, 1994.

Hobsbawm, Eric, *Industry and Empire: an economic history of Britain since 1750*, Penguin, London, 1968.

Hobsbawm, Eric, 'The Invention of Tradition', in Eric Hobsbawm and Terence Ranger (editors), *The Invention of Tradition*, Cambridge University Press, Cambridge, 1983, pages 1–14.

Hobson, J.A., *The Evolution of Modern Capitalism*, George Allen & Unwin, London, 1926.

Hobson, J.A., *Imperialism: a study*, George Allen & Unwin, London, 1902.

Hobson, J.A., *Rationalisation and Unemployment: an economic dilemma*, George Allen & Unwin, London, 1926.

Hodges, Andrew, *Alan Turing: the enigma*, Vintage, London, 1992.

Hodgson, Geoffrey, 'Walt Rostow' (obituary), *Guardian*, 17 February 2003, page 24.

Hoffman, Abbie, *Woodstock Nation: a talk–rock album*, Vintage, New York, 1969.

Hofstadter, Richard, *The American Political Tradition – and the men who made it*, Vintage Books, New York, 1948.

Hofstadter, Richard, *Anti-Intellectualism in American Life*, Vintage Books, New York, 1962.

Hofstadter, Richard, 'Status Politics', in Edward Saveth (editor), *American History and the Social Sciences*, Free Press, New York, 1964, pages 190–195.

Holquist, Peter, 'State Violence as Technique: the logic of violence in Soviet totalitarianism', in David Hoffmann, *Stalinism*, Blackwell, London, 2003, pages 133–156.

Honda, 'Asimo: world's most advanced humanoid robot', <world.honda.com/ASIMO>, accessed 14 September 2006.

Horowitz, Irving Louis, *Ideology and Utopia in the United States, 1956–1976*, Oxford University Press, New York, 1977.

Horowitz, Irving Louis, *The War Game: studies of the new civilian militarists*, Ballantine, New York, 1963.

Howe, Irving, *Steady Work: essays in the politics of democratic radicalism 1953–1966*, Harvest, New York, 1966.

Hudson, David, 'There's No Government like No Government', interview with Louis Rossetto, *San Francisco Bay Guardian*, 6 November 1996, pp. 30–34.

Hunt, Richard, *The Political Ideas of Marx and Engels, Volume 1: Marxism and totalitarian democracy 1818–1850*, University of Pittsburg Press, Pittsburg, 1974.

Hunt, Richard, *The Political Ideas of Marx and Engels, Volume 2: Classical Marxism 1850–1895*, University of Pittsburg Press, Pittsburg, 1984.

Huntington, Samuel, 'The Bases of Accommodation', *Foreign Affairs*, July 1968, Volume 46, Number 4, pages 642–656.

Huntington, Samuel, *The Clash of Civilisations and the Remaking of World Order*, Free Press, London, 2002.

Hyam, Ronald, *Britain's Imperial Century, 1815–1914: a study of empire and expansion*, Palgrave Macmillan, Basingstoke, 2002.

IBM, 'System/360 Announcement', *IBM Archives*, <www-1.ibm.com/history/exhibits/mainframe/mainframe_PR360.html>, accessed 30 September 2005.

Ibn Khaldûn, Muhammad, *The Muqaddimah: an introduction to history*, Princeton University Press, Princeton, 1969.

Inkeles, Alex, 'The Modernisation of Man', in Myron Weiner (editor), *Modernisation: the dynamics of growth*, Basic Books, New York, 1966, pages 138–150.

Innis, Harold, *Empire and Communications*, University of Toronto Press, Toronto, 1972.

Isaacs, Jeremy and Taylor Dowling, *Cold War: for 45 years the world held its breath*, Bantam, London, 1998.

ITER, 'Cadarache – the European Site for ITER', ITER, <www.itercad.org>, accessed 14 September 2006.

James, C.L.R., 'The USSR Is a Fascist State Capitalism', in Sean Matgamna (editor), *The Fate of the Russian Revolution: lost texts of critical Marxism, Volume 1*, Phoenix Press, London, 1998, pages 319–324.

Jasny, Naum, *Soviet Economists of the Twenties: names to be remembered*, Cambridge University Press, Cambridge, 1972.

Jefferson, Thomas, 'First Inaugural Address', 4 March 1801, *Avalon Project at Yale Law School*, <www.yale.edu/lawweb/avalon/presiden/Inaug/jefinau1.htm>, accessed 14 September 2006.

Jeffreys-Jones, Rhodri, *The CIA and American Democracy*, Yale University Press, New Haven, 2003.

Johnson, Bobbie and Andrew Clark, 'Free Music Download Service Wants a Bite out of Apple', *Guardian*, 30 August 2006, <arts.guardian.co.uk/netmusic/story/0,,1860925,00. html>, accessed 14 September 2006.

Johnson, Lyndon, 'Peace Without Conquest: address at Johns Hopkins University', 7 April 1965, *Lyndon Baines Johnson Library and Museum*, <www.lbjlib.utexas.edu/ johnson/archives.hom/speeches.hom/650407.asp>, accessed 14 September 2006.

Johnson, Lyndon, 'Remarks at the University of Michigan', 22 May 1964, *Lyndon Baines Johnson Library and Museum*, <www.lbjlib.utexas.edu/johnson/archives.hom/speeches. hom/640522.asp>, accessed 14 September 2006.

Joll, James, *Gramsci*, Fontana, London, 1977.

Judah, Tim, *Kosovo: war and revenge*, Yale University Press, New Haven, 2000.

Kahn, Herman, *On Thermonuclear War*, Princeton University Press, Princeton, 1960.

Kahn, Herman, 'Toward a Program of Victory', in Frank Armbruster, Raymond Gastil, Herman Kahn, William Pfaff and Edmund Stillman (editors), *Can We Win in Vietnam? the American dilemma*, Pall Mall, London, 1968, pages 304–343.

Kahn, Herman and Anthony Wiener, *The Year 2000: a framework for speculation*, Macmillan, Toronto, 1967.

Kalecki, Michal, *The Last Phase in the Transformation of Capitalism*, Monthly Review, New York, 1972.

Kampfner, John, *Blair's Wars*, Free Press, London, 2004.

Kant, Immanuel, 'To Perpetual Peace: a philosophical sketch', *Perpetual Peace and Other Essays*, Hackett, Indianapolis, 1983, pages 107–143.

Kantorovich, Leonid, 'My Journey in Science: supposed report to the Moscow Mathematical Society', in Lev Leifman, *Functional Analysis, Optimisation and Mathematical Econonomics: a collection of papers dedicated to the memory of Leonid Vital'evich Kantorovich*, Oxford University Press, Oxford, 1990, pages 8–45.

Kapor, Mitch, 'Where Is the Digital Highway Really Heading?', *Wired*, 1.3, July/August 1993, pages 53–59, 94.

Kautsky, Karl, *The Class Struggle*, W.W. Norton, New York, 1971.

Kautsky, Karl, *The Dictatorship of the Proletariat*, University of Michigan Press, Ann Arbor, 1964.

Kehoe, Brendan, *Zen and the Art of the Internet*, January 1992, <www.cs.indiana.edu/ docproject/zen/zen-1.0_toc.html>, accessed 14 September 2006.

Kelly, Aileen, *Mikhail Bakunin: a study in the psychology and politics of utopianism*, Clarendon, Oxford, 1982.

Kelly, Daniel, *James Burnham and the Struggle for the World: a life*, ISI Books, Wilmington, 2002.

Kelly, Kevin, *New Rules for the New Economy: 10 ways that the network economy is changing everything*, Fourth Estate, London, 1998.

Kelly, Kevin, *Out of Control: the new biology of machines*, Fourth Estate, London, 1994.

Kennedy, John, 'Special Message to Congress on Urgent Needs', 25 May 1961, *Internet Public Library*, <www.jfklibrary.org/Historical+Resources/Archives/ Reference+Desk/Speeches/JFK/003POF03NationalNeeds05251961.htm>, accessed 14 September 2006.

Kennedy, Paul, *The Rise and Fall of Great Powers: economic change and military conflict from 1500 to 2000*, Fontana, London, 1989.

Keynes, John Maynard, *The Economic Consequences of the Peace*, Project Gutenberg, 2005, <www.gutenberg.org/etext/15776>, accessed 14 September 2006.

Keynes, John Maynard, *The General Theory of Employment, Interest and Money*, Macmillan, London, 1936.

Khrushchev, Nikita, *Report on the Programme of the Communist Party of the Soviet Union to the 22nd Congress of the CPSU, 18th October 1961 and Reply to Discussion, 27th October 1961*, Soviet Booklet, London, 1961.

Kidron, Michael, *Western Capitalism since the War*, Penguin, London, 1970.

Kolko, Gabriel, *Anatomy of a War: Vietnam, the United States and the modern historical experience*, Phoenix Press, London, 2001.

Kolman, Arnost, 'The Adventure of Cybernetics in the Soviet Union', *Minerva*, Volume 3, Number 16, 1978, pages 416–424.

Kolman, Arnost, 'What is Cybernetics?', *Behavioral Science*, Volume 4, Number 2, 1955, pages 132–146.

Kotkin, Stephen, *Magnetic Mountain: Stalinism as a civilisation*, Unversity of California Press, Berkeley, 1995.

Kovel, Joel, *Red Hunting in the Promised Land: anticommunism and the making of America*, Cassell, London, 1994.

Kravchenko, Victor, *I Chose Freedom: the personal and political life of a Soviet official*, Robert Hale, London, undated.

Kristol, Irving, 'Forty Good Years', *The Public Interest*, Spring 2005, <www.thepublicinterest.com/current/article1.html>, accessed 30 September 2005.

Kristol, William and Robert Kagan, 'National Interest and Global Responsibility', in Irwin Stelzer (editor), *Neoconservatism*, Atlantic Books, London, 2004, pages 52–74.

Kubrick, Stanley (director), *2001: a space odyssey*, Turner Entertainment, Burbank, 2001.

Kuhn, Annette, 'Remembrance', in Jo Spence and Patricia Holland (editors), *Family Snaps: the meaning of domestic photography*, Virago, London, 1991, pages 17–25.

Kuhns, William, *The Post-Industrial Prophets: interpretations of technology*, Harper & Row, New York, 1971.

Kuron, Jacek and Karol Modzelewski, 'Open Letter to the Polish United Workers Party', in Pierre Frank (editor), *Revolutionary Marxist Students in Poland Speak Out (1964–1968)*, Pathfinder, New York, 1972, pages 15–90.

Kurzweil, Ray, 'The Intelligent Universe', <www.kurzweilai.net/meme/frame.html?main=memelist.html?m=3%23534>, accessed 14 September 2006.

Kutulas, Judy, *The Long War: the intellectual People's Front and anti-Stalinism 1930–1940*, Duke University Press, Durham, N.C., 1995.

Landau, Susan, 'The Transformation of Global Surveillance', in Robert Latham (editor), *Bombs and Bandwidth: the emerging relationship between information technology and security*, New Press, New York, 2003, pages 117–131.

Lange, Oskar, 'The Computer and the Market', in C.H. Feinstein (editor), *Socialism, Capitalism and Economic Growth: essays presented to Maurice Dobb*, Cambridge University Press, Cambridge, 1967, pages 158–161.

Lasswell, Harold, 'The World Revolution of our Time: a framework for basic policy research', in Harold Lasswell and Daniel Lerner (editors), *World Revolutionary Elites: studies of coercive ideological movements*, MIT Press, Cambridge, Mass., 1966, pages 29–96.

Laurence, William, *Science at the Fair*, New York World's Fair Corporation 1964–65, New York, 1964.

Lazzarato, Maurizio, 'General Intellect: towards an inquiry into immaterial labour', *Multitudes*, <multitudes.samizdat.net/General-intellect.html>, accessed 14 September 2006.

Leadbetter, Charles, *Living on Thin Air: the new economy with a new blueprint for the 21st century*, Penguin, London, 2000.

Lefebvre, Henri, *Introduction to Modernity*, Verso, London, 1995.

Lenin, V.I., *Imperialism: the highest stage of capitalism*, Communist Party of Great Britain, London, 1928.

Lenin, V.I., *'Left Wing' Communism: an infantile disorder – an attempt at a popular discussion on Marxist strategy and tactics*, Martin Lawrence, London, 1934.

Lenin, V.I., *State and Revolution*, Martin Lawrence, London, 1933.

Lenin, V.I., *The Threatening Catastrophe and How to Fight It: including the Russian Revolution and Civil War*, Martin Lawrence, London, 1932.

Lenin, V.I., *What Is to Be Done? burning questions of our movement*, Foreign Languages Press, Beijing, 1975.

Lenoir, Timothy, 'Programming Theatres of War: gamemakers as soldiers', in Robert Latham (editor), *Bombs and Bandwidth: the emerging relationship between information technology and security*, New Press, New York, 2003, pages 175–198.

Leonard, Andrew, 'The Saint of Free Software', *Salon*, 31 August 1998, <www.salonmagazine.com/21st/feature/1998/08/cov_31feature.html>, accessed 14 September 2006.

Leontieff, Wassily, *The Structure of the American Economy 1919–1939: an empirical application of equilibrium analysis*, Oxford University Press, Oxford, 1951.

Leslie, Stuart, 'The Biggest "Angel" of Them All: the military and the making of Silicon Valley', in Martin Kenney (editor), *Understanding Silicon Valley: the anatomy of an entrepreneurial region*, Stanford University Press, Stanford, 2000, pages 48–67.

Leslie, Stuart, *The Cold War and American Science: the military–industrial complex at MIT and Stanford*, Columbia University Press, New York, 1993.

Lessig, Lawrence, *Code: and other laws of cyberspace*, Basic Books, New York, 1999.

Levy, Steven, *Hackers: heroes of the computer revolution*, Penguin, London, 1994.

Lewin, Moshe, *Political Undercurrents in Soviet Economic Debates: from Bukharin to the modern reformers*, Pluto Press, London, 1975.

Lewis, Helena, *Dada Turns Red: the politics of Surrealism*, Edinburgh University Press, Edinburgh, 1990.

Lewontin, R.C., 'The Cold War and the Transformation of the Academy', in André Schiffin (editor), *The Cold War and the University*, New Press, New York, 1997, pages 1–34.

Leyden, Peter, Peter Schwartz and Joel Hyatt, *The Long Boom: a future history of the world 1980–2020*, Texere, New York, 2000.

Licklider, J.C.R., 'The Computer as a Communications Device', in System Research Centre, *In Memoriam: J.C.R. Licklider 1915–1990*, Digital, Palo Alto, 1990, pages 21–41.

Licklider, J.C.R., 'Man–Computer Symbiosis', in System Research Centre, *In Memoriam: J.C.R. Licklider 1915–1990*, Digital, Palo Alto, 1990, pages 1–19.

Liebman, Marcel, *Leninism under Lenin*, Merlin, London, 1975.

Life International, 'Vacationland USA', 23 March, 1964.

Lin Biao, 'People's War', in John Gerassi (editor), *Towards Revolution, Volume 1: China, India, Asia, the Middle East, Africa*, Weidenfeld & Nicolson, London, 1971, pages 70–90.

Lipietz, Alain, *L'Audace et l'enlisement: sur les politiques économiques de la gauche*, Editions la Découverte, Paris, 1984.

Lipietz, Alain, *Mirages and Miracles: the crises of global Fordism*, Verso, London, 1987.

Lippmann, Walter, *The Good Society*, George Allen & Unwin, London, 1937.

Lipset, Seymour Martin, *American Exceptionalism: a double-edged sword*, W.W. Norton, New York, 1996.

Lipset, Seymour Martin and Gary Marks, *It Didn't Happen Here: why socialism failed in the United States*, W.W. Norton, New York, 2000.

Locke, John, *Two Treatises of Government*, Mentor, New York, 1965.

Longstaff, S.A., 'The New York Intellectuals and the Cultural Cold War, 1945–1950', *New Politics*, Volume 2, Number 2 (new series), 1989, pages 156–170.

Luce, Henry, *The American Century*, Time, New York, 1941.

Lukács, George, *History and Class Consciousness: studies in Marxist dialectics*, Merlin, London, 1971.

Lyotard, Jean-François, *The Post-Modern Condition: a report on knowledge*, Manchester University Press, Manchester, 1986.

Machiavelli, Niccolò, *The Prince*, Penguin, London, 1961.

Machlup, Fritz, *The Production and Distribution of Knowledge in the United States*, Princeton University Press, Princeton, 1962.

Maclear, Michael, *Vietnam: the ten thousand day war*, Thames Methuen, London, 1981.

Makhijani, Arjun and Scott Saleska, 'The Nuclear Power Deception', *IEER Reports*, April 1996, <www.ieer.org/reports/npd.html>, accessed 14 September 2006.

Malinovskiy, B.N., 'Viktor Mikhaylovich Glushkov', in Georg Trogemann, Alexander Nitussov and Wolfgang Ernst (editors), *Computing in Russia: the history of computer devices and information technology revealed*, Vieweg, Braunschweig/Wiesbaden, 2001, pages 133–147.

Mandelbaum, Michael, 'Vietnam: the television war', *Daedalus*, Volume 4, Number 111, 1987, pages 157–169.

Mao Zedong, 'Analysis of the Classes in Chinese Society', *Selected Works of Mao Zedong, Volume 1*, Foreign Languages Press, Beijing, 1967, pages 13–21.

Mao Zedong, *Quotations of Chairman Mao Zedong*, Foreign Languages Press, Beijing, 1967.

Mao Zedong, 'Report on an Investigation of the Peasant Movement in Hunan', *Selected Works of Mao Zedong, Volume 1*, Foreign Languages Press, Beijing, 1967, pages 23–59.

Mao Zedong, *Six Essays on Military Affairs*, Foreign Languages Press, Beijing, 1971.

Mao Zedong, 'We Must Learn to Do Economic Work', *Selected Works of Mao Zedong, Volume 3*, Foreign Languages Press, Beijing, 1965, pages 239–245.

Marchand, Michel, *The Minitel Saga: A French Success Story*, Larousse, Paris, 1988.

Marchand, Philip, *Marshall McLuhan: the medium and the messenger*, Ticknor & Fields, New York, 1989.

Marchetti, Victor and John Marks, *The CIA and the Cult of Intelligence*, Dell, New York, 1974.

Marx, Karl, *Capital: a critique of political economy, Volume 1*, Penguin, London, 1976.

Marx, Karl, *Capital: a critique of political economy, Volume 2*, Penguin/New Left Review, London, 1978.

Marx, Karl, *Capital: a critique of political economy, Volume 3*, Penguin/New Left Review, London, 1981.

Marx, Karl, *The Civil War in France*, Martin Lawrence, London, 1933.

Marx, Karl, 'Critique of the Gotha Programme', in *The First International and After: political writings, Volume 3*, Penguin, London, 1974, pages 339–359.

Marx, Karl, *Critique of Hegel's Philosophy of Right*, Cambridge University Press, Cambridge, 1967.

Marx, Karl, 'Debates on Freedom of the Press', in Karl Marx and Friedrich Engels, *Karl Marx and Frederick Engels Collected Works, Volume 1: Marx 1835–1843*, Progress, Lawrence & Wishart, London, 1975, pages 132–181.

Marx, Karl, 'The Eighteenth Brumaire of Louis Bonaparte', in *Surveys from Exile: political writings, Volume 2*, Penguin, London, 1973, pages 143–249.

Marx, Karl, *Grundrisse*, Penguin, London, 1973.

Marx, Karl, 'Letter to Nicolai Danielson in Petersburg, 19 February 1881', *The Letters of Karl Marx*, Prentice Hall, Englewood Cliffs, 1979, pages 331–332.

Marx, Karl, 'Letter to Vera Ivanovna Zasulich, 8 March 1861', in Karl Marx and Friedrich Engels, *Selected Correspondence*, Progress, Moscow, 1975, pages 319–320.

Marx, Karl, 'On the Jewish Question', *Early Writings: political writings, Volume 1*, Penguin, London, 1975, pages 212–241.

Marx, Karl, 'Speech to the Hague Conference', *The First International and After: political writings, Volume 3*, Penguin, London, 1974, pages 323–326.

Marx, Karl and Friedrich Engels, *The Communist Manifesto*, Lawrence & Wishart, London, 1983.

Marx, Karl and Friedrich Engels, *The German Ideology*, Progress, Moscow, 1964.

Mauss, Marcel, *The Gift: the form and reason for exchange in archaic societies*, Routledge, London, 1990.

Mays, Benjamin, 'Race in America: the Negro perspective', in Huston Smith (editor), *The Search for America*, Prentice Hall, Englewood Cliffs, 1959, pages 65–72.

McCarthy, Mary, *Vietnam*, Penguin, London, 1968.

McCoy, Donald, *Coming of Age: the United States during the 1920s and 1930s*, Penguin, London, 1973.

McCulloch, Warren and Walter Pitts, 'A Logical Calculus of the Ideas Immanent in Nervous Activity', *Bulletin of Mathematical Biophysics*, 1943, Volume 5, pages 115–133.

McLelland, David, 'The Impulse to Modernisation', in Myron Weiner (editor), *Modernisation: the dynamics of growth*, Basic Books, New York, 1966, pages 28–39.

McLuhan, Marshall, 'Cybernation and Culture', in Charles Dechert (editor), *The Social Impact of Cybernetics*, University of Notre Dame Press, Notre Dame, 1966, pages 95–108.

McLuhan, Marshall, *Gutenberg Galaxy: the making of typographic man*, University of Toronto Press, Toronto, 1962.

McLuhan, Marshall, 'Letter to Prince Bernhard of the Netherlands', 14 May 1969, in Matie Molinaro, Corinne McLuhan and William Toye (editors), *Letters of Marshall McLuhan*, Oxford University Press, Oxford, 1987, pages 372–373.

McLuhan, Marshall, 'Letter to Jacques Maritain', 6 May 1969, in Matie Molinaro, Corinne McLuhan and William Toye (editors), *Letters of Marshall McLuhan*, Oxford University Press, Oxford, 1987, pages 369–371.

McLuhan, Marshall, *The Mechanical Bride: folklore of industrial man*, Routledge & Kegan Paul, London, 1967.

McLuhan, Marshall, *Understanding Media: the extensions of man*, Routledge & Kegan Paul, London, 1964.

McNamara, Robert, with Brian VanDeMark, *In Retrospect: the tragedy and lessons of Vietnam*, Times Books, New York, 1995.

Medosch, Armin, 'Piratology', in Armin Medosch (editor), *Dive*, Fact, Liverpool, 2003, pages 8–19.

Melancholic Troglodytes, 'The Star Trek Myth: towards a historical materialist critique', <www.geocities.com/redgiantsite/startrek.html>, accessed 14 September 2006.

Melly, George, *Revolt into Style: the pop arts in Britain*, Penguin, London, 1972.

Michels, Robert, *Political Parties: a sociological study of the oligarchical tendencies of modern democracy*, Free Press, New York, 1962.

Middlemas, Keith, *Politics in Industrial Society: the experience of the British system since 1911*, André Deutsch, London, 1980.

Miège, Bernard, *The Capitalisation of Cultural Production*, International General, New York, 1989.

Mikulak, Maxim, 'Cybernetics and Marxism–Leninism', in Charles Dechert (editor), *The Social Impact of Cybernetics*, University of Notre Dame Press, Notre Dame, 1966, pages 129–159.

Miller, John, *The Wolf by the Ears: Thomas Jefferson and Slavery*, Free Press, New York, 1977.

Millikan, Max and Donald Blackmer (editors), *The Emerging Nations: their growth and United States policy*, Little, Brown, Boston, 1961.

Minsky, Marvin, 'Matter, Mind and Models', <web.media.mit.edu/~minsky/papers/MatterMindModels.txt>, accessed 14 September 2006.

Minsky, Marvin, 'Steps Towards Artificial Intelligence', <web.media.mit.edu/~minsky/papers/steps.html>, accessed 14 September 2006.

Mises, Ludwig von, *Planned Chaos*, Foundation for Economic Education, Irvington-On-Hudson, 1947.

Monroe, James, 'Monroe Doctrine: December 2, 1823', *Avalon Project at Yale Law School*, <www.yale.edu/lawweb/avalon/monroe.htm>, accessed 14 September 2006.

Morris, Errol (director), *The Fog of War*, Sony Pictures, 2004.

Morrison, Philip and Emily Morrison, 'Introduction', in Charles Babbage, *On the Principles and Development of the Calculator and Other Seminal Writings*, Dover Publications, New York, 1961, pages xi–xxxii.

Mosca, Gaetano, *The Ruling Elite*, McGraw-Hill, New York, 1939.

Motion Picture Association of America, 'DVD-deCSS', Motion Picture Association of America, <www.mpaa.org/Legal_cases_dvddecss.asp>, accessed 14 September 2006.

Motion Picture Association of America, 'Film Studios Bring Claim Against DVD Hackers', 14 January 2000, <www.mpaa.org/final_response_1–14.asp>, accessed 14 September 2006.

Mulgan, Geoff, *Connexity: how to live in a connected world*, Chatto & Windus, London, 1997.

Narayana Gurukula, 'Contemplation Gaia Mind', <www.geocities.com/Athens/Agora/4241/Pages/Contemplations/Gaia1.html>, accessed 14 September 2006.

Neale, Jonathan, *The American War: Vietnam 1960–1975*, Bookmarks, London, 2001.

Negri, Toni, 'Keynes and the Capitalist Theory of the State', *Revolution Retrieved: selected writings on Marx, Keynes, capitalist crisis and new social subjects 1967–83*, Red Notes, London, 1988, pages 9–42.

Negri, Toni and Michael Hardt, *Empire*, Harvard University Press, Cambridge, Mass., 2000.

Nelson, Ted, *Computer Lib*, Tempus, Redmond, 1987.

Neumann, John von, *The Computer and the Brain*, Yale University Press, Yale, 2000.

Neumann, John von, 'The General and Logical Theory of Automata', *Collected Works, Volume 5: design of computers, theory of automata and numerical analysis*, Pergamon Press, Oxford, 1976, pages 288–326.

Neumann, John von, *Theory of Self-Reproducing Automata*, University of Illinois Press, Urbana, 1966.

Neumann, John von and Oskar Morgenstern, *Theory of Games and Economic Behaviour*, Princeton University Press, Princeton, 1944.

Newquist, H.P., *The Brain Makers: genius, ego and greed in the quest for machines that think*, Sams, Indianapolis, 1994.

Newton, Huey P., *Revolutionary Suicide*, Wildwood House, London, 1974.

New York City Department of Parks and Recreation, 'Flushing Meadows Corona Park Virtual Tour', <www.nycgovparks.org/sub_your_park/vt_flushing_meadows/vt_flushing_meadows_park.html>, accessed 14 September 2006.

New York World's Fair 1939, *Official Guide Book of the New York World's Fair 1939: building the world of tomorrow*, Exposition Publications, New York, 1939.

Nietzsche, Friedrich, *The Will to Power*, Vintage, New York, 1968.

Nitussov, A.Y., 'Leonid Vitalyevich Kantorovich: Cybernetics in Economy', in Georg Trogemann, Alexander Nitussov and Wolfgang Ernst (editors), *Computing in Russia: the history of computer devices and information technology revealed*, Vieweg, Braunschweig/Wiesbaden, 2001, pages 283–291.

Nitussov, A.Y. and B.N. Malinovskiy, 'Economic Changes in the Sixties and the Internationalisation of Soviet Computing', in Georg Trogemann, Alexander Nitussov and Wolfgang Ernst (editors), *Computing in Russia: the history of computer devices and information technology revealed*, Vieweg, Braunschweig/Wiesbaden, 2001, pages 163–167.

Norberg, Arthur, Jody O'Neill and Kerry Freedman, *Transforming Computer Technology: information processing for the Pentagon 1962–1986*, Johns Hopkins University Press, Baltimore, 1996.

Norden, Eric, 'The Playboy Interview: Marshall McLuhan', *Playboy*, March 1969, <www.digitallantern.net/mcluhan/mcluhanplayboy.htm>, accessed 14 September 2006.

Norton, Anne, *Leo Strauss and the Politics of American Empire*, Yale University Press, New Haven, 2004.

Nove, Alec, *An Economic History of the USSR*, Penguin, London, 1976.

Nuttall, Jeff, *Bomb Culture*, Paladin, London, 1970.

Nye, Joseph, *Soft Power: the means to success in world politics*, Public Affairs, New York, 2004.

nywf64.com, 'Unisphere', *New York World's Fair 1964/1965*, <nywf64.com/unisph01.shtml>, accessed 14 September 2006.

Oberdorfer, Don, *Tet! the turning point in the Vietnam War*, Johns Hopkins University Press, Baltimore, 2001.

Orwell, George, 'In Defence of Comrade Zilliacus', *Collected Essays, Journalism and Letters: Volume 4 – in front of your nose 1945–1950*, Penguin, London, 1970, pages 449–455.

Orwell, George, *Nineteen Eighty-Four: a novel*, Penguin, London, 1954.

Owen, Robert, *A New View of Society and other writings*, Everyman, London, 1972.

Pareto, Vilfredo, *Sociological Writings*, Pall Mall Press, London, 1966.

Parsons, Talcott and Edward Shils (editors), *Toward a General Theory of Action*, Harvard University Press, Cambridge, Mass., 1951.

Pelling, Henry, *Origins of the Labour Party, 1880–1900*, Oxford University Press, Oxford, 1965.

Peters, Mike, 'Bilderberg and the Origins of the EU', *Lobster*, Number 32, December 1996, pages 2–9.

Peters, Tom and Robert Waterman, *In Search of Excellence: lessons from America's best-run companies*, Harper & Row, New York, 1982.

Pilj, Kees van der, *The Making of an Atlantic Ruling Class*, Verso, London, 1984.

Porterfield, Keith, 'Information Wants to Be Valuable: a report from the first O'Reilly Perl conference', <www.netaction.org/articles/freesoft.html>, accessed 14 September 2006.

Pospelov, D.A., 'The Establishment of "Informatics" in Russia', in Georg Trogemann, Alexander Nitussov and Wolfgang Ernst (editors), Computing in Russia: the history of computer devices and information technology revealed, Vieweg, Braunschweig/Wiesbaden, 2001, pages 231–260.

Potel, Jean-Yves, The Summer Before the Frost: Solidarnosc in Poland, Pluto Press, London, 1982.

Preobrazhensky, Eugeni, The New Economics, Clarendon Press, Oxford, 1965.

Progress and Freedom Foundation, Cyberspace and the American Dream: A Magna Carta for the Knowledge Age, <www.ifla.org/documents/libraries/net/magna.txt>, accessed 14 September 2006.

Project for the New American Century, Rebuilding America's Defenses: Strategy forces and resources for a new century, September 2000, <www.newamericancentury.org/RebuildingAmericasDefenses.pdf>, accessed 14 September 2006.

Pugh, Emerson, Building IBM: shaping an industry and its technology, MIT Press, Cambridge, Mass., 1995.

Pugh, Emerson, Lyle Johnson and John Palmer, IBM's 360 and Early 370 Systems, MIT Press, Cambridge, Mass., 1991.

Rand, Christopher, Cambridge U.S.A., Oxford University Press, New York, 1964.

Rapoport, Anatol, Fights, Games and Debates, University of Michigan Press, Ann Arbor, 1960.

Rawnsley, Andrew, Servants of the People: the inside story of New Labour, Hamish Hamilton, London, 2000.

Raymond, Eric, 'The Cathedral and the Bazaar', First Monday, Volume 3, Number 3, March 1998, <www.firstmonday.org/ issues/issue3_3/raymond>, accessed 14 September 2006.

Raymond, Eric, 'Homesteading the Noosphere', First Monday, Volume 3, Number 10, October 1998, <www.firstmonday.org/issues/issue3_10/raymond/index.html>, accessed 14 September 2006.

Reaven, Sheldon, 'New Frontiers', in Robert Rosenblum (editor), Remembering the Future, Queen's Museum, New York, 1989, pages 74–103.

Recording Industry Association of America, 'RIAA Lawsuit Against Napster', <www.riaa.com/News/filings/napster.asp>, accessed 14 September 2006.

Reed, John, Ten Days That Shook the World, Penguin, London, 1966.

Reich, Charles, The Greening of America, Penguin, London, 1971.

Reich, Robert, The Work of Nations: a blueprint for the future, Simon & Schuster, London, 1991.

Retort, Afflicted Powers: capital and spectacle in a new age of war, Verso, London, 2005.

Rheingold, Howard, Tools for Thought: the history and future of mind-expanding technology, MIT Press, Cambridge, Mass., 2000.

Rheingold, Howard, The Virtual Community: finding connection in a computerised world, Secker & Warburg, London, 1994.

Ricardo, David, The Principles of Political Economy and Taxation, Everyman, London, 1911.

Richta, Radovan (editor), Civilisation at the Crossroads: social and human implications of the scientific and technological revolution, Australian New Left Review, Sydney, 1969.

Roosevelt, Eleanor and Huston Smith, 'What Are We For?', in Huston Smith and Richard Heffron (editors), The Search for America, Prentice Hall, Englewood Cliffs, 1959, pages 3–12.

Rose, Julie, 'Reactions to the Fair', *World's Columbian Exposition*, <xroads.virginia. edu/~ma96/WCE/reactions.html>, accessed 14 September 2006.

Rosemont, Franklin, 'Karl Marx and the Iroquois', <www.geocities.com/cordobakaf/ marx_iroquois.html>, accessed 14 September 2006.

Rosenblueth, Arturo, Norbert Wiener and Julian Bigelow, 'Behaviour, Purpose and Teleology', *Philosophy of Science*, January 1943, Volume 10, Number 1, pages 18–24.

Rosenthal, Bernice, *New Myth, New World: from Nietzsche to Stalinism*, Pennsylvania State University Press, University Park, 2002.

Rossetto, Louis, '19th Century Nostrums Are Not Solutions to 21st Century Problems: a trans-Atlantic jet streamer on European ideology and political eternal returns', *Mute*, Number 4, Winter/Spring 1996, page 17.

Rostow, W.W., 'The Case for the Vietnam War: on McNamara's "In Retrospect"', *Parameters*, Winter 1996–97, <www.carlisle.army.mil/USAWC/Parameters/96winter/ rostow.htm>, accessed 14 September 2006.

Rostow, W.W., *Concept and Controversy: sixty years of taking ideas to market*, University of Texas Press, Austin, 2003.

Rostow, W.W., *The Diffusion of Power 1957–1972: an essay in recent history*, Macmillan, New York, 1972.

Rostow, W.W., *Essays on a Half-Century: ideas, policies and action*, Westview Press, Boulder, 1988.

Rostow, W.W., 'The National Style', in Elting Morison (editor), *The American Style: essays in value and performance*, Harper, New York, 1958, pages 246–313.

Rostow, W.W., *The Process of Economic Growth*, W.W. Norton, New York, 1962.

Rostow, W.W., *The Prospects for Communist China*, Technology Press of the Massachusetts Institute of Technology and John Wiley, New York, 1954.

Rostow, W.W., *The Stages of Economic Growth: a non-communist manifesto*, Cambridge University Press, Cambridge, 1960.

Rostow, W.W., *The United States in the World Arena*, Harper & Brothers, New York, 1960.

Rostow, W.W., *View from the Seventh Floor*, Harper & Row, New York, 1964.

Rostow, W.W. and Edward Rozek, *The Dynamics of Soviet Society*, W.W. Norton, New York, 1953.

Roszak, Theodore, *The Cult of Information: a neo-Luddite treatise on high-tech, artificial intelligence and the true art of thinking*, University of California Press, Berkeley, 1994.

Roszak, Theodore, *The Making of a Counter Culture: reflections on technocratic culture and its youthful opposition*, Faber, London, 1970.

Rubin, Jerry, *Do It! scenarios of the revolution*, Simon & Schuster, New York, 1970.

Rubin, Isaac, *Essays on Marx's Theory of Value*, Black & Red, Detroit, 1972.

Ryckelynck, Xavier, 'L'Expo de 1937', *Gavroche*, Number 35, 1987, pages 17–21.

Saint-Simon, Henri, *Selected Writings on Science, Industry and Social Organisation*, Holmes & Meier, New York, 1975.

Sale, Kirkpatrick, *SDS*, Vintage, New York, 1974.

Samuelson, Paul, *Economics: an introductory analysis*, McGraw-Hill, New York, 1951.

Saunders, Frances Stonor, *Who Paid the Piper? the CIA and the cultural cold war*, Granta Books, London, 1999.

Schaffer, Simon, 'Babbage's Dancer and the Impresarios of Mechanism', in Francis Spufford and Jenny Uglow (editors), *Cultural Babbage: technology, time and invention*, Faber and Faber, London, 1996, pages 53–80.

Schefter, James, *The Race: the definitive story of America's battle to beat Russia to the moon*, Century, London, 1999.

Schlesinger, Arthur, Jr., *The Bitter Heritage: Vietnam and American democracy 1941–1966*, Sphere, London, 1967.

Schlesinger, Arthur, Jr., *A Thousand Days: John F. Kennedy in the White House*, Houghton Mifflin, New York, 2002.

Schlesinger, Arthur, Jr., *The Vital Center: the politics of freedom*, Houghton Mifflin, Cambridge, Mass., 1949.

Schiffin, André (editor), *The Cold War and the University: towards an intellectual history of the postwar years*, New Press, New York, 1997.

Schwartz, Peter, 'Shock Wave (Anti) Warrior', *Wired*, 1.5, November 1993, pages 61–65, 120–122.

Servan-Schreiber, Jean-Jacques, *The American Challenge*, Penguin, London, 1969.

Scott-Smith, Giles, 'The Organising of Intellectual Consensus: The Congress for Cultural Freedom and Post-War US European Relations (Part 1)', *Lobster*, Number 36, Winter 1998/9, pages 8–13.

Scott-Smith, Giles, 'The Organising of Intellectual Consensus: The Congress for Cultural Freedom and Post-War US European Relations (Part 2)', *Lobster*, Number 38, Winter 1999, pages 15–20.

Shamberg, Michael and Raindance Corporation, *Guerrilla Television*, Holt, Rinehart & Winston, New York, 1971.

Shanin, Theodor, *Late Marx and the Russian Road: Marx and 'the peripheries of capitalism'*, Routledge & Kegan Paul, London, 1983.

Shannon, Claude and Warren Weaver, *The Mathematical Theory of Communication*, University of Illinois Press, Urbana, Ill., 1963.

Shaw, George Bernard, 'Sixty Years of Fabianism', in George Bernard Shaw, Sidney Webb, Graham Wallas, Lord Olivier, William Clarke, Annie Besant and Hubert Bland (editors), *Fabian Essays*, George Allen & Unwin, London, 1960, pages 295–315.

Sheehan, Neil, *A Bright Shining Lie: John Paul Vann and America in Vietnam*, Pimlico, London, 1998.

Sheehan, Neil, Hedrick Smith, E.W. Kenworthy and Fox Butterfield, *The Pentagon Papers: the secret history of the Vietnam war*, Bantam Books, New York, 1971.

Shelley, Mary, *Frankenstein: the modern Prometheus*, Oxford University Press, Oxford, 1969.

Shields, Rob (editor), *Cultures of Internet: virtual spaces, real histories, living bodies*, Sage, London, 1996.

Shirikov, V.P., 'Scientific Computer Networks in the Soviet Union', in Georg Trogemann, Alexander Nitussov and Wolfgang Ernst (editors), *Computing in Russia: the history of computer devices and information technology revealed*, Vieweg, Braunschweig/Wiesbaden, 2001, pages 168–176.

Short, Philip, *Mao: a life*, John Murray, London, 2004.

Silone, Ignazio, 'The Initiates', in Richard Crossman (editor), *The God That Failed: six studies in communism*, Hamish Hamilton, London, 1950, pages 83–119.

Simon, Herbert, *Administrative Behaviour: a study of decision-making processes in administrative organisation*, Free Press, New York, 1965.

Simon, Herbert, *The Shape of Automation for Men and Management*, Harper, New York, 1965.

Simpson, Christopher, *Science of Coercion: communication research and psychological warfare 1945–1960*, Oxford University Press, Oxford, 1994.

Skinner, B.F., *Science and Human Behaviour*, Free Press, New York, 1965.

Smith, Adam, *An Inquiry into the Nature and Causes of the Wealth of Nations, Volume 1 and Volume 2*, University of Chicago Press, Chicago, 1976.

Smith, Michael, *Station X: the codebreakers of Bletchley Park*, Channel 4 Books, London, 1998.

Snow, Edgar, *Red Star over China*, Victor Gollancz, London, 1937.

Sobel, Robert, *IBM: colossus in transition*, Truman Talley, New York, 1981.

Social Democratic Party, 'Basic Programme of the Social Democratic Party of Germany adopted by an extraordinary conference of the Social Democratic Party held at Bad Godesberg, 13–15 November 1959', in Susanne Miller and Heinrich Potthoff, *A History of German Social Democracy from 1848 to the present*, St Martin's Press, New York, 1986, pages 274–287.

Sola Pool, Ithiel de, 'Communications and Development', in Myron Weiner (editor), *Modernisation: the dynamics of growth*, Basic Books, New York, 1966, pages 98–109.

Sola Pool, Ithiel de, 'The Necessity for Social Scientists Doing Research for Governments', *Background*, Volume 10, Number 2, August 1966, pages 111–122.

Sola Pool, Ithiel de, *The Technologies of Freedom: on free speech in the electronic age*, Harvard University Press, Cambridge, Mass., 1983.

Space Adventures, 'DSE Lunar Orbital', <www.deepspaceexpeditions.com>, accessed 14 September 2006.

SpiralFrog, <www.spiralfrog.com>, accessed 14 September 2006.

Stalin, Joseph, *Economic Problems of Socialism in the USSR*, Foreign Languages Publishing House, Moscow, 1952.

Stalin, Joseph, 'Foundations of Leninism', in *Problems of Leninism*, Foreign Languages Publishing House, Moscow 1954, pages 15–111.

Stalin, Joseph, 'New Conditions – New Tasks of Socialist Construction', in *Problems of Leninism*, Foreign Languages Publishing House, Moscow 1954, pages 459–482.

Stalin, Joseph, 'Report to the Seventeenth Congress of the CPSU (B) on the Work of the Central Committee: 26th January 1934', in *Problems of Leninism*, Foreign Languages Publishing House, Moscow 1954, pages 576–655.

Stalin, Joseph, 'The Right Deviation in the CPSU (B)', in *Problems of Leninism*, Foreign Languages Publishing House, Moscow 1954, pages 287–373.

Stallman, Richard, 'Why Software Should Not Have Owners', *Free Software Foundation*, 27 March 1997, <www.fsf.org/philosophy/why-free.html>, accessed 14 September 2006.

Starski, Stanislaw, *Class Struggle in Classless Poland*, South End, Boston, 1982.

Startrek.com, 'Data', <www.startrek.com/startrek/view/series/TNG/character/1112457. html>, accessed 14 September 2006.

Startrek.com, 'Star Trek – the original series', <www.startrek.com/startrek/view/series/ TOS>, accessed 14 September 2006.

Steele, Jonathan, *Eternal Russia: Yeltsin, Gorbachev and the mirage of democracy*, Faber and Faber, London, 1994.

Sterling, Bruce, *The Hacker Crackdown: law and disorder on the electronic frontier*, Viking, London, 1993.

Stern, Robert A. M., Thomas Mellins and David Fishman, *New York 1960: architecture and urbanism between the Second World War and the Bicentennial*, Benedikt Taschen, Köln, 1997.

Stewart, Michael, *Keynes and After*, Penguin, London, 1972.

Stoll, Clifford, *Silicon Snake Oil: second thoughts on the information highway*, Pan, London, 1996.

Sussman, Gerald, *Communication, Technology and Politics in the Information Age*, Sage, London, 1997.

Taber, Robert, *The War of the Flea: a study of guerrilla warfare theory and practice*, Paladin, London, 1970.

Tales from the Thousand and One Nights, Penguin Books, London, 1973.

Taylor, Frederick Winslow, *The Principles of Scientific Management*, W.W. Norton, New York, 1967.

Theall, Donald, *The Virtual Marshall McLuhan*, McGill–Queen's University Press, Montreal, 2001.

Tocqueville, Alexis de, *Democracy in America, Volume 1*, Vintage Books, New York, 1945.

Tocqueville, Alexis de, *Democracy in America, Volume 2*, Vintage Books, New York, 1945.

Toffler, Alvin, *Future Shock*, Pan, London, 1970.

Toffler, Alvin, *The Third Wave*, Pan, London, 1981.

Toynbee, Arnold, *A Study of History*, Oxford University Press, Oxford, 1946.

Triple Revolution, 'Manifesto of the Triple Revolution', in Priscilla Long (editor), *The New Left: a collection of essays*, Extending Horizons, Boston, Mass., 1969, pages 339–354.

Trotsky, Leon, *Art and Revolution: writings on literature, politics and culture*, Pathfinder Press, New York, 1970.

Trotsky, Leon, *The Class Nature of the Soviet Union*, New Park Publications, London, 1968.

Turing, Alan, 'Can Digital Computers Think?', in *The Essential Turing: seminal writings in computing, logic, philosophy, artificial intelligence and artificial life plus the secrets of the Enigma*, Oxford University Press, Oxford, 2004, pages 482–486.

Turing, Alan, 'Chess', in *The Essential Turing: seminal writings in computing, logic, philosophy, artificial intelligence and artificial life plus the secrets of the Enigma*, Oxford University Press, Oxford, 2004, pages 567–575.

Turing, Alan, 'Computing Machinery and Intelligence', in *The Essential Turing: seminal writings in computing, logic, philosophy, artificial intelligence and artificial life plus the secrets of the Enigma*, Oxford University Press, Oxford, 2004, pages 433–464.

Turing, Alan, 'Intelligent Machinery', in *The Essential Turing: seminal writings in computing, logic, philosophy, artificial intelligence and artificial life plus the secrets of the Enigma*, Oxford University Press, Oxford, 2004, pages 410–432.

Turing, Alan, 'Intelligent Machinery, a Heretical Theory', in *The Essential Turing: seminal writings in computing, logic, philosophy, artificial intelligence and artificial life plus the secrets of the Enigma*, Oxford University Press, Oxford, 2004, pages 472–475.

Turing, Alan, 'Lecture on the Automatic Computing Engine', in *The Essential Turing: seminal writings in computing, logic, philosophy, artificial intelligence and artificial life plus the secrets of the Enigma*, Oxford University Press, Oxford, 2004, pages 378–394.

Turing, Alan, 'On Computable Numbers, with an Application to the Entscheidungsproblem', in *The Essential Turing: seminal writings in computing, logic, philosophy, artificial intelligence and artificial life plus the secrets of the Enigma*, Oxford University Press, Oxford, 2004, pages 58–90.

Ullman, Harlan and James Wade, 'Shock and Awe: achieving rapid dominance', <www.shockandawe.com/index1.htm>, accessed 14 September 2006.

US Constitution, 'The Bill of Rights: Amendments 1–10 of the Constitution', <usinfo.state.gov/usa/infousa/facts/funddocs/billeng.htm>, accessed 14 September 2006.

US Government, 'Digital Millennium Copyright Act', *Library of Congress*, <thomas. loc.gov/cgi-bin/query/D?c105:6:./temp/~c105VBH1v5::>, accessed 14 September 2006.

US Steel, 'Biggest World on Earth', <nywf64.com/unisph06.shtml>.

Vaneigem, Raoul, 'Notice to the Civilised Concerning Generalised Self-Management', in Ken Knabb (editor), *Situationist International Anthology*, Bureau of Public Secrets, Berkeley, 1981, pages 283–289.

Vaneigem, Raoul, *The Revolution of Everyday Life*, Practical Paradise, London, 1975.

Venturi, Franco, *Roots of Revolution: a history of the Populist and Socialist movements in 19th century Russia*, Phoenix, London, 2001.

Vinge, Vernor, 'The Coming Technological Singularity: how to survive in the post-human era', *VISION-21 Symposium*, 30–31 March 1993, <www-rohan.sdsu. edu/faculty/vinge/misc/singularity.html>, accessed 14 September 2006.

Vonnegut, Kurt, Jr., *Player Piano*, Panther, St Albans, 1969.

Waddell, Brian, 'Limiting National Interventionism in the United States: the welfare–warfare state as restrictive governance paradigm', *Capital and Class*, Number 74, Summer 2001, pages 109–139.

Wald, Alan, *The New York Intellectuals: the rise and decline of the anti-Stalinist Left from the 1930s to the 1980s*, University of North Carolina Press, Chapel Hill, 1987.

Walker, Martin, *The Cold War*, Vintage, London, 1994.

Wallace, James, *Overdrive: Bill Gates and the race to control cyberspace*, John Wiley, New York, 1997.

Walton, C. Dale, *The Myth of Inevitable US Defeat in Vietnam*, Frank Cass, London, 2002.

Wark, McKenzie, *A Hacker Manifesto*, Harvard University Press, Boston, Mass., 2004.

Webb, Sidney, 'Introduction to the 1920 Reprint', in George Bernard Shaw, Sidney Webb, Graham Wallas, Lord Olivier, William Clarke, Annie Besant and Hubert Bland (editors), *Fabian Essays*, George Allen & Unwin, London, 1960, pages 268–281.

Weiner, Myron, 'Modernisation of Politics and Government', in Myron Weiner (editor), *Modernisation: the dynamics of growth*, Basic Books, New York, 1966, pages 205–217.

Weiner, Myron, 'Preface', in Myron Weiner (editor), *Modernisation: the dynamics of growth*, Basic Books, New York, 1966, pages v–vi.

Wells, H.G., *The Open Conspiracy: blue prints for a world revolution*, Victor Gollancz, London, 1928.

Westmoreland, W.C., 'Address to the Association of the United States Army: 14th October 1969', in Paul Dickson, *The Electronic Battlefield*, Marion Boyars, London, 1977, pages 215–223.

White, Donald, *The American Century: the Rise and Decline of the United States as a World Power*, Yale University Press, New Haven, 1996.

Wiener, Norbert, *Cybernetics: or command and control in the animal and the machine*, John Wiley, New York, 1948.

Wiener, Norbert, *God and Golem, Inc.: a comment on certain points where cybernetics impinges on religion*, MIT Press, Cambridge, Mass., 1966.

Wiener, Norbert, *The Human Use of Human Beings: cybernetics and society*, Avon Books, New York, 1967.

Wilcox, Fred (director), *Forbidden Planet*, Turner Entertainment, New York, 1999.

Williams, Raymond, *Television: technology and cultural form*, Fontana/Collins, London, 1974.

Wilson, Andrew, *The Bomb and the Computer*, Barrie & Rockliff, London, 1968.

Winston, Brian, *Media, Technology and Society: a history from the telegraph to the Internet*, Routledge, London, 1998.

Winter Soldier Investigation, 'Third Marine Division, Part 2', <www3.iath.virginia.edu/sixties/HTML_docs/Resources/Primary/Winter_Soldier/WS_14_3Marine.html>, accessed 14 September 2006.

Winter Soldier Investigation, 'Third Marine Division, Part 3', <www3.iath.virginia.edu/sixties/HTML_docs/Resources/Primary/Winter_Soldier/WS_15_3Marine.html>, accessed 14 September 2006.

Wired, 1.1, March, 1993.

Wolfe, Tom, *The Right Stuff*, Jonathan Cape, London, 1979.

Wolfe, Tom, 'What If He Is Right?', in *The Pump House Gang*, Bantam, New York, 1969, pages 107–133.

Wood, Ellen Meiksins, *Empire of Capital*, Verso, London, 2003.

Wood, Ellen Meiksins, *The Pristine Culture of Capitalism: a historical essay on old regimes and modern states*, Verso, London, 1991.

World Summit on the Information Society, 'Second Phase, Tunis: the Summit', WSIS, <www.itu.int/wsis/tunis/index.html>, accessed 14 September 2006.

Wreszin, Michael, *A Rebel in Defence of Tradition: the life and politics of Dwight MacDonald*, Basic Books, New York, 1994.

Wright Mills, C., 'Letter to the New Left', in Chaim Waxman (editor), *The End of Ideology Debate*, Simon & Schuster, New York, 1968, pages 126–140.

Wright Mills, C., *The Power Elite*, Oxford University Press, New York, 1956.

Zeman, Z.A.B., *Prague Spring: a report on Czechoslovakia 1968*, Penguin, London, 1969.

Zhdanov, A.A., *On Literature, Music and Philosophy*, Lawrence & Wishart, London, 1950.

Zinn, Howard, *A People's History of the United States: 1492–present*, Pearson, London, 2003.

Žižek, Slavoj, *NATO as the Left Hand of God?* Bastard Bibliotheque, Zagreb, 1999.

Zuboff, Shoshana, *In the Age of the Smart Machine: the future of work and power*, Heinemann, Oxford, 1988.

INDEX

Compiled by John Barker